HENRY JAMES'S EUROPE:
HERITAGE AND TRANSFER

Dennis Tredy is a tenured associate professor (*maître de conférences*) at the University of Paris III – Sorbonne Nouvelle, where he teaches American Literature and Creative Writing. He has published numerous articles on the works of Henry James, Truman Capote and Vladimir Nabokov, and his doctoral thesis of 2002 dealt with *The 'Innocent Reflector' and Its Function in the Works of Henry James's 'Experimental Period'*. His most recent studies of Henry James have dealt with the reception of James's work in Europe, with James's reception of English and French authors, and with film adaptations of the works of James.

Annick Duperray is Emeritus Professor of American Literature at the Université of Provence (Aix-Marseille Université). She is volume editor for two of the four volumes of the critical edition of Henry James's *Nouvelles complètes* (Editions Gallimard/Bibliothèque de la Pléiade, 2003). Her publications include an analytical study of Henry James's tales, *Echec et écriture : essai sur les nouvelles d'Henry James* (1993) and a contribution to *Henry James in Context* (David McWhirter ed., Cambridge University Press, 2010). She also edited *The Reception of Henry James in Europe* (Continuum Books, 2006).

Adrian Harding teaches Comparative Literature at the American University of Paris and American Literature at the University of Provence (Aix-Marseille). Besides poetry, his publications include *Blinds, a Study of the Aesthetics of Fiction* (Lebeer Hossmann, 1985) and *A Survey of English Literature: the 20th Century* (Dunod, 1992). He has written extensively on modern narrative, on poetics and on contemporary art, including articles on realism and narrative poetics in Henry James. His most recent book, with photographs by Alecio de Andrade and a preface by Edgar Morin, is *Louvre Blinds: Le Louvre et ses visiteurs* (Le Passage, 2009).

Henry James's Europe:
Heritage and Transfer

Edited by
Dennis Tredy, Annick Duperray and
Adrian Harding

Cambridge

2011

Open Book Publishers CIC Ltd.,
40 Devonshire Road, Cambridge, CB1 2BL, United Kingdom
http://www.openbookpublishers.com

© 2011 Dennis Tredy, Annick Duperray and Adrian Harding

Some rights are reserved. This book and digital material are made available under the Creative Commons Attribution-Non-Commercial-No Derivative Works 2.0 UK: England & Wales License. This license allows for copying any part of the work for personal and non-commercial use, providing author attribution is clearly stated. Details of allowances and restrictions are available at:

http://www.openbookpublishers.com

As with all Open Book Publishers titles, digital material and resources associated with this volume are available from our website:

http://www.openbookpublishers.com/product.php/72

ISBN Hardback: 978-1-906924-37-9
ISBN Paperback: 978-1-906924-36-2
ISBN Digital (pdf): 978-1-906924-38-6

Cover photo: Henry James in the garden by Alvin Langdon Coburn. Used with the permission of the George Eastman House, Rutherford. All rights reserved.

All paper used by Open Book Publishers is SFI (Sustainable Forestry Initiative), and PEFC (Programme for the Endorsement of Forest Certification Schemes) Certified.

Printed in the United Kingdom and United States by
Lightning Source for Open Book Publishers

Contents

	Page
Contributors	viii
Preface	xiii
Dennis Tredy	
On 'The European Society of Jamesian Studies'	xxiii
Adrian Harding	

I: Ethics and Aesthetics

1. Henry James on Opening the Door to the Devil	3
Jean Gooder	
2. From Romance to Redemption: James and the Ethics of Globalization	17
Roxana Oltean	
3. James's Sociology of Taste: *The Ambassadors*, Commodity Consumption and Cultural Critique	39
Esther Sánchez-Pardo	
4. Bad Investments	51
Eric Savoy	

II: French and Italian Hours

5. 'The Crash of Civilization': James and the Idea of France, 1914-15	61
Hazel Hutchison	
6. The Citizens of Babylon and the Imperial Imperative: Henry James's Modern Parisian Women	71
Claire Garcia	
7. French as the Fantasmal Idiom of Truth in *What Maisie Knew*	81
Agnès Derail-Imbert	
8. Figures of Fulfilment: James and 'a Sense of Italy'	93
Jacek Guthorow	
9. *The Aspern Papers*: From Florence to an Intertexual City, Venice	103
Rosella Mamoli Zorzi	
10. The Wavering Ruins of *The American*	113
Enrico Botta	

III: Appropriating European Thematics

11. Balzacian Intertextuality and Jamesian Autobiography in *The Ambassadors* — Kathleen Lawrence … 123

12. A Discordance Between the Self and the World: The Collector in Balzac's *Cousin Pons* and James's 'Adina' — Simone Francescato … 137

13. The '*déjà vu*' in 'The Turn of the Screw' — Max Duperray … 147

IV: Allusion

14. Some Allusions in the Early Stories — Angus Wrenn … 157

15. *C'est strictement confidentiel*: Buried Allusions in *Confidence* (1879) — Rebekah Scott … 169

16. James and the Habit of Allusion — Oliver Herford … 179

V: Performance

17. The Absent Writer in *The Tragic Muse* — Nelly Valtat-Comet … 193

18. James and the 'Paradox of the Comedian' — Richard Anker … 203

19. Benjamin Britten's Appropriation of James in *Owen Wingrave* — Hubert Teyssandier … 215

VI: Authorship and Self-Representation

20. Narrative Heterogeneity as an Adjustable Fictional Lens in *The American Scene* — Eleftheria Arapoglou … 229

21. James's Faces: Appearance, Absorption and the Aesthetic Significance of the Face — Jakob Stougaard-Nielsen … 237

22. From Copying to Revision: *The American* to *The Ambassadors* — Paula Marantz Cohen … 247

23. Friction with the Publishers, or How James Manipulated his Editors in the Early 1870's — Pierre A. Walker … 255

24. Losing Oneself: Autobiography, Memory, Vision — John Holland … 263

Bibliography of Works Cited … 273

Index … 287

Supplemental chapters available on-line at:
http://www.openbookpublishers.com/product.php/72

Introduction   s5
   Dennis Tredy

Contributors   s8

I. Re-Readings and Re-Workings of the International Theme   s10

1. Tourist Attractions, Stereotypes and Physiognomies in   s11
The American
   H. K. Riikonen

2. 'Haunting and Penetrating the City': The Influence of Emile   s20
Zola's *L'Assommoir* on James's *The Princess Casamassima*
   David Davies

3. The Mother as Artist in "Louisa Pallant": Re-casting the   s29
International Scene
   Larry A. Gray

4. James's Romantic Promises: *The Golden Bowl* and the Virtual   s38
   Leman Giresunlu

II. Beyond Biography   s47

5. Father and Son: The Divided Self in James's *Notes of a Son*   s48
and Brother
   Mhairi Pooler

6. "Fond Calculations": The Triumph of James's Mathematical   s56
Failure
   Isobel Waters

7. A Multiplicity of Folds of an Unconscious 'Crystal' Monad: s68
James, Benjamin, and Blanchot
   Erik S. Roraback

8. "Life after Death": James and Postmodern Biofiction   s78
   Madeleine Danova

Bibliography of Works Cited   s86

Contributors

Richard Anker is a tenured Associate Professor (*maître de conférences*) at Université Blaise Pascal, Clermont-Ferrand 2, where he teaches American literature. He defended a thesis on James in 2007 entitled *Le principe spectral de la representation: Déconstruction mimétique dans l'oeuvre de Henry James*. His current interest in James attempts to situate the author in the European cultural tradition, alongside such writers as Nietzsche and as a precursor to Blanchot.

Eleftheria Arapoglou received her B.A. in English from Aristotle University of Thessaloniki, Greece, in 1995. She completed her M.A. as a Fulbright grantee at the University of Texas at San Antonio, U.S., in 1998 and her PhD in 2005 at Aristotle University. Currently, she is an adjunct member of faculty in the Department of American Literature and Culture of Aristotle University. She has co-edited two volumes—*Transcultural Localisms* (2006); *[City in (Culture] in City)* (2005)—and a special issue of the journal *Gramma* entitled *Comparative Literature and Global Studies: Histories and Trajectories* (2005). She recently completed her book *A Bridge Over the Balkans: Demetra Vaka Brown and the Tradition of Women's Orients*, which is forthcoming from Gorgias Press. Her research interests include the cultural production of space in the modernist tradition, literary sociology, and cultural studies.

Enrico Botta is a PhD student in Literary Genres at the University of L'Aquila, Italy. Botta is currently writing his doctoral thesis on nineteenth-century American epics—in particular on the relationship between the epic mode and the International Theme. He has published his essay "Transatlantic Intertextuality in *The American*" in the volume *Revisionary Interventions into Henry James* (2008) and has presented his research, 'From Barlow to James: Some Epic Features', at Dartmouth College.

Agnès Derail-Imbert is a tenured Associate Professor (*maître de conférences*) at the ENS-Ulm and at the Sorbonne (Paris IV) in Paris. In 2000 she published *Moby-Dick, allures du corps*. She also co-edited and co-translated *Melville: Derniers poèmes* (2010). She has written numerous articles on nineteenth-century American literature.

Max Duperray, professor of English studies at the University of Provence, is a specialist in Gothic fiction. In the last ten years, his main publications have been *Lecture de Frankenstein* (1997); *Le roman anglais dit gothique* (2000); *La Folie et la méthode : essai sur la déréalisation en littérature* (2001); *Confessions by Thomas de Quincey* (2003); *Londres : promenade sous un ciel couvert* (2005); "In a Glass Darkly: Reflexions of a Gothic Past," in *The Remains of the Gothic* (Caliban 15/ 2004), and *Bram Stoker's Dracula* (2005). He has recently edited *Eclats du noir: généricité et hybridation dans la littérature et le cinéma anglophone* (2008) and *Gothic News: Exploring the Gothic in Relation to New Critical Perspectives and Geographic Polarities* (2009).

Simone Francescato earned his PhD from the Università Ca' Foscari of Venice (Italy). He is currently Lecturer in American Literature and Studies at the same university. He has recently published a book entitled *Collecting and Appreciating: Henry James and the Transformation of Aesthetics in the Age of Consumption* (2010). His main area of research is late nineteenth-century American fiction (realism, naturalism and decadence).

Claire Garcia is Professor of English at Colorado College. She writes on diverse topics, including gender and modernism, African American and francophone women's writing, teaching ethnic studies, and Henry James. She is the author of "Jesse Redmon Fauset, Reconsidered" in *The Harlem Renaissance Revisited: Arts, Politics, and Letters*, "Black Bourgeois Women's Narratives in the Post-Reagan, 'Post-Civil Rights', 'Post-Feminist' Era," in *From Bourgeois to Boojie: Black Middle-Class Performances*, and "A 'Native Expatriate' Reads Henry James" in *The Henry James Review*, as well as other articles.

Jean Gooder, a Fellow Emerita of Newnham College, Cambridge, has edited the Penguin edition of *The Education of Henry Adams* and published on Henry James and Edith Wharton. Her interests are in connections between Anglo-American and French writing.

Jacek Gutorow is a poet, a literary critic and a translator. He has published five volumes of poetry, four books of critical essays (recently *Luminous Traversing: Wallace Stevens and the American Sublime*, 2007) and numerous translations of British and American poetry (Simon Armitage, Charles Tomlinson, Wallace Stevens, John Ashbery). He won the 2004 Ludwik Fryde Award granted by the International Association of Literary Critics. His poems, essays and reviews have been reprinted in important anthologies and translated into several languages. Currently he is Assistant Professor at the University of Opole, Poland.

Oliver Herford is a Darby Fellow and Tutor in English Literature at Lincoln College, Oxford. He received his PhD (2009) from the University of London for a thesis on Henry James's late non-fiction, which he is currently revising for publication; other work in progress includes essays on some ethical problems of personal correspondence (for letter-writers and editors), and on the vocal dimensions of late Jamesian style. He will edit *The Prefaces* in the forthcoming Cambridge Edition of *The Complete Fiction of Henry James*.

John Holland received a doctorate in English and American literature from Princeton University and a *Diplôme d'études approfondies* in Psychoanalysis from the Université de Paris VIII (Vincennes-St.-Denis). He is the translator of Colette Soler's *What Lacan Said About Women* (2006) and Markos Zafiropoulos's *Lacan and Lévi-Strauss: The Return to Freud, 1951-1957* (2010). He has taught English at Michigan State University, at the American University in Paris, and at several French universities, including the University of Nantes. He is also a member of the editorial board of the journal *Psychanalyse*.

Hazel Hutchison lectures in British and American literature at the University of Aberdeen. Her research focuses on the literature of the late nineteenth and early twentieth centuries. Her publications include *Seeing and Believing: Henry James and the Spiritual World* (2006) and articles on James, D. G. Rosetti, and Rupert Brooke. She has edited *The Forbidden Zone* by Mary Borden (2008), and is currently writing a monograph on American writing of the First World War.

Kathy Lawrence is a professor at George Washington University, where she teaches a wide range of courses on American literature and art, including Emerson and his Circle, Henry James and his Family, American Romanticism, Literature and Film of American Suburbia, and Hollywood in the American Imagination. Her research interests focus on Henry James and his relation to his American past, on missing members of the Transcendental movement, and on the intersection of fiction, sculpture, and painting in 19-th century American culture. Her most recent work has uncovered the art of transcendentalist Caroline Sturgis as well as that of sculptor Waldo Story and painter Julian Story, and their relation to Henry James's memoirs and his late style.

Rosella Mamoli Zorzi is professor of American Studies and Director of the Graduate School in Languages, Cultures and Societies at the University of

Venice. She has worked on the relationships between American writers and Venetian painters (Titian, Tintoretto, Tiepolo). Her works include *In Venice and in the Veneto with Henry James* (2005), *Henry James: Letters from the Palazzo Barbaro* (1998), *Beloved Boy: Letters to Hendrick Andersen* (2004) and *Letters to Isabella Stewart Gardner* (2009).

Paula Marantz Cohen is Distinguished Professor of English at Drexel University. She is the author of four nonfiction books and four novels, including, most recently, *What Alice Knew: A Most Curious Tale of Henry James and Jack the Ripper* (2010). She is also the host of the *Drexel InterView*, a cable TV show broadcast on 300 public television and university-affiliated stations throughout the U.S., and a co-editor of *jml: Journal of Modern Literature*.

Roxana Oltean is Associate Professor at the English Department in the Faculty of Foreign Languages at the University of Bucharest, and holds a PhD in Philology. She has published articles in international journals of American literature and culture, including *The Henry James Review*, and two books on transatlantic and global imagology in the works of Henry James. She teaches courses in American utopian models, in Transatlantic Relations and in nineteenth-century American literature and culture.

Esther Sanchez-Pardo is is an Associate Professor of English at Complutense University in Madrid (Spain). Apart from Henry James, she works on modernism, poetics and psychoanalysis. She has recently edited *Mina Loy: Critical Anthology* (2009), and has published *Cultures of the Death Drive: Melanie Klein and Modernist Melancholia* (2003), co-authored *Ophelia's Legacy: Schizotexts in Twentieth CenturyWomen's Literature* (2000) and co-edited *Women, Identities and Poetry* (1999) and *Feeling the Worlds* (2001).

Eric Savoy is associate professor of Comparative Literature at Université de Montréal. The 2009 President of the Henry James Society, he has published widely on Henry James and various issues related to queer theory. His book, *Conjugating the Subject: Henry James and Queer Formalism* will appear in 2011.

Rebekah Scott recently completed her PhD on Henry James at Cambridge University, where she now teaches. She is also a post-doctoral researcher at the University of Ghent. She has published essays on Henry James and Charles Dickens and is one of the volume editors of *The Complete Fiction of Henry James*, to be published by Cambridge University Press.

Jakob Stougaard-Nielsen is Lecturer in Scandinavian Literature at UCL. His PhD thesis (2007) concerned Henry James's New York Edition of his collected novels and tales in the context of the visual culture and print culture of the late-nineteenth and early-twentieth century. He has published articles in *The Henry James Review* on authorship and the figure of attention in James's work, and is a contributor to the anthology *Henry James in Context* (2010).

Hubert Teyssandier is professor (emeritus) of English literature at the Université Paris 3- Sorbonne Nouvelle, where he has taught the nineteenth- and twentieth-century English novel since 1974. He founded and directed a research centre for studies on intertextuality in literature and the arts and has recently published articles on Henry James and Virginia Woolf. He is currently working on Henry James and Benjamin Britten.

Nelly Valtat-Comet is a tenured Associate Professor of English at the University of Tours, France. She studied at the École Normale Supérieure and defended a doctoral dissertation on *Vision and Voice in the Tales of Henry James*. She has published several articles on Henry James and is the author of a monograph on Edith Wharton's *The Custom of the Country* (2000).

Pierre A. Walker is Professor of English at Salem State University. He is the author of *Reading Henry James in French Cultural Contexts* and of articles on Henry James, African American literature, and literary theory; editor of *Henry James on Culture*; and co-general editor of *The Complete Letters of Henry James*.

Angus Wrenn teaches English Literature and Comparative Literature at the London School of Economics and has published articles on Ford Madox Ford and Harold Pinter, as well as an interdisciplinary study of James, Ford and Hans Holbein. He contributed the chapter on Paul Bourget and Marcel Proust in *The Reception of Henry James in Europe* (ed. Annick Duperray, 2007) and has published a monograph on *Henry James and the Second Empire* (2009). He is editing a volume of the shorter fiction in the Cambridge Complete James Edition (forthcoming in 2016). A study of the influence of Soviet Russia on the work of George Bernard Shaw is also forthcoming (2011).

Preface
Dennis Tredy

As an American in Europe, Henry James may have often felt as "bewildered" and "beguiled" as some of his most memorable American protagonists abroad, such as Christopher Newman or Lambert Strether. However, in spite of statements that many assume to be critical of a certain lack of sophistication and lightness of cultural baggage among Americans abroad, James also spoke of this status with a good deal of praise. He considered that being an American was in fact "an excellent preparation for culture," in so far as Americans, he felt, could deal, more freely than Europeans, "with forms of civilization not their own" and could "pick and choose and assimilate and in short (aesthetically) claim their property wherever they found it."

This ability to appropriate both European culture and space is at the heart of James's famed "International Theme," and that theme, though much expanded and reworked, was at the heart of discussions held and papers given at the first conference organized by the "European Society of Jamesian Studies" in Paris in April of 2009. Of the nearly sixty papers given by speakers from twenty different countries, twenty-four have been selected for this collection—two dozen studies that, collectively, expand and redefine the 'International Theme' both in James's life and in his fiction and that demonstrate the various manners in which James achieved this aesthetic (re)appropriation—that "vast intellectual and fusion and synthesis" he had dreamt of as a young writer bound for the Old World.

The papers in this collection thus aim to take into account the myriad aspects of this intellectual game of transfer, appropriation and heritage. How did this concept and dynamic of cultural differences between the Old and New World develop throughout James's life and fiction? James would indeed move, in distinct stages, from early notions of American innocence abroad to the arcane poetics of redemption and reconciliation of his 'major phase'. How were James's trans-Atlantic connections affected by the political issues and ethical concerns of the turn of the century? How accurate are the parallels drawn between the author's experiences as an American abroad and those of his protagonists? How did James perceive certain European countries and how did he appropriate their people and their culture within his fiction? Which European authors and thinkers had the greatest influence on James's literary and cultural development, and how were they absorbed into James's fiction? What picture did James draw, in both his fictional and non-fictional works, of the literary culture, the people, the politics or even the landscape of specific European countries? Perhaps most importantly, how did this ever-evolving dynamic of trans-Atlantic transfer and (re)appropriation affect the way James saw himself—or chose to represent himself—when, at the dawn of the twentieth century, he set out to take stock of his career and to look back on the choices he had made?

The twenty-four papers in this collection, divided into six sections, develop all of these points and provide a detailed picture of James's trans-Atlantic aesthetics, one that is steeped in profound notions of transtextuality and of cultural appropriation.

I. Ethics and Aesthetics

In the first part of this collection, there are four papers that, collectively, demonstrate how Jamesian aesthetics, particularly at the turn of the century, were greatly influenced by matters of ethics, by sociological concerns, and by new notions of 'capital' (both financial and political) and of 'capitalism'. The first two articles, by keynote speakers at the conference, go into great depth when exploring the interconnectedness both between ethics and aesthetics and between textual analysis of specific works by James and insight into the author's views of dangers of the coming century. Jean Gooder, for example, focuses on James's aesthetic and ethical concerns when writing his answer to the *roman dialogué, The Awkward Age,* a novel conceived when James's experimentation with technical and formal innovations in his writing as well as his fears of a society on the verge of a "great modern collapse" were both at their peak. Gooder shows, through analysis of both the novel itself and the author's literary influences at the time, that intellectual freedom (that is, freedom of mind, of expression, of speech) may "open the door to the Devil," but it was nevertheless, in James's eyes, a heavenly virtue as the twentieth century loomed on the horizon. Similarly, Roxana Oltean also uses insightful textual analysis to bring to light James's ethical concerns—in this case those concerning globalization and cosmopolitanism—at the turn of the century. Oltean, however, focuses mainly on works written during James's "major phase," at the very onset of the twentieth century. She demonstrates how James's late novels and more autobiographical works focused on the theme of redemption and proposed a new model of "cosmopolitan ethics" that was a far cry from the comparatively simple themes of romantic discovery and bewilderment that made up his earlier 'International Theme'. Then, in Esther Sánchez-Pardo's study of *The Ambassadors*, the ethical and aesthetic dimensions of James's art at the turn of the century are again underscored. Sanchez-Pardo analyzes James's sophisticated and nuanced understanding of "capitalism" at the dawn of the twentieth century, a representation of a changing economic world that was still grounded in aesthetics, culture and matters of taste. By coordinating textual analysis of James's late novel with theoretical work by sociologists such as Thorstein Veblen, Sanchez-Pardo points out how James's notions of bourgeois possession, materialism and consumption illustrate a specifically Jamesian form of capitalism, one relying notably on "the currency of appearances." In the final paper in this section, Eric Savoy similarly seeks to show how James managed to re-appropriate and redefine certain concepts lifted, as it were, from the world of finance. Savoy demonstrates that there is a confluence and a congruity between James's formalist concepts of narrative "economy," "investment" and "speculation," and their lexical counterparts found in modern economic theory and the world of finance. Savoy's comparative and deconstructive approach again stresses the intense interplay between ethics and aesthetics in late James, just as it illustrates another way in which James re-appropriated certain aspects of capitalism and materialism as the author stepped, ever so gingerly, into the twentieth century.

II. French and Italian Hours

The six articles to be found in this section focus on a different kind of re-appropriation and seem to cast James himself in a role commonly associated with the protagonists of his early and even later fiction—that is, that of the observant American in Europe. Here, through James's letters, travel writings and certain works of fiction, the author's impressions of France and Italy are explored in great depth, taking us beyond the simple 'travel sketch' to reveal a more detailed and more subjective portrait of two places dear to James and central to widespread notions of what 'European culture' actually entailed during his lifetime.

The first three papers deal with James's impression of France, focusing in turn on what the country, the people and the language represented to James as both a traveller and a writer. Hazel Hutchison, for example, studies James's late letters and his wartime essay "France," which were written as an elderly James, driven to despair by the pending "crash of civilization" that World War I represented, tried to work out exactly what France meant to him. In those late writings, James tries to put his finger on that "unnameable something" that had always made France stand out in his mind, on that indefinable yet undeniable "otherness" that had the power to modify British and American values, and on his own seemingly ambivalent assessment of French "civilization" that seems to teeter between *bona fide* praise and thinly veiled criticism.

Then, Claire Garcia looks more specifically at the way James represented Parisian women, most notable in *The Ambassadors*, and at what this reveals about James's changing notions of gender at the turn of the century. James's portrayal of Parisian women, Garcia shows, seems to embody challenges and new possibilities for the "modern metropolitan consciousness" and move away from more conventional views of women that are often associated with James and his fiction. To complete the portrait of France, Agnès Derail-Imbert takes on the French idiom itself and the symbolic value it seemed to have for James, notably in his experimental novel *What Maisie Knew*, the final third of which is set in France. Much like the overall image of France sketched out in Hutchison's paper, the French language, within James's novel, is associated with an indefinable otherness, with elusive circumlocution, and with a truth or desired sum of knowledge that remains unattainable to the outsider. What better backdrop for the story of a young girl who knows "far too much" for her age and yet whose actual degree of knowledge is curiously denied to both readers and her fellow characters?

The two papers that follow then offer a similar approach to James's impressions of Italy, and to the symbolic value James attributed to cities such as Venice, Rome or Florence—impressions that go far beyond the romanticized or cliché visions of the time. Jacek Gutorow analyzes how different James's representations of Italy were from those of France and England, noting how James's Italy was one of peregrination and of crossing of thresholds, a place of floating, suspended aesthetic images. Gutorow leads us through James's vision of Venice, Rome and even Naples, and this circuitous journey into James's aesthetic re-appropriation of Italy is concluded by Rosella Mamoli Zorzi's paper on the representation of Florence and Venice in James's "The Aspern Papers." Why did James choose to switch the setting from Florence to Venice? What was it about Venice's cultural, artistic and literary heritage that made it, in James's eye, an ideal backdrop for his story of intrigue and allusive aesthetic bliss?

Finally, Enrico Botta re-evaluates James's age-old 'International Theme' by analyzing the way James represents the ruins of the Old World that his American characters discover on their journeys through Europe. Through the prism of Italian scholar Francesco Orlando's theory on non-fictional objects in literature, Botta studies how the ruins of the Old World, when seen through the eyes of characters such as Christopher Newman, allow James to redefine the relationship between the Old and the New World and to overcome the apparent opposition between the two cultures by combining and overlapping them. In this new dialectic, James assigns much more than aesthetic value to these places, as they become landmarks to both an older order pitted against American values and to the decadence of both the past and the present.

III. Appropriating European Thematics

James's fascination with Europe was, of course, not limited to its people, languages, landmarks and observed cultural differences—it was also deeply rooted in its literary heritage, which James would also reinterpret, re-evaluate and make his own. This section will then focus on a few European literary masters from the 'Old World' who would have a lasting effect on James and his art. For example, much has been written, even by James himself, on the great 'lessons' he learned from Balzac. The first two papers in this section take a closer look at those supposed teachings and provide a more thorough exploration of the influence of two specific works by Balzac: *Louis Lambert* (1832) and *Cousin Pons* (1847). Kathy Lawrence starts things off with an intertextual reading of Henry James's novel *The Ambassadors* and of Balzac's earlier novel, *Louis Lambert*, whose protagonist was the namesake for James's character Lambert Strether. Lawrence's study reveals convincing but subtle ties between the two works and even manages to draw parallels between the fictional worlds and the actual lives of both authors. Then, Simone Francescato uncovers a connection between Balzac's late novel *Cousin Pons* and a very early story by James entitled

"Adina." As Francescato demonstrates, the parallels can be drawn on many levels, from characterization to plot to shared but disenchanted views of art collecting and of the rise of a seemingly misguided materialism in Europe. Then, Max Duperray explores the connection between Charlotte Brontë's *Jane Eyre* and James's "The Turn of the Screw," showing how the texts overlapped and in particular how James borrowed from the well-known tale so as to better subvert it and play with its romantic pretext. As Duperray shows, the reader's moment of *déjà vu* is actually recognition defamiliarized. It also seems to be situated somewhere in between parody and tribute, as James used many literary devices and dramatic situations borrowed from Brontë's novel in order to mislead readers' expectations and forge, as Duperray suggests, "a transcript of romantic sinister overtones as archetypal."

IV. Allusion

If, in the previous section, the focus was on comparative studies of certain French and English works that James used as key subtexts, the discussion now focuses on James general methodology when it came to incorporating myriad literary and cultural allusions into his works. Although all three papers here focus primarily on James's references and allusions to Shakespeare, all three also show how such references were intertwined with allusions to other European writers and thinkers. Angus Wrenn, for example, explores such allusions in James's early stories, including "A Passionate Pilgrim" (1871), "The Madonna of the Future" (1873) and "The Siege of London" (1883). From Shakespeare to Balzac and Cherbuliez, from contemporary European history to nineteenth-century cultural trends and debates—Wrenn covers a wide range of allusions made in James's early fiction, paying a good deal of attention to the often subtle ways these allusions were made and to the different narrative voices that provided them. Following Wrenn's lead, Rebekah Scott also deals with subtle allusions in early James, though her main focus concerns those "buried" in James's little-known 1879 novel *Confidence*. She unearths a great deal of "buried" or glancing allusions in the work—from Shakespeare and Milton, to Balzac and Feuillet, to Augier and Sardou, among others. She also draws a key parallel between James's notorious elusiveness and his allusions, and she explores the question of whether these allusions were ever intended to be "unburied" by the reader, as well as whether they were conscious or unconscious subtexts for the author. Finally, Oliver Herford approaches the question from a different angle and traces a single allusion to a line from Shakespeare's *Hamlet* ("My father, in his habit, as he lived!" —III, 4, 130) through the last two decades of James's writing. He discovers that allusions to this key line abound—in James's fiction as well as in his autobiographies and other retrospective works of his late career. Herford thus focuses on James's method of allusion and stresses the importance of "continuity" and "recurrence" within that method, which often allows a single allusion to prompt a series of others.

V. Performance

The papers in this section focus on two very different aspects of stage performance in James, as the first two deal with James's use of the nuanced metaphors of the playwright and of the actor in James's fiction, particularly in his 1890 novel *The Tragic Muse*, while the third paper focuses on a specific operatic adaptation of James by Benjamin Britten. Thus Nelly Valtat-Comet begins with the notion of the absent author or playwright in James and demonstrates how James staged, in a way, his own absence from the stage of his work of fiction, using a multitude of indirect methods borrowed from drama (e.g., the use of props, of characters as mouthpieces, of key dialogue scenes) in order to stage the absence of the key male writer-figure. In Richard Anker's work, it is the paradoxical figure of the actor in James's novel that is the main focus. Anker also studies James's *The Tragic Muse*, working off Diderot's notion of the "paradox of the comedian," a paradox that somehow marries both a "native lack of identity" and a "strictly mimetic identity." Thus a key dynamic in *The Tragic Muse* is a sort of role play of the tension between the rhetorical and the phenomenological, a dynamic that, as Anker shows, spreads to other key works by James, including the earlier *The Bostonians* and the later "The Turn of the Screw."

The third paper is from Hubert Teyssandier, who gives a very thorough and insightful analysis of Benjamin Britten's 1970 adaptation of James's 1892 ghostly tale, "Owen Wingrave." Though far more attention has been paid by scholars to Britten's earlier adaptation of James's "The Turn of the Screw," Teyssandier here provides a detailed study of the dramatic, literary and musical devices used by Britten to bring "Owen Wingrave" to life, as if were. We discover that many of James's own literary devices for representing the 'ghostly', some of which were used by James himself when adapting his own stories for the stage, are also used by Britten. Teyssandier also draws informed parallels between the visual devices and the musical devices used in the production, thereby providing a most masterful analysis.

VI. Authorship and Self-Representation

The five final papers in this collection all deal with ways that James chose to represent *himself*—in fiction and autobiography, in his private correspondences and in editing choices—throughout his career, focussing specifically on his very early and, especially, his very late career—as the latter often dealt quite heavily with re-telling and re-evaluating the former.

Eleftheria Arapoglou starts things off by focusing on *The American Scene*, in which James revisits America, observes how it had changed since he moved to Europe and hints at his motives for leaving in the first place. Arapoglou demonstrates how James seemed to cast himself in the role of one of his own "centres of consciousness," giving himself a position on the threshold between two cultures, both inside and outside the world he was observing, and providing a multi-voiced presentation that is nevertheless harmonious. Similarly, Jacob Stougaard-Nielsen deals with the way James represented himself at the end of his career, though the focus this time is on James's relation to his own visual representation—that is, his choice of portraits and frontispiece for the New York Edition. James had to decide how to establish himself as the central consciousness and main character, as it were, of his collected works. He also had to establish a certain visual 'exchange' with those who read his collected works (as the portrait does indeed "stare back" at readers). Thus, both Arapoglou and Stougaard-Nielsen demonstrate how James's questioning of his own identity and sense of self led him to cast himself, in many ways, in the role of some of his main characters.

Then, Paula Marantz-Cohen takes a comparative view of the early and late stages of James's career and traces certain surface patterns for each of the two periods that correspond to two key writing processes—that of copying and of revision. Both in his writing and in his personal life, James seemed to gradually move from one stage to the other, and it is also through detailed textual analysis of an early work (*The American*) and a later one (*The Ambassadors*) that Marantz-Cohen defends this distinction. As if to illustrate this point, the last two papers deal, in turn, with each of the two stages Marantz-Cohen defines. Pierre A. Walker thus focuses on the so-called 'copying' phase, as he describes in great detail how a very young James tried to act the role of the powerful, established author in order to manipulate his publishers. By bringing to light key passages from both professional and personal correspondences, Walker shows how James managed to play *Scribner's*, *The Galaxy* and *The Atlantic Monthly* off of each other with insolent skill. Finally, John Holland takes one last look at the 'revision' stage that is late James, paying particular attention to James's autobiographies. He provides us with a detailed analysis of the thought processes involved in James's endeavour to translate his former self and his own experiences into text, which includes a discussion of how the reader is made a part of the process.

In addition to the studies found here in the print edition, the online version of this publication will include eight other papers by Jamesian scholars that together broaden the scope of this study and further explore the ways in which James sought to redefine himself as an American in Europe, to rework his famed International Theme and his representation of Europeans, and to reappropriate European authors, artifacts and landmarks.

Thus, the papers in this collection seek to re-evaluate the ethical quality of the whole process of transfer and appropriation, situated as it was at the meeting point between historical and inner culture. For James, transtextual and cross-cultural relations "stop nowhere," as the scholars who contributed to this collection aim to demonstrate.

February 2011

On 'The European Society of Jamesian Studies'

Adrian Harding

That the Society should be housed in the Comparative Literature Department of The American University of Paris is, we hope, an appropriately Jamesian augury for the pursuit of the enterprise. As our department co-chair, Geoff Gilbert, said in opening words for our inaugural conference in April 2009, AUP could be imagined as a quintessential, if protean, protagonist of the international theme, a young(ish) American finding their way in Europe, garnering the unpredictable experience of their own education, to change themselves and those who encounter them. And how nicely the familiar pronominal slippage of that, between the singular subject and the plural possession, suits the indeterminacies common to both James's writing and to the perspectives motivating a comparatist experience of literature and its relations to the world. We might even say, without pushing the boat out too far, that the Society is reflecting that exploratory experience back upon itself, as a European entity exploring what is also such a carefully American oeuvre with its specific ironies of knowledge, its own ways of troping the world toward meaning. We come quickly to the limits of these grander essentialisms, however, to try and find our place between and among these things, seeing values come into existence as they come into play, in the encounters of reading James, and reading James reading.

This institutional and cultural identity of the Society will, we hope, reflect in its community of readers and scholars something of the multifarious interests of James's work, Our mission will be to contribute to the promotion of Jamesian studies in European countries by offering further opportunities for Jamesian scholars and other interested persons who cannot regularly participate in the events organized by the transatlantic "Henry James Society." The Society means to contribute to the development of scientific cooperation on an international scale by fostering conference meetings in different European institutions and by promoting publication and doctoral research generated on both sides of the Atlantic. We hope the particular structure of a European Society of Jamesian Studies will enable a field of creative interaction of texts and contexts, foregrounds and backgrounds, a turbine of *topoi* both atlantic and continental, inner and outer, synchronic and diachronic, intellectual and economic.

We mean to confront and refine methodologies and practices by developing intertextual approaches, focussing on :

the theoretical dimension of the "house of fiction" James built and the interrelations between theory and text.

the genesis of his work and the writers that influenced him

the multiple and multiform reverberations of his own work in modern and contemporary fiction and literary criticism.

As a consequence the Society will be open to the study of other fiction writers and to all nineteenth- and twentieth-century specialists willing to envisage James's texts, paratexts and critical essays from a comparatist and receptionist angle.

Because Henry James was also a cultural historian, dreaming of "a vast intellectual fusion and synthesis of the national tendencies of the world," the Society will privilege "the international theme," encouraging the exchange between new currents and older traditions of Humanities research on both sides of the Atlantic. And because Europe had such an impact on James's life and work, one of the Society's particular missions will be to examine the many ways in which the American writer can be considered as part of a European heritage, interconnecting the culturally distinct European identities. In these various senses of "reception" we hope the literary and cultural will come close enough together to illustrate a particularly Jamesian character of attention, and to determine a strong and distinctive intellectual identity for our activities.

The Society has already benefited from the administrative and financial help of the American University for its first two conferences, in April 2009 and October 2010, for which we are extremely grateful, especially as we enjoy both our university affiliation and the complete freedom of an academic society. Our founding members, Annick Duperray (with whom the idea of the Society originated), Dennis Tredy and Adrian Harding, have quickly been joined by an international gathering of scholars committed to the study of James's work and of its world. Three of these members—Nicola Bradbury, Richard Gooder and Georges Hughes—deserve special recognition for their invaluable help as readers for the current volume.

We would also like to express our sincere gratitude to Alessandra Tosi, the Managing Director of Open Book Publications, and to their editor, Bérénice Guyot-Réchard, for their patience, hard work and dedication in putting together this publication

Our October meeting in Paris has allowed us to take stock of our first two years of activity, our first conferences and publications with Open Book Publishers in England, in order to consolidate our constitution, develop our core membership and plan ahead. Future conferences and publications may now develop under different institutional auspices and in various editorial hands while we continue to enjoy our affiliation with the Comparative Literature Department at AUP.

November 2010

I
ETHICS AND AESTHETICS

1. Henry James on Opening the Door to the Devil

Jean Gooder

We begin on 26 January 1900, the start of the new century. Past midnight James dashed off one of his countless notes to a writer who had sent him their work for comment. That night—in exuberant vein—it was to a Mrs. Everard Cotes. She'd implied some resemblance between her novel, *His Honour and a Lady,* and the Master. Politely puzzled by her claim, James responds with his freest gallantry. "We are both very intelligent and observant," he writes, "and conscious that a work of art must make some small effort to *be* one; must sacrifice somehow and somewhere to the exquisite..."

> So we open the door to the Devil himself—who is nothing but the sense of beauty, of mystery, of relations, of appearances, of abysses of the whole— *and* of EXPRESSION! That's *all* he is [...]
>
> (*Letters* IV 131).

This Devil is a long way from the figure James had watched and reduced to bathos, in Henry Irving's *Faust* (1887)—a production about whose "little mechanical artifices" and "spurting flames" he was scathing. "That blue vapours should attend on the steps of Mephistopheles is a very poor substitute for his giving us a moral shudder" ("The Acting in Mr. Irving's 'Faust'" 222). The kind of "moral shudder," perhaps, that is palpable at the end of "The Turn of the Screw," as the governess sees, pressed against the window, "the hideous author of our woe." Looking (as she believes) on "the white face of damnation" she challenges Miles to "confess," insists that he *name* what he thinks is "there"—only to draw from him the climactic ambiguity of his cry: "Peter Quint—you devil!" (*"The Turn of the Screw"* [1908] 308-9). But this is my disclaimer: I'm not here engaging with the supernatural, or even the satanic, though on occasion James may have done both. The Devil of that midnight letter to Mrs. Cotes offers a more engaging prospect. He is an Arnoldian spirit delighting in the "free play of mind"—a true 'familiar' to the writer: a Devil with the potency of metaphor.

The metaphor here has a hidden history. In 1900 James was reading the new "Life" of George Sand by Wladimir Karénine. Two volumes had appeared in Paris in 1899: James knew René Doumic's notice in the *Revue des Deux Mondes* and himself wrote a long piece on George Sand for the *North American Review* (April 1902). Neither Doumic nor James mentions Karénine's striking introduction to her "Life," but it sets the stage for her whole account of George Sand. Karénine describes a curious anthology published in 1845 by the editor and writer Jules Hetzel, called *Le Diable à Paris* (I 1-8). Why the bizarre title? In a light-hearted preface Hetzel jokes that Satan, bored in Hell, has taken a quick trip round his other domains, but pressed for time he had left out Earth. He returns to find some newly arrived sinners making a *fracas* at the gates of hell. Asked where they're from, the sinners shout: "*Nous arrivons tous de Paris.*" [We're all coming from Paris.] Pressed further, they give such contradictory accounts of the city that Satan can draw only one conclusion: Paris must be an extraordinarily interesting place. A minor devil is sent to gather the fullest information on the city and its people. Disguised as a *flâneur*, he hardly sets foot on the boulevards before falling in love. This, alas, incapacitates him for the serious analysis his task requires. He has a bright idea: why not "*faire travailler les hommes à sa place!*" [Get men to do his work.] Material floods in from writers, artists, thinkers and poets—from Balzac, Musset, Gautier, Gavarni, Nerval, George Sand and many others. Happily the *diablotin* tosses this composite 'report from Paris' into space, with the cry: "*Va au diable!*"[Go to Hell!]

Most of the pieces in this urbane anthology share the wit and the cynicism of Hetzel's infernal framework. Karénine's point is that George Sand's does not. A reluctant collaborator in the project, George Sand had stuck to her own terms—those of a spiritual daughter of Rousseau and admirer of the Socialist, Pierre Leroux. This essay of 1844 defines for Karénine the true measure of her subject: the passionate idealism and outspoken personal commitment for which George Sand was most admired or disliked. Her survey of Paris is a stunning indictment of inequalities of wealth, of exploitation, of the intellectual superficiality of urban life. The Devil is indeed abroad—not as a bright literary fiction, but as a political and cultural reality.

I.

James's midnight letter welcomes the Devil in the name of art. Consider his attributes: "beauty," "mystery," "relations," "appearances," and above all, in capital letters, "EXPRESSION." This is the vocabulary of an aesthete, of a contributor to *The Yellow Book*, perhaps, but with no suggestion of a political dimension, or of the "moral shudder" of a direct encounter with evil. Yet the airy insistence that this is *"all"* the Devil is carries its own dare-devilry. Isn't the implication that the reality of evil is to be detected precisely *in* appearances, *in* the "relations" of men and women, *in the expressive resources of language*? "Mysteries" and "abysses" are the very materials of art. "No themes are so human [says the Preface to *What Maisie Knew*] as those that reflect for us out of the confusion of human life, the close connexion of bliss and bale, so dangling before us for ever that bright hard medal [....] one face of which is somebody's right and ease and the other somebody's pain and wrong" (1158). Phrases that echo Dr. Johnson's lines on Shakespeare's "mixed" plays, "exhibiting the real state of sublunary nature," where "the chaos of mingled purposes and casualties" serves to show the "crimes" and "absurdities" of life. That is, the world around the novelist is sufficient material, its signs—the manners of particular social groups—enough to yield the measure of ease or pain, of "crimes" and "absurdities." James wasn't obsessed with origins, but absorbed by the present. His art is fuelled by the need to pose difficult questions about the world he inhabited. So his Devil is a contemporary, who collaborates with an imagination fed by relations, appearances, uncertainties—by what might become a defining moment, or even a defining turn of phrase.

I offer one such moment in the spirit of comedy. In 1876 (some 30 years after Hetzel) James was mailing his own reports from Paris to the *New York Tribune*. By August the city was deserted and he had joined the vacation exodus to the coast. Sitting idly on the beach at Étretat, he recognised an actress from the Palais-Royal (no less!) sporting a bathing dress in which, as he saw, "even the minimum has been appreciably scanted." He watches the actress survey her "breezy nether limbs" and with a casual "*C'est convenable, j'espère, eh?*" ['I trust I'm decent!'] trot up onto a springboard to make a great aerial dive, executing in mid-air the most graceful of somersaults. James muses on

> the curious and delicate question why a lady may go so far as to put herself into a single scant, clinging garment and take a straight leap, head

> downwards, before 300 spectators, without violation of propriety—leaving the impropriety with her turning over in the air in such a way that for five seconds her head is upward. The logic of the matter is mysterious; white and black are divided by a hair. But the fact remains that virtue is on one side of the hair and vice on the other
>
> ("A French Watering Place" 204-05).

That critical hair's breadth dividing virtue from vice—or at least, the *perception* of this fine line—was to figure in his fiction on many occasions. Not always with such unqualified delight. Paris proved as interesting (and contradictory) a city to James as it had to Hetzel's Satan. It had the attraction of an intellectual magnet, where opposites meet, where life and art are pushed to (and beyond) the limits of the *convenable*. The "restless analyst" was to note the beauty and mysteries of the place and its people over a life-time. For all his wide reading, James's material isn't only literary. His 'map' of France came to have a rare density of reference—one that rightly prompts the European dimension of this conference.

France was both familiar and 'other,' as instanced by the "curious and delicate" question James put to himself at Étretat. Propriety and impropriety are codes by which a social group exerts control over its members. George Sand, James knew, had eluded such control. Even before the sensation of *Indiana* (1832), "this woman" (as he put it) was "too imperious a force, too powerful a machine, to make the limits of her activity coincide with those of wifely submissiveness." She had, abundantly, the determination and the capacity for "making acquaintance with life at first hand" ("George Sand" 1877, 716). Claiming the highest of moral vantage points, George Sand had crossed every line of "conventions and proprieties, and even decencies." 'Anglo-Saxon' notions of 'discretion' didn't figure either in her volatile domestic life or in her prolific literary output. When the political pressures of the Second Empire forced her from Paris, she reinvented her image as "*la bonne Dame de Nohant.*" But to those around her and within her family she remained as uninhibited, as frank, as ever—on her own terms.

The riddle was how to square George Sand's "distinction" with her "vulgarity"—her beautiful manner with her dubious matter. When it came to handling "relations between the sexes," James jibbed: she was "*too* explicit, too business-like" and altogether "too technical" ("George Sand" 727). Later Karénine was to shed a different light on the case: she cites a long letter from Balzac to his future wife, Mme Hanska, written in the spring of 1838 while staying with George Sand at Nohant. By chance they had had three days alone, when (James speculates) "the wonderful friends [...] could endlessly talk and smoke by the fire. For once we feel sure fundamental questions were not shirked" ("George Sand" 772). Balzac's account of his hostess and their talk touched truths that James hadn't been able to formulate: fundamental questions of his own about the mysterious logic of gender and propriety. He was revising those hair's breadth distinctions between white and black. The questions become less formulaic: forget about supposedly *feminine* "sensibility" and "graces" and "the scene quite changes." You see that:

> As a man Madame Sand was admirable—especially as a man of the dressing-gown and slippers order, easy of approach and *tutoiement*, rubbing shoulders with queer company and not superstitiously haunted by the conception of the gentleman
>
>   ("George Sand: The New Life" 773).

Relax *gendered* roles and she becomes "comprehensible." In 1899, more than thirty years after her death, it was clear that "this woman" had shown quite how far a first-hand acquaintance with life might take you. At the turn of the century "change" was more than ever "in the air." "Women [James saw] are turned more and more to looking at life as men look at it and to getting from it what men get" (774). Reading Balzac's letter was to overhear actual voices, to catch the quick of human realities, then—and *now*.

II.

George Sand had simply *assumed* an intellectual freedom that compromised neither her public reputation nor her private life. Hers was a world of principles without proprieties. The "marvel" was that she had "positively got off from paying" for it ("George Sand: The New Life" 751). Quite how *much* she had "got away with" was only just coming into the public domain. James read as avidly as Edith Wharton the newly appearing volumes of letters by George Sand, Marie Dorval and Hortense Allart—women who had executed moral somersaults of the most daring kind, flouting the *convenable* in dress and conduct alike. Yet by the 1890's social codes had tightened significantly. Boundaries were under pressure, the costs of infringing them higher. For good reason the *jeune fille* became a key fictional *topos*. The young yet-unmarried girl is a social point where that line between white and black is most in question, where the Devil could well lie in appearances—in what is seen and what is said. James's Maisie Farange owes something to the young Olga Caracciolo, goddaughter to the Prince of Wales, whose mother (a dubious Duchess) he had provided with a villa at Dieppe. Painted by Jacques-Emile Blanche (infanta-style, in a pink dress), Olga was already in the *longer* skirts worn by girls who were to "come out." Yet, silent and melancholy, "a prisoner, without friends of her age and rank," she was the object of audible adult speculation about her marriage prospects. James (like Proust) knew Olga and the social world of Dieppe well. He found it "a reduced Florence" where "every type of character for a novelist seems to gather." "That enchanting Olga [he added] learnt more at Dieppe than my *Maisie* knew" (Blanche 52). An instance of life and art re-crossing.

In 1895 James was noting another version of this theme—to become, three years later, the masterpiece that is *The Awkward Age*. This very *English* novel is premised on a theoretical issue dividing London from Paris. The tactic of cultural contrast "doubles" the effect, catching "reflected light from across the Channel." It has some odd French sources and a larger French dimension. The *Notebooks* suggest where James got his start: "a little volume of *Notes sur Londres* by one 'Brada'" that he'd come across in the library of the Athenaeum. He was sufficiently struck by this French observer of London to copy several passages. They confirmed the deterioration in English society taking place before his very eyes. He was focussing "the rich theme of a large satirical novel" that would treat of "the great modern collapse of all the forms and 'superstitions' and respects, good and bad, and restraints and mysteries [...]. The lost sense, the brutalized manner [...]."[1]

James wasn't alone in sensing a "great modern collapse." Henry Adams ironically called the late 1890's an "Indian Summer." He recalls staying with his friends the Camerons at the beautiful place in Kent that they'd taken in 1898. International events were dominating public attention, the talk all of atrocities in the Boer War and other impending disasters. For James, England was tarnished by the trial of Oscar Wilde and the tawdry Diamond Jubilee celebrations. And he was estranged from old friends in France (like the Bourgets) by the bitterly divisive course of the Dreyfus Affair—a case of the Devil abroad if ever there was one.[2] James translates the political laterally into art. London is registered through the Buckingham Crescent circle. No

---

1 'Brada' was the pen-name of Henrietta Consuelo (Sansom), Contessa di Pulago. James's entry is dated 4 March 1895, but extends over several pages.
2 "I eat and drink, I sleep and dream Dreyfus. The papers are too shockingly interesting." To Elizabeth Cameron, 15 October 1898 [Edel, *Henry James* IV 83]. Dreyfus spent almost five years' solitary confinement in the penal colony of Devil's Island in Guyana.

public event is mentioned, yet we're always aware of economic pressures, of failures of social and aesthetic forms, of moral confusion. Appearances and relations in themselves "vulgar and empty enough" become, as James deals with them, "the stuff of poetry and tragedy and art" (Preface to *What Maisie Knew* 1162). The alchemy of transformation lies in that key attribute of the Devil of the midnight letter: "EXPRESSION."

III.

"Language most shows a man: Speak that I may see thee…"
(Ben Jonson)

A failure when it first appeared, *The Awkward Age* may still be the least read of James's late novels. "I'm sorry to say," wrote his publisher, "the book has done nothing to speak of; I've never in all my experience seen one treated with more general and complete disrespect" (Preface to *The Awkward Age* 1129). Yet re-reading the novel as he prepared the New York Edition, James felt how well it stood up to his *own* keenest scrutiny, quite *how* good it was. Copy sent to Scribners in September 1907 had the lightest of revisions. The Preface that followed in October recognises what the novel was really taking on. *The Awkward Age* is a crucial work: absolutely contemporary, radically new in style and substance. London and its "complications" enact "the real state of sublunary nature." From a "chaos of mingled purposes and casualties" (Dr. Johnson's words again), this strange, compelling fiction deals in the "crimes" and "absurdities" of ordinary life. It pushes the idiom of the 'modern' to the point of anticipating Modernism itself.

But it's a taxing read, even by late Jamesian standards. The novel's "architecture" (James's word) was designed to "open the door wide to ingenuity," to the technically innovative. There's no authorial voice, no attempt (as James says) to "go behind." The text is largely dialogue, speech which follows the contours of the speaker's mind: deceptively naturalistic, its rhythms colloquial, fluid, opaque. In effect we 'overhear' a succession of conversations with some stage directions. There's no formal narrative: the story has to tell itself. Like the speakers, we supply the sense of unfinished phrases, of allusions, and gestures; deduce intentions, motives and meanings in what is said or left unsaid. We learn to see *through* appearances—"by indirection find direction out." Of course these are problems for James's characters, as well as his readers. He had, he knew, gone way beyond his French model, the ingenious and inexhaustible 'Gyp.' ('Gyp's entertainingly quirky characters, speaking in their own distinct idioms, had become an embarrassment, tainted by her open anti-Semitism.) What James took from this "muse of general looseness" was her gift for making "talk" a sufficiently flexible medium. He liked her lightness of touch. A classic case of finding what you want in unlikely places: James was a shameless snapper-up of unconsidered trifles.

What *kind* of "large satirical" theme did he have in mind? Hardly that of *The Rape of the Lock*, but still one where a small social circle registers larger issues, and in a text almost as steeped as Pope's in Miltonic allusions. Maisie was a child. Here the *jeunes filles* are unambiguously in full-length skirts. Nanda Brookenham and 'Little Aggie' must "come out" (or "come down") for their rite of passage into the adult world, where it will be their parents' duty to marry them with due diligence. There are powerful imperatives: first, the strain on the family purse. Then, a less quantifiable calculation about the shelf-life of the item on offer, of the young female so "deliberately prepared for consumption" (238). The "preposterous fiction" of innocence cannot be kept up for long or she risks passing her 'sell by' date. The theme is familiar. Let in the Devil and it metamorphoses into a fable for our times—poised between the comic and the tragic.

'Mrs. Brook's' circle prizes its 'modern' character. The friends enjoy what they call "intellectual elbow room": that is, the freedom of intelligent adults to discuss whatever they want without the "editing" required for the *jeune fille*. The drawing room at Buckingham Crescent is a place for "good talk"— part "circus" part "temple of analysis." The talk has high-wire performance value, but the analysis is more often prurient speculation about each other's indiscretions—Lord Petherton and the Duchess, Carrie Donner and Mr. Cashmore... Will Lady Fanny or will she *not* "bolt," like Anna Karenina, to "one of the smaller Italian towns"? (280). These Londoners, however, are no 'Bloomsburies': their *intellectual* life is philistine. There's no reference to music, to art, or the theatre: their advanced ideas are of the sketchiest; their reading consists of *risqué* French novels. "Vanity" and "inexpertness" are precisely part of their tale. The more, with choric voice, they claim to be "simple," "natural," and "sincere," the more the reverse is implied. The guiding principle, literally as well as metaphorically, is to cover up the obvious in talk—talk over tea, after dinner, and, finally, in the room Nanda calls her own.

Everything turns on notions of propriety, present or, precisely, absent. France has protocols to provide against social "awkwardness." French upbringing (theoretically at least) does not permit "good talk" before the "hovering female young." The better the talk "the more organised, the more complete" must be the exclusion of the *jeune fille*. For an adult to sacrifice the free exercise of "social intelligence" — something "perfectly preventable by wise arrangement" — would be "barbarous." But across the Channel you find "the inveterately English trick of the so morally well-meant and so intellectually helpless compromise" (1124). In "the mixed English world" 'Mrs. Brook' (as the Duchess puts it) is "in a prodigious fix — she must sacrifice either her daughter or [...] her intellectual habits" (255). Each scheme is of course an artifice, an exercise in social manipulation, with its price-tag. Aggie's innocence is a "pious fraud," an absurdly contrived ignorance. The central ambivalence is in what Nanda so unavoidably "knows." It is *compromise* that brings Nanda into question — that awkward compromise between code and practice. For James, a theme bristling with possibilities: "What will happen, who suffer, who not suffer, what turn be determined, what crisis created, what issue found?" (1123). Questions for the artist, rather than the social historian. Understanding Nanda is what 'happens' in the novel: through her the *topos* of the *jeune fille* is turned on its head.

IV.

Later D.H. Lawrence saw that "The 'Jeune Fille' Wants to Know": her *father* now trembles in his study, while "the innocent maiden knocks you flat with her outspokenness in the conservatory." Nanda does not exactly knock anyone flat, but she asks awkward questions. She *is* "positively and helplessly modern": she "knows too much," knows "everything." She has "unlearned surprise through the habit, in company, of studiously not compromising her innocence by blinking at things said" (*The Awkward Age* 232). Life at first hand is already familiar. But why, for whom, is this a moral taint? Nanda's case is (again) "odd." "Girls understand now," she explains. "It has to be faced." Van is "just trying to dodge it." "The real old thing" *might* have a special value, but anything short of that and she'd "rather brazen it out as [her]self" (341). Her mother complains that Nanda's exposure has been only to talk, to "mere words." The girl puts it differently: "Doesn't one become a sort of little drain-pipe with everything flowing through?" (358). Mitchy asks why she shouldn't (more gracefully) see herself as "a little aeolian harp set in a drawing-room window and vibrating in the breeze of conversation." Both images are passive. Neither reflects Nanda's wish to be herself. "'The trouble is,'" Van concludes,"—but quite as if uttering only a general truth—"'that it's just a thing that may operate as a bar to pity'" (378). The impersonal has a disturbing chill. A modern Eve does not need to eat of the tree of carnal knowledge: she is already fallen, fatally tainted by association. Within a few paragraphs, language shifts in register through the idioms of current slang to the sinister. The tone is indefinable— unless it's what James meant by "brand[ing] it all, but ever so tenderly, as monstrous" (Preface to *The Awkward Age* 1120).

In such exchanges we hear a change of direction. Take the scene where Vanderbank makes his "great blind leap," blurting out to Mrs. Brook Mr. Longdon's "proposition": to settle an undisclosed fortune on Nanda if he, Van, marries her. Van has so far "funked" saying anything about it and is not sure now that he is "within his rights" to do so. Mrs. Brook, taken by surprise, manoeuvres carefully: she's been "backing" the wealthy Mitchy for her daughter, keeping Van for herself.

> She had reached now, with her extraordinary self-control, the pitch of quiet bland demonstration. 'I wanted the poor thing, *que diable*, to have another string to her bow and another loaf, for her desolate old age, on the shelf. When everything else is gone Mitchy will still be there. Then it will at least be her own fault— !' Mrs. Brook continued. 'What can relieve me of the primary duty of taking precautions," she wound up, "when I know as well as that I stand here and look at you— '
>
> 'Yes, what?' he asked, as she just paused.
>
> 'Why that so far as they count on you they count, my dear Van, on a blank.' Holding him for a minute as with the soft low voice of his fate, she sadly but firmly shook her head. 'You won't do it' (295).

That is the 'noise' of a decision. Mitchy is shown in, and she turns to him with the "wonderful piece of news"—of Mr. Longdon's wish to "make it worth somebody's while to marry my child." At this blatant betrayal of his confidence, Van stiffens.

> He was not angry—no member of the inner circle at Buckingham Crescent was ever angry—but he looked grave and rather troubled. He addressed his hostess straight—'I can't make out quite why you're doing *this*. I mean immediately making it known.' (304)

Mrs. Brook threads her way through various possible outcomes for her daughter, till Vanderbank protests at the tone of "high intellectual detachment": "'What are we playing with, after all, but the idea of Nanda's happiness?' 'Oh I'm not playing!' Mrs. Brook declared with a little rattle of emotion" (306).

Indeed she is not: insisting on the note of special collusion among friends, Mrs. Brook seals the 'fate' not just of Nanda but of her entire circle. Can we, a century later, still feel the shock—the *shockingness*—of these words?

James's goes in for *leitmotifs*. Some are pure comedy—the wonderfully obnoxious Harold cadging £5 notes (in today's terms worth some £400), and the wonderfully telling notations of dress. Then there are books: compromising French novels, their covers carefully colour-coded. Circulated in London their implications only multiply. All these *motifs* are acrobatically in play on the January night of Tishy Grendon's party. The evening begins with Mrs. Brook's unfortunate fib to Mr. Longdon—the improbable fiction that she wanted Nanda back, comically exposed by her own husband. Then there is the game of "hunt the book"— a book that proves to be the French novel lent by Van, too "bad" even to be returned except under cover of darkness. Altogether too much is revealed by Tishy's unnerving *décolleté*: but what is revealed in Mrs. Brook's staged exposure of Nanda before the circled friends? Publicly challenged, Nanda is forced to admit that she *has* read the "hideous" thing. The party—already a "civilised saturnalia"—becomes a catastrophic 'outing' as Mrs. Brook chalk-marks her daughter as damaged goods. Afterwards Mitchy asked her why, Samson-like, she should have pulled down the whole temple. Was it by impulse or design? The casuistry of the moment is diabolical.

Some months later, Vanderbank calls at Buckingham Crescent. He had come for Nanda, but instead has tea with Mrs. Brook. With double tongue she invokes their old comradeship in obliquity: he leaves without seeing Nanda. On a June afternoon, Nanda arranges to see Van, Mitchy, and finally Mr. Longdon. The three interviews that close the novel raise questions to which there are no answers. Nanda reassembles the scattered "atoms" of what Mitchy calls her mother's "saloon." Behind her careful agenda is an omission: what is at stake for her, her own end-game. The Duchess had seen earlier (as her mother had not) that Nanda's "fairly sick—as sick as a little cat—with her passion" for Vanderbank (252). Mitchy too knows the unspoken fact, and wants to believe that a "passion so great, so complete is—satisfied or unsatisfied—a life" (488). The girl's self-control cracks only once, as Mr. Longdon pities her plight. She breaks down in a torrent of tears, "in a passion as sharp and brief as the flurry of a wild thing for an instant uncaged" (540). The cost is finally plain—the price-tag of being (in her words) "the horrible impossible," of being herself. "I'll come," she tells

Mr. Longdon, "if you'll take me as I am." Unlike George Sand, Nanda pays in full for a transgression too subtle for *words*.

Absurdities abound, yet where in all this is the crime? James knew a letter George Sand wrote to her son, Maurice, in 1851—a despairing letter about her daughter, knowing full well the "evil" Solange was up to. "Burn this letter but don't forget it," she ends:

> Crime isn't always what we think. It's not a set purpose, a fatal drive that slowly takes root in monsters. More often it's a blind act, a flash of rage. Catholics call it the devil's breath, *le souffle du diable*—a fanciful metaphor, that catches nicely the destructive and unpredictable impulses of human nature
>
> (Karénine III 609).[3]

James doesn't ask us to believe in monsters, but in the present figures of evil; not in Fate, just in the way things happen. Yet we are very close to things that prompt a "moral shudder." Mrs. Brook's destructive impulse is naked. But what of her "comrade in obliquity"? Initiating Mr. Longdon into the Buckingham Crescent set at the start, Vanderbank had told him: "You see we don't in the least know who we are. We're lost..." (35). Words that come to have the weight of the whole novel behind them. Unable to commit himself, to act or not to act, Van is the "blank" Mrs. Brook predicted—one of the Hollow Men, brushed by "the devil's breath." "What in the world, Mr. Van, are you afraid of?" Nanda asks (503). He is simply evasive, as constrained as the speaker in Eliot's "Portrait of a Lady":

> I take my hat: how can I make a cowardly amends
> For what she has said to me
> I feel like one who smiles, and turning shall remark
> Suddenly, his expression in a glass,
> My self-possession gutters; we are really in the dark [...] (21)

There is a final somersault. Nanda, the modern daughter, assumes her mother's role and puts back together again the ruined "temple." "Without these friendships—life, what *cauchemar*!" (18). Quietly she connives with the world that has destroyed her; only she has no place in it. Is her stoic clairvoyance the heroism of the present? Or is Nanda so much 'of' the shabby world of Buckingham

---

3 George Sand to Maurice Sand, 2 janvier 1851. "Brûle cette lettre, mais ne l'oublie pas. Le crime n'est pas toujours ce qu'on croit. Ce n'est pas un parti pris, une tendance fatale qui germe lentement chez les monstres. C'est une acte de délire le plus souvent, un mouvement de rage. Les Catholiques attribuent cela au souffle du diable, c'était une métaphore fantastique qui caractérisait assez bien les mouvements terribles et imprévus de l'être humain" (Karénine III 609).

Crescent that she can do no other? Is it an act of conformity, or a declaration of independence? Intelligent and natural, Nanda sees that "everything's different from what it used to be" (*The Awkward Age* 544). Tragically compromised, she is way ahead of the 'compromises' of the London circle.

Satire is never simple. For Flaubert, James said, "the bad smell of the age was the main thing he knew it by." Flaubert looked down on his theme as *"une blague supérieure"* ['the finest of jokes']—that is, with "the amused freedom of an observer as irreverent as a creator" ("Correspondance de Gustave Flaubert" 311). James knew well that "horror of the *cliché*" which had led Flaubert to collect over a lifetime the cultural banalities of his *Dictionnaire des idées reçues*—a demonstration of that thin membrane between irony and the absurd. But he admired the "extraordinary ingenuity" with which Flaubert could find a "middle way into grandeur," could "edge off from the literal without forsaking truth." James too revelled in the technical challenges of writing. Artistic integrity, for both, was in "objectivity." But *James* also loved to drag out "odds and ends from the 'mere' storyteller's great property-shop of aids to illusion" (Preface to *The Awkward Age* 1131). It was not by its bad smell that James knew *la Belle Époque*. He is never the judge; always the detached yet connected observer—imaginatively both inside and outside his "labyrinth of mere immediate appearances." The Preface to *The Awkward Age* argues the need for art to be "shut up wholly" in its own terms—with the crucial *caveat*: "save, of course, by the relation of the total to life" (1134). Those phrases about finding a middle way to grandeur, of edging off the literal to get at truth, perfectly fit what is new in *The Awkward Age*. The multiple idioms of the surface allow for mockery, for the release and the focus of tensions. They guarantee that distance from available resources so distinctively the note of Modernism. By 1910 Eliot had written "Portrait of a Lady" and was drafting "Prufrock." Proust had begun *À l'Ombre des jeunes filles en fleurs*.

V.

There is another (unnamed) French figure behind the Preface. Marcelle Tinayre is less known than Colette (or even 'Gyp') but she was a far more interesting player on the Parisian scene than she's been given credit for. A friend of Lina Sand (George Sand's daughter-in-law), her portrait was painted by Frédéric Lauth, married to George Sand's grand-daughter. Her background was politically radical, and included working for Marguerite Durand's newspaper *La Fronde*, run entirely by women. Her novel *Avant l'Amour* (1897) was one of the pleasures James shared conspiratorially with Edith Wharton.[4] The heroine, Marianne, makes her own acquaintance with life at first hand: she exposes the "conspiracy" of education, religion, and upbringing to distort and suppress the "facts of life," the double standard in sexual relations, and makes her own painful journey to selfhood. Like George Sand's Valentine, Marianne affirms her right to happiness, to equality in love, despite the fate, the plight of her destiny as a woman. ["*J'ai revendiqué ma part de bonheur sur la fatalité, sur la misère de ma destinée de femme*" (Tinayre 336) ['I've exacted my share of happiness from all that's failed, from the plight of my destiny as a woman.'] James called her "the demonic little Tinayre" (*Letters, Vol. IV* 386).

In 1876, at Étretat, James had been amused by an actress's scant bathing-dress. After 1910, he was watching the *Ballets Russes*.[5] Léon Bakst's costume designs for the dancers were frankly explicit: they pushed the limits of the *convenable* even for sophisticated audiences at Covent Garden and le Châtelet. When Diaghilev took *The Firebird* to St Petersburg, the "appreciably scant" tunic Nijinsky had worn in Paris was deemed *not* "*convenable*" for a performance at the Mariinsky Theatre before the tsarina (Wulshlager 122). Despite a back-stage row Nijinsky insisted on wearing it. The tsarina was not amused. Nijinsky was sacked, and the *Ballets Russes* left in a hurry—for Paris. The Devil really is in EXPRESSION.

---

4 See letter of 8 November 1905 to Mrs. Wharton, in Horne *A Life in Letters*, 419; and letter of 18 December 1905 to Mrs. Wharton, in *Letters* 386-87.
5 James's diary for 6 November 1911 reads "Covent Garden — to Russian Ballet." That night he would have seen Nijinsky and Pavlova in *Giselle* and *Le Carnaval*. On 25 June 1913 he went with Mrs. Hunter to the London *première* of "Jeux" at Drury Lane. See *The Complete Notebooks of Henry James* 345 and 375.

2. From Romance to Redemption: James and the Ethics of Globalisation

Roxana Oltean

James's novels abound in memorable dictums about home and belonging, with both Europe and America re-appropriated as essential ways of being and of relating to the world. As Ralph puts it in *The Portrait of a Lady*: "One doesn't give up one's country any more than one gives up one's grandmother" (99).[1] Christopher Newman's American origin makes him, in the words of Mrs. Tristram, "the great Western barbarian" (*The American* 546), while Strether's Woolett makes an indelible mark on his identity: "'It sticks out of me, and you knew surely for yourself as soon as you looked at me' [...] 'Well, the fact of where I come from'" (*The Ambassadors* [1987] 63). However, the undeniable mark of home can also be integrated into an openness towards the other that is part of the cosmopolitan encounter couched, I will argue, in inevitable ethical terms. For example, the manner in which Milly puts forth and meets, with her typically American wealth—expressed as the pearls—but also with the "value of her life" and the "candour of her smile," the gaze of Kate and Densher can be read as a transatlantic encounter between American innocence/gullibility and European scheming, but also as an ethical encounter expressed in terms of Levinas's revelation of the face of the other, who "precisely reveals himself in his alterity not in a shock negating the I, but as the primordial phenomenon of gentleness" (Levinas 150). So too Milly reveals herself to Kate and Densher in full "candour":

> Milly, from the other side, happened at the moment to notice them, and she sent across toward them in response all the candour of her smile, the lustre

---

[1] In this paper I use the the New York Edition version of the novels with the exception of *The American*, where the revisions substantially alter the early transatlantic representation that is instrumental to the argument of this paper.

of her pearls, the value of her life, the essence of her wealth. It brought them together again with faces made fairly grave by the reality she put into their plan. Kate herself grew a little pale for it, and they had for a time only a silence

(*The Wings of the Dove* II 229).

This paper proposes to analyse James's contribution to discourses about cosmopolitanism, globalisation and ethics (all areas acknowledged by Jamesian critics) by arguing that the Jamesian imagination actually shifts from early romance plots involving America and Europe in a neo-colonial relationship to the later redemptive plots, in which America and Europe are re-appropriated as elements in what one might call a cosmopolitan ethics. In this sense, I propose the term 'ethics of globalisation' to capture the rich node of meanings in which geography, globalisation and ethics intersect.[2]

After a discussion of James's early phase, what I aim to suggest is that, in his late writings, James developed a view in which an ethical standpoint is inseparable from a global outlook. The other of a Levinasian ethical approach is, in this sense, the other of a Jamesian cosmopolitan encounter. Thus while the early international writings seem to cast Europe as a place of regenerative renewal, corresponding to an emancipatory colonisation scenario,[3] the later writings cast America, once again, as the site of—albeit belated—moral revelation.

In addition to the Levinasian reading of self, other, and the world, my reading of the ethical dimension of Jamesian global encounters[4] also draws

---

2 The term 'global ethics,' also used in this paper, is associated with political science, with ethical, global movements that attempt to deal with the moral questions arising from globalisation—for example, the UNESCO Global Ethics Observatory, or The Global Ethic Foundation, and the Declaration toward a Global Ethic issued by the Parliament of the World's Regions. James's late novels, I would argue, adumbrate these contemporary issues in a remarkable way.

3 The emancipatory scenario of exploration in James's earlier international tales is discussed in Oltean, *Spaces of Utopia*, ch. 4 and 5.

4 In light of the issues addressed in this paper, a brief reference to what has been called the "ethical turn" of criticism is also in order. While there is increasing talk of an "ethical turn" in the contemporary American novel in the wake of 9/11, the return of ethical criticism reaches even further back. Thus in *Deconstruction and the Ethical Turn*, Peter Baker points to the "ethical turn" of deconstructive criticism, matching the "linguistic turn." While arguing that "it seems crucial [...] to acknowledge that both Derrida and Foucault follow Nietzsche in rejecting the possibility of a normative ethics based on a universal human subject [...] we must also note, however, that Derrida's critique of the self-presence of the self is related to questions of power and violence, and Foucault's view of power relations undermines the self-consistency of the self" (Baker 2-3). After striking out the Enlightenment image of man as the basis of a description of who we are and of what is, the question to be addressed

upon post-Saidian visions of cosmopolitanism. Thus Appiah speaks of an outlook that is located in between imperialist appropriation and the claim for local unreadability, and James might have made a particularly telling example. In this sense, cosmopolitanism embodies an aspect of identity open to the other, as illustrated in Appiah's *Cosmopolitanism*, where travel and the description of otherness do not necessarily pertain to an orientalising gaze but rather to an ethical approach and respect for otherness.[5]

The Romance of Discovery

Musing back on his early writings in the New York Edition prefaces, Henry James speaks with a certain nostalgia of his own early international scenarios, based on a polar opposition between two interdependent, allegorical entities, "ingenuous young America" and "dramatic" Europe:

> It does thus in true come home to me that, combining and comparing in whatever proportions and by whatever lights, my 'America' and its products would doubtless, as a theme, have betrayed gaps and infirmities enough without such a kicking-up of the dramatic dust (mainly in the foreground) as I could set my 'Europe' in motion for; just as my Europe would probably have limped across our stage to no great effect of processional state without an ingenuous young America (constantly seen as ingenuous and young) to hold up its legendary train
>
> (Preface to Vol. XIV vii).

Moreover, this scenario belongs to a 'golden age' where the two continents were kept in ideal isolation, making for a 'romance' of exploration and discovery:

> "[the] classic years of the great Americano-European legend; the years of limited communication, of monstrous and unattenuated contrast, of prodigious and unrecorded adventure. The comparatively brief but

---

is thus how to re-imagine intersubjective relations: "One could say that, for each, alterity emerges as the sign of intersubjective relations and the ethical subject of discourse as its necessary corollary" (Baker 3). Stressing that "ethical criticism implies a transactive theory of reading where texts shape reader, and reader shapes text" (Schwarz 6), and also addressing the ethical turn of criticism and philosophy, Schwarz boldly states that "we are in the midst of a humanistic revival or at least a neohumanist burst of energy" (Schwarz 3). Henry James himself has almost always been part of a compulsory corpus dealing with ethical approaches to literature and is often placed, for example, in an "Anglo-American humanistic tradition— stretching from Matthew Arnold and Henry James to J. Hillis Miller and Raymond Williams" (Schwarz 4).
5 Put otherwise, in *Cosmopolitanism*, but also in *Ethics of Identity*, Appiah suggests an approach that departs from what Venn would characterize as Occidentalism.

infinitely rich 'cycle' of romance embedded in the earlier, the very early American reactions and returns (medieval in the sense of being, at most, of the mid-century), what does it resemble today but a gold-mine overgrown and smothered, dislocated, and no longer workable?

(Preface to vol. XI xvii).

This early imaginative construction permeating the novels and stories that consecrated James's international theme in the early phase is perhaps most concisely illustrated in the allegorical piece "Benvolio" (1875). "Benvolio," in fact, could be read as a blueprint allegory of the early oppositional geography also developed in "Daisy Miller," *The American*, or *The Portrait of a Lady*, suggesting a world view that pertains, it is argued, to the romance of discovery. The term 'romance of discovery' is thus used here to refer to neo-colonial patterns of appropriation in early novels of the international theme, based on the element of contrast between Europe and America, entities essentially unknowable to each other.

While Tintner has pointed out that "Benvolio" encodes James's dilemma "over whether to choose Europe or America as his permanent home" (Tintner *Museum World* 66-67), it can also be argued that the two feminine figures at the center of the story, the Countess and Scholastica, correspond to the two allegorical entities of James's transatlantic imagination: the vibrant Countess is akin to young America, while the melancholy Scholastica is reminiscent of the Old World, a "Europe" of the "legendary train."

In this sense, the Countess is an image of New World energy, "expressive," "fascinating," and revealing a frontier of possibilities, as she represents "a dozen different women":

> Few faces were more expressive, more fascinating. Hers was never the same for two days altogether; it reflected her momentary circumstances with extraordinary vividness, and in knowing her you had the advantage of knowing a dozen different women

("Benvolio" 88).

It is in this spirit that one might read the Watteau references associated with the Countess. While the relationship between James and Watteau is a complex one, as Tintner pointed out, it can be argued that, in "Benvolio," the reference to Watteau enhances the New World associations resonating in descriptions of the Countess, particularly with regard to Watteau's visions of discovery and utopian bliss in paintings such as *Pilgrimage to Cythera* (see Figure 1). In this sense, the glimpse of the Countess's "joyous Watteau groups" encodes Benvolio's romance of discovery associated with the Countess's New World spirit: "He saw them in envious fancy, studded with joyous Watteau-groups, feasting and making music under the shade of ancestral beeches" (97).

Figure 1. Jean-Antoine Watteau, *Pilgrimage to Cythera* (1719). Charlottenburg Palace, Berlin

By contrast with the expansive Countess, the nun-like Scholastica, the other object of Benvolio's interest, is a melancholy representation of the *contemptus mundi* tradition, inhabiting a space marked by old age, meditation and introspection: her house is "an ancient grizzled, sad-faced structure, with grated windows on the ground floor; it looked like a convent or a prison" ("Benvolio" 96). In opposition with the atmosphere of the "joyous Watteau-groups," space around Scholastica is imbued by dimness and reaches back towards the past of old books: "the light of the low western sun shining through the wet trees of the famous garden. Everything else was ancient and brown; the walls were covered with tiers upon tiers of books" (99).

The ending of James's allegory reconfirms the writer's vision upon his own early international novels expressed in the above-cited Preface, that Europe and America make sense through the romance of discovery made possible by irresolvable opposition. After the Countess banishes her rival Scholastica to a New World space (the antipodes), hoping to win Benvolio's undivided affection, the latter retreats to the world of meditation (the "poetic brow"), exclaiming to the Countess that (much like Europe and America) the two women were significant only through their opposition:

> 'Can't you imagine that I cared for you only by contrast? You took the trouble to kill the contrast, and with it you killed everything else. For a constancy I prefer *this!*' And he tapped his poetic brow
>
> ("Benvolio" 125).

The polarised view of the world illustrated in "Benvolio" is played out more fully in the other novels of the early phase, also capitalising on the romance of discovery sustainable only in a world of oppositions. Part of the international legend, Europe is, as James would put it later in *The Wings of the Dove*, the "great American sedative" (I 115), an answer to America's problems, reversing the geography of colonisation; as Mrs. Touchett explains in *The Portrait of a Lady*: "'[the Americans] all regard Europe over there as a land of emigration, of rescue, a refuge from their superfluous population'" (*Portait of a Lady* [1995] 53-54). These oppositions entail a colonial scenario of appropriation in *The American* (1877), for example,[6] where Europe is inscribed in a polarised view of the world and answers Christopher Newman's conquistadorial impulse:

> 'I feel something under my ribs here,' he added in a moment, 'that I can't explain—a sort of a mighty hankering, a desire to stretch out and haul in'
>
> (*The American* [1983] 545).

What is striking in *The American* is the overlap between Europe's Old World attributes—melancholy, old age, spaces imbued by the past, echoing the figure of Scholastica—and the frontier attributes with which it is invested. In this sense, one can speak of a conquest of Europe by the American, or the "great Western Barbarian," as Mrs. Tristram puts it to Christopher Newman, whose name is a transparent reference to Christopher Columbus (519):

> 'You are the great Western Barbarian, stepping forth in his innocence and might, gazing a while at this poor effete Old World and then swooping down on it' (546).

In fact, it could be argued that *The American* clearly captures the sense of New World romances ringing with Watteau-like utopias staged in Europe, a space of discovery. The romance dimension of the novel is a frequent subject of critical attention, and it has been argued for example that *The American* stages a cultural collision between two romances, that of the Old World and

---

6 For further discussion of this see my *Spaces of Utopia*.

that of the New (Lucking 94), the romance dimension also being inherent in the novel's fascination for national typologies (Banta *New Essays* 9).

Interestingly, Newman's love for Madame de Cintré begins to flourish under the sign of a *fête champêtre*. Before announcing the ball in Newman's honour, Mme de Bellegarde looks at her fan (a model?) depicting a *fête champêtre* that quite explicitly recalls the "joyous" Watteau image associated with the Countess: the painting on the fan "represented a *fête champêtre*—a lady with a guitar, singing, and a group of dancers round a garlanded Hermes" (*The American* [1983] 701).

However, the New World romance that Newman was to have enacted in Europe, under the sign of a Watteau *fête champêtre*, is finally defeated by the ultimate incomprehensibility of Old and New World, which remain unreadable to each other, beyond the agonic colonial scripts of conquest and assimilation. In this sense, the *fête champêtre* is followed by another utopian space, only not of love but of lack of communication: the Carmelite monastery where Madame de Cintré retreats. Newman's visit confirms the physical and figurative "blank wall" that ultimately separates the two poles of the world:

> On Sunday morning, at the hour which Mrs. Tristram had indicated, he rang at the gate in the blank wall. It instantly opened and admitted him into a clean, cold-looking court, from beyond which a dull, plain edifice looked down upon him (832).

Attending the service, Newman becomes aware of the "unintelligible drawl" that has replaced any notion of transatlantic dialogue, and responds with "wrath" towards what he perceives to be the "aids and abettors of Madame de Cintré's desertion" from the *fête champêtre*:

> That was the convent, the real convent, the place where she was. But he could see nothing; no light came through the crevices. He got up and approached the partition very gently, trying to look through. But behind it there was darkness, with nothing stirring. He went back to his place, and after that a priest and two altar boys came in and began to say mass. Newman watched their genuflections and gyrations with a grim, still enmity; they seemed aids and abettors of Madame de Cintré's desertion; they were mouthing and droning out their triumph. The priest's long, dismal intonings acted upon his nerves and deepened his wrath; there was something defiant in his unintelligible drawl; it seemed meant for Newman himself (832).

Marked by the failure of the Americano-European legend, *The American* already adumbrates, in a sense, the melancholy of the waning world of romance and discovery. Ultimately, Europe proves "defiant" in its unintelligibility, apparently directed at Newman himself, and the dream of communion results in a collapse of understanding, revealing the hostility of the other.

Transatlantic Misperceptions

While the early phase imagines a geography where Europe and America only make sense in a scenario of opposition, with the other as a repository of often frightening irreducible differences, James's late phase nuances this scheme by introducing the possibility of transatlantic overlap and misperceptions of the earlier "Americano-European legend."[7] This complex encounter might be interpreted through the prism of Levinas's question relating self and other: "But how can the same, produced as egoism, enter into relationship with an Other without immediately divesting it of its alterity? What is the nature of this relationship?" (Levinas 38). Imagining an alternative to the romance of discovery that actually divests otherness of alterity by subsuming its manifestations into a colonial script, James's late novel *The Ambassadors* (1903) can be read as an intermediary model towards a fully-fledged global ethical encounter.

In this sense, *The Ambassadors* reiterates the earlier colonial pattern, only under the sign of loss, errancy, and in a belated key. In opposition to Newman's active assimilation of Paris, *The Ambassadors* is centered on Strether's famous postponement, described as imbued with the "sweetness of vain delay":

> [H]is final appreciation of what he had done—his appreciation on the spot— would provide it with its main sharpness. The spot so focussed upon was of course Woollett, and he was to see, at the best, what Woollett would be with everything there changed for him […] Well, the summer's end would show; his suspense had meanwhile exactly the sweetness of vain delay
>
> (*The Ambassadors* [1987] 489).

---

7 The international theme is notoriously absent from the middle phase. However, it is possible to discern traces of this in the multiple valences of Mr. Longdon's innocence as an 'oncle d'Amerique' in *The Awkward Age* (1899), in the colonial fables staged by Maisie as "untutored and unclaimed subject" engaged in a play of knowledge and innocence in *What Maisie Knew* (1897) or the kitsch Arcadias of *The Turn of the Screw* (1898), all suggesting, in addition, an adumbration of the veritable Lolita complex that Nabokov was to develop fully-fledged.

2. The Ethics of Globalization

Moreover, transatlantic space itself is altered, and no longer functions according to transatlantic oppositions. The image of Chad formed in Strether's mind is inappropriate to the likable reality Strether finds in Paris, and the image of Chad as a "brute" is in fact a "violence" that Strether actually misses, as it would have simplified his reading:

> [T]he turn taken by his affair on the whole was positively that if his nerves were on the stretch it was because he missed violence. When he asked himself if none would then, in connexion with it, ever come at all, he might almost have passed as wondering how to provoke it. It would be too absurd if such a vision as THAT should have to be invoked for relief; it was already marked enough as absurd that he should actually have begun with flutters and dignities on the score of a single accepted meal. What sort of a brute had he expected Chad to be, anyway? (183)

Unlike the symmetric oppositions staged in *The American* and reflected in what could be termed the straight planes of allegory, corresponding to Euclidian geometry, Strether inhabits a space of curvatures, in which planes are not flat but curved. Images from across the Atlantic come modified and Strether has to account for the "extravagant curve of the globe" in interpreting Mrs. Newsome's messages, marked by a "primal crudity" pertaining to the afore-mentioned "violence" of transatlantic oppositions:

> He could himself, comparatively recent as it was—it was truly but the fact of a few days since—focus his primal crudity; but he would on the approach of an observer, as if handling an illicit possession, have slipped the reminiscence out of sight. There were echoes of it still in Mrs. Newsome's letters, and there were moments when these echoes made him exclaim on her want of tact. He blushed of course, at once, still more for the explanation than for the ground of it: it came to him in time to save his manners that she couldn't at the best become tactful as quickly as he. Her tact had to reckon with the Atlantic Ocean, the General Post-Office and the extravagant curve of the globe (183).

The "extravagant curve of the globe" suggests what one might call an international Riemannian geography that results in the distortion of information or, on the contrary, in efforts to recompose the message in the receiver's mind, the latter having to allow for warped distance. The situation is strikingly similar with the effort of anamorphosis demanded by the painting *The Ambassadors* by Holbein the Younger, a possible source of inspiration for James's title, of course (see Figure 2 and Figure 3).[8]

---

8 See Tintner *Museum World*, for example.

Figure 2. Hans Holbein the Younger, *The Ambassadors* (1533)
National Gallery, London

Just as the viewer of Holbein's painting has to recompose the death's head from an angle, so Strether's dialogue with Mrs. Newsome is fraught with transatlantic misperceptions which no longer allow straight-forward readings or symmetrical oppositions.

In this sense, *The Ambassadors* complicates the geometry and geography of conquest outlined in *The American* (and reiterated, to an extent, in Waymarsh's appropriation of the European frontier).[9] In keeping with warped visions of self and other, communication requires, as in Holbein's

---

[9] The vast frontier of European space is a script still present especially in Waymarsh's assimilation of European space. Thus the Catholic Church is, for Waymarsh "the enemy, the monster of bulging eyes and far-reaching quivering groping tentacles," while society is "the multiplication of shibboleths, exactly the discrimination of types and tones, exactly the wicked old rows of Chester, rank with feudalism; exactly in short Europe" (*The American* [1983] 82).

2. The Ethics of Globalization 27

anamorphosis, the effort of reinterpretation and the risk of misreading. Europe, and Paris in particular, imply an excess of impressions, as "wherever one paused in Paris the imagination reacted before one could stop it":

> Many things came over him here, and one of them was that he should doubtless presently know whether he had been shallow or sharp. Another was that the balcony in question didn't somehow show as a convenience easy to surrender. Poor Strether had at this very moment to recognise the truth that wherever one paused in Paris the imagination reacted before one could stop it. This perpetual reaction put a price, if one would, on pauses; but it piled up consequences till there was scarce room to pick one's steps among them
>
> (*The Ambassadors* [1987] 123).

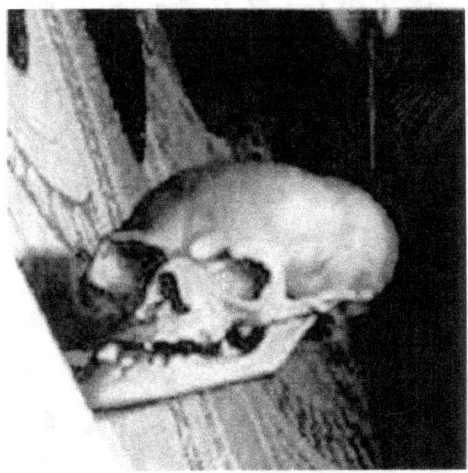

Figure 3. The recomposed head of death from Hans Holbein the Younger's
The Ambassadors

Paris, in this sense, is over-signified, yielding surprising consequences and reactions. In Strether's eyes, the temptation of Paris is that consequences and interpretations can hardly be contained: "it piled up consequences till there was scarce any room to pick one's way among them. What call had he, at such a juncture, for example, to like Chad's house?" (123-24).

If, as argued earlier, the 'golden years of the Americano-European legend' freeze the two poles of James's world into a (failed) romance of discovery and love, in *The Ambassadors* the colonial pattern is present as a simulacrum, revealing senseless repetitions and its inherent belatedness.[10]

---

10 Critics have pointed out the function of refigured transatlantic spaces. Méral,

The distance separating the continents dramatises the mutual gaze that the two loci fix on each other, and transatlantic space, in fact, is as distorted as Holbein's skull. Europe, in this sense, is the space of delay, a warped space of geography, no longer offering the consolations of a confrontational encounter. Both America and Europe, in fact, read and misread each other as modified by an extravagant curve of the globe, and appear distorted, only to come into focus in a Riemannian geography that accounts for extravagant curves, as with death's head in Holbein's *The Ambassadors*.

Cosmopolitan Ethics

Transatlantic distortions pervade the two other novels of the major phase, *The Wings of the Dove* (1902) and *The Golden Bowl* (1904). What this paper aims to emphasise, however, is the extent to which these two novels suggest a global ethic expressed as a cosmopolitan encounter that is necessarily paralleled, as in Appiah's vision, by an ethical attitude towards the other. This ethical attitude is, as I shall try to show, readable through the prism of Levinas's understanding of the ethical duty towards the other. In this sense, while *The Wings of the Dove* is marked by the melancholy of waning worlds, and while *The Golden Bowl* suggests a New America of love, both can be inscribed in a global ethic in which cosmopolitanism is an ethical stand towards the other and towards the world.

In *The Wings of the Dove*, Milly belongs to a long line of *Americana* figures,[11] assimilated to "the American mind as sitting there thrilled and dazzled" (I 277), while Europe seems to open up a frontier of vast geographies stimulating rather than quenching the explorer's thirst, or "the eagerness without point and the interest without pause":

> [T]he vagueness, the openness, the eagerness without point and the interest without pause—all part of the charm of her oddity as at first presented—had become more striking in proportion as they triumphed over movement and change (114-15).

However, Europe fails to work for Milly as the "great American sedative," and functions instead as the background for "American intensity." Susan Stringham ponders on the effects of Europe on Milly:

---

for example, speaks a "transatlanticised" Paris (Méral 243). However, what I am focusing on is the extent to which *The Ambassadors* implies a model from an early colonial script to a late ethical encounter with otherness.

11 This aspect is discussed more at length in my *Eternal America*, ch. 5.

2. The Ethics of Globalization

It was not Milly's unpacified state, in short, that now troubled her—though certainly, as Europe was the great American sedative, the failure was to some extent to be noted: it was the suspected presence of something behind the state—which, however, could scarcely have taken its place there since their departure. [...] The nearest approach to a personal anxiety indulged in as yet by the elder lady was on her taking occasion to wonder if what she had more than anything else got hold of mightn't be one of the finer, one of the finest, one of the rarest—as she called it so that she might call it nothing worse—cases of American intensity (115).

Moreover, Mrs. Stringham's failure to completely understand Milly's state is translated as being in presence of the "muffled" and the "intangible." The earlier script dominated by the romance of discovery is superposed with misperceptions reminiscent of Strether's melancholy space of Europe as "vain delay":

> She had just had a moment of alarm—asked herself if her young friend were merely going to treat her to some complicated drama of nerves. At the end of a week, however, with their further progress, her young friend had effectively answered the question and given her the impression, indistinct indeed as yet, of something that had a reality compared with which the nervous explanation would have been coarse. Mrs. Stringham found herself from that hour, in other words, in presence of an explanation that remained a muffled and intangible form, but that assuredly, should it take on sharpness, would explain everything and more than everything, would become instantly the light in which Milly was to be read (115-16).

The 'light' in which one might read Milly's experience in Europe is, in this sense, not only from the perspective of the encounter with otherness staged in a romance of discovery, as in *The American*, or of the space of transatlantic misperception and postponement, as in *The Ambassadors*, but also as an encounter with the world and the worldly. Thus when Susan Stringham contemplates Mrs. Lowder's life, she is not simply "carried away" by the thrill of the "spectacle," but is also confronted with "the world" which Puritan America has insulated itself from:

> They had plenty, on these lines, the two elder women, to give and to take, and it was even not quite clear to the pilgrim from Boston that what she should mainly have arranged for in London was not a series of thrills for herself. She had a bad conscience, indeed almost a sense of immorality, in having to recognise that she was, as she said, carried away [...]; and the principle of her uneasiness was that Mrs. Lowder's life bristled for her with elements that she was really having to look at for the first time. They represented, she believed, the world, the world that, as a consequence of the cold shoulder turned to it by the Pilgrim Fathers, had never yet boldly

crossed to Boston—it would surely have sunk the stoutest Cunarder—and she couldn't pretend that she faced the prospect simply because Milly had had a caprice. She was in the act herself of having one, directed precisely to their present spectacle (I 170).

Ruled by the principle of economy and indexing the colonial world of raw material, as denoted by Mrs. Lowder's presence as "The Britannia of the Marketplace" (I 30), the city of London occasions Milly's encounter with the specter of the world(ly). Aware that Milly's social success in London is partly due to European curiosity for American exoticism, Mrs. Stringham watches uneasily the arena where Milly is "caressingly martyred:"

> [B]ut it brought them back to the fact of her success; and it was at that comparatively gross circumstance, now so fully placed before them, that Milly's anxious companion sat and looked—looked very much as some spectator in an old-time circus might have watched the oddity of a Christian maiden, in the arena, mildly, caressingly, martyred. It was the nosing and fumbling not of lions and tigers but of domestic animals let loose as for the joke. Even the joke made Mrs. Stringham uneasy, and her mute communion with Densher, to which we have alluded, was more and more determined by it (II 42).

The potentially tragic encounter encounter between the self and the world is explored by Levinas in his *Totality and Infinity*:

> The world, foreign and hostile, should, in good logic, alter the I. But the true and primordial relation between them, and that in which the I is revealed precisely as preeminently the same, is produced as a soujourn [séjour] in the world. The way of the I against the "other" of the world consists in *sojourning*, in identifying oneself by existing here *at home with oneself* [chez soi]
>
> (Levinas 37).

Returning to James, it might be argued that Milly ends up embodying a strikingly similar "true and primordial relationship" between self and world. A scapegoat[12] figure martyred by the worldly that America had shunned beginning with the Pilgrim fathers, a motor of action for the mechanism set into motion by Kate's plan, Milly is largely unaltered by the world.

In a Venetian interior as the one painted by Sargent (see Figure 4), the Palazzo Barbaro, she is "at home," *chez soi* in Levinas's sense. While it has been argued that Milly belongs to a long line of Jamesian collector figures,[13] the Palazzo Barbaro is a home in the Levinasian sense. Described by Milly as

---

12 King, for example, analyzes the instances of martyrdom and sacrifice in the novel.
13 See Freedman (1990), for example.

2. The Ethics of Globalization   31

her "shell," the Palazzo denotes Milly's capacity to "sojourn" in a "foreign and hostile world." In a conversation with Lord Mark, Milly describes the Venetian interior as a "gilded shell" suggesting both her life and her death:

Figure 4. John Singer Sargent, *An Interior in Venice* (1898).
Royal Academy of Arts, London

'This is more, as you say there, my form.'
'Oho, oho!'—he laughed again as if to humour her. 'Can't you then buy it—for a price? Depend upon it they'll treat for money. That is for money enough.'
'I've exactly,' she said, 'been wondering if they won't. I think I shall try. But if I get it I shall cling to it.' They were talking sincerely. 'It will be my life—paid for as that. It will become my great gilded shell; so that those who wish to find me must come and hunt me up.'
'Ah then you WILL be alive,' said Lord Mark.
'Well, not quite extinct perhaps, but shrunken, wasted, wizened; rattling about here like the dried kernel of a nut' (II 151).

A space of sojourning in which the self, "shrunken, wasted, wizened" is able to live ultimately unaltered by the world, or, as Levinas puts it, "preeminently the same," the "gilded shell" also allows Milly to engage in a "primordial relation" to the world (Levinas 37).

Moreover, Milly is not only "at home" in a world which does not alter her, as in Levinas's primordial encounter, but she is also able to ultimately redeem the heavy materiality of the "world." Continuing the play of absence and presence suggested by the image of the shrunken yet unaltered self in the gilded shell, Milly is indirectly present at the end of the novel through the letter from the solicitors in New York and the sum of money left for Densher. Discussing the sum of money, Kate and Densher are aware of the change operated by Milly's absence, imagined as the wings of a dove:

> 'I never was in love with her,' said Densher.
>   She took it, but after a little she met it. 'I believe that now—for the time she lived. I believe it at least for the time you were there. But your change came—as it might well—the day you last saw her; she died for you then that you might understand her. From that hour you DID.' With which Kate slowly rose. 'And I do now. She did it FOR us.' Densher rose to face her, and she went on with her thought. 'I used to call her, in my stupidity—for want of anything better—a dove. Well she stretched out her wings, and it was to THAT they reached. They cover us.'
>   'They cover us,' Densher said (II 403-04).

The ethical relationship embodied by Milly and her way of being "at home" holds regenerative potential for the Old World protagonists, including Densher (who feels "forgiven, dedicated, blessed") and Mrs. Lowder, who had denoted, in Susan Stringham's eyes, the very essence of the "world," and who now stands "at the door" of the scene of redemption:

> The essence was that something had happened to him too beautiful and too sacred to describe. He had been, to his recovered sense, forgiven, dedicated, blessed; but this he couldn't coherently express. It would have required an explanation—fatal to Mrs. Lowder's faith in him—of the nature of Milly's wrong. So, as to the wonderful scene, they just stood at the door. They had the sense of the presence within—they felt the charged stillness; after which, their association deepened by it, they turned together away (343).

An even more powerful scenario of redemption at a global dimension is acted out in James's highly cosmopolitan novel *The Golden Bowl*. The last scene of the novel, arguably a scene both of love and of capitulation, sketches a possible type of global ethics in which otherness is comprehended, as the Prince's embrace "encloses" Maggie, but also an essential movement of separation and uncommunicability, expressed through Maggie's "buried" eyes:

> He tried, too clearly, to please her—to meet her in her own way; but with the result only that, close to her, her face kept before him, his hands holding

her shoulders, his whole act enclosing her, he presently echoed: "'See"? I see nothing but you.' And the truth of it had, with this force, after a moment, so strangely lighted his eyes that, as for pity and dread of them, she buried her own in his breast

(The Golden Bowl II 369).

While the story of marital reconciliation is replete with geopolitical overtones and American reappropriations[14] and while the novel fascinates readers in the context of today's new world order,[15] it can also be argued that James's allegory of globalisation and story of love suggests an exemplary ethical encounter with the other in Levinas's terms.

The very indirectness of the crisis in *The Golden Bowl* seems to illustrate the ethical relationship to otherness and, more particularly, its inevitable correlation with the issue of cosmopolitanism, especially in the evolution from the colonial pattern of appropriation established at the beginning of the novel. At the start, the Prince is quite clearly a collectable in the Ververs' museum, described as a tent "suggesting that of Alexander furnished with the spoils of Darius" (I 19). In the same logic, when Maggie averts her doubts regarding the Prince's infidelity by reading about his family at the British Museum, she contemplates the "associations" she had "secured" for herself, her son and her father:

> [S]he had felt more at her ease than for months and months before; she didn't know why, but her time at the Museum, oddly, had done it; it was as if she hadn't come into so many noble and beautiful associations, nor secured them also for her boy, secured them even for her father, only to see them turn to vanity and doubt […]. 'I believed in him again as much as ever' (II 155).

The crisis produced by the revelation occasioned by the golden bowl illustrates a departure from this pattern, a departure embraced with the curiosity of viewing a pagoda in the garden:

> This situation had been occupying for months and months the very centre of the garden of her life, but it had reared itself there like some strange tall tower of ivory, or perhaps rather some wonderful beautiful but outlandish pagoda, a structure plated with hard bright porcelain, coloured and figured and adorned at the overhanging eaves with silver bells that tinkled ever so charmingly when stirred by chance airs (II 5).

---

14 Tambling shows how Maggie seeks to craft her marriage in the image of a "purer America" (Tambling 181); Anderson argues that Maggie's office is to "consummate a wedding between America and Europe" (Anderson 739), while Burrows argues that Maggie, akin to a settler, uses the projection of innocence to achieve her purpose. Also see *Eternal America*, ch. 6.
15 See Rowe, O'Hara.

In this vein, the pagoda revealed to Maggie in her garden of the mind is not only a symbol of a half-glimpsed truth—the revelation that something is wrong in the comfortable arrangement through which the Prince and Charlotte manage social relations for the whole family. The pagoda implies a break in the utopian father-daughter relationship Maggie had continued after her marriage:

> The pagoda in her blooming garden figured the arrangement—how otherwise was it to be named?—by which, so strikingly, she had been able to marry without breaking, as she liked to put it, with her past. She had surrendered herself to her husband without the shadow of a reserve or a condition and yet hadn't all the while given up her father by the least little inch. She had compassed the high felicity of seeing the two men beautifully take to each other, and nothing in her marriage had marked it as more happy than this fact of its having practically given the elder, the lonelier, a new friend (II 5).

The father-daughter relationship, in fact, is inscribed in a space of innocence—even childishness—inevitably associated with their blindness towards the implications of the family arrangement and with their American lineage—"children of good children:"

> They knew, it might have appeared in these lights, absolutely nothing on earth worth speaking of—whether beautifully or cynically; and they would perhaps sometimes be a little less trying if they would only once for all peacefully admit that knowledge wasn't one of their needs and that they were in fact constitutionally inaccessible to it. They were good children, bless their hearts, and the children of good children; so that verily the Principino himself, as less consistently of that descent, might figure to the fancy as the ripest genius of the trio (I 333-34).

In this sense, by shedding new light on this innocent—even "grotesque" (I 335)—view of the world, the pagoda can also signify the glimpse of the worldly that Maggie has to look at for the first time, perhaps not unlike Susan Stringham and Milly. Prompting an awareness of the "darkening shadow of a false position," Maggie contemplates having "taken a cold" without having actually having fallen in the water of full awareness of infidelity:

> Moving for the first time in her life as in the darkening shadow of a false position, she reflected that she should either not have ceased to be right— that is to be confident—or have recognised that she was wrong; though she tried to deal with herself for a space only as a silken-coated spaniel who has scrambled out of a pond and who rattles the water from his ears. [...] She hadn't, so to speak, fallen in; she had had no accident nor got wet; this at any rate was her pretension until after she began a little to wonder if she mightn't, with or without exposure, have taken cold (II 6-7).

One of the landmarks of the ethical movements in the novel is that the crisis—like the pagoda and the world—is approached with a curiosity that might illustrate Levinas's exemplary unintrusive relationship to otherness, in which the self deals with otherness without attempting to alter it. Maggie walks around the glimpsed crisis at the center of the garden of her mind, and becomes dimly conscious of the difficulty of grasping the situation, "never quite making out as yet where she might have entered had she wished":

> She had walked round and round it—that was what she felt; she had carried on her existence in the space left her for circulation, a space that sometimes seemed ample and sometimes narrow: looking up all the while at the fair structure that spread itself so amply and rose so high, but never quite making out as yet where she might have entered had she wished. She hadn't wished till now—such was the odd case; and what was doubtless equally odd besides was that though her raised eyes seemed to distinguish places that must serve from within, and especially far aloft, as apertures and outlooks, no door appeared to give access from her convenient garden level (II 3-4).

Denoting the worldly that Maggie is confronting for the first time, the pagoda reveals itself gently, yet firmly, as "foreign," resorting again to Levinas's vision of the possibly tragic encounter between self and otherness. "Impenetrable" and "inscrutable," the pagoda is akin to an exotic object that not only continues the marked imperial chain of imagery in the novel by being compared with a mosque as well but also encodes, mutely, the possibility of violence and the image of the sacrifice of the I in the world. Much as Milly is "caressingly martyred" (*The Wings of the Dove* II 42) at the hands of the worldly in London, so Maggie feels like an "interloper" who might pay with her own life if found "unprecedently near" the odd mental construction:

> The great decorated surface had remained consistently impenetrable and inscrutable. At present however, to her considering mind, it was as if she had ceased merely to circle and to scan the elevation, ceased so vaguely, so quite helplessly to stare and wonder: she had caught herself distinctly in the act of pausing, then in that of lingering, and finally in that of stepping unprecedentedly near. The thing might have been, by the distance at which it kept her, a Mahometan mosque, with which no base heretic could take a liberty; there so hung about it the vision of one's putting off one's shoes to enter and even verily of one's paying with one's life if found there as an interloper
>
> (*The Golden Bowl* II 4).

In the series of scenes through which the crisis is resolved, the hostility of the world is also related, to the ultimate unknowability of the face of the other, when, according to Levinas, the other reveals himself "in his alterity" (Levinas 150). The situation of the four characters at Fawns is eloquent of the difficulty of relating to the face of the other:

> [T]he facts of the situation were upright for her round the green cloth and the silver flambeaux; the fact of her father's wife's lover facing his mistress; the fact of her father sitting, all unsounded and unblinking, between them (II 232).

The scene of four characters facing each other blankly is transmuted, however, from a domestic masquerade into a veritable encounter with alterity—this time, a blank face of the other. Pervaded by the melancholy of a baroque season at Fawns, the hitherto colonial scenario of appropriation changes into a cosmopolitan openness to otherness for Maggie.

The cue to this ethical approach to otherness and to the world, that is, the cue to the capacity of the self to sojourn in the world and to embrace the alterity of the other lies in the scene of the pagoda, when Maggie finds a way of relating to the unprecedented situation represented by the pagoda by waiting and by producing, by her mere presence and touch, a recognition of her consciousness, as indicated by the "sound sufficiently suggesting that her approach had been noted":

> She hadn't certainly arrived at the conception of paying with her life for anything she might do; but it was nevertheless quite as if she had sounded with a tap or two one of the rare porcelain plates. She had knocked in short— though she could scarce have said whether for admission or for what; she had applied her hand to a cool smooth spot and had waited to see what would happen. Something HAD happened; it was as if a sound, at her touch, after a little, had come back to her from within; a sound sufficiently suggesting that her approach had been noted (II 4).

The last scene in the novel, invoked earlier, rehearses the scene of the characters facing each other at a card game, no longer blankly, but involved in a profoundly ethical encounter with otherness. In fact, the last scene bears a striking resemblance to Levinas's "face to face" encounter, in which, in the epiphany of the face of the other, proximity and distance are both felt: "The Other precisely reveals himself in his alterity not in a shock negating the I, but as the primordial phenomenon of gentleness" (Levinas 150).

The scene between Maggie and the Prince can be interpreted as a repetition with a difference of the world closing in earlier on the Prince and Charlotte. They had made up a "tightened circle" based on an intense relationship of reflection between self and other: "their lips sought their lips, their pressure their response and their response their pressure" (*The Golden Bowl* I 312). The scene between the Prince and Maggie, however, is built on an ethical act where the Prince's capitulation is met by Maggie's acknowledgement of the alterity of the other, rather than its assimilation or reflection. To the Prince's "See? I see nothing but *you*," Maggie acknowledges alterity, as in Levinas's ethical model, not as a shock negating the I, but with gentleness: "for pity and dread of [his eyes], she buried her own in his breast" (II 369).

Returning to the transatlantic allegory staged in *The Golden Bowl* and doubling the realist plot of adultery and reconciliation, James stages a progression from a neo-colonial appropriation of Europe as a collectable in an American inventory, to an encounter with otherness as a blank, to a final ethical encounter based on recognition of the ultimate unknowability of the other.

Redemptive America

By way of a conclusion, one might make brief mention of the overtly redemptive role America plays in what Haviland calls James's fourth phase of revisionism (Haviland 214). Re-staging an ethical encounter on a global level, the redemptive potential of the American presence appears, to lesser or greater degrees, in the late tales of New York, for example in the figure of the melancholy absentee in "The Jolly Corner," the vision of Old New York in "Crapy Cornelia" or more amply in "The Round of Visits," where the New World experience oscillates for Mark Monteith between a vision of a nightmarish place of miscomprehension and a capacity to empathise with Phil Bloodgood, who had swindled him out of his money. An even richer vision of the role of America in a global ethic is displayed in *The Ivory Tower*, left unfinished, and intended as a story of dispossession and forgiveness: as James indicated in his Notebooks, "I want Gray absolutely to inherit the money, to have it, to have had it, and to let it go" (*The Ivory Tower* 295).

An appropriate coda is provided, however, by James's *The Sense of the Past*, a fantasy of time-travel begun in 1900, abandoned as James commenced work on *The Ambassadors* and interestingly taken up again in 1914, at the beginning of the World War I "with such a tremendous lot of possibilities in it that I positively quake in dread of the muchness with which they threaten me" (*The Sense of the Past* 295). A "ghost hit" (*Henry James: Letters IV* 158), James's fantasy provides an interesting counterpoint to the allegory in "Benvolio," the first text discussed in this paper. Like Benvolio, the hero of the story, Ralph Pendrel, is torn between two women and their two worlds: Aurora, the spirit of America, of the future and, like the Countess, a figure of energy, and Nan, a character from the European past and, akin to Sholastica, a melancholy presence. Tempted by a trip into the past and to Europe, Ralph Pendrel ultimately yearns for his America of the future and tells Nan about the wonders of the world represented by Aurora:

> [H]e now, at last now, opening up, opening out, everything that he has had before to keep back, tells her such things about those fruitions of the Future which have constituted his state, tells her of how poor a world she is stuck fast in compared with all the wonders and the splendors that he is straining back to, and of which he now sees only the ripeness, richness, attraction and civilization, the virtual perfection without a flaw
>
> (*The Sense of the Past* 337).

No longer valuable only for its opposition to Europe, the New World spirit in James's last allegory and in the late Jamesian imagination returns and explicitly fulfills the redemptive potential of Milly's and Maggie's America, rehearsing the ethical scenario of James's global "hits."

3. James's Sociology of Taste: *The Ambassadors*, Commodity Consumption, and Cultural Critique

Esther Sánchez-Pardo

This paper aims at elucidating James's complex position at the crossroads of impression—in his late "impressionist novels"—versus possession, examining how he weaves together a systematic focus on the workings of perception and desire and an analytical representation of plots that involve possession—of art or aesthetic objects, or of money in most cases. The oscillation between both is enhanced in the confrontation of America and Europe in the midst of major social and economic changes in the West. The early twentieth century witnessed fundamental transformations, such as the shift from industries filled with manual labourers, producing tangible commodities, to a new middle class of mental labourers who produced intangible products or services, such as the manufacture of cultural commodities. More than it has been acknowledged, James's late fiction focuses on the nascent cultural milieu of this emerging middle class, the rise and visibility of corporate white-collar workers, entrepreneurs, and businessmen, and their impact on literature and aesthetics, in particular on the way their mental labour altered the forms and symbolic logic of mass culture. James's responses to these major transformations in his writing testify to his engagement, rather than resistance, to these social and economic developments. The stylistic innovations cosmopolitan modernists later adopted from James were a competitive response to changes in contemporary European and American economic systems.

I would like to argue that James took up the challenge of representing American society through a sophisticated and nuanced understanding of capitalism that very seldom has been addressed in previous studies. Novels such as *The Wings of the Dove* (1902), *The Ambassadors* (1903), and *The Golden Bowl* (1904), along with a few less well-known stories and essays, demonstrate that James distinguishes between an older stage of British capitalism and an emerging American brand of corporate capitalism. Marxist critics have ignored James's writings in their focus on economic and class issues because James does not directly address material production in his novels. In his book on the melodramatic imagination, Peter Brooks has observed how the category of realism could not sufficiently contain writers like James and Balzac. Instead, these writers seemed to operate in excess of realist ideals rather than in a dialectical relationship to them, and it is this deviation from materialism that makes it difficult to apply Marxist theory to James across the board. In this paper, I will argue that James's stylistic representations of the new middle class, along with the consumption of cultural commodities, affect the relations between American "Realism" and cosmopolitan "Modernism," and that a repositioning of James's late fiction at the intersection of these polarised literary movements may shed light on why they were less opposed than scholars often assume.

In James's narratives, possession figures neither as a state in which objects are 'held' or preserved, nor as a stable narrative of their harmonious and continuous transmission. In contrast to the proprietary relation of ownership, possession here reflects the status of becoming rather than of being. Whereas property is a socially conservative force, James underlines the disruptive power of possession. The Jamesian pursuit of coveted 'objects,' particularly in the late novels, represents an agonistic struggle, in sociologist Thorstein Veblen's (1857-1929) sense of the term.[1] The stakes of possession here (as, James insinuates, in late nineteenth-century bourgeois

---

[1] I quote Veblen: "the term is used in a technical sense as describing a comparison of persons with a view to rating and trading them in respect of relative worth of value— in an aesthetic or moral sense—and so awarding and defining the relative degrees of complacency with which they may legitimately be contemplated by themselves and by others. An invidious comparison is a process of valuation of persons in respect to worth" (Veblen 34). Social class status mediates these categories, transforming acquired material differences, through the viewpoint of James's central characters, into the signs of a "moral" difference in nature. The majority of the objects referred to in James's novels should be understood as symbolic in their rhetorical aspects, as signs within a network of coded signifiers which come to be "naturalised" and fixed within a virtually unmovable social system.

society) are primarily social: the pattern of acquisitions does not merely reproduce or reflect the hierarchy of class relations but also serves as a means of transforming that structure.

I have invoked Veblen's terminology to describe the stakes of Jamesian possession, for Veblen's theoretical account of the late nineteenth- and early twentieth-century "leisure class" strikes at certain key elements which we may recognise as characteristic of the *haut-bourgeois* stratum James depicts: its emulatory character and predatory practices, its preference for the rhetoric of warfare over trade, its fetishism of material wealth, and its peculiar 'aesthetic' taste for ornamental excess. In *The Theory of the Leisure Class*, Veblen incorporates these elements within a theoretical account of the "barbarian" leisure class, a class whose socially dominant status belies, according to Veblen, its ethical incompatibility with advanced industrial capitalism. Veblen argues that the leisured classes in advanced industrial society maintain their ascendancy, in effect by performing a relation to production and consumption, which symbolically negates the values of the industrial economy.

Veblen's leisure class functions according to an alternative, honorific prestige economy which valorises objects and appearances that appear incompatible with the 'mechanical' virtues of utility or work. Leisure requires value as a representation of freedom from labour; conspicuous consumption evidences wealth and power by 'liberating' consumption from reference to use-value or need. Predicated upon a material basis which it displaces and conceals, the prestige economy of Veblen's leisure class essentially sublimates an acquired pecuniary power into the aesthetic signs of a static class distinction.

This transubstantiation of money values comes under fire in James's novels of the late 1980's and early 1900's. Capitalist wealth and consumption prove an embarrassment to James's aspirant bourgeois characters because they signify a dependence on the industrial, working classes rather than a 'liberation' therefrom. Maria Gostrey questions Lambert Strether as to whether Chad Newsome's virtual exile in Paris reflects an abashed retreat from the source of his industrial fortune: "Is it perhaps then because it's so bad—because your industry, as you call it, is so vulgar—that Mr. Chad won't come back? Does he feel the taint?" Strether, in turn, confirms that Chad's money is a sign of his dependence upon production: "'Oh,' Strether laughed... 'He's glad enough of the money from it, *and the money is his whole basis*. There's appreciation in that [...]'" (98, emphasis mine). Chad,

Strether implies, is not one to feel "taints" — although he himself is. Unlike Chad, Strether strives to deny the monetary basis for his own sojourn in Paris: this he accomplishes, in a reversal of Chad's reconciliatory gesture, by breaking relations with Mrs. Newsome. James represents Chad's compromise between industrial production and 'aesthetic' consumption as a reprehensible bargain, but Strether hardly fares better in the novel: his refusal to acknowledge either basis necessarily leads him to a dead end.

James's bourgeois characters, who are typically drawn from the new middle class, likewise seek to conceal the instability of bourgeois financial power by covering it in the image of a 'natural,' solid and traditional (or aristocratic) taste. Not only do they disclaim their own impulses toward conspicuous consumption, James's "centres of consciousness" — Lambert Strether, Maisie Farange, Fleda Vetch, Merton Densher — distort or refract the traces of consumption that they observe in other 'honorific' characters. James uses the main character's perspective on material objects to dramatise the process by which the appearance of consumption is transformed, outwardly as well as inwardly (i.e. mentally) into the guise of its opposite: solid, stable *possession*.

Veblen's leisure class, by contrast, is openly infatuated with wealth and seeks to display it in forms sufficiently transparent. According to Veblen, social 'esteem' accrues to displays of wasteful excess (such as conspicuous consumption) because these displays serve as a patent "evidence of wealth" (Veblen 74). "Wealth or power must be put in evidence," Veblen argues: "in order to gain and to hold the esteem of men, it is not sufficient *merely to possess wealth or power*" (36, emphasis mine). Mere possession, however, takes center stage in Jamesian narratives. In James's novels bourgeois wealth registers (as it is 'seen' or represented by the narrator) as an object of desire or esteem only where it appears covered or dressed in the alluring, and presumptively legitimising, garb of precious and preserved 'objects.' Covering the bare and unadorned face of financial power, James's *grand-bourgeois* characters strive to hide their money in 'things' — or in persons. What we find in these novels, consequently, is the attempt among James's bourgeois characters to cleanse bourgeois wealth by covering it in the 'aesthetic' signs of natural taste, or class.

Possession, to be honorific, in these novels, must be predicated upon a pretended horror of the object's consumption. James represents this *grand-bourgeois* antipathy toward consumption, moreover, as all the more intense for its hypocrisy: with scenes of shopping and theatrical performance, and allusions to the nascent boom of advertising. *The Ambassadors* aptly illustrates that consumption has become the dominant mode in which the late nineteenth and early twentieth-century bourgeois treats of objects and social relations. Nonetheless, in this novel, as typically in James's late fiction, it is the avowed contempt for wasteful excess or expenditure—which is a posture of conservatism, in spite of its true nature—that effectively gains social 'esteem' for James's characters. In the late novels, James's characters entertain the illusion that possession reveals not wealth primarily, but social distinction.

The prestige economy of possession that James's late novels represent and criticise is one which Pierre Bourdieu has described, in his major work *Distinction*, as "an enchanted experience of culture" (Bourdieu 3).[2] In this system of possession, the consumption of goods—even the remembrance of their acquisition—is seemingly banished from consciousness. In possessing coveted *objets d'art* and other symbolic representations of wealth, James's bourgeois characters aspire to an expressive model of possession, in which possession represents "the acquisition of legitimate culture by insensible familiarization *within the familial circle*" (3, emphasis mine). Naturalising possession in this manner, as Bourdieu observes, necessarily "implies forgetting the acquisition" (3). In James's narratives, likewise, the basis of possession is acquisition through monetary exchange, yet its social function demands repudiation of this basis. Hence Lambert Strether, as we will see, chronically 'forgets'—or displaces—the monetary basis of Madame de Vionnet's collection, envisioning her acquired objects as putatively natural 'reflections' or 'expressions' of the possessor.

Objets d'art, likewise, acquire value in the represented viewpoint of James's characters by possessing a special capacity to signify integrity, wholeness, and constancy over time. The value imputed to these objects, however, proves to be odds with the manner of their acquisition. James represents bourgeois possession as an act which, in claiming the historical object as a value, simultaneously, violates that claim.

For the aspirant bourgeois characters of James's fiction, objects of possession—and the 'aesthetic' desire for them—function as means of

---

[2] Bourdieu's work mounts a strong critique of Kantian disinterest and the tradition which distinguishes categorically between the "taste of sense" and the "taste of reflection" (measuring the former by physical gratification and the latter by its independence of such gratification). We may observe a similar dynamic of negation-through-mimesis in James's treatment and representation of bourgeois possession *qua* consumption.

cloaking, or signifying indirectly, this collusive relation between economic and class power. James's characters employ aesthetic objects to perform, and thereby attain, social status and personal power, as Madame de Vionnet, styling herself an aristocrat, manages to ensnare Chad Newsome and to fascinate Lambert Strether. Such characters nonetheless disclaim the fact by imagining that aesthetic objects are transcendent of 'base' relations, and by projecting an aesthetic disinterest in the manipulation of objects for social ends. The bad faith of bourgeois possession, as James represents it, lies in this pretence to define itself in contrast to the very mechanism it employs.

James undercuts this bourgeois romanticism of objects in his late, 'impressionist' novels. In these narratives, James once again traces the source of values imputed by his characters not to objects—or to the histories in which they figure—but rather to desiring subjects. Through the narrator and those he observes, James represents the esteem of the late nineteenth-century bourgeois for aesthetic wholeness and historical continuity as a function of the bourgeois' own social lack, and consequent desire for an integral, continuous, and historical class identity, or 'family' structure. In the ironic consciousness of the observing narrator, James's novels symbolically entertain the illusion that outward 'things' reflect a 'natural' social legitimacy.

In *The Ambassadors,* Lambert Strether's narrative is intimately bound up with his desire to possess the city of Paris—visually and epistemologically—along with all that it represents. In the preface, however, James argues that Strether was not to be drawn back into temptation but rather "thrown forward...upon his lifelong trick of intense reflexion" (*Art of the Novel* 316). By means of this "reflexion," James asserts, Strether managed to be "very much in Paris" without being very much of it: "with the surrounding scene itself a minor matter, a mere symbol for more things than had been dreamt of in the philosophy of Woollett." James goes so far as to assert that "another surrounding scene would have done as well," but then he adds one qualification that entirely undoes the pretence: "could it have represented a place in which Strether's errand was likely to lie and his crisis to await him." This errand and crisis, again, are confirmations of the 'trivial' and 'vulgar' association of Paris with sexual and sensual temptation. Chad has lingered in Paris to carry on an illicit affair; and Strether himself prolongs the situation, for he himself has fallen in love with the sensations of Paris—especially those he experiences in the Faubourg-Saint Germain drawing-rooms of Madame de Vionnet.

Strether permits himself the indulgence of memory, sensation and fantasy by holding desired objects at a distance—whether these be romantic objects like Maria Gostrey, or perceptual ones, such as Paris: "it hung *before him* this morning, the vast bright Babylon, like some huge iridescent object" (*Ambassadors* [1986] 11)—and by possessing them only vicariously. He does so, ironically enough, by identifying with Chad, the displacement for his own "stray spirit of youth" (122). Strether does, after all, participate in the competition over Chad's 'profits,' however indirectly: initially, by summoning him back to Woollett, and later by encouraging Chad's relationship with Madame de Vionnet. Despite Strether's defensive assertion to the contrary, James's impressionist novels figure the narrator's observations as actions of possession, even of consumption. Seeing pivotal scenes before shop windows and within theatre boxes, James reminds us that consumption in this late capitalist world is increasingly a scopic activity.

When Strether first meets Madame de Vionnet, she impresses him with an English that appears effortless, "clearly of the easiest to her, yet unlike any other he had ever heard" (210). But his fascination ceases when she is caught off-guard, and Strether realises that Madame de Vionnet has been performing all this time when she reverts to her native French. Strether remembers later that

> the wonderful woman's overflow of surprise and amusement was wholly into French, which she struck him as speaking with an unprecedented command of idiomatic turns, but in which she got, as he might have said, somewhat away from him, taking all at once little brilliant jumps that he could but lamely match (464).

Madame de Vionnet cannot keep up the performance of familiarity for Strether, and "the present result was odd, fairly veiling her identity, shifting her back into a mere voluble class or race to the intense audibility of which he was by this time inured" (464).

Madame de Vionnet uses language strategically to further assist in her performance of identity. Both words and images work together to create the illusion that she is not different from the kind of women Strether is used to encountering back at home. She uses innocuous, uncontroversial topics for conversation which are typical of the American women of Strether's acquaintance; and he therefore wonders, "[W]hat was there in her, if anything, that would have made it impossible he should meet her at Woollett? And wherein was her talk during their moments on the bench together not the same as would have been found adequate for a Woollett garden-party?—unless perhaps truly in not being quite so bright" (212). Strether doesn't perceive the French woman's use of artifice in her language to gain the older American's approval. Madame de Vionnet also takes care to speak an English that does not sound too alien to Strether's ears:

> [S]he had spoken to him, very simply and gently, in an English clearly of the easiest to her, yet unlike any other he had ever heard. It wasn't as if she tried; nothing, he could see after they had been a few minutes together, was as if she tried; but her speech, charming, correct and odd, was like a precaution against her passing for a Pole. There were precautions, he seemed indeed to see, only when there were really dangers (210).

The French gentlewoman's manner of delivery, as well as the simplicity of her choice of words, makes it seem that she speaks English without effort; like Chad she too has an 'easy' style. This impression of facility allows her to pass off as intentional any noticeable oddity in her idiom or accent. Madame de Vionnet successfully deflects attention away from being judged as not being a native English speaker by drawing attention to her performance as a Polish refugee who isn't a native French speaker.

It is only when some French guests interrupt Strether's and Madame de Vionnet's *tête à tête* that Strether becomes aware of the important role that language also plays in French society. Again, visual cues such as a new cast of characters, costumes, deportment, and gestures signal that Madame de Vionnet responds in a French rather than an American dramatic scene. The duchess "had more of a bold high look, the range of expensive reference, that he had, as might have been said, made his plans for" (212). Strether notices how in Madame de Vionnet's milieu, the French use words in a different way than Americans do. And he realises he cannot fully engage in social interaction because he isn't fluent in French. When Madame de Vionnet reverts back to speaking French to the other guests and does not introduce Strether to them, she no longer strikes him as "the usual thing," an American, because an American lady would have introduced the strangers; he senses instead "a note he was conscious of as false to the Woollett scale and the Woollett humanity" (213). Due to Paris's fascination with and celebration of the visual sense, the word would seem to place a distant second as a representational form. James nonetheless depicts a society that values the power of the word, one that has traditionally viewed the visual and verbal arts in harmony. Although in the novel Strether surrenders possession of the central object which is at stake in the novel's plot—the Newsome fortune, as represented in Chad—he nonetheless seeks to abet its possession by Madame de Vionnet. Strether stands to profit, materially, by his own marriage to Mrs. Newsome, yet upon being introduced to Parisian society he conceives, as it were, of a higher goal: not to marry money himself, but indirectly to marry money with taste—that is, with the upper class and its history—by strengthening Chad 'virtuous' alliance with Madame de Vionnet.

Barred by his own "want of money, of opportunity, of positive dignity" — in other words, practical pecuniary power or effective symbolic status— from "raising up... the temple of taste" (117), Strether seeks to discover the image of this "temple" in theatrical Europe, and purports to find it in the home of Madame de Vionnet. James dwells repeatedly and at length upon Strether's appreciation for the well-appointed apartments of Madame de Vionnet: the theme appears, strategically placed, in the opening chapters of books six, nine, and twelve (the final book). In rehearsing Strether's aesthetic and affective estimations of Madame de Vionnet's possessions, James reveals the basis for their appeal to him. This appeal lies in the objects' reference to a social historical past, a pre-revolutionary, ancient Paris, and the succeeding post-revolutionary period of imperial and Napoleonic glory (236). This past, for Strether, becomes mythical rather than historical as it moves into a cipher for his own subjective desire.

James also underlines the persistence with which Strether strives to see Madame de Vionnet as being continuous with, or even reflected in, her things. In the process of this reflection, Strether effaces all distinctive and historical qualities of the objects and comes to see in them only the possessor's image, the reflection of her avowed 'hereditary' relation.

Strether knows this illusion to be a lie: he has been told that Mme de Vionnet is a "celebrated" collector (203). But he nonetheless persists in denying the fact to himself. Disclaiming the acquisitive efforts taken on Mme de Vionnet's part to assemble these 'things' into the appearance of an aristocratic legacy, Strether imagines the collection as a natural integrity, passed down from generations. He disclaims any perception of Mme de Vionnet's commercial activity. The collection, like its mistress, becomes beautiful to the extent that he may credit it with detachment from the marketplace.

Approaching Mme de Vionnet's character through her relation to possession—patently, as a negation of consumption—Strether enacts what Bourdieu has described as "the ideology of natural taste" (*Distinction* 68).

Explicitly or tacitly, as Bourdieu points out, this ideology, "naturalises real differences, converting differences in the mode of acquisition of culture into differences of nature" (68). Here, Bourdieu's arguments clearly reinforce Thorstein Veblen's views. In Strether's response to Madame de Vionnet's possessions, we observe the "sense of costliness masquerading under the name of beauty," in Veblen's terms (182). Veblen reminds us that this "blending and confusion of the elements of expensiveness and beauty is, perhaps, best exemplified in articles of dress and of household furniture" (131): it should not surprise us that Strether conceives of Madame de Vionnet's identity and allure precisely in terms of these articles. What is at issue, however, is not simply an attraction to money coded as aesthetical appeal: Madame de Vionnet and her possessions appear attractive to Strether by virtue of their *indirect* relation to money.

Strether persists in his illusions through the remainder of the novel: he 'dresses' the appeal of Mme de Vionnet's money—like her sexual relation—in vagueness. He does so, moreover, because he wishes to. Strether has not gone undeceived. When the sexual nature of her relationship with Chad is exposed to Strether—in the infamous boating scene which stands as the quintessentially impressionist moment in the novel—he concedes to himself merely what the reader has already granted above: that Mme de Vionnet's "manner," like her calculated performance of possession, "had been a performance" (*Ambassadors* [1986] 466). While no longer in the dark, Strether feels the charm, even after this, of the lady and her 'things.' It is not, as we just said, that Strether is undeceived; rather, he wishes to be deceived. It is not repression but rather repudiation, finally, which maintains Strether in ignorance of the sexual and monetary relations he will not submit to see—relations which would altogether undo his assertion that Mme de Vionnet represents the 'old' aristocratic manner of 'good taste.'

In his parting meeting with Mme de Vionnet, Strether understands Mme de Vionnet's manner of possession—sexual as well as material—as the very opposite of despoilment or contamination; Strether imagines 'possession' in 'good taste' as entailing the sublimation of 'things,' a refinement of their 'values.' He maintains the illusion of 'good taste' and refinement by evacuating the material, 'immoral', (i.e. sexual) and economic content to which all signs point. James figures Strether's credulous view of possession as a wilful illusion, one, James suggests, the reader must learn to see through.

As it has been widely discussed, the primary site of discursive complexity in Jamesian narrative is the layered orchestration of perspectives: no longer plot, but narration, and therefore style. Subordinating his materialist plots to an aesthetic focus in narration, James brings subjects and their perspectives to the foreground of his texts, while permitting action to recede from direct view. With this technical gesture, James incurs charges of having suppressed a historical process, namely, the socio-economic foundations for the 'privilege' of consciousness. This is Terry Eagleton's argument about Jamesian narrative[3]. He holds that James mediates story by subjective perception in order to suppress "certain real conflicts and divisions" (Eagleton 141) that are at stake in his plot. Eagleton identifies the typical plot of these narratives as "the struggle for material acquisition." But he asserts something more: in Jamesian narrative, he claims, that material struggle is displaced by a parallel quest for putatively immaterial objects: consciousness, epistemological mastery, a detached but "encompass[ing] view" (141). This epistemological pursuit, Eagleton argues, takes over the quest narrative, effectively repressing the plot of material struggle and thereby conjuring away the social underpinnings of James's text. Although plot pays tribute to the "conflicts and divisions" that "generate the wealth which makes such privileged consciousness possible in the first place" (141), in the guise of a quest for consciousness, Eagleton asserts, James purports to transcend those very conflicts. He locates the central dynamic of Jamesian narrative in his 'aesthetic' turn, so to speak, from a social and material world directly grasped to an interior harmony constructed by thought.

Eagleton's position is a forceful and compelling one. It rests, however, upon certain premises, both social and narratological. Eagleton is correct in observing that 'things' and 'consciousness' occupy parallel positions in the grammar of Jamesian narratives. A number of James's novels and tales from the turn of the century, as we have discussed, integrate these objects in a two-fold quest for possession: the quest represents, in plot, a social contest for material acquisition, and in narration, an interior, subjective struggle on the part of the centre of consciousness for epistemological mastery. Eagleton presumes, however, that these two narrative lines are fungible and mutually exclusive, positioned in an either-or relation with respect to one another. His argument implies, moreover, that James's narrative enacts and exchange between them, repressing plot in foregrounding narration — surrendering 'things,' in short, for ideas.

---

3 Terry Eagleton developed the argument in *Criticism and Ideology* (1975) and holds very closely to it in his *Introduction to the English Novel* (2005). Here we follow his first views.

Through the narrator's discourse of a social contest over material acquisition, James's impressionist narratives digest and reflect upon the novel's own implication in narratives of 'aesthetic' possession. Formally, the impressionist novels seek to articulate a reflective distance between the novel's 'vision' of material values and the practices of consumption in which it is engaged.

James's fiction reminds us that the currency of appearances—of class, or the associated distinction of 'taste'—requires endorsement at both ends: both in its display and imputed recognition. In Bourdieu's words, "Taste classifies, and it classifies the classifier" (*Distinction* 6). In James's impressionist novels, desire—in particular aesthetic desire—serves to reinscribe reference to the social and economic bases which underlie the display of 'historical' or aristocratic tastes and which fuel, as well, the material and aesthetic 'plots' for possession. Representing "aesthetic" appeal as an ideology grounded in a dissimulation of its social and economic base, James's stories of possession bring the contents of this aesthetic ideology to consciousness.

4. Bad Investments
Eric Savoy

Everybody knows that Henry James, like Balzac, was keenly interested in money, particularly in the nefarious entanglements that arise between those who have it and those who want it. Money is never *merely* money in James's fiction: as the pre-requisite for any experience of self-realisation, it has both a pragmatic function in the matrix of emplotment and a sort of spiritual office. In order to be buoyant, a character needs a certain, emphatically non-metaphorical liquidity. As Ralph Touchett observes in *The Portrait of a Lady*, "'I call people rich when they're able to meet the requirements of their imagination.'" His father, a hard-headed banker from Vermont who knows money first-hand, shares neither his son's spectatorial pleasure in the prospect of a rich Isabel Archer nor his idealised expectation of Isabel's imaginative fulfillment, for he knows that she may well "'fall a victim to the fortune-hunters'" (*The Portrait of a Lady* [1986] 236-37). Not surprisingly, James's commentators have followed the elder Mr. Touchett's line: "'I don't think I enter into your spirit,'" he responds, "'It seems to me immoral'" (237). Early and late criticism has focused exclusively on the corrupting influence of American capital, whether it be the traditional moral and ethical implications of Jamesian realism (according to which money is the root of all evil), or more recent post-colonial critiques of American empire-building and acquisition. This is hardly a misguided project, but it confines itself to the conventional perspectives of the literary humanities, both textual and historical, that do not engage with explanatory paradigms or systems of thought beyond the frontier of the humanities. In the argument that follows, I shall attempt to outline another way of thinking about James's economics—an approach that is not particularly attentive to moral or political agendas and that is not concerned with money as such. Under the auspices of new directions in comparative literature—directions that locate the specificity of the literary in relation to other disciplinary quests for meaning—I shall trace the confluence, or the congruity among, two very specific concepts of *economy*.

The first is 'narrative economy,' by which I mean the circulation, in narrative time and in the spatial emplotment of inter-subjective relations, of the complex, figurative signifier. My perspective on the return and repetition of the signifier—which is the prime 'currency' of narrative—is deconstructive: far from binding the text into coherent unity, the signifier detaches itself from punctual meaning as it evolves in the escalating spirals of *différence*. In direct proportion to the collapse of the signifier's grounding in the material reality of actual things, it loses all referential value in a process of hyper-inflation. It continues to circulate as a debased currency or as a form of waste paper, but it has lost the symbolic efficacy of language that constituted, for the New Criticism, its gold standard. The career of the free-floating and highly attenuated signifier is basic to James's narrative economy, for it occasions the encounter with the Lacanian 'Real'—with trauma and nothingness—that is the salutary corrective to his characters' bad investments. The other 'economy' I take up is, predictably, economics itself—in particular, the system of finance and investment banking that depends upon derivatives, which are instruments whose values are derived from something else. Derivates can be used to mitigate the risk of loss arising from changes in the value of the underlying asset: this process, known as hedging, is the basis of trading, for example, in commodities like oil and agricultural products. Alternatively, derivatives can be used to acquire risk rather to hedge against it. Here, investors engage in derivative contracts to speculate on the value of the underlying asset, betting that it will rise in value. Both types of derivates, when bundled together and traded on an exchange, are known as futures. In recent years, the combination of excessive risk-taking, wild speculation leading to investment bubbles, and unregulated trading in derivatives has led to a severe contraction of the international economy. At issue for my immediate project is the meaningful connection between recent economic history, particularly the speculation in futures, and fictional narratives of high-risk investment in a model of 'futurity.' Such fictions involve characters who live in the mode of expectancy; their narrative present is impoverished, if not vacant, for everything is sacrificed for the life to come. Always imminent yet endlessly deferred, this future time is anticipated as the arrival at a fully authentic subjectivity, a realization of a potential that must remain latent until that unveiling. My object of scrutiny is James's 1903 tale, "The Beast in the Jungle": in what ways might James's story of John Marcher's wild speculation about futurity illuminate the predicament in which the global economy now finds itself? What they have in common, I suggest, are the consequences that arise from the failures of accounting.

In his history of the Great Depression, John Kenneth Galbraith observes that "the autumn of 1929 was, perhaps, the first occasion when men succeeded on a large scale in swindling themselves" (Galbraith quoted by Paumgarten 44). Galbraith's point is easily transferred to the case history of John Marcher, who spends his life with the conviction that, sooner or later, in one way or another, something momentous is going to happen to him — something that will utterly transform his way of being in the world, and that will realise his potential, for good or for bad. "'I don't focus it. I can't name it'" ("The Beast in the Jungle" 372), he explains to the companion of his watch, May Bartram. On the one hand, Marcher might be understood as following the advice of legendary investor, Warren Buffett, who counselled his followers to "[p]ut your eggs in one basket, and then watch the basket." On the other hand, Marcher's speculative investment assumes a very high risk, for it concentrates all his resources, and to that extent, may be said to be leveraged — that is, under-written by borrowing from today in the hope of a magnificent return tomorrow. In order to revalue the striking modernity of "The Beast in the Jungle," it is worth exploring the possibility that a form of speculative 'leveraging' might occur in forms of social behaviour other than the economic. As Buffett observes, in modernity, "[d]ebt now became something to be refinanced rather than repaid." For Marcher, it would appear, needs to continually 're-finance' his speculation.

The underlying asset upon which Marcher bases it is his concept of his 'self' as pure potentiality, the potentiality that Lacan locates in the unconscious: it is as nebulous, as unverifiable, as the future transformative event upon which he reckons enormous profit or loss. The opacity of the entire situation, particularly in terms of 'asset,' compounds over time. Marcher's 'derivative,' then, in the sheer unaccountability of its basis, is uncannily similar to the protocols of contemporary finance, which are summed up by the concept of securitisation: this is the process by which loans — most notoriously, sub-prime mortgages given to risky borrowers in the United States — were bundled together and sold on to other institutions as packages of debt. As John Lanchester explains, "these packages of debt were then sold on and resold in the form of horrendously complex and sophisticated financial instruments... so complicated that no one knows who owns what underlying debt, and furthermore, no one knows what the assets are worth" ("Cityphobia" 3). The point is that the 'derivation' of dubious securities has been so multiplied and protracted that any concept of 'real' value has gone out the window. Normally, 'value' is determined by the market: derivatives are worth what somebody is willing to pay for them. But in recent months, because nobody is buying, nobody has a clue what they are worth, if anything. As a result of weak accounting practices, then, banks are reluctant to lend to each other, and the entire financial system has ground to a halt. Or, as Ben Bernanke, chairman of the Federal Reserve put it, there is a "chaotic unwinding" of the financial system (Weissman).

In order to embark upon speculation in futures, James's narrative economy requires that Marcher post a paper instrument—a signifier—that can circulate in that economy in good faith as a security worthy of his psychic investment and our readerly engagement. In banking terms, this instrument can be understood only in a very limited fashion as collateral or as a promissory note, because it isn't exactly a loan, nor are its terms subject to specification. It is however a binding contract with futurity itself, by the terms of which Marcher invests 'everything.' Required to pony up what he cannot 'name' or 'focus,' Marcher's 'terms' are never *not* a figural derivative: "something or other lay in wait for him, among the twists and turns of the months and the years, like a crouching beast in the jungle" (365). We can see immediately, in James's figurative economy, what I have called the 'multiplication and protraction' that has rendered illegible the underlying value of derivatives in contemporary finance. Marcher's asset in literal terms is merely 'something or other,' a nominally vacant this-or-maybe-that, a grammatical place-holder, that is exchanged for a series of different rhetorical currencies. As a "thing" that "lay in wait for him," the "something or other" is converted to prosopopeia, but the whereabouts of this animate "thing" is rebundled with metaphor, by which time—"the months and the years" ahead, or futurity itself—is imaged as a spatial maze of "twists and turns." Within this syntactic bundle is the delivery of a sharper, more gaugable prosopopeia, for the thing that "lay in wait" is specified as "a crouching beast in the jungle" ("The Beast in the Jungle" 365) of time and space—yet the specificity of this ultimate clarification is mitigated by its being only "like" such a creature, whereby the certainty of overarching metaphor is undercut by the attentuations of simile. As Warren Buffet might say, this is a hell of a risky investment: for not only are there no eggs, there isn't even a discernable basket.

John Lanchester argues that, like other forms of cultural production, finance in the twentieth century, in its turn toward self-referentiality and abstraction, underwent successive modernist and postmodernist transformations. As a result of arcane mathematisation, the total market in derivatives around the world is counted in the hundreds of trillions of dollars, a purely notional amount that exceeds the total value of the world's actual economic output by a factor of tenfold. "It seems wholly contrary to common sense," Lanchester writes, "that the market for products that derive from real things should be unimaginably vaster than the market for things themselves. With derivatives, we seem to enter a modernist world in which risk no longer means what it means in plain English" ("Melting into Air" 83). Late in the last century, it became virtually impossible for even the most sophisticated investor to assess the risks that lurk in derivatives. As a result of rampant bundling and re-selling, nobody knows who is at risk from the 'toxic debt' at the heart of the system: Warren Buffet compared the new world of financial products (strange creatures such as credit-default swaps) to "'weapons of mass destruction'—first, because they are lethal, and, second, because no one knows how to track them down" (Buffet quoted by Lanchester, "Melting into Air" 83). Lanchester concludes that "if the invention of derivatives was the financial world's modernist dawn, the current crisis is unsettlingly like the birth of postmodernism. For anybody who studied literature in college in the past few decades, there is a weird familiarity about the current crisis: value, in the realm of finance capital, evokes the elusive nature of meaning in deconstruction. According to Jacques Derrida "[...] meaning can never be precisely located; instead, it is always 'deferred,' moved elsewhere, located in other meanings, which refer and defer to other meanings" (Lanchester "Melting into Air" 84).

It is precisely in relation to Lanchester's broad cultural argument that I situate the prescient narrative economy of James's "The Beast in the Jungle," written at the outset of modernity itself. From an economic point of view, James offers a cautionary tale about bad investments—both in the model of futurity that drives speculation, and in the specific rhetoric instruments upon which such speculation is based. There are two things to observe about the circulation of these toxic instruments. First, as I have partly demonstrated, the prosopoetic figure of 'the beast' is generated by the text in order to suture the non-commensurability between words and things. Meaningless from the moment of its articulation, it is a figural derivative that brings nothing to presence in the present, apart from a determination to speculate on an equally implausible future value. Intended to manage risk, prosopopeia ends up magnifying it. As it circulates and recirculates in the narrative, it functions as a kind of junk bond, the rhetorical name of which is *catachresis*—that is, a figurative image for which there is no literal nor denotative referent. James offers an extreme case of the arbitrary signification that Paul de Man locates in *catachresis*, which, he claims, like prosopopeia is "hallucinatory" (49). As symptom of obsessional disorder rather than merely as signifier, Marcher's waste paper can be framed by the impasse, the undoing of the distinction between reference and signification, that de Man locates in the field of tropic derivatives: "it is impossible to say whether prosopopeia is plausible because of the empirical existence of dreams and hallucinations or whether one believes that such a thing as dreams and hallucinations exists because language permits the figure of prosopopeia" (49-50).

Secondly, the human drama that unfolds in "The Beast in the Jungle" is made possible by a process that I would describe as prosopoetic contagion. John Marcher's speculative investment in the futuristic 'beast' is not his alone, but requires the psychic capital of his collaborator, May Bartram. Because the catachrestic 'beast' is not subject to negotiation, James sets in motion a tightly interlaced imagistic economy of other, supporting signifiers—eyes, faces, hands and feet—that laminate the indescribable properties of the 'beast' onto May. In life, May gazes at Marcher from an undisclosed knowledge of his fate, from across "some mystic line that she had secretly drawn round her" (373), her eyes "beautiful with a strange, cold light" (382); in death, "the face of [her] tomb did become a face for him [...] because her two names were like a pair of eyes that didn't know him" (396). It would be absurdly reductive to suggest that May 'becomes' the 'beast,' yet it would seem that "the deep disorder in her blood" (376) is to be understood as resulting from prosopoetic contagion, from the toxic shock of her own bad investment.

Early in 2007, pundits issued dire warnings that the international economy had been infected by untraceable, bad assets and was on the verge of collapse. Interest rates began to rise in order to cool a vastly overheated economy. Ironically, it was already far too late to repair the overextended protocols of investment, let alone the pervasive and unregulated culture of pathological greed that subtended it. The culture was in the grip of the death drive. Midway through "The Beast in the Jungle," May Bartram has the cold comfort of advising John Marcher that whatever his investment had anticipated, its return had already been delivered. Incredulous, Marcher asks, "[W]hat then has happened?" "What *was* to," is May's enigmatic riposte (387). Like his repetitive compulsion, Marcher's sense of time is circular and tautological: "Since it was in Time that he was to have met his fate, so it was in Time that his fate was to have acted" (379). Under the auspices of James's queer temporality, in which *catachresis* pays its dividends to an unmarked account in a Swiss bank, May as investment counsellor delivers the bad news: "It has done its office. It has made you all its own [...]. It's past. It's behind. [...] Before... Before, you see, it was always to *come*. That kept it present" (389-91).

It is entirely debatable whether John Marcher arrives at any corrective epiphany at the conclusion of "The Beast in the Jungle." To argue, as most critics have done and as the tale itself seems to suggest, that Marcher ought to have invested in May Bartram—to 'have loved her for herself'—invokes both a heterosexual economy and a normative model of 'futurity' that the tale itself discounts as its very *donnée*. To explain this further would require a detour into another economic model—the psychoanalytic, both Freudian and Lacanian, in which the drives circulate around the impossible object in persistent unpleasure. In my forthcoming book, *Conjugating the Subject: Henry James and Queer Formalism*, I take up the psychoanalytic dimensions of John Marcher's case to demonstrate the transformation of his symptom into *sinthome*, the process by which he coheres as subject by learning to enjoy his symptom. For the moment, I leave him with his bad investments—seeing in his speculations, and in James's complex rhetorical derivatives, the image of what Lewis Lapham diagnoses as the absurdity of investors, the "Wall Street achievetrons folding and refolding sets of imaginary numbers into paper hats and airplanes" (Lapham 11). Like every investor in the world, John Marcher "had but one desire left—that he shouldn't have been 'sold'" ("The Beast in the Jungle" 379).

II
FRENCH AND ITALIAN HOURS

5. 'The Crash of Civilisation': James and the Idea of France, 1914-15

Hazel Hutchison

In the opening days of the First World War in August 1914, one word echoes through the many letters which Henry James wrote to his friends in an attempt to order his feelings about events: civilisation. To Howard Sturgis he expressed his horror at "the plunge of civilization into this abyss of blood and darkness," and to Edith Wharton he wrote that he felt "unbearably overdarkened by this crash of our civilization" (Lubbock 28). To Rhoda Broughton he wrote on 10th August:

> Black and hideous to me is the tragedy that gathers, and I'm sick beyond cure to have lived on to see it. You and I, the ornaments of our generation, should have been spared this wreck of our belief that through the long years we had seen civilization grow and the worst become impossible. The tide that bore us along was then all the while moving to *this* grand Niagara— yet what a blessing we didn't know it. It seems to me to *undo* everything, everything that was ours, in the most horrible retroactive way (403).

Six days into the war, James was shrewdly articulating the disillusionment, the rupture with the past, and the sense of futility that many cultural commentators would only recognise much later, and which would come to be the hallmarks of First World War literature.

However, James's reaction to the war was far from static. As weeks became months, James, like most other people, ran the gamut of emotions about the war, swinging from horror to enthusiasm and back again. James found it almost impossible to write fiction about the contemporary world during the war, although he did attempt some further work on his autobiography and the MS of *The Sense of the Past*, which had lain untouched since 1900 and which would be still unfinished at his death (Lubbock 442). He involved himself in relief work, visiting soldiers and serving as the honorary president of the American Volunteer Motor Ambulance Corps, for which he raised funds. But James was clearly troubled by this rupture with his writing routine and, as his letters and wartime essays show, felt the need to make sense of the conflict, not just as a political event, but also as a cultural one. I had anticipated that this paper would show that James saw France as the exemplar of European civilisation, however, on examination, James's opinions about civilisation and about France are not as clear-cut as one might imagine. What this paper does do is to explore James's war-time essay "France," and to ask exactly what it was that France represented to James in 1914-15. It also asks what James meant by "civilization" and how he thought it could be best saved from the abyss—if indeed it was worth saving.

"France"

James's essay "France" was written in the spring of 1915 as part of a fund-raising venture in aid of "The French Parliamentary Committee's Fund for the Relief of the Invaded Departments." *The Book of France* was edited by Winifred Stephens and, like Edith Wharton's later venture *The Book of the Homeless* (1916), it included a starry array of contributors from the worlds of art, literature and politics. The venture was headed by an honorary committee, which boasted five government ministers, including Winston Churchill (and his mother), various knights and ladies of the realm, and many of James's circle of friends and contacts, including Sidney Colvin, Edmund Gosse, Lucy Clifford, Thomas Hardy, Rudyard Kipling, Mary Ward, and H. G. Wells, as well as James himself. The book was a bi-lingual project. Stephens collated contributions from French writers and thinkers such as Maurice Barrès, André Gide, Anatole France and Pierre Loti, and then asked prominent British figures, mostly members of the committee, to provide translations. The only original pieces in English were a poem by Rudyard Kipling entitled "France" and James's short essay of the same title. James's piece was first delivered as "Remarks at the Meeting of the Committee held on June 9, 1915" and was published as the prologue to the collection (Stephens 1). James's prominent and privileged role in the project suggests that in the months since the previous August, he had quickly established his position as one entitled to speak on behalf of the British cultural community on the subject of the war—which is in itself remarkable, given James's usual avoidance of public and political affairs. The book was published, on a non-profit basis, by Macmillan in London and Edouard Champion in Paris in July 1915, which was a busy month for James. During July, he also adopted British nationality, wrote his long memorial essay on Rupert Brooke, and still found time to fall out with H. G. Wells. The essay was later collected with his other war essays by Percy Lubbock and published posthumously in *Within the Rim and Other Essays* (1917).

"France" is a complex essay, which draws much of its character from its context. James's writing about the war is often caricatured as jingoistic and nostalgic. Adeline Tintner dismissed all of James's war essays as "propaganda" (Tintner "First World War" 170). However, compared with the other pieces of writing in *The Book of France*, James's short essay is remarkably measured and restrained. He does not, like many contributors, denounce the ignorance or barbarity of the German nation, or pretend that the present conflict will be the war to end all wars. The essay seems on one level simply to voice James's appreciation of French intellectual and artistic style, which he sums up as "the life of the mind and the life of the senses taken together, in the most irrepressible freedom of either" (5). This is not exactly the sort of thing over which nations usually go to war. And yet, this vague but passionate celebration of the intellectual glories of France pervades other contributions too. Rudyard Kipling, ever ready with a catchy jingle, expresses it thus:

> First to follow Truth and last to leave old truths behind—
> France beloved of every soul that loves its fellow kind!
>
> ("France" 336)

However, it may be worthy of note that Kipling's poem mostly talks about how France and England have spent the last thousand years at war with each other. Nevertheless, the voguish idealisation of France as the cradle of civilisation and right feeling also appears in other wartime contexts—not simply in the pages of Stephens's collection. For example, Edith Wharton's novel *A Son at the Front* (1923), about a group of exiled Americans in Paris during the war, voices a similar idea:

> An Idea: that was what France, ever since she had existed, had always been in the story of civilization; a luminous point about which striving visions and purposes could rally. [...] to thinkers, artists, to all creators, she had always been a second country. If France went, western civilization went with her; and then all they had believed in and been guided by would perish
>
> (Wharton 193).

In 1917, as the young poet E.E. Cummings embarked on an Atlantic crossing from New York to serve as a volunteer ambulance driver, his father sent this telegram:

> As I said in advance
> I envy your chance
> of breaking a lance
> for Freedom in France
> by driving and mending
> an ambulance
>
> (Sawyer-Lauçanno 106)

Clearly James was right that the idea of France held a cultural currency that extended far beyond its geopolitical borders. As James expresses it in "France": "What happens to France happens to all that part of ourselves which we are most proud, and most finely advised, to enlarge and cultivate and consecrate" (5).

The Other France

What is striking in all of these examples, and I could have given many more from other writers, is the complete lack of specificity about what it is that France represents. The nation does not just stand, as Wharton suggests, for an idea, but for *any* idea that can be projected upon it. Indeed James seems to acknowledge this in his opening sentence:

> I think that if there is a general ground in the world on which an appeal might be made, in a civilized circle, with a sense of its being uttered only to meet at once and beyond the need of insistence a certain supreme recognition and response, the idea of what France and the French mean to the educated spirit of man would be the nameable thing
>
> (Wharton 1).

Throughout the rest of the essay however, France seems rather to be the *unnameable* thing. There is no mention of any of the tokens by which one might gain access to French life or culture—not a place name, not a region, not a writer, not an artist, a politician, a historical figure, a fictional character, a cathedral, a museum, nor an item of food or clothing. The only thing you might gather about the nation if you didn't know much about it already is that it is "our great neighbour" ("France" 5). And given James's ambivalent national status in the summer of 1915, this use of first person plural could quite logically locate France somewhere in northern Mexico.

If you don't know what you mean by "France" before you start, this essay will do nothing to explain, and I suspect this is the point. Like the title of the essay, France here is a word merely, a sign which invites multiple forms of signification, thus forcing readers to supply their own details. Of course, this is one of the key tactics of propagandist writing, to abstract and generalise, thus inviting a quick judgement rather than a thorough investigation. However, the call to certainty is undercut (as ever) by James's syntax in this sentence. A personalised and conditional opening clause: "I think that if," and the deviations and diversions of the sentence structure remind us that the wartime James remains as hesitant and introspective as usual.

The one thing that James does appear to say about France is that it is somewhere else. Indeed this seems to be its primary appeal—not in a crass escapist way, but in its constant challenge to and extension of familiar values. It is "a native genius so different from our own" which prompts "our growth of criticism and curiosity" ("France" 3). It is another family, which has "a way […] of interesting us more than our own" (4). Unlike Wharton, who repeatedly insisted on her immersion in and identification with French culture and society, James appears to value France as the embodiment of some kind of otherness or alternative identity. This is particularly interesting given the place that France, especially Paris, plays in James's own psychological alterity. In *A Small Boy and Others* he recounts the nightmare scene of being pursued by some hideous form through the Gallerie d'Apollon in the Louvre, and then turning to pursue the phantom figure in turn, thus assuming the predatory role of the other form. There is also the poignancy of James's deathbed dictations in which he speaks as Napoleon, suggesting that his debilitating stroke provided access to some fractured element of James's personality that saw itself as quintessentially French. This seems initially odd, but is not entirely nonsensical. France fascinated James by the tension which it appeared to perpetuate between form and freedom in all areas of public, private, and artistic life. This tension also lies at the core of James's ideas about his own art, and characterises much of what we know about his own personality. So it is perhaps not surprising that his splintered self should, as it were, seek resolution there. However, the tension between cultural form and material excess also informs James's ideas about civilisation in ways that are complex and unsettling.

Civilisation

This tension was not just appealing to James. As Jean Méral points out in his study *Paris in American Literature,* the idealisation of France as an alternative location of identity was seductive to many nineteenth-century American writers, for whom Paris operated not simply as a site of projection, where forbidden desires and aspirations could be explored, but also as a cipher which represented the entirety of European experience and tradition (Méral 44). By extension, it comes to represent, as Wharton notes, the very history of civilisation, without (from an American perspective) the political and religious complications of London and Rome.

James is often assumed to buy wholesale into this picture of Paris and of French culture in general. Many faulty readings of *The Ambassadors,* for example, are due to the assumption that James venerates French culture as the height of civilisation, and that by civilisation, James means something in the line of Matthew Arnold's faith in European high culture as a redemptive social force. However, as both Tim Lustig and Pierre Walker point out, James's terminology is not interchangeable with Arnold's. Lustig notes that for Arnold, civilisation and culture are two separate things: civilisation refers to the infrastructure of a society, its buildings, machinery and systems, while culture refers to the intellectual and artistic activity of a society. Thus, for Arnold, as Lustig notes, America could be civilised but was not yet "cultured" (Lustig "James, Arnold" 175). In *Civilization in the United States* (1888), Arnold argues that America has material comfort and urban organisation, but is not "interesting." There is a lack of "the elevated and the beautiful" (Arnold 357-58). It has no history, no castles, no Elizabethan houses. James appears to offer a similar viewpoint in his earlier study of *Hawthorne* (1879) where he notes the lack of "high civilization" in American life in the 1840's:

> No sovereign, no court, no personal loyalty, no aristocracy, no church, no clergy, no army, no diplomatic service, no country gentlemen, no palaces, no castles, nor manors, nor old country-houses, etc...
>
> (*Hawthorne* [London 1967] 55).

This list is, of course, notorious and there is much more of it. However, what is generally overlooked is that James's point here is that Hawthorne *did not* need these things to write. Life was interesting enough to him without them. When we recall this, James's use of the term "high civilization" takes on a mocking and sarcastic tone, undercutting the supposed superiority of European tradition in order to celebrate Hawthorne's American ingenuity in doing without such things. Indeed, James's account of "civilization" is often less than respectful—especially where France is concerned. His early essays on Paris written for the *New York Tribune* in 1875-76 and collected as *Parisian Sketches* take a light view of French civilisation—perhaps as part of James's desire to reach his American newspaper audience. Certainly, the word appears rather less than you might expect for one supposedly in awe of European sophistication, and is rarely used seriously. When it does appear, it is more often used in connection with the fripperies and frivolities of Parisian life, such as extravagant clothes, light opera and candy boxes:

> The *bonbonnière*, in its elaborate and impertinent uselessness, is certainly the consummate flower of material luxury; it seems to bloom, with its petals of satin and its pistals of gold, upon the very apex of the tree of civilization
> (*Parisian Sketches* 41).

James's anxiety about the proximity of material luxury and civilisation lingers on throughout his writing career. It is especially prominent in his late novels where we see James eliding the Arnoldian distinction between material wealth and aesthetic culture. Increasingly, James appears to accept that culture costs money, but also that one can buy culture without acquiring either good taste or good behaviour or even, like Adam Verver, without being very "interesting." James's distrust of civilisation is still evident as late as 1907 in *The American Scene*, where he uses the word both with and without heavy sarcasm. There is the "breathless civilization" reflected in the ever changing brick and marble of the New York cityscape which foretells the "defeat of history," there is the multifaceted "idea of civilization" that takes form in the historical "richness" of Richmond Public Library, and there is finally, and damningly, the Pullman car's "pretended message of civilization" which piles up its arrears against the poor, the dispossessed and the racially excluded (*The American Scene* [1987] 81; 279; 334).

Conclusion

James's track record with "civilization," therefore, makes it tricky to draw any firm conclusions about his uses of the word in his war essays and letters. Did he really condone a war to defend an idea that over the years he had associated with French chocolate boxes, Native American clearances, English public schools and *opera bouffe*? It is hard to believe either that James instantly abandoned his scepticism about civilisation on the brink of the war, or that he continued to use the term with its usual double-edged asperity. Tim Lustig argues that James's really important statement about the war is his declaration "for I believe in Culture" at the end of "The Long Wards" ("James, Arnold" 125). Lustig's reading of this statement suggests that for James it was not the material trappings of civilisation that mattered so much as the intellectual and artistic values of society. But is it something material or something aesthetic that James mourns after the bombing of the Rheims Cathedral in September 1914?—an outrage which he characterises as "the most hideous crime ever perpetrated against the mind of man" (Lubbock 421). Civilisation, like France itself, appears to have been for James contradictory, sometimes sublime, sometimes false and shabby, something which blurred the boundary between the material and the abstract, a concept onto which many associations can be projected and yet one which offered an ideal of form which James could not quite do without.

I for one don't mind James's lack of finality in his war essays. It suggests to me that his remarkable mind was still open to contradiction and reorganisation and was therefore still flexible and responsive to experience. The war clearly tested James's values, as it tested those of so many others, and we should remember that none of his responses to the conflict, whether in letter or essay form, were ever intended to be his final words on the subject. So, it is perhaps not so surprising that his essay on "France" is rather speculative and impressionistic in tone. James himself was feeling his way forward cautiously, revising his own vocabulary, hoping that something could be saved from the past, but vividly aware that civilisation required remaking in the light of new events. And the more optimistic of his war letters (to a range of contacts including Wharton, Scribner's and Hugh Walpole) point to his desire to do just that through his writing. As he wrote to Alfred Sutro's wife early in the war:

> I hold that we can still, he and I, *make* a little civilization, the inkpot aiding, even when vast chunks of it, around us, go down into the abyss—and that the preservation of it depends upon our going on making it in spite of everything and sitting tight and not chucking up
>
> (Lubbock 402).

Civilisation, in his war writings, seems to signify for James not so much a place or a fixed set of cultural values as a process of creation, the ability to make something out of experience. And this is in the end what he celebrates about France—her ability to "gather the rarest and sweetest fruits of our so tremendously and so mercilessly turned up garden of life" ("France" 6).

When he says that she remains "our incalculable, immortal France," he is not looking back but ahead to the many ways in which she will reinvent herself in the future (8).

6. The Citizens of Babylon and the Imperial Imperative: James's Modern Parisian Women

Claire Garcia

"'Be for me,'" implores Lambert Strether to Madame de Vionnet in his head as he ventures into the countryside in search of the original model for the painting he couldn't afford to buy, "'please, with all your admirable tact and trust, just whatever I may show you it's a present pleasure to me to think you'" (*The Ambassadors* [1994] 307). This sentiment echoes other Jamesian male characters' demands upon the women they love. Peter Sherringham, in trying to save Miriam Rooth from becoming the actress that her own genius determines she *must* be, demands of her, "'Be anything you like, except this','" to which Miriam laughingly responds, "'Except what I want most to be?'" (*The Tragic Muse* [1995] 233). Christopher Newman challenges Mrs. Tristram: "'Present to me a woman who comes up to my notions, and I will marry her tomorrow'" (*The American* [1978] 44). In her essay, "Walking on Water: The Metropolitan Feminine in *The Ambassadors*," Marianne DeKoven claims that, "Strether's opening shopping trip chaperoned by Maria Gostrey signals the text's preoccupation with the reconstruction of gender in urban modernity; the reversal of that chaperone relation at the end—the reinstatement of the conventional patriarchal gender relations—signals James's retreat from that reconstruction" (DeKoven 5). While I don't make claims about James's own anxieties about the modernist reconstruction of gender roles, I argue here to the contrary: that this novel exposes the inadequacy and untenability of the narratives and attitudes which sustain the "conventional patriarchal gender relations."

Henry James, in both his fiction and non-fiction, often critically engages a concept of masculinity which dominated American culture at the end the century—a masculinity epitomised by Theodore Roosevelt and associated with the virile exploration, conquest, and capitalist exploitation of the domestic frontier and non-Western countries. Of course, this masculinity has been mythic since its inception: the romance of the American frontier is an idea born of nostalgia long after the frontier was closed. The men who derived vast fortunes from the gold and silver ore of the American West were not rugged individual miners in lonely campsites in the remote mountains, but shareholders in corporations who had bought up the rights to vast tracts of land long before individual miners staked their claims. The majority of those who struck it rich in the gold and silver rushes were retailers who supplied the miners and went on to become department and grocery store magnates. By the turn into the twentieth century, the power of this myth was primarily discursive and rhetorical, and lay in its ability to shape narratives of nation, identity, and gender to further American colonial projects around the world. The western encounter with the Other always involves a struggle for mastery and control. Written during an era when Theodore Roosevelt's government and popular culture were associating American national identity with a particular vision of virile masculinity associated with business prowess and physical stamina (Banta "Men, Women..." 23), *The Ambassadors*, like other novels of the New Woman era, posits Woman as a site of aesthetic, cultural, and political arguments within discourses of the modern nation and the anxieties of empire (Berman 3).

Dreamy as they are, Strether's often Magoo-like misperceptions are attempts to understand and thus control, and we would be remiss not to realise the significance of the ways in which Madame de Vionnet and Paris itself remain "Other" to Strether simply because they suggest realities and perspectives for which his interpretive tools are inadequate. Already subject to a variety of social, cultural, and economic challenges, including the emergence of the New Woman, the waves of non-Anglo-Saxon immigrants, the creation of sexuality as a field of scientific inquiry, the Rooseveltian narrative of American masculinity would reach a point of rupture during the Great War, and inspired a generation of male and female modernist writers to both reflect and create new understandings of gender and sexuality for the twentieth century. By the end of *The Ambassadors*, Paris and its women have already initiated Strether into a new, distinctly modern consciousness, which questions the power and authority of past narratives and takes as an existential condition what are now accepted as the characteristics of Anglo-American modernist consciousness: fluidity and multiplicity of identities; states of permanent dislocation or dispatriation; a skepticism toward accepted sources of authority, including the links between seeing, knowing, and mastering; a critical stance toward capitalism and a valorisation of individual freedom.

Years before he brings his ambassadorial portfolio to Paris, Strether's masculinity has been thrown into question. His quest for the "France" of the Lambinet landscape is spurred by a moment of failure—the "only adventure of his life in connexion with the purchase of a work of art" (*The Ambassadors* [1994] 303)—which highlighted his financial impotence and the frustration of his desire: "The little Lambinet abode with him as the picture he *would* have bought" (303). Many years later, as he takes the train into the *banlieue* of Paris, Strether is seeking not only to possess the original of the representation that he could not afford—the particular light, colors, and vegetation of the French countryside—but also to triumph over the urban, commercial world which determined the painting's value and so painfully thwarted his desire. For Strether, the painting's commercial value (beyond his means) is inextricable from its aesthetic appeal. Thus, he wanders from Paris not just to encounter the "original" which inspired the painting, but also to accomplish "the restoration to nature of the whole far-away hour: the dusty day in Boston, the background of the Fitchburg Depot, of the maroon colored sanctum, the special green vision, the ridiculous price, the poplars, the willows, the rushes, the river, the sunny silvery sky, the shady woody horizon" (303). This sentence levels and blurs the distinctions between the price, the real landscape, and representation of the poplars, the silvery sky, the dusty day. So when Strether achieves "success" (305) in possessing, finally, "what he wanted" (304), it is clear that what he wanted involves a collapse of distinctions between the aesthetic and the commercial, downtown Boston and suburban Paris, the painter and the spectator: "it was Tremont Street, it was France, it was Lambinet" (304). Everything is so exactly the answer to his desire that he might have walked "freely" through the landscape "to the maroon-colored wall" (304). The significance of the painting cannot be abstracted from the emotional context and physical setting which gives it its value for Strether. The urban gallery, and the social and economic power it represents, challenges his financial and sexual authority. Strether, at the moment of his failure before the shop window, is the antithesis of the Rooseveltian male: his 'adventure' is a sorry thing compared to months of battling wildlife, natives, and Amazonian currents. Like the failed initiation symbolised by the lemon-coloured books he did purchase but never got bound, Strether's adventure is testimony only to his "long grind and his want of odd moments; his want moreover of money, of opportunity, of positive dignity" (63).

During the final moments of his elaborately self-imposed innocence before the shock of the famous recognition scene, Strether feels free in a world which seems to have perfectly met his expectations—what he sees is exactly what he wanted to see— he almost, for a few pages, approximates a Christopher Newman. His imperative plea to the absent Madame de Vionnet characterises both the moral and epistemological hazards of Strether's failed narratives. Ironically, of course, the very real Madame de Vionnet, in inadvertently providing the "right thing"—the parasoled lady in a boat which completes the picture to Strether's satisfaction—provides the final stage of Strether's fall into modern consciousness.

Although, as Peter Brooks and others have pointed out (Brooks *Henry James Goes to Paris* 28), James himself resisted the modernism associated with Paris in the visual arts and other genres, and his own later novels anticipate some of the basic aesthetics and ideologies of modernist fiction. I am particularly interested in how James's female Parisian characters embody and enact the challenges and possibilities of the modern metropolitan consciousness which provides the ground note for twentieth century modernist writing.

Lambert Strether, upstanding citizen of Woollett, Massachusetts, arrives in Paris to reel in his fiancée/employer's son from the what are presumed to be the well-known hazards of Paris, epitomised by the 'bad woman' with whom he has entangled himself. Strether's portfolio is stuffed with conventional nineteenth-century identity narratives about sexuality, morality, and national identities. Early in his mission to Paris, Strether fears the challenge of Paris— or more specifically, any receptivity on his part to Parisian or radically 'Other' perspectives and values—poses to his 'authority':

> His greatest uneasiness seemed to peep at him out of the imminent impression that almost any acceptance of Paris might give one's authority away. It hung before him, this vast, bright Babylon, like some huge iridescent object, a jewel brilliant and hard, in which parts were not to be discriminated nor differences comfortably marked (64).

The use of Babylon as a metaphor for a decadent imperial city is common Orientalism in nineteenth-century writing (Greenslade 100); the term "*babylonisme*" refers to an appetite for grandiosity, especially huge buildings (Cassells French/English Dictionary). By the mid-19th century, references to Paris as "the New Babylon" were *cliché*; even William James, in his letters to his brother during the latter's first adult sojourn there, repeatedly referred to the city as "the new Babylon" (Brooks 10). What is interesting in this context, though, is that French opponents to Haussmann's modernisation efforts used the term "Babylon" much as people in Colorado use the term "Californication" in discussing the threat of over-development: the French associated it with *American* cities. According to historian Alistair Horne,

> At the time [Haussmann's new Paris] had its vigorous critics. The conservative Goncourt brothers said it made them think of 'some American Babylon of the future'; Gautier agreed, 'This is Philadelphia; it is Paris no longer!' [...] . Emile Zola [...] depict[ed] the city as 'an enormous storm-tossed ocean, or a distant and alien Babylon'
>
> (Horne 240).

Babylon had connotations of destruction and loss in the name of modernity; Haussmann was a self-professed 'demolition artist' and proud of it.

Paris, from the middle of the 19th century to the eve of the Second World War, has been considered a city which represents the paradoxes, perils, and promises of modernity: the flame-keeper of Enlightenment values which was also a notoriously ruthless imperial power; the cosmopolitan, polyglot city which drew refugees, artists, and tourists from all over the world but still to this day scrupulously maintains one of the most narrow and calcified narratives of national identity; the epitome of urban space that is both technologised and aestheticised. While many critics read *The Ambassadors* as James's nostalgic return to the Paris he missed truly experiencing during his earlier sojourn there, and it has been duly noted that Strether never takes the Métro, it is necessary to Strether's transformation that the Paris-Woollett binary be demolished once and for all, and that the 'international theme' of James's earlier work is replaced by a metropolitan form of perception which deconstructs national identities based upon different 'types.' As noted earlier, Woman in nineteenth-century literature often serves as a site of discourses of the modern nation, so it is not surprising that James's Parisian women take on a major role in dismantling the truisms of the nineteenth-century imperial narratives. In *The Ambassadors*, it is the women who embody resistance to and rejection of familiar American national narratives. It is the women Strether encounters in Paris, the citizens of

Babylon, who challenge Strether's American patriarchal authority, and position him at the end of the novel as a man who cannot live according to the conventional understandings of gender and nation.

In aspects both momentous and trivial, when Strether is struck by the 'Otherness' of Paris it is usually through his encounters with its women. Strether's relationships with the women in *The Ambassadors* force him to experience the collapses and flattening out of differences that challenge the world view which informs his mission to Paris. It is the women of the novel, especially Chad's lover, who disrupt the extravagant explanatory narratives Strether unsuccessfully attempts to impose upon the baffling barrage of perceptions which constitute his Paris. Such a consciousness as Strether's can only be developed in the modern metropolis, as Raymond Williams defines the term in relation to the development of modernism:

> For a number of historical and social reasons the metropolis of the second half of the nineteenth century and the first half of the twentieth century moved into a quite new cultural dimension. It was now much more than the very large city or even the capital city of an important nation. It was the place where new social and economic and cultural relations, beyond both city and nation in their older senses, were beginning to be formed
> ("Metropolis and Modernism" 20).

Within "major metropolises," Williams asserts, "there was at once a complexity and sophistication of social relations, supplemented in the most important cases—Paris above all—by exceptional liberties of expression" (Williams 20). Key to understanding the disruptive and creative role played by the women in these Parisian novels is looking at the specific historical and geographical settings with which they are associated. Strether's Paris is a city of performance and spectacle, where women particularly are 'on view.'

The Women's Spaces in Paris

Maria Gostrey's apartment, cluttered with the bounty of numerous shrewd shopping expeditions in a variety of European cities and towns, is located in the Quartier Marboeuf, described in a footnote in the Norton Critical edition of the novel as "[i]n 1900 a modern and handsome section of Paris" (*The Ambassadors* [1994] 79), although she has decorated it with the debris of other people's histories (342). Her collection of antiques is, ironically, testament to her modernity. Unlike Strether, Gostrey is a successful participant in the global economy, who can initiate him, without "vulgarity," into the border-crossing currents of consumer goods. The past which is present in her apartment is not her own or her family's: it is an imaginative and aesthetic appropriation of the forms and connotations, detached from the original contexts which had given them meaning.

More importantly, Gostrey also initiates Strether into an alternative way of understanding and engaging reality. Rather than retreating into what DeKoven has characterised as "the old patriarchal scripts," at the end of the novel, Strether adapts (or more accurately, perhaps, 'absorbs') Maria Gostrey's rhetorical as well as perceptual strategies such as 'embroidering,' 'filling in,' absenting oneself rather than insisting on one's presence, and allowing events to organically unfold on their own terms rather than controlling. These ways of being in the world are inevitably disruptive of the stabilising fictions which have sustained the identities and fortunes of Woollett.

In his final conversation with Maria Gostrey, Strether acknowledges his own new disruptive power: he is, according to Chad, "exciting" and he has "pretty well to have upset everyone." He has accepted the impossibility of his ever being "in harmony" with any surroundings—Woollett, Paris, London—in which he may conceivably find himself (343). He has changed—yet he has not changed to another, fixed state, but rather an identity of being "different," in relation to Mrs. Newsome's "more than ever the same" (345). His returning 'home' will not be returning to a familiar, stable, and natural environment, but a return "[t]o a great difference" from which he will attempt to create something new and meaningful. Whatever Strether 'makes' of his newfound and hard-earned consciousness of this external and internal "difference," it will elude the criteria of value established by American capitalist dynamics; he will not gain or profit from his experience in Paris, even metaphorically. If there is any 'logic' to his Parisian adventure, it is "'Not, out of the whole affair, to have got anything for [him]self'" (346). Whatever his future holds, it will involve rupture from past narratives of identity and value.

Strether initially tries to read Mme de Vionnet as the repository of old and enduring values. From his early impression that her possessions are somehow "transmitted" rather than exchanged for money, unlike those in Gostrey's "little museum of bargains" (145), to his final impression of her as Madame Roland, the sentences which describe his perceptions of her are often shaped around *bouleversements* and contradictions which undermine his readings. From her putting her elbows on the table in that very Parisian modern invention, the restaurant, to her entrepreneurial dealings on the marriage market, to her sexual discretions, Mme de Vionnet cannot be accounted for by Strether's perceptions of her. His various narrative templates for female sexuality—Cleopatra, the Madonna, or a maidservant weeping over the loss of her 'follower'—cannot contain or even address her being. What Strether wants to see as her magical and passive embodiment of transcendent 'antique' values is really, after all, very clever advertising— her manipulation of images and associations for the consumption of a desirous observer. As Maria Gostrey tells Strether, Madame de Vionnet is multiple and polyglot: "It would doubtless be difficult, today […] to name and place her" (139). An example of the syntactic bouleversements which are associated with Strether and de Vionnet's encounters occurs in the scene in Notre Dame. Without recognising her, Strether spends quite a bit of time making the woman he observes at prayer into "a heroine of an old story […] that […] he might himself have written," noting that "his impression absolutely required that she be young and interesting" (174). However, Madame de Vionnet does recognise Strether a few moments later, and quickly reads him and takes control of the situation: "[s]he checked, quickly and gaily, a certain confusion in him, came to meet it, turned it back, by an art of her own; the confusion having threatened him as he knew her now for the person he had been observing" (175). She not only resists but manipulates the narratives Strether's very act of seeing her attempts to impose upon her. Thus they leave Notre Dame, the medieval cathedral resurrected by Victor Hugo's 19th-century novel, for a restaurant, "a place of pilgrimage for the knowing, they were both aware, the knowing who came for the great renown, the homage of restless days, from the other end of town" (177). Other Parisian women, too, confound Strether, and his confusion is often enacted in sentences which contain paradoxes, reversals, and inversions within their syntax and imagery. [Miss Barrace, who, to Strether-the-tourist's surprise and delight, smokes cigarettes publicly and incessantly, "is "so oddly […] both antique and modern" (156); Strether cannot tell if he has either "soared above or sunk below" Maria Gostrey's explanations (178).] These modern women are citizens of a public sphere: introducing themselves, as Maria Gostrey does, to strange men in public spaces. They are denizens of hotels, restaurants, streets, and shops. Paris is peopled by women, such as "the prompt Parisian women […] driving the public pen" at the telegraph office (317) in the novel's final pages, who give a sharper and more threatening focus to Strether's earlier impression of Paris's distinctive "promptness" (59). Though Madame de Vionnet professes that she has never been to the left-bank restaurant with Chad "'because I don't go about with him in public'" (178), she is clearly at ease as a modern woman moving through urban spaces, as she invites him to stroll aimlessly and comfortably through the city streets. What for Strether is the inevitable 'smash' at the end of a 'runaway' is her natural habitat: "The smash was their walk, their déjeuner, the omelette, the Chablis, the place, the view, their present talk and his present pleasure in it" (179).

Strether first meets Madame de Vionnet in the artist Gloriani's garden. The physical location of Gloriani's garden and its allusions to *The American* set the stage for the revision of the role Paris plays in the transformation of each novel's protagonists. Gloriani lives in "the heart of the Faubourg Saint-Germain and on the edge of a cluster of gardens attached to old noble houses [...] which spoke of survival, transmission, association, a strong indifferent persistent order" (119). This is the neighborhood where James's earlier American ambassador on a failed mission to Paris, Christopher Newman, found the quiet privacy of the "grey and silent streets [...] a queer way for rich people to live; his ideal of grandeur was a splendid façade, diffusing its brilliancy outward" (*The American* [1978] 50). The aristocratic Bellegarde Hotel "answered Newman's conception of a convent" (50). Ironically, the convent Claire de Cintré actually ends up immured in is located in "a quarter [which] has an air of modern opulence and convenience" (275) on the other side of the river. The Carmelite convent in the novel is next to the Parc Monceau, the meticulously preserved remnant of a ducal garden surrounded by Haussmanian-era high intensity real-estate development. The convent, and Claire's fate, is an archaic disruption of both setting and narrative.

The Faubourg St.-Germain surroundings of Gloriani's garden remind Strether, too, of a convent: "Strether had presently the sense of a great convent, a convent of missions, famous for he scarce knew what, a nursery of young priests, of scattered shade, of straight alleys and chapel bells" (*The Ambassadors* [1994] 119-20). In the later novel, this air of the convent—suggestive to Strether of aristocratic immutability—encircles the bohemian vivacity and hybridity of Gloriani's guests, with their ambiguous nationalities and indeterminable social ranks, polyglot conversations, and suggestions of migratory and perhaps *louche* lives.

Madame de Vionnet has replaced the chaste and victimised Claire de Cintré as the exoticised and eroticised 'Other' of desire. Both women have been married to husbands who were 'brutes,' and thus deserve better men.

Madame de Vionnet lives on Rue de Bellechasse, which crosses the Rue de l'Université, where the Bellegardes lived (Fussell *The Ambassadors* 185).

While Claire's names evoke purity and strong connections between opposites (a *cintre* supports the center of a bridge or arch) and speaks to Newman's failed fantasies of uniting the values of the Old and New Worlds, of amassing centuries of European history to sit atop his New World spoils, Mme de Vionnet's names playfully evoke a range of competing femininities, among them 'notre dame'; her foil and perhaps romantic rival, Maria Gostrey; and the French designer Madeleine Vionnet. Although she did not open her own atelier until 1912, Vionnet, the inventor of the bias-cut gown, by turn of the century had developed her own reputation, when she worked for designers such as Doucet, for garments which stylishly allowed her customers to move freely and naturally. Other readers, most amusingly Fussell, have pointed out that Strether's sense of Madame de Vionnet's historical connections is based on Strether's very limited and inaccurate perceptions of French history.

Strether's mission to Paris fails because the Woollett/Paris binary upon which he builds his interpretive apparatus fails. The hierarchised differences and distinctions which he must make—between virtuous and bad attachments, for example—are confounded by his adventures in Paris. Yet the confusions, connections, and ambiguities which baffle him during his sojourn in the modern Babylon will also be present in Massachusetts, as he brings this new consciousness back with him to the United States. Chad, the other Woollett adventurer, is also bringing something back to the United States: his commitment to new advertising methods, which he transports from London—where he has the "revelation" of the "great new force" that advertising can be (341), which opens the possibility that perhaps Mrs. Newsome, as her company employs the latest marketing techniques to disseminate the product too quotidian to be worthy of naming, is as much a citizen of Babylon as Madame de Vionnet.

7. French as the Fantasmal Idiom of Truth in *What Maisie Knew*

Agnès Derail-Imbert

Simultaneously published in England and in the United States, *What Maisie Knew* is set in end-of-the-century London and winds up in Boulogne, making France the place 'abroad' where she achieves an ultimate form of knowledge which the preface calls "the full ironic truth" of the novel. While the novel's Victorian backdrop has received much critical attention, the choice of France as the location of the spectacular *dénouement* has not been thoroughly interrogated.

Maisie's cognitive predicament can be traced back to a deficiency in linguistic command, preventing her from making sense of the punning and cunning use of language practised among the adulterous adults she lives with. If Maisie is exposed to deceptive words because she is caught in an entangled web of illegitimate relationships, this 'adulteration' of speech is also symptomatic of the corruption of English in decadent London — London as the hub of the Empire, the centre of monetary and sexual transactions marked by a lack of discrimination resulting in a debasement of meaning. In this context of pervasive falsification, France appeals to Maisie's imagination as the fictional land of truthful love. Scattered throughout the novel in preliminary fragments, the image of France finally coheres in Maisie's expanding consciousness as the epitome of her quest for knowledge and wonder. Her increasing awareness is matched by her growing understanding and even her bold uttering of a few French words that the 'English' text incorporates in their original version.

Whereas James's non-fictional considerations on the erosion of American English may have conservative, almost nativist overtones, my assumption is that the sum of Maisie's knowledge, which encompasses nothing less than the whole novel, obscurely gestures toward a foreign or strange idiom, a fantasised language capable of accommodating its untranslatable, fictional truth. French, in the book, would then be the figure of this circumlocutionary language—in other words, the secret name of James's own 'un-homed' literary English.

The dramatic knot of the novel can be identified as a cognitive and linguistic crisis: how and what does one know when one does not master language? As a child, which she remains till the end of the story, Maisie, is, metaphorically at least, an infant, a "register of impressions" deficient in words. Those words, as the preface argues, are supplied for her by a narrator who acts as a 'translator' whose role is supposed to be limited to the transcoding of her thoughts and affects into an elaborate English prose, akin to that of James himself. This cognitive issue is caught in a network of social transformations affecting Maisie's London at the turn of the century. These mutations create an environment in which the new instability of signs can only add to the confusion already entailed by Maisie's linguistic limitations, and thicken the maze (encoded in Maisie's name) in which she tries to find clues on her way to knowledge. The historical context, accessible obliquely through Maisie's restrictive prism, constitutes a reservoir of tropes which shape the action and the unfolding of Maisie's consciousness: the new cultural context conditions the opening of a narrative stating the legal account of the parents' divorce case, made possible only through recent changes in the laws regulating marriage and subsequently patrimony, procreation, filiation, etc. Among other things, Maisie's initiation requires her understanding of the conventions ruling the social microcosm, namely upper-class Kensington, where she grows up. Her fate, decided at the end of an "interminable litigation" (13), is the result of new marital laws allowing Maisie's parents to divorce on the ground of flagrant infidelities. Not only does the trial publicise sex as illicit, but the financial settlement of Maisie's case overtly correlates sexual transactions with monetary dealings. Even if both parents remarry their sexual partners, they remain involved in a round of notorious adulterous affairs that are all determined by economic interest. She will meet some of her mother's partners—some of them men of the City, who can become bankrupt overnight, others who are involved in international business, like the last lover, possibly of Jewish origin, that she will join in South Africa. As for the father's last mistress, an American woman, ironically designated by the non-American title of "Countess" (a brown, "almost black" lady), she is said to have "great interests in America" and "no end of money" (137, 155, 151). The proliferating economic allusions testify to the narrator's indictment of a general loss of faithfulness—both conjugal and financial—as it becomes impossible to discriminate between real countesses and false ones, real governesses and fake ones, wealthy lovers and frauds.

The erosion affecting the criteria of truth also involves a blurring of distinctions between the sexes. Sir Claude depicts himself as an old grandmother; women, who are masculine and flirtatious, do not want babies anymore, and Maisie herself is repeatedly called "my dear boy" (108, 183), "old boy" (69, 198), or "old chap" (73, 253). Genders are as shifting as national and racial identities or places of residence, in the cosmopolitan setting across which Maisie is dragged along according to the adults' passing whims. In this variety of places of entertainment, museums, exhibitions, parks, shops, cafés, which serve as the sole unfit substitute for school, she is exposed to "an abuse of visibility" (16). Her "sense of spectatorship" (90), meant to compensate for her lack of verbal command, is sharpened by an exposure to degraded forms of visibility that characterise the modern metropolis. One of the novel's crucial scenes takes place in the gardens of Earl's Court, which was the setting of one of the Great Exhibitions in London. These exhibitions with their optical gadgets accompanied the rise of a Victorian "mass visuality," which also served as a medium of propaganda for the Empire at a time when the United States was taking the lead of a globalised capitalistic world order.[1] The decadent subtext of the novel's London is implicitly linked with the Americanisation or the vulgarisation of British manners and institutions. This degradation affects art as well–art, which is notably absent from the characters' preoccupations. One scene, set in the National Gallery, revealingly stages Sir Claude and Maisie equally bored by the quattrocento paintings of "ugly Madonnas." While Maisie submissively endorses Sir Claude's statement that the "affectation of admiring such ridiculous works" is only "silly superstition," we, readers, are nevertheless aware of the narrator's dissenting opinion.

> Maisie sat beside him staring rather sightlessly at a roomful of pictures which he had mystified her much by speaking of with a bored sigh as a "silly superstition." They represented, with patches of gold and cataracts

---

[1] In "Technologies of Vision," Christina Britzolakis shows how James imbricates modernist narrative technique and the novel's exploration of the new optical technologies which shape the modernity of the imperial metropolis (Britzolakis 369-90).

of purple, with stiff saints and angular angels, with ugly Madonnas and uglier babies, strange prayers and prostrations; so that she at first took his words for a protest against devotional idolatry—all the more that he had of late often come with her and with Mrs. Wix to morning church, a place of worship of Mrs. Wix's own choosing, where there was nothing of that sort; no haloes on heads, but only, during long sermons, beguiling backs of bonnets, and where, as her governess always afterwards observed, he gave the most earnest attention. It presently appeared, however, that his reference was merely to the affectation of admiring such ridiculous works—an admonition that she received from him as submissively as she received everything

(*Maisie* 94).

This rampant fictitiousness contaminates the language Maisie is steeped in. The adults' speech is cryptic, not only because she is too young to understand, but because it is voluntarily deceptive since most of the time exchanges revolve around sexual transactions. What Maisie, as any child brought up in a Victorian background, is supposed *not* to know, is sex itself. But as the book's title teasingly suggests, the suspicion is strong that she knows more than she ought to, that such knowledge is potentially available for purposes of seduction. Hence the inevitable distortion in a discourse that is contrived with a view of hiding what it nevertheless tries to convey. Witnessing improper behaviour, Maisie is required to listen to emphatic claims of decency or to false avowals of affection, aimed at enrolling her as a lure for lustful games. Conversely, she is used as a messenger of hard-edged words that serve as missives or missiles in the never-ending warfare between members of ever-splitting couples. Language keeps swinging from euphemism to overstatement. The protagonists of Maisie's world continually resort to conflictual hyperboles, increasing the strain of her life. Sir Claude is at once "an angel" and "an awful fraud," or an "idle beast" (58, 77). Her mother is termed an angel by one of her lovers, while Sir Claude calls her "a damn old b—" (118), a word either unknown to Maisie or one at least she refrains from repeating verbatim, filling the dash with the hardly more decent "brute." Overstatements are especially salient as they emerge from a general evasiveness of discourse that equally bars access to meaning. Unspecification, abstraction, and equivocation produce in Maisie, and in the reader as well, a sense of elusiveness that defeats the securing of a consistent meaning. From her young age, Maisie gathers that "affairs are involved" (182), that women may be "compromised" (267), that her mother is likely to "come down" on her husband (38, 86), that people have to "square" their former partners (94, 100, 105, 110, 133), that they may "bolt" with (89, 149), "settle" (21, 203), "dodge" (47), or "funk" one another (255), and that they do not want her to be "mixed" (135) while expecting her, as Mrs. Beale says, to "save us—from one thing and another" (106). If her governess copies for her the big easy words that the girl might clutch to, in order to soothe the strain of her removal from one parental house to the other, Maisie finds that the words she overhears are actually not easily attachable to meanings. The "childish dusk" (20) of her consciousness is a dark closet where meanings and forms are kept separate waiting to be rightly connected. In this general drift, anything might come to mean anything, in an endless series of permutations, just as the adulterous round opens a potentially unlimited series of substitutions.

In this respect, it is not by chance that the adulteration of language is connected to the adulterous games of the plot. The cleavage between the parental couple at the origin of Maisie's existence initiates a split between signifiers and signifieds, which in turn obfuscates the possibility of knowledge. The first thing in the book Maisie knows she feels is a sense of inadequacy. This 'strain' is first marked on her body, precisely in something wrong with her legs whereby, as her nurse says, she differs from other children: "'Oh my dear, you'll never find such another pair as your own,'" adding the cryptic, but "terribly truthful," "'you feel the strain—that's where it is; and you'll feel it worse, you know'" (19). This pair of too skinny legs induces a sense of being inadequate—inadequate, possibly, to satisfy male desire. First located in or between the pair of legs, the strain, obviously referring to the sexual self, might also concern the strain between another 'pair,' this time the pair of parents, the embattled, dislocating origin of Maisie's life. Knowledge, in that case, amounts to the perception of an original strain. Seeking to reestablish a continuity between adults (either parents or parental substitutes), Maisie's strategy consists in literalising the dubious metaphors she hears, or in conveying messages strictly identical to their initial utterance, for instance, scrupulously repeating to her mother that her father calls her a "nasty horrid pig" (21). Making herself an obedient signifier faithful to the others' spurious statements, she incorporates the discordance she wishes to smooth out. The truthfulness of her language only increases difference and discord. This emanates however from a constant wish that words might speak the truth, the truth of love, or even truth as love.

My assumption is that such language is imagined as a fantasised French idiom, assumed to be markedly different from the adulterated British English which is the only medium available in the novel. Maisie's resistance to the trauma of this degraded medium, through which she is to rescue or idealise "the vulgar little comedy" that unfolds about her, involves a recourse to fiction—a fiction that would redeem the fictitiousness of sordid experience. France, as the ultimate location of Maisie's initiation, plays a major role as a counterpart to decadent London, as it nurses the dream of a language of truth. I would argue that idioms in the novel are distributed along a demarcation line that makes London the stage of bourgeois comedy involving vile intrigues of adultery, while France early looms in Maisie's fancy as the homeland of romance, medieval romance, set in *châteaux*, the land of chivalry, of courteous love, or *fin'amor*.[2] Cast off against the English spoken by the theatrical society of fashionable London, the French of the novel would then rather be the language of high (or genuine) literature, poetry, romance, tragedy, a literature that could extend to the vernacular idiom spoken by the fishermen or native old women in Boulogne, or again the *roman* made of the 'stories' of all the lives she has encountered including her own, of her discovery of love, and ultimately of the impossible life with the man she knows she loves.

The long French *dénouement*, which covers about a third of the novel, has been carefully prepared throughout the story. If Maisie's absence of education has committed her exclusively to fiction, France has occupied a privileged place in this fiction, dangled before her childish imagination as a promise of romance. Besides the thousand stories she has been through with her governess (Mrs. Wix), there have been the "richest romances" (139) of her French doll, called Lisette or Elise with a possible reference, through a translinguistic pun on *lire*/to read, to the reading of French books, the books Sir Claude will buy for her at the station in Boulogne. Sir Claude's incongruous present to Mrs. Wix of a "history of France" (64), added to the never fulfilled pledge to take Maisie to 'lectures' on French literature (109, 113, 132), interestingly coupled to "sacred history" (109), the French ring to Claude's name, his command of the language—all these scattered clues, in the English context of the book, have contributed to fashion France in Maisie's consciousness as the desired image of knowledge, pleasure, adventure, initiation, wonder. It is appropriate that it is in France that she

---

2 For other generic divisions in the novel, see Martha Banta, "The Quality of Experience."

gains the freedom of making "a claim for herself" (199), of choosing her destiny.

The final phase of the novel deploys the inaugural chord struck by Sir Claude at the end of chapter XXI and repeated by an enraptured Maisie: "To-morrow we go to France" (179). Once Maisie's parents have given up their former partners and abandoned her for good, various arrangements are possible for her future. She might consent to live somewhere in France with Mrs. Beale and Sir Claude, offering a cover of respectability to their illegitimate couple, or she might renounce this stepfather for whom she has "a more than filial gaze" (204) and go back to England for an unpromising future with drab Mrs. Wix. Before she is asked to make a choice, the trip to France has taken the thrilling accents of an elopement with Sir Claude who treats her to seaside hotels and fine restaurants. But mostly, the experience of being "abroad" is set forth as a decisive move away from both sham innocence and sham guilt, and towards abandonment to enlarged perceptions. Maisie's first moments in France are depicted in terms of an aesthetic experience, which produces the impression of a larger life, a sense of 'poetic justice' which redeems the London past, whose last remnants still linger in the character of the ignorant cockney maid, impervious to the charms of France. In Maisie's heroic mood, crossing the Channel means leaving behind the dangers of England, which recedes in the distance, perceived as the grey horizon held at bay by the French light.

> She was 'abroad' and she gave herself up to it, responded to it, in the bright air, before the pink houses, among the bare-legged fishwives and the red-legged soldiers, with the instant certitude of a vocation. Her vocation was to see the world and to thrill with enjoyment of the picture; she had grown older in five minutes and had by the time they reached the hotel recognised in the institutions and manners of France a multitude of affinities and messages. Literally in the course of an hour she found her initiation; a consciousness much quickened by the superior part that, as soon as they had gobbled down a French breakfast—which was indeed a high note in the concert—she observed herself to play to Susan Ash (180).

While the sordid English vaudeville goes on in the hysterical dialogues between struggling adults, Maisie's final quest is pursued in a literary reverie that includes much of French ancient lore and tradition. Walking on the ramparts of Boulogne, in the medieval *haute ville*, Maisie gives free rein to her "historical imagination" which recaptures the "courtesy of romantic forms" enhanced by an aura of sacredness. The full knowledge that she is to achieve is coloured by the purified sense of worship she experiences in the church situated on the bastion and dominated by the statue of a gilt Virgin which is the redeemed version of the National Gallery's "ugly Madonnas."

> They sat together on the old grey bastion; they looked down on the little new town which seemed to them quite as old, and across at the great dome and the high gilt Virgin of the church that, as they gathered, was famous and that pleased them by its unlikeness to any place in which they had worshipped. They wandered in this temple afterwards and Mrs. Wix confessed that for herself she had probably made a fatal mistake early in life in not being a Catholic. Her confession in its turn caused Maisie to wonder rather interestedly what degree of lateness it was that shut the door against an escape from such an error (206).

The highly calculated presence of the Virgin in the novel's ending gives an almost mystic hue to Maisie's epiphany. Her name, a diminutive for Margaret, which means "pearl," a classic emblem for virginity, figuratively connects Maisie to the gilt Virgin, who, according to old legends was said to have come miraculously on a boat (just like Maisie). Maisie's access to knowledge occurs when she makes the decision to live with Sir Claude alone, asks him to give up his mistress and take her to Paris, fancied as the romantic heart of France. It is no coincidence that the appointment she fixes him is close to the gilded Virgin. What she offers, with the acknowledgment of her love for him, is her virginity. When she urges him to buy the train tickets to Paris, her first and last words uttered in French, *"prenny, prenny"* (261), reproduced with her English accent, are charged with sexual urgency. The moment of her awakening, or full awareness, is also a moment of loss, a loss of consciousness, a syncope in which she can only utter "'I don't know.'" Her overflowing knowledge is manifested by bodily responses, the visible jerk of an arm, but also a spasm within her, invisible to the narrator yet reported as an intimate corporeal opening "of something deeper than a moral sense." The spasm is here the unrepresentable spasm both of love and knowledge— simultaneously a new birth and the death of her childhood. When Mrs. Wix accuses Sir Claude of having "nipped [her moral sense] in the bud," expanding the underlying metaphor of defloration, he can only answer that on the contrary he has "produced life," ultimately admitting that he has figuratively taken the offered maidenhood, fathering Maisie's love, fathering Maisie as "a beautiful thing" that is as "sacred and exquisite" as a work of art (268). Maisie's offered yet untouched virginity, her discovery of a love at once recognized and ignored are images for a knowledge which is not figurable otherwise than in the form of such tropes.[3] What Maisie knows is only the totality of what the book *What Maisie Knew* figures. Such "full ironic truth" (4) is not convertible into a definite content. Its untranslatability is itself, in turn, presented tropically in the untranslated French of the novel. The final scenes are strewn with French phrases or words which, we may surmise, belong to the list of "the things of which [Maisie] knew the French name" (215), the *plage*, the *table d'hôte, café complet, omelette aux rognons, poulet sauté, vous n'y êtes pas*, or again the humorously apt motto, *honni soit qui mal y pense*... Hanging over the rail of the balcony in the summer night, dropping "into the manners of France," Maisie listens to a serenade sung in the café below:

> She hung again over the rail; she felt the summer night; she dropped down into the manners of France. There was a café below the hotel, before which, with little chairs and tables, people sat on a space enclosed by plants in tubs; and the impression was enriched by the flash of the white aprons of waiters and the music of a man and a woman who, from beyond the precinct, sent up the strum of a guitar and the drawl of a song about 'amour.' Maisie knew what 'amour' meant [...] (218).

What she knows, called "*amour*," remains untranslated. The foreign word, the letters and the sound of the signifier, are less an equivalent for the English "love" than the emblem of Maisie's untranslatable knowledge or again the fiction of her truth. If we know that "amour," at any rate, could be translated into English, the novel also signals towards another form of French which, this time, is definitely lost in translation, incomprehensible, even by native French speakers. Sitting by the golden Madonna, Maisie, falling into a reverie, listens to the "hum of French insects."

> She watched beside Mrs. Wix the great golden Madonna, and one of the ear-ringed old women who had been sitting at the end of their bench got up and pottered away. '*Adieu mesdames!*' said the old woman in a little cracked civil voice—a demonstration by which our friends were so affected that they bobbed up and almost curtseyed to her. They subsided again, and it was shortly after, in a summer hum of French insects and a phase of almost somnolent reverie, that Maisie most had the vision of what it was to shut out from such a perspective so appealing a participant. It had not yet appeared so vast as at that moment, this prospect of statues shining in the blue and of courtesy in romantic forms (209).

---

[3] In *Versions of Pygmalion*, James Hillis Miller shows how Maisie's achievement of knowledge coincides with her vanishing from the narrator's and the reader's circuit of knowledge (Hillis Miller 23-81).

How such hum, through a striking hypallage, can be identified by Maisie as French, distinct from the hum of English, or even, for that matter, American insects, may remain puzzling to a reader of any nationality. In the bold weirdness of the phrasing itself,[4] the text provides Maisie's vision with an unintelligible foreign sound track that has no verbal, articulate counterpart but is the imaginary idiom of courtesy in romantic forms, the forms of the novel *What Maisie Knew*, fantasised as a 'French' romance which 'un-homes' and rescues the English in which it is actually written. French in that case will not be translated by *"français"* but is only the hum of truth haunting the English novel.

In the controversial conference known as *The Question of Our Speech*, addressed to Bryn Mawr's female students in 1905, James warned his audience against the degradation of American language and manners. He urged the young women to display the same "conservative interest" "for the institution of speech as for the institution of matrimony." He argued that unlike all great European idioms, American English found itself unattended by the protection of ancestry, of tradition, while required, under this ordeal, to give birth to the national community.

> [W]hereas the great idioms of Europe in general have grown up at home and in the family, the ancestral circle (with their migrations all comfortably prehistoric), our transported maiden (English in America), our unrescued Andromeda, our medium of utterance, was to be disjoined from all the associations, the other presences, that had attended her, that had watched for her and with her, that had helped to form her manners and her voice, her taste and her genius (39).

Coming over to America, the English tongue experiences, much like Maisie herself, the situation of the young maiden abandoned by her parents.[5] This parallel, however, raises a problem: indeed the language undergoing a degradation that can be ascribed to the corruption of institutions, marriage in particular, is not, in the novel, American English but British English, as it is spoken among its family, to continue James's metaphor. As if the risk of declension were not due to historical conditions, but inherent in language itself, whose fate it is, even at home, to depart from its origin.

---

4 Interestingly, Marguerite Yourcenar recoils from translating the audacity of the hypallage, which her French translation simply cancels: "au milieu du bourdonnement des insectes d'un été français" (*Ce que savait Maisie* 293).

5 On a cross reading of *Maisie* and the 1905 conference and on the parallel between Maisie's situation and the English language in America, See Marotta. "*What Maisie Knew*: The Question of Our Speech."

This contradiction betrays, I think, a double impulse in James towards the question of language: the fear of adulteration, of "grossness of alienism" (*The American Scene* [1994] 96), prompts him to conservative responses, but this dream of purity does not eradicate the fascination for the intrinsic foreignness of language, for its unintelligible part, its unknown residuum, which is what the fantasmal French of *Maisie* gestures towards as the "best residuum of truth." Pondering over the facts that make up the "American character," the autobiographical writer of *The American Scene* says that "he doesn't *know*," that he "can't *say*," that these facts are as syllables "too numerous to make a legible word." This illegible word, which pictures the impossible expression of an American identity, looms in the writer's imagination as "something fantastic and *abracadabrant*" (93). Here again, it is a strange French signifier which is summoned to evoke at once the failure of any language to be adequate to national or personal origin, and its longing to incorporate or to 'fiction' the fantastic hum of foreign or alien truth.

8. Figures of Fulfillment: James and "a Sense of Italy"

Jacek Gutorow

I.

In his *Images of Italy*, one of the most beautiful books on Italian *Wanderjahre*, Pavel Muratov writes:

> The words *traveling to Italy* are tale-telling, as they grasp our experience and our life in the Italian element, the liberation of new spiritual forces, the birth of new faculties, as well as a lengthening of the scale of our desires. Occurring in time and space, this is also a journey through the depths of our being and a firing of a resplendent circle at the bottom of our soul (370).[1]

Such words would be sympathetic to Henry James, who discovered in Italy not only an element novel and unknown to him—that of beauty and unraveled existence—but also a promise, and both traces and tropes of the metamorphosis taking place in the consciousness of the "sentimental tourist" (as James called himself) and in the deepest being of his soul. Both Muratov and James found in Italy a separate space that was free of the ambient reality and existed in its own right. Muratov has a wonderful intuition of this in "The Waters of Lethe," the essay opening *Images of Italy*. Referring to a painting by Giovanni Bellini, the Russian writer recalls his own trips to Venice and outlines a vision of an experience on the verge of existential transgression. Going to Italy is for him a journey of forgetting, as if his existence was suddenly erased:

> For us, people of the North, who enter Italy through the golden gates of Venice, the waters of the Venetian lagoon are in fact the waters of Lethe. When we stand in front of the paintings found in the churches of Venice,

---

[1] All the quotes from Muratov are in my translation, as his book has not been translated into English.

when we sail in a gondola or roam in the silent streets or through the tides of crowding tourists on St. Mark's, we drink some gentle and sweet wine of forgetting (18).

Thus, a journey to Italy resembles a rite of passage, a breakthrough to a new form of life. Interestingly and perhaps not surprisingly, such an aspect of ritual may be found in Henry James's travel sketches, particularly in his *Italian Hours*, a collection of essays, notes, and diary-entries written between 1872 and 1909. The book is my point of departure and constitutes the most important frame of reference for those interested in James's 'Italy of the mind.'

It should be noted first that it is the very moment of entering Italy that becomes ritualistic. In his early sketch "From Chambéry to Milan," James speaks of the "mysterious delights in entering Italy by a whiz through an eight-mile tunnel, even as a bullet through the bore of a gun" (*Italian Hours* [1995] 77). What we have in other essays is an almost obsessional rhetoric of, first, anticipation, and then transgression, going-through. Descriptions are detailed, sometimes even hallucinatory, as in this fragment:

> After leaving Modane you slide straight downhill into the Italy of your desire; from which point the road edges, after the grand manner, along those great precipices that stand shoulder to shoulder, in a prodigious perpendicular file, till they finally admit you to a distant glimpse of the ancient capital of Piedmont (100).

A rhetoric of fulfillment may be detected a bit later—reaching Italy is like a certain experience coming to a close, which becomes a 'past' experience. However, James does not let his Italian impressions ossify into a snapshot memory. On the contrary, he stresses their fragile uniqueness immune to all attempts, on the part of reason, to keep, rationalise, and retain moments of fulfillment. The latter precedes acts of consciousness and cannot be frozen— while articulated, it becomes solid and loses its own character.

One can say that Italy became for James a *figure* of fulfillment. It might be described as hypothetical and speculative—something separating life from the existential rhetoric that distorts it, be it a rhetoric of time or of space. Obviously enough, any figurative moment—and the idea of the figurative in general—is necessarily rhetorical. However, it may point to a sense of fulfillment as something present but potential. Figures defer fulfillment but at the same time reveal its possibility. The dimension achieved is that of present fulfillment or fulfilled presence. It is kept at bay, not articulated— but it is there, with no doubt.

8. 'A Sense of Italy'   95

My contention is that James himself experienced such a presence during his Italian peregrinations. When we read subsequent sketches from *Italian Hours*, either chronologically or in the order suggested by the writer, we pass through stages of initiation into the nature of things. Italian landscapes, buildings, and paintings are viewed so intensely, so attentively, in so detailed a manner, that after a while they become transparent, as in Vladimir Nabokov's *Transparent Things*, where trivial objects reveal their past and their uniqueness, as if they were endowed with subjectivity. In the eyes of the devoted observer—and James was definitely such an observer—the smallest items are vibrant with life. They do not add up but remain unique, one appearing after the other.

What kind of experience was this? How did Italy differ from England and France, which were also important loci of perception for James, but remained sites of perception, and not of experience? Maybe we should speak here of *genius loci*? Would it be a genius understood as 'absolute consciousness,' elevated so high that it goes beyond itself in a sublime experience, or genius seen as an external agent, something alien to consciousness, a moment of resistance? Such questions guided me in my subsequent readings of *Italian Hours*.

II.

In James there are many spirits and their nature is quite problematic. Sometimes these are specters of places—reflections and recollections that haunt the tourist and take him out of the traditional *topoi* of time and space. Sometimes we can speak of the spirit which is collective, doubly so in the context of the Romantic idea of the Grand Tour. The Romantic tourist is in search of his transnational identity, and he tries to arrive at the universal mind of Europe that would crown his life with a kind of abstract fulfillment—a congregation of spirits from different places and epochs.

The sketches gathered in *Italian Hours*, however, break the pattern of the Grand Tour, even if they do so discreetly and in a peripheral manner. With James structures of perception and cognition are anarchic and centrifugal—casual impressions are as important as essential recognitions, experiences are often so random and chaotic that they cannot be gathered into any logical exposition, and the conclusions arrived at are less significant than the premises that gave rise to them.

The coordinates of the Jamesian map of Italy are movable. We know that James carefully traced the routes of his Italian trips. But in his notes he was not so provident. Many impressions are indeterminate, many descriptions vague and indefinite. Instead, they disseminate into a chaotic series of observations. They may be rendered in neat and beautiful passages—however, a sense of excess and overflowing wealth of reality is there.

James's anarchic sensibility may be seen at work in his treatment of space and time. Someone reading *Italian Hours* for the first time may have an impression that the writer follows both a very detailed itinerary and a well-planned calendar. A more attentive reading, however, reveals that Italy became for James a site and a place of puzzling spectrality, which does not let time and space consolidate into any whole. Images multiply and branch out in all directions so that no sense of the place is preserved. Moments are repeated, or ignored, or forgotten, or underrated, or overrated. Time does not flow but moves in jerks of anticipations and flashbacks. This is the essential paradox of James's Italy: it is a promise of experiencing something infinitely different, but at the same time it does not let individual impressions add up in a synthesis that could be a formula of the experience. So instead of the genius or spirit hovering over the place we have specters haunting the writer, taking on various shapes and leading him to more and more places.

Significantly, James often describes Italian towns and cities in terms of a labyrinth. Here is how he perceives Perugia:

> The small, dusky, crooked place tries by a hundred prompt pretensions, immediate contortions, rich mantling flushes and other ingenuities, to waylay your attention and keep it at home; but your consciousness, alert and uneasy from the first moment, is all abroad even when your back is turned to the vast alternative or when fifty house-walls conceal it, and you are forever rushing up by-streets and peeping round corners in the hope of another glimpse or reach of it (*Italian Hours* [1995] 211).

On the one hand, James's Italy loses its coordinates and continuum, and becomes a tourist site, a paradise for nomads. On the other hand, we have the writer who opts for the Nietzschean unconditional affirmation of things-as-they-are, and manages to evade the constraints of time and space. As a matter of fact, we should use here the plural form and speak about Italian hours and spaces that overlap one another and do not cohere into any whole.

That was also how time passed with James—not in a linear continuum but in parallel times. James's Italy was not a one-time phenomenon. And just as one could apply the Deleuzian concept of rhizome to the writer's perceptions of Italian spaces, so one could go to Bergson and Husserl to account for James's perception of Italian times. James's sentimental tourist is entangled in a web of crossing recollections and anticipations. This is particularly true of the past, which in James is rarely viewed as a chronological sequence of facts—its time is spectral, potential, parallel to the time measured by clocks. So, the Italian experience was for James not only a process of gathering impressions, but also an experience of the temporality of this process, which resulted first of all in making chronology problematic.

Examples of this may be found in "Roman Rides" (1873) and "From a Roman Notebook," a diary kept from December 1872 to May 1873:

> This unbroken continuity of the impressions I have tried to indicate is an excellent example of the intellectual background of all enjoyment of Rome. It effectually prevents pleasure from becoming vulgar, for your sensation rarely begins and ends with itself; it reverberates—it recalls, commemorates, resuscitates something else (149).

> The impression of Rome was repeatedly to renew itself… to overlay itself again and again with almost heavy thicknesses of experience, the last of which is, as I write, quite fresh to memory (194).

Italy became for James an accumulation of different times—the time measured by clocks, the time of one's own experiences, the time of memories, the time lost on the way.

III.

James's encounters with Italian towns and cities, as recorded in his travel sketches, provide us with interesting cases of what Raymond Williams called "structure of feeling" (*Marxism* 128). Descriptions of particular places are characterised by distinct rhetorical tendencies and climates. The differences are not big, but James definitely, if unconsciously, modified his rhetoric depending on the place depicted. Also, James's Italian sketches cannot be considered apart from his biography. For example, the Venetian and Florentine essays are fully understandable only in the context of such biographical information as the history of his relationship with Constance Fenimore Woolson, or James's fascination with such figures as Robert Browning or Richard Wagner. The biographical moment gives a specific flavour to ostensibly impersonal topographical moments; seeing is often tinged by a mood and pure perception turns out to be a foreshortening of perspective, and thus fiction.

But existence is not a prism diffracting the light of perception. On the contrary, the genius of James consisted in his ability to abandon the role of the sentimental tourist and discover a point of view that would reveal the uniqueness and singularity of the scene. So if I use the phrase "structure of feeling" in reference to *Italian Hours*, I do so to the effect that the moment of rhetorical consciousness exceeds the monologues of feeling. In other words, perception traces a trajectory that cannot be embraced by what Wittgenstein called "logical space," because it opens a possibility of going beyond life understood as rhetoric.

This can be seen in the Venetian essays. James's fascination with the city began during his first journey to Italy in 1869. It was not only a fascination with monuments and paintings. Rather, Venice became an almost perfect scene of perception. Its basic effect was due to a play of surfaces and reflections (the surface of the water, carnival masks, frescoes and canvas), which helped the writer understand the mechanics of sensibility. One's sight stops on the surface and does not reach the depth; the city becomes a conglomerate of fragments and is devoid of history; seeing is limited to here and now. Chance is also an important factor: an aimless walk, a conversation with a gondolier, or some accidental encounters.

One can notice James aiming at a sort of 'atemporal reductiveness,' a tendency to see Venice as a set of suspended images that should be approached in purely aesthetic ways. James the sentimental tourist is decidedly after detached scenes and disconnected pictures, ignoring the city's historical frames of reference. His interest in the Venetian painters is also there—James is interested mainly in impressionistic effects, even in the case of his favorite Tintoretto.

James's casual sightseeing and drifting through the city provided him with many such images. It is amazing, for instance, how often James depicted the classical 'gondola scene,' both in his novels and essays. Already in his 1872 "early impression" he noted: "Your brown-skinned, white-shirted gondolier, twisting himself in the light, seems to you, as you lie at contemplation beneath your awning, a perpetual symbol of Venetian 'effect'" (52). In his second essay on Venice he wrote:

> There is something strange and fascinating in this mysterious impersonality of the gondola [...] From my windows on the Riva there was always the same silhouette–the long, black, slender skiff, lifting its head and throwing it

back a little, moving yet seeming not to move [...] Sometimes, as you see this movement in profile, in a gondola that passes you—see, as you recline on your own low cushions, the arching body of the gondolier lifted up against the sky—it has a kind of nobleness which suggests an image on a Greek frieze (18).

In "The Grand Canal" (1892), James presents a "gondola piled with references" (35), and there is a splendid image of a solitary gondolier, a "somewhat melancholy figure" who "always has a little the look of an absent-minded nursery-maid pushing her small charges in a perambulator" (39). The gondola passages are symptomatic and provide us with a formula of the Jamesian Venice: detached but always in focus, haunting the writer with its unique character. James's imaginary Venice floats through his texts with rare grace and precision. It marks the experience of fleeting time, so dear to the sentimental tourist.

IV.

On 30 September 1869, James visited Rome for the first time. His first reaction was enthusiastic:

> At last—for the time—I live! It beats everything: it leaves the Rome of your fancy—your education—nowhere. It makes Venice – Florence – Oxford – London – seem like little cities of pasteboard. I went reeling and moaning thro' the streets, in a fever of enjoyment. In the course of four or five hours I traversed almost the whole of Rome [...] Even if I should leave Rome tonight I should feel that I have caught the keynote of its operation on the senses
> (quoted by Edel *Henry James: A Life* 102).

This resembles James's early impressions of Venice and Florence. The writer stressed that the first encounter with a new place was decisive and made it possible to grasp its essence: "First impressions, memorable impressions, are generally irrecoverable; they often leave one the wiser, but they rarely return in the same form" (*Italian Hours* [1995] 132). James's initial fascinations followed the same pattern and were mainly connected with the perception of discovering new spaces: new arrangements of streets and squares, new perspectives, different ways the light touches the walls and is absorbed by them. That was also how Rome affected James—singularly and totally.

There were other impressions characteristic for the time and place James found himself in. The writer was hypnotised by Pope Pius IX and the surrounding crowd of cardinals and ambassadors. In a letter to Alice he would call the Pope "the Grand Llama" and would express both respect and disgust. Rome was for James a site of struggles with his own religiosity, apparently absent but manifested in curious and sometimes tantalising forms. A few years later the writer would be stricken by a scene that was ostensibly insignificant, but in fact emblematic of James's "spectral Rome." During the Roman carnival James found himself, quite accidentally, in the little church of St. Bonaventure on the Palatine hill and saw there a young, solitary priest kneeling in front of the altar and giving him "a sidelong glance" as he entered. It is not unlikely that it was then that the writer came closest to the religious side of his personality; he would approach it in his best novels and stories.

Later both the Pope and the young priest would seem to him nostalgic shades of the past. Unlike other Italian cities of the North, Rome was undergoing quick and radical changes. After the 1870 Risorgimento the Eternal City was becoming more and more secular. When James revisited it in 1873, the Pope was almost its prisoner. The next visits would witness the decline of the city. In 1907 James came to Rome by car and he saw a pseudo-modern, vulgar metropolis: "the abatements and changes and modernisms and vulgarities, the crowd and the struggle and the frustration [...] are quite dreadful [...] I quite revel in the thought that I shall never come to Italy at all again" (quoted by Edel *Henry James: A Life* 632).

Thus, Rome became for James a figure of time as a constant flow of forgetting. The past haunted him and the present eluded his consciousness. The Roman Campagna brought not only a sense of nostalgia but something more: "the light was full of that mellow purple glow, that tempered intensity, which haunts the after-visions of those who have known Rome like the memory of some supremely irresponsible pleasure" (*Italian Hours* [1995] 139). This is different from James's impressions of Venice. The stress here is not on trivia and details that suddenly reveal their uniqueness, but on the time of perception. It is as if objects cast shadows and filled the writer with a sense of melancholia.

It is perhaps not surprising that in his later essays on Rome James felt strong nostalgia for the Catholic city and the Pope (yet another affinity with Henry Adams). Unlike his brother William, for whom Rome was always a place of corruption and rotten religiosity, Henry had a taste for the city's Baroque flavor, the sun setting behind the Piazza del Popolo, and afternoons spent by the graves of Keats and Shelley in the Protestant cemetery. The gradual modernisation of the city filled him with terror, as it marked a slow reorganisation of memory, both individual and collective. What was left were traces, drifting images, distorted after-visions of something that had never really existed.

V.

Italian Hours concludes with an excellent essay on Naples and Capri: "The Saint's Afternoon." It is also James's farewell to Italy—James's visits to Naples were his last Italian trips. The Neapolitan impressions are sparing but there are no doubts that this is late James. The reader is struck by two keys: the key of serenity and balance, of finding a golden mean, and the key of fascination with the everyday giving way to a sense of liberation and joy. Naples, which was viewed by Americans as a dangerous and corrupt place, became for James an antidote for the melancholic moods brought to him by Florence and Rome.

What is significant is that James could not put his Neapolitan experiences into rhetorical frames as he had done with Venice and Rome. Naples seemed too elemental and vehement, too unrestrained and uncontrollable to be mediated and articulated. But perhaps that was what James really wanted it to be: down-to-earth, physical, opaque, and immediate. What the writer discovered in Naples was a silent appeal to integrate one's self and do so through liberating the repressed contents of one's consciousness. After all, that was the fulfillment he was looking for, consisting of letting things appear and cohere. Like Venice, Naples flooded James with images and impressions. But now there was a sense of the physical aspect of the process—impressions got consolidated and integrated into the material substratum of his life.

This had to do with James's repressed sexuality as well. The Naples essay is permeated with, as the writer puts it, a "sound and fury" of strongly physical impressions (315). Typically for James, allusions to his sexuality are scattered and take on a form of strangely convoluted, external phenomena, like the image of "delightful amphibious American children, enameled by the sun of the Bay as for figures of miniature Tritons and Nereids on a Renaissance plaque" (316). One is struck by the sheer force with which James depicts bodies. A corresponding and a somewhat surprising sense of serenity is there as well, and the main impression we can draw from the essay is that of the artist trying desperately to integrate two extreme aspects of his self.

Commenting on the Roman and Neapolitan stories of Matilde Serao, a then-famous Italian novelist, James used characteristic words. He would refer to her "poetry of *passione*," and then would write: "a feeling revives at last, after a timed intermission, that we may not immediately be quite able, quite assured enough, to name, but which, gradually clearing up, soon defines itself almost as a yearning"—and we can guess that the yearning is connected with Serao's "evocation of the absolute ravage of Venus" (quoted by Auchard xxviii). Once and again, James would point to the need for integration and integrity, and 'his' Naples would provide him with the ultimate form of fulfillment.

The Neapolitan experience was decisive. It resulted in a sense of completion. Not a synthesis, perhaps—James was too particular for that—but a heightening of one's existence, an elevation of the spirit. "The Saint's Afternoon" ends with a fantastic note so characteristic for James—the note of near-accomplishment and a corresponding joy:

> The charm was, as always in Italy, in the tone and the air and the happy hazard of things, which made any positive pretension or claimed importance a comparatively trifling question [...] we practiced intimacy, in short, an intimacy so much greater than the mere accidental and ostensible: the difficulty for the right and grateful expression of which makes the old, the familiar tax on the luxury of loving Italy (320).

9. *The Aspern Papers*: From Florence to an Intertextual City, Venice

Rosella Mamoli Zorzi

It is a well-known fact that James heard the 'germ' of the story developed in *The Aspern Papers* in Florence:

> Hamilton (V.L.'s brother) told me a curious thing of a Capt. [Edward] Silsbee—the Boston art critic and Shelley-worshipper; that is of a curious adventure if his. Miss Claremont, Byron's *ci-devant* mistress (the mother of Allegra) was living, until lately, here in Florence, at a great age, 80 or thereabouts, and with her lived her niece, a younger Miss Claremont—of about 50. Silsbee knew that they had interesting papers—letters of Shelley's and Byron's—he had known it for a long time and cherished the idea of getting hold of them. To this end he laid the plan of going to lodge with the Misses Claremont [...]
>
> (Florence, 12 January 1887, *Notebooks* 33).

It is also common knowledge that James presented some reasons for his transposition of the story from Florence to Venice in the Preface to *The Aspern Papers*: "Delicacy had demanded, I felt, that my appropriation of the Florentine legend should purge it, first of all, of references too obvious; so that, to begin with, I shifted the scene of the adventure" (*Henry James: Literary Criticism II* 1179).

These are of course quite acceptable reasons, but one wonders if there may be less obvious reasons behind the change in the setting,[1] that is if in

---

1 See Giorgio Melchiori's questioning of these passages in "Henry James: Burbank or Bleistein," in *Henry James e Venezia*, pp. 9-10, where the answer is found in James's appreciation of Venice as "a place of the mind" by 1888. See also Giuliano Gramigna, pp. 111-112, on the "sedimentazione più intensa, e per così dire più disperata, di passato," and on the theatrical quality of the city.

addition to fairly evident historical reasons, the traditional literary image of Venice as the city of beauty *and* intrigue may have acted on James's imagination.

As the anecdote referred to the letters of Byron and Shelley preserved by Miss Claremont, it could be considered equally appropriate that the story should be set in Venice, since Byron had lived in Venice from 1816 to 1819. James also specified: "Juliana, as I saw her, was thinkable only in Byronic and more or less immediately post-Byronic Italy;" (1179). James was well aware of the haunting presence of the memory of Byron in the city, as he wrote in his essay "The Grand Canal":

> There are persons who hold this long, gay, shabby spotty perspective, in which, with its immense field of confused reflections, the houses have infinite variety, the dullest expanse in Venice. It was not dull, we imagine, for Lord Byron, who lived in the midmost of the three Mocenigo palaces, where the writing table is still shown at which he gave rein to his passions
> (*Italian Hours* [1992] 48; Mamoli Zorzi, *In Venice* 43).

The literary presence of Byron is part of James's perception of the city when mentioning the Mocenigo palaces. The mention of Byron's presumed writing desk underlines Byron's activity as a poet, but the reference "it was not dull" might hint at Byron's sexual encounters, displayed and celebrated by Byron himself in his letters.

The presence of Browning, mentioned in the same essay, shows James's awareness of the presence of another poet in the city:

> Those who have a kindness for Venetian gossip like to remember that it [Palazzo Montecuccoli] was once for a few months the property of Robert Browning, who, however, never lived in it, and who died in the splendid Rezzonico, the residence of his son [...]
> (*Italian Hours* [1992] 42)

Byron, for his life in Venice, for his famous Canto IV of *Childe Harold's Pilgrimage*, for his *Ode on Venice*, for his vision of a decayed and fallen Venice, more than for the humorous, 18th-century vision of the city in his *Beppo*, is on one hand the obvious reason for James's transposition of the story from Florence to Venice, and on the other the first stitch in the tissue of transtextuality regarding the representation of Venice which I will try to illustrate.

As regards the actual letters mentioned in Florence (Shelley and Byron's), Shelley is also important, not so much for his horseback riding on the Lido with Byron as for his Venetian lines in *Lines Written among the*

Euganean Hills and *Julian and Maddalo*. In James's early story "Travelling Companions" the sunset described by the narrator returning from the Lido with Miss Evans ["the lagoon is sheeted with *a carpet of fire*" (*Complete Stories* 524)] evokes quite closely the sky "roofed with clouds of rich emblazonry, /Dark purple at the zenith" and the *"lake of fire"* of the lagoon, in Shelley's *Julian and Maddalo* (327). Sunsets are amply present in *The Aspern Papers*: the lagoon is "aglow with the sunset,"[2] Juliana exhorts Tina to go out with the narrator: "He will show you the famous sunsets [...]" (232), and Colleoni continues to look "at the red immersion of another day" (295). The lexicon is, however, different. Perhaps Shelley's *fire* may be seen as turning into the fire of the burning of the letters. Shelley's famous portrait by Amelia Curran has been seen as the source of Aspern's portrait (Hoeveler "Romancing Venice"155).

With Byron, Shelley, and Browning, we start seeing a 'Venetian' literary network, to which Ruskin's *Stones of Venice* is an essential addition, a literary network that has been studied by several scholars, such as Leon Edel, Marilla Battilana, Tony Tanner, John Pemble, Adeline R. Tintner, Manfred Pfister, and others.

If no specific and explicit references to Ruskin[3] seem to appear in *The Aspern Papers*, Ruskin's observations on the dilapidated exteriors and interiors, echoed in Sargent's paintings of bare halls used for low purposes, all infuse in the description of the Misses Bordereau's empty sala (Mamoli Zorzi, "'A Knock-down Insolence of Talent" 152-55), "in a sequestered and dilapidated old palace" (163):

> It [the sala] had a gloomy grandeur, but owed its character almost all to its noble shape and to the fine architectural doors, as high as those of grand frontages, which, leading into the various rooms, repeated themselves on either sides at intervals. They were surmounted with old, faded, painted escutcheons, and here and there in the spaces between them hung brown pictures, which I noted as speciously bad, in battered and tarnished frames [...] (176).

To Byron, "Otway, Radcliffe, Schiller, Shakespeare's art/ Had stamp'd" the image of Venice in him ("Her Image in Me," Canto IV, XVIII, *Childe Harold's Pilgrimage*). For Byron, then, four authors come into the picture in creating an imaginary Venice, one known before going there: Thomas

---

2 Although this refers to the Northern side of the lagoon, the narrator has come back from the Lido (like Shelley); the contiguity of the passage might suggest an influence.
3 On Ruskin and James see Clegg (1981, 1987) and Follini (2008).

Otway, the author of *Venice Preserved* (1680); Ann Radcliffe, the author of *The Mysteries of Udolpho* (1794), which presents an imaginary, melancholy Venice; Shakespeare; and Schiller.

Of Schiller's novel Byron also wrote, in a letter to Murray (April 2, 1817), as follows:

> Schiller's *Armenian*, a novel which took a great hold of me when I was a boy. It is also called *The Ghost Seer*, and I never walked down St. Mark's by moonlight without thinking of it, and 'at nine o' clock he died'
>
> (*A Self-Portrait* II 405).

Schiller's unfinished novel, *The Visionary* (*Der Geisterseher* 1788-89) was a very popular text in the 19th-century, with its protagonist haunted in the Piazza San Marco by a mysterious stranger (the "Armenian"), who announces a death that will actually take place ("at nine o' clock he died").[4] This was a Gothic novel, similar in a way to Brockden Brown's novels, for the principle of the "explained supernatural." The evocation of the spirits of the dead, for instance, is first represented in all its romantic terror, but then explained through the presence of such devices as a magic lantern, stones falling down to cause noise, etc. The novel, however, seems to have impressed its readers above all for the phrase quoted above.

James was well aware of the existence of Schiller's novel, which is explicitly mentioned in the Venetian pages in *William Wetmore Story and his Friends* (1903). After quoting a long letter on "black" Venice by William Wetmore Story, James added: "He [Story] ends his throbbing day by the inevitable evening in the Piazza, thronged and brilliantly lighted, and remembers Schiller's 'Geisterseher'" (I 190).

In *William Wetmore Story and His Friends*, James foregrounded Story's black vision of Venice, taking his distance from it: this was at a later date than *The Aspern Papers*, but James's insistence in quoting passages by Story on the Venice of the Inquisition and the Venice of crime and deceit shows his awareness of this representation: "Before me" —wrote Story, later quoted by James— "the dagger of the cloaked bravo or of the jealous husband gleams, and I hear the splash of the body as it falls into the dark canal" (194).

James was certainly aware of this 19th-century literary tradition in the

---

4 Washington Irving also happened to quote this phrase in a story—again of mystery and intrigue—partly set in Venice, *The Adventure of the Mysterious Stranger* (1824). Poe's tale, *The Visionary* (1833, published 1834), which is set in Venice, echoed Schiller's title, before it was changed to *The Assignation*. See Mamoli Zorzi "The Text is the City" (1990), for this and references to other authors.

representation of Venice, some examples of which we have just seen.[5]

The perception of places by James was always heavily filtered, as one may well expect, by his readings: London is seen very much through the lens of Dickens; Tour, Touraine, and Paris, through the lens of Balzac; Florence through that of President des Brosses, etc.; Venice through Shakespeare, Schiller, Byron, Shelley, Browning, and Ruskin.

For Venice, James himself recognised the innumerable representations—literary and visual—which conditioned a traveller's perception of the city, representations that even allowed the traveller to imagine the city without going there. James himself reminds us of this in the well-known opening paragraph of his 1882 essay on Venice:

> Venice has been painted and described many thousands of times, and of all the cities of the world is the easiest to visit without going there. Open the first book and you will find a rhapsody about it; step into the first picture-dealer's and you will find three or four high-coloured 'views' of it
>
> (*Italian Hours* [1992] 1).

What could these paintings have been?[6] Of course some "perfidious Canalettos," of which Britain was so rich, contribute, however, to the "glorious" view of Venice that goes together with the negative representation we are focusing on. But, also, in addition to the glorious Venetian paintings where the city was represented in its splendor (Titian, Veronese), James must have been necessarily aware of some of the most popular paintings underlining the black myth of Venice, such as William Etty's *The Bridge of Sighs*. This was perhaps the most famous 19th-century representation of the black legend, illustrating, in a night scene, in the canal of the Bridge of

---

5 Of course one can refer to many other texts. In James Fenimore Cooper's *The Bravo* (1831), a warning against corruption aimed at the USA, Venice is again the city of intrigue and plotting. Cooper placed a quotation at the beginning of each chapter of his novel: several of these are drawn from two unavoidable texts, Byron's *Childe Harold's Pilgrimage* (Canto IV) and the tragedy *Marin Faliero*. One must also remember that the black legend of Venice was intensified by such interpretations of her history as the post-Napoleon *Histoire de la Republique de Venise* by Daru (1819, explicitly mentioned by Cooper as one of his sources). See Mamoli Zorzi, "Intertextual Venice," 225-36.

6 To the literary lens, one should of course add the 'visual' lens, just as important in James: his perception of Florence, for instance, was surely influenced by the Thomas Cole painting of Florence "which covered half a side" of the Jameses' New York "front-parlour" (*Autobiography* [1983] 153), the Campagna is seen through Claude Lorraine ("A months' rides in different directions will show you a dozen prime Claudes." "Roman Rides," *Italian Hours* [1992] 149). For the hidden presence of Giorgione in *The Aspern Papers*, see O'Gorman.

Sighs, the action of two men loading onto a boat a man's corpse, to be taken out and thrown into the lagoon. James, a great esteemer of Delacroix, might have known this painter's *The Execution of the Doge Marin Faliero* (*Venezia nell'Ottocento*, 149, no. 179), again recalling Byron and the black legend.[7]

There were also innumerable prints and etchings illustrating both the romantic and the negative view of Venice: an example could be the collection of etchings printed in *Legends of Venice by J. R. Herbert Esq.* (1840) (*The Fatal Curiosity*, 246; *Aloisi Sanuto and the Ambassador's daughter*, 247; *The Elopement of Bianca Capello*, 248; *Lady Viola*, 249) illustrating such subjects as "Marin Faliero Imprecating Vengeance on his Wife's Traducer," "The Doge Foscari Pronouncing Sentence of Exile upon his Son," subjects obviously made popular by Byron's dramas. Any image of a lover serenading his sweetheart on a balcony, of a romantic elopement, of heroic deeds, can be seen as a background to which *The Aspern Papers* offers an ironic commentary.

These paintings and prints were the popular, and widely-circulating, visual translations of the black myth of Venice, which started, for the English-speaking world, together with the myth of beauty, in the Elizabethan time, and was present of course also in Shakespeare. Echoes of Shakespeare's *Othello* and *The Merchant of Venice*, but also of *Macbeth*, have been identified in the revisions of *The Aspern Papers* by Philip Horne (Horne *Revision* 265-68), the most relevant among them, for our purpose, being the narrator's "super-subtle inference" in front of the secretary containing the letters, recalling the "supersubtle Venetian" (*Othello* Act I Scene III, 357 in Horne *Revision* 281).

The 19th century representations of Venice had deep roots further back in time: I would like to refer more explicitly to three texts: Thomas Nashe's *The Unfortunate Traveller, or the Life of Jack Wilton* (1594); Roger Ascham's *The Schoolmaster* (1570, published posthumously); and Coryat's *Crudities* (1611).

In Nashe's book, a young lord, who has swapped clothes with his servant, arrives in Venice and is taken to the house of Tabitha, a courtesan. Dressed as a servant, he soon learns that Tabitha and her friend Petro de Campo Frego want him to kill his master: "stab, poison, or shoot him through with a pistol, all is one; into the vault he shall be thrown when the deed is done" (301).

This hyperbolic choice of possibilities does not take anything away from the real intention of the courtesan, who also wants to get rid of the young gentleman's servant later on. The plotting is eventually unsuccessful.

---

7 Hayez also painted some famous pictures such as *The Revenge of a Rival* (*Venezia nell'Ottocento* 244), the *Last adieu of Doge Francesco Foscari*, painted also by Grigoletti (243). One can also mention Meissonnier's *The Bravos* (1852), so popular as a subject in the tableaux vivants of British and American expatriates in Venice in the 1880's.

It is interesting to observe that Tabitha's house appears as a "saint's" house, with its "books, pictures, beads (i.e., rosaries), crucifixes" (300) spread all around, even near the bed on which she exercises her profession. The reference to these objects of religion is an obvious hint at Roman Catholic depravity.

In Roger Ascham's *The Schoolmaster*, "Papistrie" is quite evidently the cause of corruption. The "schoolmaster" writes:

> I was in Italy my selfe: but I thank God, my abode there was but IX. dayes: And yet I sawe in that little tyme, in one Citie (Venice), more libertie to sinne, than euer I hard tell of in our noble citie of London in IX. Yeare. I sawe, it was there, as free to sinne, not onelie without all punishment, but also without any mans marking, as it is free in the citie of London, to chose, without all blame, whether a man lusts to weare Shoo or pantocle. And good cause why: For being unlike in troth of Religion, they must nedes be unlike in honestie of living (234).

The duplicity of the attraction of Venice, with its sexual dangers and its plots of murder, is present in these Elizabethan texts, where one can clearly see the protestant suspicion as regards a Roman Catholic, and therefore corrupt, country, in the presence of the misleading rosaries and crucifixes, covering up the activity of a prostitute.

A slightly later book, Thomas Coryat's very famous *Crudities Hastily Gobbled up in Five Months Travel* (1611), celebrates the wealth and beauty of the Republic, its magnificent "milk-white palaces" that "stand very near the water," the new Rialto bridge (whose cost Coryat annotates, to show the wealth of the city); all this beauty "did even amaze or ravish my senses" (314). Senses are always alerted in Venice, and the visitor should be careful, as

> the boatmen [...] are the most vicious and licentious varlets about all the City. For if a stranger entereth into one of their Gondolas, and doth not presently tell them whither he will goe, they will incontinently carry him of their owne accord to a religious house forsooth, where his plumes shall be well pulled before he commeth forth again (...). Therefore I counsaile all my countrimen whatsoever, Gentlemen or others that determine hereafter to see Venice, to beware of the Circaean cups, and the Syrens melody, I meane these seducing and tempting Gondoleers of the Rialto bridge, least they afterward cry Peccavi when it is too late
>
> (Coryat I 311).

The "religious house" to which the "diabolical" gondoliers will take the British gentlemen is of course the house of a courtesan, similar to Tabitha's, the trap of a Roman Catholic country.

Coryat goes on to describe the courtesans, and only after fascinating his reader with a detailed and enchanted descriptions of their charm does he warn him about the dangers of the place:

> For thou shalt see her decked with many chaines of gold and orient pearle like a second Cleopatra, (but they are very little) divers gold rings beautified with diamonds and other costly stones, jewels in both her eares of great worth. A gowne of damaske (I speake this of the nobler Cortizans) either decked with a deep gold fringe [...] or laced with five or six gold laces each two inches broade. Her petticoate of red chamlet edged with gold fringe, stockings of carnasion silke, her breath and her whole body, the more to enamour thee, most fragrantly perfumed (I 404-05).

Having seduced his reader, Coryat adds that the courtesan "will either cause thy throate to be cut by her Ruffiano, [...] or procure thee to be arrested [...] and clapped up in prison" (I 405-06), if the customer does not pay up. The house of Coryat's courtesan also has a sacred image:

> And amongst other amiable ornaments she will shew thee one thing only in her chamber tending to mortification, a matter strange amongst so many irritamenta malorum; even the picture of our Lady by her bedde side, with Christ in her armes, placed withing a cristall glasse (I 405).

The negative myths of Venice that we find in Nashe, Ascham, and Coryat, Papistry being the cause of all this sexual license, crime, and dissimulation, can be found in many other British writers. Ben Jonson chose a Venetian setting for his play *Volpone or the Fox* (1606), to stage a warning against plots in England.

Other authors could come into the picture, such as Voltaire, with his Venetian pages in *Candide,* George Sand, with her Venetian novels, "her masterpiece *Consuelo*" (Sand 707), *La Dernière Aldini* (explicitly quoted in "Travelling Companions," 514), *Léone Léoni* (Sand 719) or Henri de Reigner and Hyppolite Taine: but what interests us here is the Protestant British tradition.

One could also mention the "queer rococo Venice of Goldoni and Casanova,"[8] of which Miss Tina's "tone, hadn't it been so decent, would have seemed to carry one back" (*The Aspern Papers* 220). We have here a macrosystem of representation, whose single items were not necessarily known in detail.

My suggestion is that the transposition of the intrigues and plotting of *The Aspern Papers* must be read also against a longer literary background: "plot" and "conspiracy" are keywords in *The Aspern Papers* (268). The

---

8 Goldoni was added in the New York Edition (Horne *Revision* 279).

"palpable imaginable *visitable* past" for James is also the centuries-long literary reading and rendering of a city. James of course, as any great writer, refined and changed this representation: there is no explicit stiletto or poison to further the drama, but the scene is filled with the representation of an explicit psychological war, which takes place in a labyrinthine Venice, an apt stage for the psychological drama. The actors are different, as are the means of the plotting, but the stage and its atmosphere of intrigue, reflected in the topography of the city, are the same.

This literary image of Venice seems to have stayed with James even in his late novels. If Tabitha the courtesan is defined as "a temptress," the art of writing, for Morton Densher, who will never actually write a word, is, in *The Wings of the Dove,* "a temptress by Titian," as is Kate Croy ("he brought out the beauty of the chance for him—there before him a temptress painted by Titian—to do a little quiet writing," [1965] 352).

The sensuality of Venetian painting, amply underlined by James in his comments on Veronese's *Europa*, chimes in with the representation of the alluring Venice as a city of corruption and intrigue, re-appropriated by James in *The Aspern Papers*. Here sensuality could only have belonged to the past, in Juliana's relation with Jeffrey Aspern. It does not belong to the present, and any offer of sexual relation, which is not so alluring, is to be rejected: the passion is all for the papers.

The background of intrigue is still there, present through the transtextual relations with the works of the past.

10. The Wavering Ruins of *The American*

Enrico Botta

> To delight in the aspects of sentient ruin might appear a heartless pastime, and the pleasure, I confess, shows the note of perversity.
>
> Henry James, *The Italian Hours*

This essay focuses on the motif of ruins in Henry James's *The American* in the light of Italian scholar Francesco Orlando's theory of non-functional objects in literature. I would like to explore how this topic traces a cause-effect relationship between the idea of an appropriation of the European artistic and cultural heritage—metaphorically outlined by Newman's initial attitude towards the ruins of the Old World—and the belief that this assimilation should be purified of its corrupt traits before being transported to the United States—symbolically suggested by the burning of the tell-tale letter at the end of the novel.

The aim of this chapter is to demonstrate how the idea of ruins—which oscillates throughout the novel between being the emblem of an artistic and cultural past to be achieved, and the tragic witness of the decline of Western civilisation—is a dialectical process that not only reflects the inevitable friction between the objectivity of physical ruin (the object itself) and the subjective perspective of the observer (Christopher Newman), but also defines the cultural relationship between the Old and the New World.

The American first sets up the themes, characters, and values of American and European culture, which it then includes and combines, thus overcoming their initial opposition. In reaction to an escalating American exceptionalism, attempting to frame the cultural identity of the United States within a nationalistic framework, James's "first international novel" (Cargill 419), epitomising both Americanism and internationalism, traces a transatlantic map where American and European culture meet and interact. If on the one hand, the man of the West and, even more importantly, the model of Americanness, desires to enrich his American self by acquiring European values and commodities in an international context, on the other hand, *The American* aims at turning into a transatlantic novel by appropriating the literary *topoi* and motifs that have made up the European canon—e.g., *The Moon-borne Madonna* by Murillo, *The Marriage at Cana* by Veronese, *Hamlet* and *Othello* by Shakespeare, *La Belle Dame Sans Merci* by Keats, *Don Giovanni* by Mozart, etc. This is a process that is made more significant by the novel's date of publication—1877, when the United States was celebrating the first anniversary of its independence and projecting itself into an international context as a new cultural as well as political power.

The motif of ruins represents a significant element in the transtextual and transatlantic operation of the novel, allowing it to explore the idea of cultural appropriation from a wide viewpoint, both spatial and temporal, both physical and metaphorical. If, as argued by Donatella Izzo, "the international theme in *The American* becomes mainly a literary theme" (*Henry James* 9), and keeping in mind Walter Benjamin's definition of quotation as a ruin that emerges from the past, we could interpret Christopher Newman's and the novel's tour amongst the (artistic and literary) ruins of the Old World as the reading and reinterpretation of that tradition, which gives a new meaning to James's present literary construction.

In my consideration of ruins, my starting point is two-fold: on the one hand, Christopher Woodward's theorisation of a time-honoured idea of ruins as having both an objective value (as an assemblage of bricks and stones) and a subjective one (as an inspiration to artists and thinkers on the themes of man, nature, art, and mutability), enabling memory to see through a paradox: the coexistence of the glory of the past and the decay of the present.[1] On the other hand, Francesco Orlando's consideration of ruins as "non-functional objects," which unlike Woodward's, seems to turn the deep cultural and moral value of the motif itself upside down, at least from a physical and materialistic point of view.

By tracing Western literature's obsession with outmoded, obsolete, and superseded objects, the Italian scholar claims that ruins—together with relics, rarities, rubbish, uninhabited places, and hidden treasures—take on

---

[1] According to Woodward, the "Ozymandias complex" is the idea of "ruins as an obvious symbol of the rise and fall of empires" (177). Ruins have long been objects of contemplation and sources of creative inspiration, and have determined different yet intermingled reflections. They are reminders of the splendor of what has been, and at the same time of the transience of human ambition.

a new meaning in the literature of the nineteenth and twentieth century. If the non-functional is something that has no function in relation to culture, especially in an age increasingly devoted to technological progress, its prominence in Western literature indicates that this is not only the place, in Freudian terms, of the returning past that refuses to die, but also the dimension in which a literary "compromise formation" turns the primary non-functionality of a physical lack of value into the moral value of its secondary refunctionalisation.² Orlando proposes twelve "strategically arbitrary" categories to describe the ways in which literature uses non-functional objects; by reading *The American* through some of these categories, it is possible to frame the Jamesian 'international theme' in a cognitive map, which would underline not only its primarily spatial identity, but also its temporal and chronological value.³

From this perspective, ruins link *The American* with the theme of time, which on the one hand wears out and destroys things, but on the other hand confers on them the prestige of rarity and antiquity. This double focus reverberates on the dialectical process between the acquisition and rejection of 'old things' — which are moral, aesthetic and cultural values — outlined by the irresolute vacillation between Newman's, James's, and American culture's desire to assimilate European values, and the need to purify them from their allegedly corrupt traits. Thus, if the "wavering" of my title first refers to the physical condition of an object, it also concerns Christopher Newman's state of uncertainty during his European journey. This swinging movement can be framed as an oscillation between the extremes of Orlando's range of categories, especially between the "positive" frame of what he terms the "precious-potential" and "prestigious-ornamental" modes, and the "negative" field of the "sinister-terrifying" and "worn-realistic" ones.

The theme of ruins is particularly significant in Henry James's *Autobiography*. Remembering his first "ecstatic vision of Europe," James

---

2 Here Orlando develops the idea of literature as a compromise-formation, produced by the conflict of the pleasure-principle and the reality-principle.
3 According to Orlando, useless and superseded objects can be conceived in twelve categories: the solemn-admonitory, the threadbare-grotesque, the venerable-regressive, the worn-realistic, the reminiscent-affective, the desolate-disconnected, the magic-superstitious, the sinister-terrifying, the precious-potential, the sterile-noxious, the prestigious-ornamental, and the pretentious-fictitious. According to the Italian scholar, these categories are "strategically arbitrary": strategic, because they can disclose patterns of thought broadening across temporal, spatial, and cultural boundaries; arbitrary, because they are potentially capable of revealing further patterns.

writes that, while looking outside the window of the train from Lyons to Geneva, he saw "a castle and a ruin" along with "the first peasant [he] had ever beheld." This picturesque frame led James to assert: "Supremely, in that ecstatic vision, was 'Europe,' sublime synthesis, expressed and guaranteed to me [...]."

Like his creator, after "long[ing] for a new world" (*The American* [1978] 536), Christopher Newman starts to contemplate European ruins, because he recognises them as a primary tool to trace a continuity between what he has left in America and what he is going to find in the Old World—that is, a new perspective connecting his past and his future. By an aesthetic and moral assimilation of the Old World values and commodities, he (unconsciously) sets up a secondary refunctionalisation of ruins, which involves the idea of *importing* them in order to *construct* American history and culture.[4] This process seems to be in line with J. B. Jackson's idea according to which the European and Western models of cultural history need the physicality of the past ruins, around which segments of memory are re-constructed and interwoven, thus giving continuity to their own evolution. This temporal theory can be translated into a transatlantic spatial structure in which American culture and history require an assimilation and re-elaboration of the Old World tradition (represented by its own ruins), thus duplicating the process through which Rome delineated its identity by synthesising indigenous elements with the heritage of ancient Greece.

This cultural move can be viewed through Orlando's "positive" category of the "precious-potential," describing the imaginary effects of ruins as an impressive cultural resource for the present. In fact, in the first part of the novel ruins are represented as very valuable tools for Christopher Newman's (and Henry James's) cultural improvement. This is how the narrator describes Newman's tour through Newman's own eyes in Chapter V:

> He [Christopher Newman] lounged through Belgium and Holland and the Rhineland, through Switzerland and Northern Italy, planning about nothing, but seeing everything. [...] When an excursion, a church, a gallery, a ruin, was proposed to him, the first thing Newman usually did, after surveying his postulant in silence, from head to foot, was to sit down at a little table and order something to drink. [...] "What is it?" he asked. "How far?" And whatever the answer was, although he sometimes seemed to hesitate, he

---

4 In this perspective, even the famous passage from *Hawthorne*—concerning the need for an American writer to seek in Europe the key elements for creating a work of art—can be considered to have a ruinistic frame.

never declined. He stepped into an open cab, made his conductor sit beside him to answer questions, bade the driver go fast (he had a particular aversion to slow driving) and rolled, in all probability through a dusty suburb, to the goal of his pilgrimage. If the goal was a disappointment, if the church was meagre, or the ruin a heap of rubbish, Newman never protested or berated his cicerone; he looked with an impartial eye upon great monuments and small, made the guide recite his lesson, listened to it religiously, asked if there was nothing else to be seen in the neighborhood, and drove back again at a rattling pace. [...] Newman, now and then, in an unguided stroll in a foreign city, before some lonely, sad-towered church, or some angular image of one who had rendered civic service in an unknown past, had felt a singular inward tremor. It was not an excitement or a perplexity; it was a placid, fathomless sense of diversion (575-76).

In his moving backward in time and space to re-discover and re-appropriate the Old World, the ruins that the new Columbus encounters are the emblems of the cultural achievements of the ancient European civilisation. Simultaneously, they stand for the tools James employs to provide moral and aesthetic lessons to America.

First, it is worth noting that Christopher travels without a definite plan but with the intention of admiring the Old World as much as possible: "I seemed to feel a new man inside my old skin, and I longed for a new world" (536) is the way he describes his reason for undertaking his journey. At a first reading, he may seem rather inexperienced and superficial; he gives the impression of not being particularly interested in his own spiritual edification, but he carefully does everything required by the Grand Tour tourists' duties as quickly as possible: he regards everything that is shown to him as having equal dignity, and listens to all stories and anecdotes. Although the narrator describes Christopher's reaction as "a sense of diversion," ironically denying any sublimity to the vision, Newman has the ambitious project to purchase every element of the European tradition. In this first part of the novel, Christopher seems to regard European culture not only as an intellectual heritage to learn, but also as a kind of unknown territory, often in ruins, to be observed, explored, and appropriated—"I have come to see Europe, to get the best out of it I can. I want to see all the great things, and do what the clever people do" (535). The *marginalia* he writes on the pages of his tour guide, after visiting cities, castles, monuments, and churches, further confirm his symbolic appropriation of the continent: "Wherever you find a scratch, or a cross, or a 'Beautiful!' or a 'So true!' or a 'Too thin!' you may know that I have had a sensation of some sort or other" (585). His desire to learn is enormous—"I find that the more I see of the world the more I want to see" (585)—and, as a new Ulysses, his goal is to return home after having experienced an ancient and magnificent universe.

Nevertheless, Newman begins to realise that Europe is also a perverse and deceptive world, and ruins are not only a precious resource for him but also—in line with Orlando's "prestigious-ornamental" mode—a sophisticated artifact of culture and time. As the spiritual and moral decadence of the Old World reveals itself to Christopher in the metaphorical ruins of certain places—the de Bellegarde's palace, the castle in Fleurières, the Convent in Rue d'Enfer, and so forth—Newman's desire to observe and assimilate gradually fades. After realising Claire's sudden change of heart, Newman goes to Fleurières to convince her to marry.

> As soon as he received this letter Newman went straight to Paris and to Poitiers. The journey took him far southward, [...] and the next morning he drove in a couple of hours to the village of Fleurières. But here, preoccupied though he was, he could not fail to notice the picturesqueness of the place. It was what the French call a petit bourg; it lay at the base of a sort of huge mound on the summit of which stood the crumbling ruins of a feudal castle, much of whose sturdy material, as well as that of the wall which dropped along the hill to inclose the clustered houses defensively, had been absorbed into the very substance of the village. The church was simply the former chapel of the castle, fronting upon its grass-grown court, which, however, was of generous enough width to have given up its quaintest corner to a little graveyard. Here the very headstones themselves seemed to sleep [...] (780-81)

As can be seen, his new state of mind does not preclude Christopher from observing the attractiveness of the place: the crumbling ruins of the castle, the fortress protecting the village, the church, and the picturesque cemetery. The feelings produced in the American by this scene are no longer those of a heroic achievement, but of a dark and melancholy lyricism, and the pathetic fallacy of the headstones that seem to sleep, duplicates the material and spiritual fading, both of Claire and of her family.

If the first part of the novel—the complication—focuses on Newman's acceptance and assimilation of ruins, the second part—the *dénouement*—is concerned with their rejection. By experiencing the Old World, Newman (James) realises that the encounter with the ruins swings between what he actually sees and feels, and his expectations regarding his own trip. Thus, when in the turning point of the novel the ruins start to indicate no longer the greatness of the past, but the immoral traits of Europe, the coordinates of a (utopian) cultural appropriation need to be changed. While the story of Christopher progressively becomes a melodramatic plot of murder and vengeance, James manages the transition from a notion of ruins as aesthetic principle to one of ruins as warning and moral teaching. The imaginary effects of ruins invest the 'supernatural' order of the entire gloomy setting of Claire's seclusion—the palace in Rue de l'Université, the castle in Fleurières, and the convent in Rue d'Enfer—with passive expectations, according to Orlando's category of the "sinister-terrifying."

If at this point ruins no longer prove the greatness of the European past but rather symbolise its most decadent aspects, it is noteworthy that the tragic and unexpected crisis of the novel begins in the same ruinistic frame of Fleurières. Newman meets Mrs. Bread at night in a secluded place: "Come to me in the old ruin there on the hill, in the court before the church. I will wait for you there, I have something very important to tell you" (797), the American says to the woman. The quotation that follows describes the encounter between the two characters:

> The path which led up the hill to the ruin was easy to find, and Newman in a short time had followed it to the top. He passed beneath the rugged arch of the castle wall, and looked about him in the early dusk for an old woman in black. The castle yard was empty, but the door of the church was open. Newman went into the little nave and of course found a deeper dusk than without. A couple of tapers, however, twinkled on the altar and just enabled him to perceive a figure seated by one of the pillars.
>
> [...] 'We shall be safer,' said Newman, 'where no one can hear us.' And he led the way back into the castle court and then followed a path beside the church, which he was sure must lead into another part of the ruin. He was not deceived. It wandered along the crest of the hill and terminated before a fragment of wall pierced by a rough aperture which had once been a door (802-03).

The introspective and psychological depth of his transatlantic quest is converted into a Gothic and melodramatic conventionalism, and his love story and European dreams seem to crumble like the walls he passes through. In the castle courtyard and in the church where his marriage to Claire would have been celebrated there is only darkness and a sense of solitude, which seem to duplicate his sinister story.

In the final chapter, we encounter the last reference to ruins. Disgusted and rejected by the de Bellegarde, before going back to America Newman moves to England, where we find him again "wandering about cathedrals, castles, and ruins. Several times, taking a walk from his inn into meadows and parks, he stopped by a well-worn stile, looked across through the early evening at a gray church tower, with its dusky nimbus of thick-circling swallows, and remembered that this might have been part of the entertainment of his honeymoon" (863-64).

When, "a sadder and wiser man," Christopher finally goes back to America, he has realised that European ruins—the evidence of its past—are the majesty symbol of its civilisation but also tell the tale of its decadence and transience. In line with Orlando's "worn-realistic" category, Newman discovers that ruins everlastingly belong to history, and not only to his story.

The last scene of the novel seems to solve the dialectical process between the acceptance of non-functionality and its rejection. Reading this scene through Orlando's mode of the "solemn-admonitory"—in which ruins indicate a perception of time that gravely reminds men of the transience of worldly things—the burning of the tell-tale sheet suggests that everything in the Old World indicates its fascinating history and culture, but also its corruption and degeneration: "Newman instinctively turned to see if the little paper was in fact consumed, but there was nothing left of it" (872).

The image of the burned sheet could be regarded as James's original re-elaboration of the motif of ruins: in fact, this is a ruin that does not leave ruins. At this point of the novel, the de Bellegardes's ideology and commodities no longer represent the ruins of a glorious yet vanishing tradition, but they become the symbol of a hierarchic order that has been trying to defend its own rights against Newman's American values. By destroying the immoral and perverse elements of the Old World, Christopher can definitely realise its artistic and cultural value and, even though the European civilisation and the de Bellegardes's tradition seem to fade away amongst the ashes in Mrs. Tristram fireplace, they will never cease to exist in his mind. In the end, while Orlando's systematic modes seem to frame Newman's understanding of ruins (as containing lessons for the United States as much as for Europe itself), the pendulum swinging between attraction and repulsion keeps on tracing the composite trajectories of the encounter of American and European culture.

III: APPROPIATING EUROPEAN THEMATICS

11. Balzacian Intertextuality and Jamesian Autobiography in *The Ambassadors*

Kathleen Lawrence

> Cette aventure arrivée sous le toit paternel, aux yeux de Louis, alors âgé de neuf ans, contribua beaucoup à le faire croire aux visions miraculeuses de Swedenborg, qui donna pendant sa vie plusieurs preuves de la puissance de vision acquise à son être intérieur.[1]
>
> Balzac, *Louis Lambert*

With recent renewed interest in Henry James's late style, and in particular the impress of autobiography on his late novels and non-fiction, it is perhaps worth revisiting the question of the meaning of Lambert Strether's Christian name, with its larger implications for the intertextual relation between Balzac's *Louis Lambert* (1835) and *The Ambassadors* (1903).[2] Adeline Tintner ominously warns critics away from the topic, maintaining that,

> Scholars have been trying for years to make some sort of identification between Lewis Lambert Strether of *The Ambassadors* and his namesake Louis Lambert, but the effort is wasted, since the hero of the late James novel of Paris has been ironically saddled with his name by two provincial parents

---

[1] "This event, under his father's roof and to his own knowledge, when Louis was nine years old, contributed largely to his belief in Swedenborg's miraculous visions, for in the course of that philosopher's life he repeatedly gave proof of the power of sight developed in his Inner Being." This and subsequent translations are taken from the 2005 edition of the story, translated by Clara Bell and James Waring.

[2] See, for example, Sheila Teahan's "My Sculptor/My Self: A Story of Reading." In *The Henry James Review* 23: 3 (Fall 2003), 246-54; Hazel Hutchison, "James's Spectacles: Distorted Vision in the Ambassadors." In *The Henry James Review* 26: 1 (Winter 2005), 39-51; and Bill Brown, "Now Advertising: Late James." In *The Henry James Review* 30: 1 (Winter, 2009).

from Woollett, Massachusetts, who did not know that *Louis Lambert* was a 'bad' Balzac novel

(Tintner *Book World* 256).³

Louis Lambert may be, from the standpoint of form, a "'bad' Balzac novel," but a close reading of Balzac's and James's novels in light of Julia Kristeva's exploration of intertextuality reveals profound resonance between Balzac's mystical novel and James's first novel of his late style. Kristeva traces the origin of literature to "concrete, historical family structures" (97), suggesting we look for intertextual correspondence on the deepest level of psychic identity and the unconscious. Kristeva's idea of "writing as a reading of the anterior literary corpus and the text as an absorption of and a reply to another text" (39) opens the possibility of reading *The Ambassadors* and *Louis Lambert* in a dialogic mode heretofore too easily dismissed.

In her denigration of Strether's provincial parents, Tintner fails to take note of their similarity with Henry James's own parents, one of many autobiographical threads woven into James's text. Apparently Mr. and Mrs. Strether, Sr. had a lot in common with Mr. and Mrs. Henry James, Sr., who called James's younger brother Garth Wilkinson James, named, like Lewis Lambert Strether, for a prominent Swedenborgian, albeit for the real British Swedenborgian J. J. Garth Wilkinson and not Balzac's fictional mystic.⁴ The name "Lewis Lambert Strether" thus implicates not only Strether's absent parents but also Henry James's own, suggesting that a powerful belief system rather than mere provinciality may have inspired such unwieldy epithets. This matrix of childhood experience had increasing importance for James as he faced failures in the theatre and literary marketplace, the

---

3 Yet, Tintner contradicts her assertion, stating, "In view of James's great attention to the nuances of the names of his characters, we cannot view [that Marie de Vionnet and Maria Gostrey share the same first name] as accidental" (Tintner *Book World* 306). James W. Gargano, "The Ambassadors and Louis Lambert." In *Modern Language Notes* 75 (1960), 213; and Hazel Hutchison, "The Other Lambert Strether: Henry James's *The Ambassadors*, Balzac's *Louis Lambert*, and J. H. Lambert." In *Nineteenth-Century Literature* 58: 2 (September 2003), 230-53, concur with Adeline Tintner. For example, Hutchison argues that "In choosing a slight, unadmired novel, James underlines Strether's marginality and the bad taste of his hometown" (237). Hutchison's argument is more nuanced, however, than Gargano's as she asserts the complexity of the connection with Balzac, for "it is not possible to dispose of the Balzacian mysticism in *The Ambassadors* as swiftly as Gargano might wish. [...] Part of Balzac's appeal was that James felt that the line between the concrete and the abstract, the material and the spiritual, should be constantly blurred" (238).

4 With a canny sense of verbal play, Henry James Sr. must have realized that "Garth Wilkinson James" simply reversed his great friend's own name "James (John) Garth Wilkinson."

loss of his sister Alice and brother "Wilky," the embarrassing dissolution of his brother Rob, and the assault of Gilded Age materialism. Strether's name and its tie to Garth Wilkinson James leads the reader from Belle Epoque Paris back to antebellum Boston, linking *The Ambassadors* through Balzac to the young James family and the cultural crucible that turned James from infant *flâneur* to artist, the very source of his genius. Henry James's Lewis Lambert Strether is thus an "ambassador" to Paris not only from a distant American land but also from a lost American age, evoking the dawn of James's own consciousness as part of his family's idiosyncratic world, as set against increasingly imperialistic and business-minded American values.

James seems at first to want to throw his readers off the track. For example, he complains vociferously in an early review of Balzac, "'Louis Lambert,' as a whole, is now quite unreadable; it contains some admirable descriptions, but the 'scientific' portion is mere fantastic verbiage" (*"Correspondance de H. de Balzac"* 76). In another review of his French master, James claims, "Balzac possessed indeed a lively interest in the supernatural: "La Peau de Chagrin, "Louis Lambert" and "Séraphîta," are a powerful expression of it. But it was a matter of adventurous fancy, like the same quality in Edgar Poe; it was perfectly cold, and had nothing to do with his moral life" ("Honoré de Balzac" 48). These statements presage Maria Gostrey's oft-quoted dismissal of the novel in the first chapter of *The Ambassadors*, the line that has confused scholars analysing the book according to conventional tenets of close reading. But, as Kristeva explains, "relationships that the nineteenth century labeled 'social value' or literature's moral 'message'" are "actualized as textual ambivalence." She continues, "Dialogue and ambivalence are borne out as the only approach that permits the writer to enter history by espousing an ambivalent ethics: negation as affirmation" (Kristeva 40). In spite of James's prosaic repudiations, autobiographical correspondences between *Louis Lambert* and *The Ambassadors* bespeak not rejection but rather ambivalence that Kristeva pairs indissolubly with the unseen psychic gears driving intertextuality and literary absorption. James rejects *Louis Lambert* in his essays and dismisses it in on the surface of *The Ambassadors* itself only to reply to it on a subtle level throughout the novel where the symbolic manifestations of his unconscious have free play. Kristeva explains this level of imaginative work as "the psychic aspect of writing as trace of a dialogue with oneself [...] as a splitting of the writer into subject of enunciation and subject of utterance" (Kristeva 44).

As Graham Robb delineates in his recent biography of Balzac, Louis Lambert's fantastical visions and pseudo-scientific epigrams are affixed to a solid armature of dates and facts derived from Balzac's actual life. Balzac begins his novel by announcing Louis Lambert's birth date as 1797, two years before his own, and continues with realist portions that correspond to Balzac own experiences during his school days as a boarder at the Oratorian College de Vendôme where he was spurned by his schoolmates and punished by his teachers for his recondite intellectual pursuits. Lambert's pamphlet "Traité de la Volonté," written in spite of the harsh circumstances of school life, matches a corresponding one written by Balzac himself, as remembered by one of his schoolmates years later. Autobiographical correspondences continue in Lambert's move to Paris where he experiences the loneliness and desperation felt by Balzac during his literary apprenticeship in his garret in Paris on the Rue Lesdiguières. Last but not least, Balzac intrudes into the text to announce his authorship and his identity as Lambert's companion: *"Ce fut en mémoire de la catastrophe arrivée au livre de Louis que, dans l'ouvrage par lequel commencent ces Études, je me suis servi pour une oeuvre fictive du titre réellement inventé par Lambert [...]"* [It was in memory of the disaster that befell Louis' book that, in the tale which comes first in these Etudes, I adopted the title invented by Lambert for a work of fiction] (*Louis Lambert* 624). Louis and the narrator become inseparable companions, known by the hyphenated epithet "Le Poète-et-Pythagore" who *"furent donc une exception, une vie en dehors de la vie commune"* [The Poet-and-Pythagoras formed an exception and led a life apart from the life of the rest] (613). Linked to Louis as his alter ego, the narrator reveals, *"Nous nous habituâmes, comme deux amants, à penser ensemble, à nous communiquer nos rêveries"* [Like two lovers, we got into the habit of thinking together in a common reverie] (615).

Analysed according to Kristeva's "psychic aspect of writing as trace of a dialogue with oneself," Balzac's novel is more than just an autobiographical *roman à clef*. Splitting himself into both the narrator and Louis, Balzac infuses the text not only with autobiographical facts, but also with symbolic logic corresponding to the deepest needs of his psyche to portray the unhealed wounds of childhood, in particular his rejection by his mother. As Balzac' scholars have long noted, Balzac's mother not only put him out to nurse as a baby but also arranged to send him away to school at a tender age. Letters home show his intense desire to please her. She also exposed him to Swedenborg as a child, parallel to James's initiation by his father. In *Louis*

11. The Ambassadors   127

Lambert, Madame de Staël discovers the young Louis reading Swedenborg's *Heaven and Hell* alone in the woods, recognises his genius, and endows him with a scholarship to school. De Staël's initial benevolence is ironically detrimental to the precocious visionary when she recklessly sends him to the conventional Collège de Vendôme where schoolmates and teachers alike torment him for his idiosyncratic genius. When he goes to Paris in search of her counsel and wisdom, he is unable to find his benefactress and suffers further desperation and loneliness. Exemplifying Kristeva's concept of "dialogue and ambivalence," Balzac again mentions Madame de Staël as a metonymic exchange for her great heroine but disparages the careless author whose largesse ironically hurt Lambert, "*déplanté par Corinne de ses belles campagnes pour entrer dans le moule d'un collège auquel chaque intelligence, chaque corps doit, malgée sa portée, malgré son tempérament* [...]" [transplanted by "Corinne" from the country he loved, to be squeezed in the mould of a collegiate routine to which every spirit and every body must yield, whatever their range or temperament] (619). "Corinne's," i.e. Madame de Staël's, carelessness ruins Lambert's life. Lambert the wounded Swedenborgian dies while his friend and alter ego the narrator lives on. Displacing his mother as Madame de Staël, Balzac re-enacts his childhood trauma but also his ambivalent relationship to his mother from whom he sought approval and who became his financial assistant during his early years as an author, enabling him to succeed and survive.

Balzac's references to Madame de Staël's novel *Corinne* (1807) tie the autobiographical aspects of *Louis Lambert* to intertextual and generic considerations. As Kristeva's writes, "any text is constructed as a mosaic of quotations; any text is the absorption and transformation of another [...]" (37). Like *Corinne*, *Louis Lambert* can be construed as a *Bildungsroman* or novel of the development of the young person. Madame de Staël's *Corinne* makes an earlier appearance in *Louis Lambert* when Balzac's narrator describes Madame de Staël's iconic portrait by Gérard where she appears dressed as her heroine and holding her lyre in a scene from the famous novel. With an ekphrastic description of this painting, Balzac's narrator again intrudes on the text, recording the moment of his primal identification with his precursor, "*j'ai vu le tableau de Corinne, où Gérard l'a représentée et si grande et si belle; hélas! la femme idéale rêvée par mon imagination la surpassait tellement, que la véritable Madame de Staël a constamment perdu dans mon esprit, même après la lecture du livre tout viril, intitulé De l'Allemagne*" [I saw at a later time the picture of Corinne, in which Gerard represents her as so tall and handsome; and, alas!

the woman painted by my imagination so far transcended this, that the real Madame de Stael fell at once in my estimation, even after I read her book of really masculine power, De l'Allemagne.] (601).The narrator's own vision of his precursor exceeds the real woman. Balzac also mentions Goethe's *Werther* (1774), the other great Romantic *Bildungsroman* that he wished to supersede. Goethe's hero, like Madame de Staël's, shares many traits with his author. In a lengthy digression, Balzac discloses his intention for his protagonist to surpass Goethe's troubled hero, *"Les soupirs de Lambert m'ont appris des hymnes de tristesse bien plus pénétrants que ne le sont les plus belles pages de Werther [...]. Werther est l'esclave d'un désir, Louis Lambert était toute une âme esclave"* [Lambert's woes had taught me many a chant of sorrow far more appealing than the finest passages in "Werther" [...] Werther is the slave of desire; Louis Lambert was an enslaved soul.] (614). Just as Louis Lambert exceeds Werther in the intensity of his suffering, so Balzac intends to supplant Goethe's Romantic fervor with his realist mode, explaining the precision of places, dates, and specific sensory memories in spite of the novel's bizarre catalogue of visionary and pseudo-scientific insights.

All three protagonists—Werther, Corinne, and Lambert—are creative geniuses suffering from exclusion and misunderstanding by the mediocre hordes, placing their fictional biographies in the generic sub-category of *Künstlerroman*, or novel of the growth of the young artist. All three novels also exhibit autobiographical overlap with their authors on both surface and symbolic levels. In *The Ambassadors*, James absorbs and replies to the generic and thematic particulars of the autobiographical *Künstlerroman* and in particular to *Werther, Corinne,* and *Louis Lambert* in subtle ways that exhibit Kristeva's idea of authorial ambivalence paired to intertextual absorption. In her discussion of intertextuality in *Revolution in Poetic Language*, Kristeva defines novels as having "borrowed from different signifying materials [...] never single, complete and identical to themselves, but always plural, shattered [...]" (Kristeva 111). For example, James transposes the plot device of the early deaths of Werther, Corinne, and Louis Lambert into the early death of Strether's son and wife, and, metaphorically, the early emotional death of Strether himself. Attributing to Strether's lost boy the Romantic passion of Werther, Corinne, and Louis Lambert, James writes in his original notebook entry, "He was wild—he was free—he was passionate; but there would have been a way of taking him" (*Notebooks* 142). As James reveals in his later synopsis for *Harper's*, "There have been special facts about the boy, his nature, his temperament, tendencies, that Strether has subsequently accused himself, with bitter compunction, of not having understood and allowed for, not handled with sufficient tenderness and tact" (549). Like his precursors in the canonical *Künstlerroman*, Strether's son is the misunderstood and sensitive type of the artist too good to survive in the world. In the finished novel, James explicitly connects the death of his wife and son with Strether's own inner death, "Beyond, behind them was the pale figure of his real youth, which held against its breast the two presences paler than itself—the young wife he had early lost and the young son he had stupidly sacrificed" (*The Ambassadors* [2009] 84). Subtly referencing *Louis Lambert*, whose protagonist turns pale, almost completely white, before he dies, Strether's youth becomes embodied as a "pale figure" that dies along with his son and wife, "two presences paler than itself." When his son dies, Strether dies emotionally and intellectually, as symbolised by the "lemon-colored volumes" of Hugo that represent his youth, purchased in Paris "back in the sixties," that are now buried in his attic, "stale and soiled and never sent to the binder" (86-87). Subsuming works of his French precursors, James hopes to supplant Romantic and even Balzacian realist modes with his psychological realism.

Kristeva's theory of intertextuality lends insight to a re-reading of *The Ambassadors* in light of its precursors in the genre of *Künstlerroman*. Kristeva discusses the intersection of "*language* (the true practice of thought) with *space*," where the word works "*horizontally* (the word in the text belong to both writing subject and addressee)" and "*vertically* (the word in the text is oriented towards an anterior or synchronic literary corpus)" (Kristeva 36-37). This conception is part of her examination of "spatial conception of language's poetic operation," the "three dimensions of textual space" that extend the work outward to "larger sequences" and "exterior texts." Enfolding *Louis Lambert* into *The Ambassadors*, James enters Kristeva's vertical space, subsuming not only Balzac's novel but also Goethe's and Madame de Staël's novels. Lambert Strether leads us to Louis Lambert, who leads us to Werther and Corinne, who tie us back to Strether, an intertextual *mise en abîme* that extends forward and backward in the "synchronic literary corpus." With the autobiographical correspondences between each of the protagonists and their creators, on the level of simple surface resemblance and deeper psychic symbolism, Kristeva's image of a "synchronic literary corpus" allows a strand of autobiographical text parallel to and shadowing the vertical line of *Künstlerromans* as the fictional and real-life figures lend each other added resonance vertically across the vast literary infrastructure.

Autobiographical parallels between James and Strether are strengthened when analysed in light of James's covert reference through Balzac and Louis Lambert to Garth Wilkinson, 'Wilky' James, implicitly calling forth the world of James's childhood and their idiosyncratic Swedenborgian and Emersonian upbringing. By specifying Strether's age as fifty-five in the year 1900, James further strengthens the link between his hero and his brother Garth Wilkinson, who also would have been fifty-five in 1900, born like Strether in 1845, just two years after James himself and a year before youngest James brother, Robertson. Just as James connects Strether's birth to his own and Wilky's, Lewis Lambert Strether and Garth Wilkinson James are exact contemporaries. More important than their vital statistics, Wilky and Strether are tied by repeated personal failure, a predicament shared with Balzac's Louis Lambert and authors Balzac and Henry James themselves. Like James's brothers Wilky and Bob, Strether "had failed, as he considered, in everything, in each relation and in half a dozen trades" (*The Ambassadors* [2009] 114), a description that fits James's sensitive and good-natured younger brothers more than it does the successful editor Howells, who is Strether's ostensible prototype. Strether edits the Woollett *Review* in order to rescue from "the wreck of hopes and ambitions, the refuse-heap of disappointments and failures, [his] one presentable scrap of an identity" (100-01). James's hypersensitive and troubled sister Alice is also implicitly included in James's record of failure through Maria Gostrey, who is herself tied to Louis Lambert's female counterpart in failure, his beloved Pauline de Villenoix, ostracised from French society by her Jewish genealogy and sensitive nature. As Maria Gostrey confesses, "'If you knew,' she sighed, 'the dreams of my youth! But our realities are what have brought us together. We're beaten brothers in arms'" (84). As for James, his brothers, and Alice, Strether and Gostrey's relationship is ultimately fraternal and their shared failures makes them "beaten brothers in arms." Of particular significance for Kristeva's psychoanalytic and semiotic reading are the deaths of Strether's wife, son, and the metaphorical death of Strether's soul. Death plays a key role for Kristeva in the artistic process. As she explains the work of the novelist,

> in order to function, he must make himself the bearer of death. In this sense the artist is comparable to all other figures of the 'scapegoat.' But he is not just a scapegoat; in fact what makes him an artist radically distinguishes him from all other sacrificial murderers and victims [...] the artist sketches out a kind of second birth (120).

As we noted earlier, Balzac displaces anger towards his mother onto Madame de Staël, who destroys Louis but not the narrator, who triumphs as Louis's alter ego and succeeds where he failed. Just as Strether gains "a kind of second birth" in Paris where "He had never expected [...] again to find himself young [...]"(*Louis Lambert* 81), so James experiences vicariously a "second birth" through symbolic deaths in his novels, surviving the loss of Minny Temple, his parents, sister Alice, and brother "Wilky." Like Werther, Corinne, and Lambert, Wilkie died too early, in 1883 at the age of thirty-eight, the first of the James children to die. James had felt the loss keenly, writing to William "It is a great weight off my spirit" (Edel *Henry James II* 256).

Between October 1895, when James first recorded receiving the 'donnée' for *The Ambassadors* from Jonathan Sturges, and his summary sent to *Harper's* five years later, James looked back with poignant meditation at a series of calamitous losses, not just the deaths but also the attending catastrophes, financial and personal, of the family fortunes as well as his own failure in the theatre and continual 'friction' with the literary marketplace, the "bitter grief" of which Michael Anesko so thoroughly recounts (Anesko 162). In his notebooks, James describes himself as having "been exactly the martyr and victim of [...] that long vain study to take the measure above-mentioned, to 'meet' the vulgar need, to violate his intrinsic conditions [...] I lost my place—my letters weren't wanted" (*Notebooks* 110). In the fall of 1900, rather than leave England for his usual peripatetic travels, James instead installed himself in Rye, beyond the reach of social entanglements, and set to work. Past fifty, wounded by his failures and those of his siblings, James thought deeply about the past, and faced a reckoning of sorts, as evidenced by his elegiac tone in a letter to Morton Fullerton that he was "face to face at my age, with every successive lost opportunity (wait till you've reached it!) and with the steady, swift movement of the ebb of the great tide—the great tide of which one will never see the turn." Referencing Strether's speech to Little Bilham from *The Ambassadors* that he was then in the midst of writing for later serialization, James added ominously, "The grey years gather; the arid spaces lengthen, damn them—or at any rate don't shorten; what doesn't come doesn't, and what goes *does*" (Edel *Henry James IV* 169). Strether had said to Little Bilham, "What one loses, one loses, make no mistake about that." While William Dean Howells may have been his original prototype for Strether, here James identifies himself with his hapless protagonist during the imaginative phase of constructing his novel, before having put pen to paper.

Failure in *The Ambassadors* parallels failure in *Louis Lambert*, both linked to the overarching sense of failure in the James family, particularly in regard to money and "business." After his arrival in Paris, Louis writes to his uncle, his sole surviving relative, "*Cher oncle, je vais bientôt quitter ce pays, où je ne saurais vivre. Je n'y vois aucun homme aimer ce que j'aime, s'occuper de ce qui m'occupe, s'étonner de ce qui m'étonne. Forcé de me replier sur moi-même, je me creuse et souffre. [...] Ici le point de départ en tout est l'argent. Il faut de l'argent [...]*" [Dear Uncle,—I shall soon be leaving this part of the world, where I could never bear to live. I find no one here who likes what I like, who works at my work, or is amazed at what amazes me. Thrown back on myself, I eat my heart out in misery... Here, money is the mainspring of everything. Money is indispensable [...]" (646-47). Representing Balzac's and James's failure in business, Lambert laments that "*Je manque essentiellement de la constante attention nécessaire à qui veut faire fortune. Toute enterprise mercantile, toute obligation de demander de l'argent à autrui, me conduirait à mal [...]* " [I am absolutely devoid of the constant attention indispensable to the making of a fortune. Any mercantile venture, any need for using other people's money would bring me to grief [...].] (647). Like his protagonist, Balzac was desperate for money, constantly in debt and living monastically in his garret while roaming the Parisian streets as a nighttime *flâneur*. Balzac's difficulties did not end with his successful entry into the literary world after publication of his first masterpiece, *La Peau de Chagrin*, in 1831. In fact, the ostensible reason for his penning of *Louis Lambert* was as a refutation to his enemies' assertions of his ineptitude and even possible madness. As he writes to his future wife Madame Hanska in a letter quoted by James in a review of Balzac's letters, *Louis Lambert* would be "a work in which I have striven to rival Goethe and Byron, Faust and Manfred. I don't know whether I shall succeed, but the fourth volume of the 'Philosophical Tales' must be a last reply to my enemies and give the presentiment of an incontestable superiority" ("*Correspondance de H. de Balzac*" 76).

James notes in this same essay, "We constantly feel that his work would have been greatly better if the Muse of 'business' had been elbowed away by her larger-browed sister. Balzac himself, doubtless, often felt in the same way; but, on the whole, 'business' was what he most cared for" ("*Correspondance de H. de Balzac*" 82). What James discusses in this essay is a duality in Balzac, wondering "what concern the poet has with so much arithmetic and so much criticism, so many statistics and documents" and conversely "what concern the critic and the economist have with so many passions, characters and adventures" (*Notes on Novelists* 114). James agrees with French critic Hippolyte Taine that Balzac was "an artist doubled with a man of business" (118). In this discussion of Balzac's duality as both artist and "man of business," James uses "business" in both its literal and figurative sense, as denoting the vocation of mercantilism but also metaphorically as significant occupation, be it commercial or artistic. Balzac embodies the literal definition of businessman in his desire to be "the impassioned economist and surveyor, the insatiate general inquirer and reporter" (117). Balzac is also business-like in his obsession with money, "'Things' for him are francs and centimes more than any others, and I give up as inscrutable, unfathomable, the nature, the peculiar avidity of his interest in them" (120). But James contrasts this faculty of economic preoccupation with art, asking "again and again what then is the use on Balzac's scale of the divine faculty. The imagination, as we all know, may be employed up to a certain point in inventing uses for money; but its office beyond that point is surely to make us forget that anything so odious exists" (120). James, in other words, ultimately rejects Balzac's "business" and recognizes his "divine faculty," equating imagination with something sacred and holy. Indeed, Balzac possesses for James "the inner vision all the while wide-awake, the vision for which ideas are as living as facts and assume an equal intensity" (116). This "inner vision" making ideas "as living as facts" is what matters most to James. By the end of the essay, James has transposed "business" from its literal to its figurative sense as endeavor. James writes that "we can think, frankly, of no one else with an equal amount of business on his hands," referring to the gargantuan project of *La Comédie Humaine* as a whole. He adds, "It is the whole business in fine—that grand total to which he proposed to himself to do high justice—that gives him his place apart, makes him, among the novelists, the largest weightiest presence" (121).

It is just this transposition of the meaning of "business," and its related cognates "office" and "errand," from the literal to the figurative that James enacts in *The Ambassadors*. This rhetorical legerdemain ties Balzac the artist to Strether and, most important, ties them both to James and his own larger project, his version of the "Human Comedy" as "American Human Comedy." Here we must return to James's own obsession with "business." As Kristeva reminds us, novels are "the result of a redistribution of several sign-systems: carnival, courtly poetry, scholastic discourse" (Kristeva 111). James's essays on Balzac have a bearing on his fiction, are implicit commentary on it, as are his two actual autobiographies, *A Small Boy and*

Others (1913) and *Notes of a Son and Brother* (1914). James's preoccupation with business is tied to his sense of failure, in particular his family's ineptitude in business. As James confesses in *A Small Boy and Others*, "our consciousness was positively disfurnished, as that of young Americans went, of the actualities of 'business' in a world of business. As to that we all formed together quite a monstrous exception; business in a world of business was the thing we most agreed [...] in knowing nothing about" (*Autobiography* [1956] 35).

In his oscillation between literal and figurative meanings of "business" in *The Ambassadors*, James employs a discourse central to the myth of America and enters an historic debate over the meaning of American statehood. Both Emerson and Thoreau in their now-classic works of American literature transpose "business" from its literal to its figurative sense to stage a polemic against the fusion in American culture of the sacred and the secular going back to John Winthrop's sermon "A Model of Christian Charity," given as the Arbella sailed into Boston harbor in 1630, followed by Crevecoeur's *Letters from an American Farmer* and Ben Franklin's *Autobiography*. Franklin uses the word "business" no less than 130 times in his short autobiography, most famously in the first instance of American public relations and advertising, as he discloses "to show that I was not above my business, I sometimes brought home the paper I purchased at the stores through the streets on a wheelbarrow" (77). Franklin, in fact, connects virtue not only to industry but also to wealth, deftly mixing American success with piousness through his compendium of aphorisms known as *Poor Richard's Almanac* that he filled, "with proverbial sentences, chiefly such as inculcated industry and frugality, as the means of procuring wealth, and thereby securing virtue; it being more difficult for a man in want, to act always honestly" (163).

Thoreau challenges this unholy American obsession with business in *Walden* (1854), where he parodies Franklin's industriousness by using the discourse of American business for his life in nature. With implicit reference to Franklin, Thoreau repeatedly uses the word "business" in the opening chapter entitled "Economy," another word he uses ironically as for him it signifies understanding "the cost of a thing is the amount of what I will call life which is required to be exchanged for it [...]" (28). Thoreau writes "How many mornings, summer and winter, before yet any neighbor was stirring about his business, have I been about mine!" Rather than ply the usual trade of farmer, lawyer, or merchant, Thoreau was "anxious to improve the nick of time, and notch it on my stick too"; or was "trying

11. The Ambassadors   135

to hear what was in the wind, to hear and carry it express"; or "was the self-appointed inspector of snow storms and rain storms, and did my duty faithfully." Making fun of the small-town bureaucrats already in existence in 1854, Thoreau concludes "I went on thus for a long time [...] faithfully minding my business, till it became more evident that my townsmen would not after all admit me into the list of town officers, nor make my place a sinecure with a moderate allowance" (16). Thoreau continues in this vein, using the words "trade," "enterprise," and "capital" ironically, culminating in his assertion,

> Finding that my fellow-citizens were not likely to offer me any room in the court house, or any curacy or living anywhere else, but I must shift for myself, I turned my face more exclusively than ever to the woods, where I was better known. I determined to go into business at once, and not wait to acquire the usual capital [...] (17).

Counter to the example of Boston worthies who engaged in the famous New England-China trade in "some small counting house on the coast, in some Salem harbor," Thoreau "thought that Walden Pond would be a good place for business" (18).

In *The Ambassadors*, James re-enacts Thoreau's parody of Franklin by his metaphorical use of the word "business" and classic business nomenclature, situating his late novel in the tradition of radical American resistance literature and connecting his own work to that of his father's contemporaries in the Transcendental movement. James employs the word "business" no less than fifty times in *The Ambassadors*, like Thoreau using the word as an implicit critique of Franklin's reductive mercantile mode of existence and its more strident manifestations in James's own Gilded Age. James alerts his reader to the significance of the metaphorical versus actual meaning of "business" in his Preface to *The Ambassadors* by calling his vocation "the business of my tale" and specifying that *The Ambassadors*, as opposed to *The Wings of the Dove*, is "this other business" (34-5). He goes on to define his art through this figurative use of the word:

> No privilege of the teller of tales and the handler of puppets is more delightful, or has more of the suspense and the thrill of a game of difficulty breathlessly played, than just this business of looking for the unseen and the occult, in a scheme half-grasped, by the light or, so to speak, by the clinging scent, of the gage already in hand (36).

Continuing with what approaches an extended metaphor or "conceit," James likens his expansion of the original germ of his tale to "the business that can least be likened to the chase with horn and hound. It's all a sedentary part—involves as much ciphering, of sorts, as would merit the highest salary paid to a chief accountant [...] He sows his seed at the risk of too thick a crop; wherefore yet again, like the gentlemen who audit ledgers, he must keep his head at any price" (38).

For James, as for Strether, the "business" of America is the 'errand into the wilderness,' which would be defined by James as art and life itself, not the errand chosen by Mrs. Newsome to return Chad to the Woollett mills. James had a lot at stake in *The Ambassadors*, enacting therein the struggle in America over the essential meaning of its creed and the parallel struggle for James to prove the validity of his family's mode of existence. Establishing the dialogic relation between *Louis Lambert* and *The Ambassadors*, we travel along three parallel strands of Kristeva's "synchronic literary corpus," that of the European *Künstlerroman*, the non-fiction American autobiography that includes Franklin, Thoreau, and James, but also, more fundamentally, the psychic autobiographies of Balzac and James imported into their works on the symbolic level, where literature happens. Kristeva's concept of intertextuality thus allows us a deeper reading of James's text as it speaks across vertical literary space to his French master Balzac.

12. A Discordance Between the Self and the World: The Collector in Balzac's *Cousin Pons* and James's 'Adina'

Simone Francescato

In a lengthy essay published in *The Galaxy* in 1875, Henry James praised Honoré de Balzac as an unsurpassed master of characterisation, underlining how much of the French master's extraordinary achievement sprang from his "mighty passion for things" (*Criticism* 52). For James, Balzac's characters were so vivid because he knew how to 'paint' with amazing precision the concrete details of their environment,[1] achieving so strong an effect that "it [was] hard to imagine how the power of physical evocation [could] go farther […]"(53). Being himself "a profound connoisseur" (50) in matters of house decoration and bric-à-brac, Balzac also managed to infuse his characters with an insatiable craving for exclusive possessions, making the latter the 'prime motor' behind all their actions.[2] The impressive portrait of the unfortunate and refined collector in his late novel *Cousin Pons* (1847) must have been a crucial source of inspiration for a writer as obsessed with collecting and collectors as James.[3] Although Balzac's influence resurfaces

---

[1] See, for instance, James's discussion of the tenants of the Maison Vauquer in Balzac's *Père Goriot* (*Criticism* 52).

[2] Balzac's skillful representation of material desire was so great that it almost compensated for the neglect of moral concern that James so much deplored in his writings.

[3] Unforgettable figures like Gilbert Osmond in *The Portrait of a Lady*, Adela Gereth in *The Spoils of Poynton* and Adam Verver in *The Golden Bowl* are all examples of this obsession.

more or less everywhere in the work of the American writer, my paper hypothesises and focuses on the influence of *Cousin Pons* on James's early story 'Adina,' written just one year before James's first important critical essay on Balzac.[4]

Balzac's introduces the protagonist of his novel as an old man in his sixties, strolling in the Boulevard des Italiens in the Paris of 1844. Pons gives the impression of being remarkably isolated from the world he lives in, almost as if time for him has stopped in the 1810's: his clothes and manners, in fact, are presented as a "caricature" of the fashions of the old French Empire. Pons's eccentric attitude—a strange combination of ugliness and melancholy—derives from a stigma which has followed him since birth and Balzac defines as the cruellest of all afflictions—the inability to please [*"le plus cruel de tous les malheurs: ne pouvoir plaire!"*] (401). Although kindhearted, dreamy, and sensitive, Pons is so unattractive that he has never had any success with women and is condemned to lead the solitary life of a bachelor. The sad discordance between Pons's inner self and the outer world—between his aching for love, beauty, and recognition, and the impossibility of getting them—is the existential drama which Balzac places at the very root of his hero's extraordinary achievement as collector.

The event which starts Pons's collecting is indeed his failure to be recognised as a creator of beauty. Having been a gifted and talented composer of romances in his youth (402), Pons spent many years in Rome, sent by his government, to become a great musician. But shortly after his return to Paris, he sees his career rapidly stopped by the castrating bureaucracy which rules competitions in his country [*"Il montrait gratis une des nombreuses victimes du fatal et funeste système nommé Concours qui règne encore en France après cent ans de pratique sans résultat"* (402): "He exhibited gratis one of the many victims of that baneful and disastrous system called Concours,—a system of competition in educational institutions which has ruled in France for over a hundred years without beneficial results."][5] and by an unexpected change in musical taste, increasingly dominated by German and Italian production [*"bientôt noyé dans les flots d'harmonie allemande, et dans la production rossinienne"* (403): "fated to be drowned

---

4 Quotes from the texts are taken from Honoré de Balzac, *Cousin Pons* in *La Comédie Humaine*, 1999, and Henry James, *The Tales of Henry James*, 1978. Page numbers are indicated within brackets.
5 The English translation of portions of the original French text, here and throughout this study, is taken from Katharine Prescott Wormeley 1896 translation of Balzac's work (Boston, Robert Bros., 1898).

12. Balzac's Cousin Pons and James's 'Adina'   139

erelong in floods of German harmony and Rossinian opera"]. His long sojourn in Italy, however, saves him from despair. In Rome, in fact, Pons develops a taste for antiques and works of art which rapidly turns into an incontrollable [*"féroce"* (403)] collecting mania.

Art-collecting soon becomes for Pons an activity that rewards him for his crumbled dreams of fame in the music world, giving him the chance to withdraw from a disappointing reality and to build himself a secret refuge of secluded and protected beauty. Since reality never comes up to the high standard of his ideals [*"les choses de la vie toujours au-dessous du type idéal qu'il s'en était créé"* (403): "the things of life lower than the ideal standard he had created for them in his own mind"] producing a kind of "discordance" with the mellow music of his soul [*"discordance entre le son de son âme et les réalités"* (403)], Pons experiences his collection as a safe space where no discordance is allowed between the Ego and the material world—that is, where any frustration is systematically excluded. Although this helps Pons preserve his inner balance, it reinforces in him a tendency towards isolation, already manifested by his limited skills as composer. As evident in the following passage, the musical analogy is recurrent in the novel and provides interesting information about the collector's psychology:

> [Pons] avouait naïvement sa faiblesse relativement à l'harmonie: il avait négligé l'étude du Contrepoint; et l'orchestration moderne, grandie outre mesure, lui parut inabordable au moment où, par de nouvelles études, il aurait pu se maintenir parmi les compositeurs modernes, devenir, non pas Rossini, mais Hérold. Enfin, il trouva dans les plaisirs du collectionneur de si vives compensations à la faillite de la gloire, que s'il lui eut fallu choisir entre la possession de ses curiosités et le nom de Rossini, le croirait-on? Pons aurait opté pour son cher cabinet (404).[6]

Pons's predilection, as composer, for the lyrical genre of the romance—a solo performance at odds with the complexity of modern orchestration—emerges in the text as a metaphor for the collector's inability to *harmonise* [*"sa faiblesse relativement à l'harmonie"*] with the complexity of a world [*"l'orchestration moderne, grandie outre mesure, lui parut inabordable"* (403):

---

[6] "...but in truth he honestly admitted his weakness on the score of harmony; he had neglected the study of counterpoint, and modern orchestration, grown utterly beyond his knowledge, became inscrutable to him at the very moment when by fresh study he should have kept himself to the level of modern composers and become, not indeed a Rossini, but a Hérold. However, he found such lively compensation in the joys of a collector for his failure as to musical fame, that if he had been forced to choose between his treasures and the glory of Rossini, he would—can it be believed?—have decided in favor of his beloved bric-á-brac."

"modern orchestration, grown utterly beyond his knowledge, became inscrutable to him] which constantly threatens his self-esteem. The ever-renewed compensation [*"vive compensation"*] offered by art-collecting is a way for Pons to get his portion of pleasure without ever compromising with a reality that he perceives as distant and hostile. Behind every purchase for his refined collection, in fact, it is easy to recognise something like a *repeated act of revenge* against life that has unjustly deprived him of physical beauty and of the advantages that derive from it. Like someone fallen victim to some secret habit [*"bien élevé en proie à quelque vice secret"* (401): "of good breeding now the prey of some secret vice"], Pons gets his portion of happiness not so much from the objects that he possesses, but from the feeling that he has managed to pay nothing for them. As Balzac explains, in fact, the pleasure of purchasing bric-à-bracs comes always second to the pleasure of a successful negotiation [*"le plaisir d'acheter des curiosités n'est que le second, le premier c'est de les brocanter"* (405): "The pleasure of buying curios is second only to the superior joy of bartering them"]. But it is important to stress that Pons's collecting is far from being compromised by 'vulgar' interest, as he does not care at all about the commercial value of his possessions. Like his fellow collector Sauvageot, Pons loves his objects as if they were a beautiful mistress [*"une belle maîtresse"* (405)] who never grows old and is always willing to please him. His private museum, in fact, is so precious because it materialises a longed-for personal history which, unlike his real one, conforms to his inner desires.[7]

Pons's eccentric attachment to his material belongings exemplifies Balzac's view of the consumerist turn that French metropolitan society (*Cousin Pons* is a Parisian novel *par excellence*) was taking in the middle of the 19th century. At that time, collecting rapidly became one of the distinctive practices of a rising middle class struggling to fill the idiosyncratic gap between being and having, between reality and desire, through the appropriation of enviable objects. Balzac was quite cynical on the success ultimately allowed by this tendency, seeing it largely as a form of self-deceit:

> Aux premiers contours de cette esquisse biographique, tout le monde va s'écrier: " Voilà, malgré sa laideur, l'homme le plus heureux de la terre ! "
> En effet, aucun ennui, aucun spleen ne résiste au moxa qu'on se pose à l'âme en se donnant une manie. Vous tous qui ne pouvez plus boire à ce que, dans tous les temps, on a nommé la coupe du plaisir, prenez à tache

---

[7] This materialisation is the individual counterpart of the institutionalisation of fictitious history performed by public museums in the 19th century. See Sherman and Rogoff, *xii*.

de collectionner quoi que ce soit (on a collectionné des affiches !), et vous retrouverez le lingot du bonheur en petite monnaie. Une manie, c'est le plaisir passé à l'état d'idée ! Néanmoins, n'enviez pas le bonhomme Pons, ce sentiment reposerait, comme tous les mouvements de ce genre, sur une erreur.

Cet homme, plein de délicatesse, dont l'âme vivait par une admiration infatigable pour la magnificence du Travail humain, cette belle lutte avec les travaux de la nature, était l'esclave de celui des sept péchés capitaux que Dieu doit punir le moins sévèrement: Pons était gourmand (405-06)[8].

In this passage collecting emerges as the pathological symptom [*"une manie"*][9] of the alienation which dominates bourgeois society. Being an activity kept separate from ordinary occupations and practised in the intimacy of one's spare time (we must remember that Pons is, first of all, a very modest music teacher and composer), collecting guarantees a perverse enjoyment which can never be attacked by the frustrations of external reality. But even when pleasure appears to be successfully transferred from the plane of concreteness to the "plane of ideas" [*"à l'état d'idée"* (405)] — Balzac seems to warn the reader — reality always finds strange ways to creep back. In fact, Pons's denial of his contingent existence — that is, of his contemptible body artificially replaced by an extra-refined and enviable collection — is ironically punished by an irrepressible and grotesque gluttony [*"Pons était gourmand"* (406)].

Balzac's disenchanted, and even cynical, portrait of this unfortunate collector captures a crucial moment of 19th-century cultural history: it shows a creator and appreciator of artistic beauty on the brink of degenerating into what we may describe as a refined consumer. Although despising the world he lives in, the refined consumer is unable really to detach himself from it through a real act of subversion (he only pretends to be an artist [*"[Pons] se comportant d'ailleurs en artiste"* (406)] and turns instead into a

---

8 "At the first outline of this biographical sketch, every one will cry out: 'Why, in spite of his ugliness, he must be the happiest man on earth!' True enough: no ennui, no spleen, resists the soothing influence a hobby sheds upon the soul. You, who can drink no longer from that chalice called through all time the 'cup of pleasure,' take up the task of collecting something, no matter what (people have ere now collected handbills), and you will recover your ingots of joy in small change. A hobby, a mania, is pleasure transformed into the shape of an idea. Nevertheless, do not envy the worthy Pons; for if you do, your sentiment, like others of its kind, will rest on error." / "This man of innate delicacy, whose soul lived by its unwearying admiration for the glories of human toil, — that noble struggle with the forces of Nature, — was the slave of a capital sin, albeit the one which God will punish least severely. Pons was a gourmand."
9 See also Pety, 45-8.

parasite who only sometimes manages to entertain the wealthy and the rich on whom he depends ["*la laideur de Pons s'appela donc originalité.* [...] *Lorsque, d'invité perpétuel, par sa décadence comme artiste, à l'état de pique-assiette*" (406-07): "Pons's remarkable ugliness was considered 'originality.' [...] When Pons, falling from reputation as an artist, fell also from the condition of honored guest to that of a poor relation sponging for a dinner on his prosperous friends..."]. By doing so, Balzac tackles in *Cousin Pons* the problematic reversal of producing and consuming which resurfaces some thirty years later, in works like Edmond de Goncourt's *La maison d'un artiste* (1880) — where refined collecting stands out as a prerequisite of — and even as a substitute for — real artistic creation.

This element must have appeared as extraordinarily modern to a writer like James, so concerned with the destiny of art in a world increasingly dominated by the rules of commodification. In his works he saw with preoccupation the late 19th-century ascent of the collector — the most refined type of consumer — as custodian, or even creator, of artistic beauty, and questioned the idea that art objects could be properly appreciated when turned into private collectibles. This is particularly evident in his 1874 short story 'Adina,' where James seems to draw on Balzac's ideas on collecting in *Cousin Pons* to give shape to his protagonist. Set in the beautiful Alban hills in the surroundings of Rome, the story deals with the aesthetic and sentimental apprenticeship of a young American scholar and collector, Sam Scrope, seen through the eyes of a friend, an amateur painter. James's Scrope is significantly younger than Balzac's Pons and decidedly more irreverent and sarcastic, but is on his way to developing the same melancholy cynicism.

Very much as Balzac does in his novel, James's narrator introduces Scrope as an *eccentric* character, describing his passion for rare bric-à-brac as a strange habit ("It was an oddity among his many oddities, but it agreed well enough with the rest of them," 351). He also underlines that "what [Scrope] looked for and relished in old prints and old china was not, generally, beauty of form nor romantic association; it was elaborate and patient workmanship, fine engraving, skillful method" (351). Although this puts Scrope somehow at odds with Pons — much more sensitive to the emotional effect of beauty —, what at first sight appears as a difference, is instead the sign of a common feature. Scrope's predilection for the technical, 'intrinsic' properties of art objects over the effect conveyed by their "romantic association" with their context is, in fact, the evidence of the sharp line he traces—like Pons—between a safe and private universe and a dangerous outer world:

> It was [Scrope's] fancy to pretend that he enjoyed nothing, and that what sentimental travelers call picturesqueness was a weariness to his spirit; but the world was new to him and the charm of fine things often took him by surprise and stole a march on his premature cynicism [...]. The truth was that the picturesque of Italy, both in man and in nature, fretted him, depressed him strangely. He was consciously a harsh note in the midst of so many mellow harmonies; everything seemed to say to him—"Don't you wish you were as easy, as loveable, as carelessly beautiful as we?" In the bottom of his heart he did wish it. To appreciate the bitterness of this dumb disrelish of the Italian atmosphere, you must remember how very ugly the poor fellow was (348-49).

In this passage there recurs the musical analogy featured in Balzac's novel. Like Pons, consciously unable to 'harmonise' with the surrounding world symbolized by contemporary music production, Scrope is unable and unwilling to 'harmonise' with the picturesque beauty of the Italian *campagna* ("he was consciously a harsh note in the midst of so many mellow harmonies" 348) because that would imply for him a confrontation with a reality that constantly reminds him of his physical and psychological shortcomings ("very ugly the poor fellow was" 349).

This resistance is even more significant for a story like this that deals with transatlantic relations, as it manifests a certain kind of paranoid and imperialist American attitude towards the Old Continent. Scrope seems to be the predecessor of other Jamesian characters, like Christopher Newman or Adam Verver, who are unable to enjoy beauty unless they manage to turn it into something to control and possess from a position of *safe detachment from its original context*—especially when the latter takes on 'human' features. This is evident in the key event of the story, when the collector tricks Angelo Beati—a very 'picturesque' poor young Italian man—out of a priceless gem of the Roman period, denying him a proper payment for it. My argument is that Scrope's unfairness towards Angelo derives entirely from his reluctance to recognise any sort of association between the object he would like to own and its possessor. Insensitive to his kindness and friendliness, Scrope perceives Angelo only as an ignorant, dishonest man who has no right to own the jewel—almost as if Angelo and the object actually came from two different dimensions.

Although disguised as an act carried out "in the interest of art, of science, of taste," Scrope's appropriation and methodical restoration of the gem ("he quietly informed himself as if from general curiosity, as to the best methods of cleansing, polishing, and restoring antique gems, laid in a provision of delicate tools and acids, turned the key in his door, and took the measure of his prize," 356) appear instead as the two steps of a *decontamination*, through which to recover an intrinsic value in the object separated as far as possible from Angelo and the "irritating Italian felicity" (356) in which the young man lives. By doing so, the collector indulges in a secret identification with the imagined past materialised by the object (the object contains an image of Emperor Tiberius), dreaming that its possession makes him—and not Angelo—a true descendant of the old and noble Roman race ("Haven't I worked all these days and nights, with my little rags and files to some purpose? I've annulled the centuries—I've resuscitated a *totius orbis imperator* […] It's the finest intaglio in the world. It has told me its secret," 357).

Scrope's decontamination of the ancient gem represents a significant departure from the aesthetic sensibility of "the sentimental traveller" (348) referred to by James—of whom the collector somehow represents the degenerate version. Whereas the sentimental traveler in this story (probably embodied by the narrator) stands out as the participant observer, who respectfully enjoys the picturesqueness of art works, places and people as something leading to an interpersonal growth, Scrope stands out as the forerunner of the modern consumerist tourist who enjoys an ambiguous position of involvement and detachment from every manifestation of alterity. As the sociologist Birgitta Nedelman points out, the distinguishing trait of this figure is that of enjoying an extreme physical proximity to art works, places, and people, but also that of keeping himself well segregated from a more intimate contact with them (Nedelman 193). One of the consequences is that his aesthetic and relational experience is inevitably restricted to the limits of his travel program, his pre-set expectations and—of course—his material appropriations.

James's story features a young American heroine entrusted with the task of revealing and challenging the shortcomings of this attitude. Along with the many female characters who confront unscrupulous male collectors in James's fiction (an obvious example is Isabel Archer vs. Gilbert Osmond), Adina Waddington is a character who has no equal in Balzac—a novelist generally uninterested in placing women in 'redeeming' roles. In the story she does not simply dismiss the collector as a suitable life partner, eloping with his rival Angelo, but she also stands out as the dismantler of Scrope's appreciation of *decontaminated* objects of art. Even before making the acquaintance of Angelo (who perhaps tells her how he was wronged by the collector), Adina is very sceptical about Scrope's manic passion for his gem. By refusing to accept Scrope's gift of the 'stolen' object as love token,[10] the young woman stands out indeed as the spokesperson of a restored dialogue between the self and the world that is deliberately thwarted by the collector.

Starting from the passage describing her visit to Villa Borghese — where she almost disappears behind the walls of the picturesque Park with Angelo — the story registers the woman's progressive *harmonisation* with a human and aesthetic dimension totally inaccessible to her paranoid suitor — to the extent that, in the eyes of the narrator, she even starts taking on the same 'picturesque' tone or attitude that characterises Angelo and the surrounding landscape ("Was she more silent than usual, was she preoccupied, was she melancholy, was she restless? *Picturesquely*, she ought to have been all these things," 369, emphasis mine). In this perspective, Adina embodies a figure that openly resists and challenges the collector's problematic equivalence between possessing and appreciating, reminding us not only of the aesthetic but also the ethical implications of such equivalence.

To conclude, the two works I have analysed can be taken as evidence of the disenchanted view that Balzac and James shared about collecting. Balzac's novel unmasks the collector as someone who only apparently manages to create and preserve artistic beauty, while he is only deeply alienated from reality. James's story goes even further, showing how the collector not only fails to replace human affection and recognition through the possession of art objects, but also contributes to the aesthetic obsolescence — and even to the destruction — of the latter. This is evident in the final part of the story. Once Scrope understands, in fact, that his collectible cannot replace the love of the woman he has lost, he completely loses interest in it, and throws it back forever into the silent waters of the Tiber.

---

10 By doing so, the woman also resists her own objectification and identification — by physical contiguity — with Scrope's treasure. For Adina as collectible, see Izzo *Portraying the Lady* 78-79.

13 'Déjà Vu' in 'The Turn of the Screw'

Max Duperray

I.

Considering hypothetical sources for 'The Turn of the Screw' in terms of generic intertext might show James apparently toying with the great tradition of the English novel and with its undercurrents of society and sex, as exemplified in fantasy (the gothic) or in manners (the realistic novel). Edel's contention is that James's attempt was to enshrine that tradition in his story: "The Brontë's rather than the modern psychological movement nascent in Vienna" (Edel *Stories of the Supernatural* 433, quoted by Perry 62). James would then rank among the practitioners of the tropes familiar among his forerunners in the novel of sentiment and its stereotypes: "the perceiving female subject, the Gothic structures […] and the explained supernatural" (Milbank 159).

One persistent reference is of course to Charlotte Brontë's *Jane Eyre*, insofar as the text of the novella relates to the "governess novel" and to the question of a "mystery" at Bly and its imprisoned inmate. A systematic study (by Alice Hall Petry) has gone a long way in demonstrating the overlap of the two texts, highlighting the concept of the role-playing governess: she would act out the character of Jane, 'The Turn of the Screw' becoming a parody of Charlotte's romantic novel. Millicent Bell, however, maintains that "*Jane Eyre* is an intertextuality which denies its model," meaning its sentimental model (225). T.J. Lustig takes a more radical view: *The Mysteries of Udolpho* and *Jane Eyre* are but "quicksilver glints of what the narrative fails to do" ('The Turn of the Screw' xviii).

The echo of the romantic novel, principally, has become enmeshed with the reader's reception of 'The Turn of the Screw.' James induces the reader to look backwards by pushing the time of his story back to the 1840s when *Jane Eyre* was published. Moreover, he relies on a well-known formula—namely, the isolated heroine confronted by a secret from which she is excluded—and this updates the reader's sense of recognition and sets in motion a search for a definable intention, which is never acknowledged as James keeps aloof from any concrete feedback. Therefore recognition is defamiliarised, as any '*déjà vu*' can be, and becomes paradigmatic in the text, in a hypnotic sort of way. One might say that James's dogged evasiveness tends to place him decidedly "in the reader-response camp," as Edward Parkinson puts it in the "Preface" to his dissertation on the history of the criticism of 'The Turn of the Screw."

Recognition might thus work as a wrong expectation turning sour. James does rely on the assumption of a romantic pretext, in the manner of fables of the supernatural: the listening ladies, in the introduction, precisely ask what the governess's "reward" was—a term reminiscent of *Pamela*. But the answer is: "She never saw him again." Douglas has no title either. He is not entitled to satisfy the public's expectation of yet another romance. From the start the mysticism of a Romantic past is being hollowed out for a modern subject to assert itself within a mysterious halo.

The preface also ushers in reading as an embedded theme. And the heroine follows suit. She refers to the pent-up inmate of *Jane Eyre* and defines mysteries as pertaining to *Udolpho*. More surprisingly, she keeps Fielding's *Amelia* at her bedside. Fielding wrote *Amelia* in the 12-book structure of Virgil's *Aeneid*, which he designated as "the noble model," with a view to writing a modern epic for his time. He notably lifted a line which reads "*Furens quid Foemina possit*" (145) ["what a woman can do in frenzy"]. Mimicry of Virgil's narrative is a parody—but also a reminder—of the epic form. *Amelia* then can be a signpost—not only in the heroine pitted against a background of a corrupt society of deceit, but in the parodic reenactment of older materials—possibly feminine romance revamped in the guise of a near psychic case.

The inserted books also repeat young Jane's mania for reading, notably *Pamela* and *Gulliver's Travels*, i.e. feminine diary vs. epic and masculine expedition. Now if Brontë stages domesticity versus escape into the world by conflating two contradictory connotations, James focuses on the thematisation of reading as visualisation… and reading in the dark to boot. Immersed in old novels, the governess reads characters into being—hence the appeal to archetypal narratives as enduring templates for all fictions.

Now *Jane Eyre* was itself a story told retrospectively, given as autobiography: a romantic story already displacing gothic tropes and deflating them. James makes his novella an alleged manuscript, lost and retrieved—according to the romantic archetype. Ironically, Brontë's feminine fantasy given as a man's piece of work (Currer Bell's) would echo inversely in Henry James's story, given as a woman's narrative. This paradoxical inversion implies that James intentionally framed this *amusette* of his in the terms of a belated pseudo-feminine fiction—tapping into the popular fantasies of the governess to be married off as reward, and of the latent psychic disorders inherent in 'woman as writer'—a tale of possession/dispossession, as if the writer was labouring under a duty of exorcism, of interrogating the past as both familiar and alien.

Writing here harks back to the epistolary mode of Richardson's novel of sentiment and beyond that to the predicaments of the gothic heroine probing the 'secret' of patriarchy. The first-person woman narrator stages her self-interrogation as a desiring subject negotiating the move from "a symbolics of blood to an analysis of sexuality," to take up Hoeveler's words in her study of feminine Gothicism; and she does that notably "through the power of language to dissemble" (*Gothic Feminism* 21-22).

James indeed kept in mind the old sentimental theme of "virtue in distress." Robert Brissenden, a specialist of the genre, asserts that "if Richardson can be called a sentimental novelist so can Henry James" (Brissenden 117). The social and theological tradition of Puritan conduct books, which was vital for Richardson to create a passion of tragic dimension, was thus imported as an undercurrent of the modern story, echoing the old appeal to divine power or Providence in order to foreground the repeated "analysis of mortally intricate and perplexing situations" (Brissenden 119).

Strong ambivalence in the concept of sensibility (more to be feared than desired, as Emily of *Udolpho* would say) fosters the ambiguity of sentimental discourse—secular experience moulded by religious exaltation. This is updated in *Pamela* by the ambiguities of espistolary intercourse being both contact and distance—or by the dubious evangelism of Jane Eyre teaching submission to God in order to withstand Rochester's advances, or opposing Rivers's Calvinistic appeal to the same submission. The governess as both Inquisitor and Saviour of the lost follows the path of her forerunners: Emily St. Aubert overwhelmed by the reenactment of the restless life of Signora Laurentini/ Sister Agnes; Jane facing Bertha, the mad woman, as in a distorting mirror; the conformist versus the carnivalesque. James has conflated the two opposites into one, also relying on the guardian figure of the housekeeper either conniving in misdeeds, like Mrs. Jervis and her evil double Mrs. Jewkes in *Pamela*, or supportive, like Mrs. Fairfax, though she does warn Jane against a wrong alliance.

Epistolary discourse becomes thematised in 'The Turn of the Screw', together with its vacuity: the letters do not reach their intended readers and the ghost (of the other—Miss Jessel) assumes the responsibility for writing—not to mention the issue of the alleged theft of the letter by Miles. It thus repeats frustration in writing moulded by the mystery of the interdict: woman called upon to take responsibility, but excluded from knowledge. In *Jane Eyre* the daughters of the gentry designate governesses as nonexistent 'incubi'—hence the concept of usurpation, woman turning masculine as "oedipal detective, rational seeker of the family's buried secret" (Hoeveler *Gothic Feminism* 32)—while vindicating her position as "orphan," orphans desiring the father's approval as the governess claims the master's agreement.

Emily was similarly summoned to investigate the mysteries of parentage and uphold the demands of patriarchy to protect the domain from dilapidation against the interdict of reading; the problematic instruction of her father reads "save the castle and burn the papers" without looking at them. Both Emily and the governess labour under that interdict which calls for a transgression: Emily does read an excerpt from the fateful papers—"a sentence of dreadful import"—and the governess does write despite the ban on writing; and they both suffer from visitations. Destiny is writ in hieroglyphic terms in *Jane Eyre*.

Topsy-turvidom in gender roles also relates to givens in gender formulae: on the side of a woman's vision are visual theatricals harking back to the masquerades of 18th century novels, Quint parading as a spurious master or whispered mysteries of hauntings, or implicit phrases and a pseudo-maternal legacy (Mrs. Grose), as pitted against the male-oriented letter writing from which the governess is excluded. Disguise and horse play occupy the episode of the ball room in *Jane Eyre* displaying the lesson of the charades: marriage as 'pantomime,' with Rochester as a gypsy and a woman to boot. The carnivalesque blurs vice and virtue. Innuendoes of libidinal pursuits bring the memory of *Amelia* and its masquerade back into the governess's experience. They notably relate to the culture of travesty and implicit sexual disorder. Parentage intricacies and confusing interrelations in *The Mysteries of Udolpho*, elaborate family criss-crossings—in *Jane Eyre*—of disappeared parents or uncles, re-emerge in the status of the nephews and the parental servants as commanding figures. The governess wonders at the children's capacity for "telling her stories, acting her charades, pouncing out at her, in disguises [...]" (*The Turn of the Screw* [1992] 167). She construes them as "Shakespearians, astronomers and navigators" and concludes: "we lived in a cloud of music and affection and success and private theatricals" (168). Midsummer is also the period of emotional crisis in *Jane Eyre*, blurring summer and stormy weather—late summer turning into autumn in "The Turn of the Screw."

The enduring guideline is predicated on the gender-oriented game of power. Studying "repetition and subversion" in the novella, John Pearson writes about "[Kierkegaard's concept of] repetition that maintains patriarchy in the voice and guise of a woman [...]" (Pearson 277). Sexual confusion or role playing thus updates textual anxiety. Jane, orally designated by Rochester as *"la petite mère anglaise"* ["the little English mother"], is imperfect as a maternal surrogate, because she is meant to assume a more important role in the patriarchy.

Remarkably, the master of Thornfield has been the victim of the law of primogeniture, exactly as women were in Victorian society. Masculinity is a dubious model. Jane is confronted with this in her own family, being roughed up at the hands of John Reed and also forced into wedlock by yet another cousin and another John, St. John Rivers. James's governess is similarly confronted with sinister resumptions of masculine legacies, Quint and Miles. Usurpation hovers above the empowerment of the evil servants or of the gradually more libidinous governess and her usage of metaphoric, pseudo heroic language, incongruous in a now realistic and secular context.

The underlying contradiction between self-effacement and egoistic heroism also informs the novel of sentiment. In both *Jane Eyre* and 'The Turn of the Screw' the school-room is a tantalising refuge for self-reflexivity. That is where Jane draws in chalk a self-portrait to materialise her introspective guilt and James's governess faces the feminine ghost as a writing double. Self-sufficiency had already made of Jane Eyre the solitary and withdrawn "eccentric," as Virginia Woolf has it (155-61), connecting to her fancied mother as the moon, when she calls upon her to flee temptation. She courts the shade and puzzles good Mrs. Fairfax, unable as she finds herself "to draw her out" (Brontë 100). The recipe for James's governess lies there. More profoundly Jane links to death from the Red Room episode onwards, by identifying with death from Lowood to Moor House. She contaminates

St. John, who will long for his own death in chapter 38. In the same way, James's governess utters her doomsday-like discourse of exorcism, sitting on "a low table-like tomb" (*The Turn of the Screw* [1992] 152) to ponder her situation, before she ultimately becomes the actual agent of death—that being mediated through *fin de siècle* sensibility.

II.

Now the concept of the lost form expands within that of the phasing out of the plot of intricate and piled up family narratives. Criticism has noted this disappearance: "The governess's frustration is a frustration of plot" (Bell 228); "The governess is in pursuit of the story itself" (Bersani "The Jamesian Lie" 65, quoted by Bell 227). Hence the alluring hidden plot which corresponds to James's avowed purpose: to make the reader imagine and connect him to the un-nameable. Whereas Currer Bell (Brontë xx) claimed responsibility in unveiling sham and underlining cant, James disclaims responsibility in downgrading the seriousness of his enterprise. The story as plot fades back into a ghostly concept of metonymic anxiety, and this calls up the 'fading' of the subject as a self in the making.

The very spectrality of the tale is obtained through the receding perspective of loss, the governess herself being affected by that fading impression—as when she depicts the evenings at Bly "in the ebbing actual, an extraordinarily sweet sadness" (*The Turn of the Screw* [1992] 215). Romantic closure is replaced by a poetics of uncertainty, but also by nearly explicit murder, whatever its nature is.

James more emphatically designated, in his preface to the New York Edition, those "simple" narratives—children's tales—of gruesome tricksters and ogres. Thus the primeval narratives and the sophisticated fiction of the great tradition merge into one and the same thing, reenacting mental categories, not so much for a discriminate emphasis on one definite type of narrative but for an all-inclusive reference to the essence of narration as repetition of things past—"the shadow of a shadow" (148). His heroine bears testimony to that paradigm: "such a place as would [...] take all colour out of story-books and fairy-tales." The castle, a "big ugly antique but convenient house," characteristically becomes "half-displaced, half utilised" (127).

James frames his story in the ellipical way of a repeated fairy-tale with its gingerbread castle and its little grandees, princes of the blood, with the air of knowing nothing but love (134 and 136). Yet children's books like Grimm's tales highlight the relevance of children as willful participants of bloody victimisation.

This very much updates the principles of 'déjà vu'. Terry Castle, in *The Female Thermometer*, argues that "The principle of dejà vu dominates both the structure of human relations and the phenomenology of reading" (Castle 127). Lisa Chinitz, studying the shift from fairy tale into ghost story, maintains that "The governess's narrative is punctuated by a series of repetitions that reminds us of the primitive compulsion to repeat and that induces an anxiety by which we rehearse our efforts to master the fear of death it awakens" (270). Rehearsing the episode of the ghost behind the glass, the governess exclaims: "I had the full image of the *repetition* of what had already occurred" (143, emphasis mine).

Abandoned children in *Jane Eyre*—Jane dreaming she lets a child fall from her lap—and motherly uncanniness in the 'The Turn of the Screw' rehearse that fear: the image of the sequestered woman as "the vampire life in death" underlines a conflation of old stories with modern neurosis. The object of fear has faded away like the beliefs in supernatural occurrences, but the problem of language as dissemblance has remained—the old overlapping the new.

Repetition is intertext—for example, in the way it recalls *Amelia* in the dramatising of homilies and of aphorisms notably about Fear, Love, and Truth (*Amelia* Book VI *iv*); repetition is neurosis, 'déjà vu' as hysteria in confronting otherness. The text invites recognition but foregrounds itself as spectral heroines seen "through a glass darkly."

As a result, fear does not spring so much, as in the poetics of Todorov, from assessing the competition between the believable and the unbelievable, as from the enduring repetition of the age-old anxiety of dispossession and usurped empowerment. Though no so romantic as older romances of elaborate plots, it has a dialectic that haunts its romantic antecedents as a necessary but displaced backdrop.

So 'The Turn of the Screw' is neither a parody nor sheer denial ("*Jane Eyre* glissades into 'The Turn of the Screw' only to signal the later text's derivations"), but a transcript of romantic sinister overtones as archetypal. Stripping them of their anecdotal substance, elliptically repeated, leaves the uncanny as the upshot of hollowing out both social messages and mystical beliefs in the redemption of literary textuality.[1] The assumption is

---

1 This being predicated on intertextuality, which Jean Perrot sees as imparting a

that repetition becomes the very substance of the heroine writing about the transmission of "ur-texts" and substantiating thereby her hysterical *'déjà vu'* embedded in the templates of primitive 'child-like' stories.

---

special tonality to narration: "[L'intertextualité donne] à la narration l'ambigüité d'un tapis complexe dans lequel l'écrivain semble avoir inscrit son secret" (Perrot 235).

IV:
ALLUSION

14. Some Allusions in the Early Stories

Angus Wrenn

The earliest of James's stories which he was willing to reprint in the New York Edition, "A Passionate Pilgrim," begins not with James's own words but with an allusion to William Shakespeare. By the strict definition of the Oxford English Dictionary (OED),[1] where the term is defined as "a covert, implied, or indirect reference," James's title only just qualifies as an allusion rather than a straight quotation, since Shakespeare's *The Passionate Pilgrim* becomes James's "A Passionate Pilgrim." By the standards of the OED many of the examples which will be adduced in this paper constitute direct, overt references and quotations rather than indirect allusions, where the later author makes some form of adaptation to the original wording. However it will also be shown that James himself understood the term in a more general and inclusive sense. In some instances the source of the words imported into James's text is fully acknowledged by James himself. Therefore the field of reference is here widened from pure allusions to something more general, partly because the context in which the words are reproduced is every bit as relevant as the actual words of the quotation, reference, or allusion by themselves.

To use another writer's title as the title for your own is a phenomenon worthy of examining in its own right. William Irwin says that "An allusion may be said to be a reference which is indirect in the sense that it calls for associations that go beyond mere substitution of a referent" (Irwin 521). To call a short story, as here, "A Passionate Pilgrim," referring to the early sequence, chiefly of sonnets, published in Shakespeare's name, has one set of implications. Many readers who have never even read the sequence will

---

[1] In the OED (1989 348-49), the entry for the verb 'to allude' brings in the etymology from the Latin *'ludus'* and with it the suggestion of the playful.

still know it as one of Shakespeare's works. The use will therefore evoke certain associations even when the reader has no more knowledge than that. Giving a work, as with Eliot's *The Waste Land*, a title derived from a passage in Malory's *Morte d'Arthur* (Book 17, Ch. 3), in which the phrase lifted is hardly the most memorable in the work, will produce comparable associations only if readers know the whole of the original intimately (Southam 72). Furthermore, the general degree of knowledge among readers changes over time. The phrase, since Eliot adopted it as his title, has an altogether different range of reference from that enjoyed in its original context. Miranda's line "O brave new world" in *The Tempest*, though already of some considerable significance within Shakespeare's play, now arguably brings with it a whole array of other, dystopian associations, essentially thanks to Huxley's novel of that name, which they never had in the original seventeenth century context.[2] James's "A Passionate Pilgrim" comes close to simply borrowing Shakespeare's title in its entirety without any adaptation to the new circumstances in which it is to be used. By contrast Alan Bennett's *Me, I'm Afraid of Virginia Woolf* is an allusion to Edward Albee's *Who's Afraid of Virginia Woolf?* (which is in turn an allusion to the oral children's tale, *Who's Afraid of the Big Bad Wolf?*, and therefore possibly an allusion without being a literary allusion).

Since the author involved is Shakespeare, perhaps the ultimate canonical figure, "A Passionate Pilgrim" is a title replete with associations, and by 1908 those associations had only multiplied for James. It of course has extra associations when an American writer, the heir, as such, of the Pilgrim Fathers, gives it to his own short story, and all the more so when that story, as here, concerns an expatriate making the pilgrimage in reverse to reclaim his inheritance in the Old World—associations which had not been available to Shakespeare himself. By 1907 the sense that his career had been a pilgrimage had of course only intensified, and by this date James had also made further allusions in his work to that of William Shakespeare. His 1900 short story "The Birthplace" had been concerned with—although it always remains allusive because the bard remains unnamed other than

---

[2] Other examples, from the many which might be cited where later authors seize for their titles upon relatively less-known phrases by earlier writers include Steinbeck's quotation of *Mice and Men* (Burns); Huxley's use of Marlowe's *Edward II* for *Antic Hay*; Hardy's use of a phrase from Gray's *Elegy In A Country Churchyard* in *Far From the Madding Crowd*; and Forster's use of Whitman's 1874 poem on the opening of the Suez Canal (hardly his most quoted) for the title of *A Passage to India*. In each case the later work has surely eclipsed the earlier.

as 'He' (like the deity)—the guardianship of Shakespeare's birthplace in Stratford-upon-Avon. And by this date James himself knew Sidney Lee, one of the great Shakespeare scholars of his day, who had indeed edited "A Passionate Pilgrim." So what looks like a wholesale borrowing of a title, unadapted, may well be, on closer inspection of the context, highly allusive.[3] It was one thing for James to use the title "A Passionate Pilgrim" in 1873, when he was still relatively young and had yet to make the decision to settle permanently in Europe. By 1907 the title becomes an allusion beyond the action of the tale to which it is given, to the history of James's own life as an expatriate.

In 1882 James's short story "The Siege of London" again has a title which possesses allusive qualities, although this time the allusions are not to literature so much as to real life and the history of his own times. For in 1870-1871, the Prussians had laid siege to Paris during the Franco-Prussian War. By the end of that war the attack on Paris became the siege of Montmartre and the Paris Commune by French Government forces. Just a dozen years later, James is using it ironically, in a story whose Parisian inspiration he mentioned on several occasions both in his notebooks and later in the New York Edition Prefaces, here perhaps bathetically, to refer to Mrs. Headway's assault upon polite London society. It may be ventured that this is arguably an allusion in dubious taste. After all, thousands had died, or been reduced to extreme privations in the putting down of the Commune. And the questionable taste of the allusion, as will be shown, is intensified by the fact that the literary references it contains, much more than to London, are to French literature and Parisian society.[4]

Inside the texts of James's fiction the next question to address is not so much identification of the exact words involved in any reference or allusion, and how they may differ from the original, but the context in which the reference or allusion occurs and what its effect may be. Irwin says that allusion can be used "to instruct an audience, to generate an

---

[3] James alludes to Shakespeare repeatedly within the story, echoing *Macbeth*, *Hamlet*, *Measure for Measure*, *The Merchant of Venice* and *Othello*. On the latter especially, see G. Melchiori's "Locksley Hall Revisited," *Review of English Literature* 6 (October 1965), 9-25. There are, in addition, important allusions to Cervantes, Smollett and Fanny Burney. (See Christina Albers, *A Reader's Guide to the Short Stories of Henry James* 1997, 671-72)

[4] After all, James's literary inspiration for this short story is Alexandre Dumas *fils*'s play *Le Demi-Monde* (1855) (acknowledged in the Prefaces to the New York Edition), where a comparable woman with a dubious past, Madame d'Ange, had 'besieged' polite Parisian society by endeavouring to make an opportunistic marriage.

aesthetic experience in an audience, and to link or connect the author with a tradition by activating themes, motifs, and symbols" (Irwin 521).

It makes a major difference whether the reference or allusion is made by the author (James) in a tale which is told in the third person, or by a character taking part in the story who is also narrating it in the first person, or alternatively by a character in the story who is not, however, the principal consciousness from whose point of view the story is seen. These all constitute different ways of instructing the audience.

James's fiction invariably gains from a frame of reference which includes the writers who formed the staple reading both of the educated British of James's class, and also their counterparts, the same educated classes in New England.[5] At the same time, Pierre Walker has observed that James reviewed French as frequently as he did English literature (Walker xi). It was at least as much a source of influence upon him. James is not averse to inserting French phrases into his own English prose. As Edwin Fussell has remarked: one can sometimes be forgiven for thinking that a James novel is actually a translation into English from an unknown French original, with a few phrases left in the original language to give local colour (Fussell *The French Side* 141). But in fact the language distinction does have an influence upon his use of the many French novels and short stories which James read from early adolescence onwards. The influence of these French texts upon James often takes forms other than direct lifting of a phrase, but which are arguably every bit as pervasive.

It is worth considering the way in which James himself understood the term "allusion." While the OED talks of "covert, implied, indirect, often passing reference," *Chambers Twenty-First Century Dictionary* describes an allusion as "any indirect reference to something else" and gives a supplementary definition in literary theory of an allusion as "a reference either explicit or veiled, to something else which an author uses deliberately, aware that only readers who are 'in the know' will understand it" (32).

Although this may seem a charter for imprecision James himself appears to have used the term "allusion" in this wide, inclusive way. Littlemore, one of the characters in "The Siege of London," describes the position of power in which he finds himself in relation to Mrs. Headway, who is in fear of being exposed as a woman with a past, which prompts his friend Waterville to refer directly to the Dumas *fils* drama written in 1855, *Le Demi-Monde*:

---

[5] I am indebted to Philip Horne for sight of his essay "Henry James and the Poetry of Association" [private communication]. For a comprehensive discussion of the phenomenon of allusion, see Gérard Genette 1982, 169-76.

"'You're in the position of Olivier de Jalin, in the *Demi-Monde*,' Waterville remarked. 'In the *Demi-Monde*?' Littlemore was not quick at catching literary allusions" (182). Here the narrator—James himself—classifies this direct reference as an allusion.

It has important implications, in James's narratives, whether the literary reference is made by the narrator—sometimes anonymous, as if it were James himself, or by a character in the story being told. In "The Siege of London" James allows one of the characters to suggest the parallel between the 'real life' of the narrative in which they find themselves and fiction, a play which two characters in the plot have both viewed.

In a tale from the previous decade, "The Madonna of the Future," James introduced the idea of basing the action of his own tale upon some previous work by another author, also French—in this case Honoré de Balzac, perhaps the French novelist whom James revered above all others. Here the story James tells of Theobald—an American expatriate artist in Florence, who passes his entire career, as he himself says, as a "dawdler," never getting round to painting the ideal portrait of his favoured model, who ends up too aged any longer to serve her purpose—is closely based, although with key differences of emphasis, upon Balzac's short story "*Le Chef-d'oeuvre inconnu*" of 1832. Balzac's tale itself purports to be, as it were, historical fiction, with two of its characters real-life seventeenth-century French painters, Nicolas Poussin and François Porbus. Moreover Poussin is not just classical but, coming after the high watermark of the renaissance, a neo-classicist—an artist for whom classical precept is all. The idea of dependence upon the past central to classicism gives it much in common with the process of allusion as practised by James.

Also of significance is the idea that the connexion with Balzac is made not directly by either James (as author) or by his American tourist first-person narrator, but by one of the story's supporting cast—the society hostess Mrs. Coventry:

> "There are people who doubt whether there is any picture to be seen. I fancy, myself, that if one were to get into his studio, one would find something very like the picture in that tale of Balzac's—a mere mass of incoherent scratches and daubs, a jumble of dead paint!"
>
> ("The Madonna of the Future" 159).

Here, in one sense, is a reference rather than allusion because the writer is mentioned by name; and at the same time it is slightly indirect, since the title of the particular tale by Balzac is not specified by name. Though the

Balzac story "*Le Chef d'oeuvre inconnu*" is not identified, it is to prove pivotal in James's tale. The unnamed narrator of the tale within a tale, 'H-', (Henry or an allusion to Honoré?) appears to recognise this particular Balzac story to which Mrs. Coventry is alluding (although James perpetuates the atmosphere of allusion by not spelling this out conclusively) and therefore conceives the idea that Theobald may be destined never to produce any masterpiece at all. And that leads him to confront Theobald with this conviction and therefore precipitate his death. This presumably explains the fact that 'H-' ends feeling "sad and vexed and bitter" and taking his leave of Mrs. Coventry, the ill-willed hostess, "with reprehensible rudeness" (178).

The allusion is also indirect in the sense that it is not made by the first person, the American tourist narrator, 'H-', but by Mrs. Coventry, who is not depicted as a sympathetic character within the tale. We therefore take her allusion to another tale with a certain caution.

And yet allusion does, in another respect, permeate this tale. Theobald, the deluded, dawdling painter, spends his life trying to produce a madonna, one of the archetypal genres of painting in the medieval and renaissance periods. As a genre it is almost by definition allusive. Every new madonna evokes in some respect or other those produced before it. But at the same time, Theobald's projected painting is billed as *The Madonna of the Future*—directed towards some ideal future rather than evoking the past. Yet the very fact that Theobald, as an American Protestant (and by the end of the tale we know that he has been buried in the Protestant cemetery), is painting a madonna is itself culturally incongruous in the nineteenth century. Simultaneously the painting is also an allusion to the debate in artistic circles between naturalism and idealism, a debate with which James would have been familiar from his reading of the French journal *La Revue des Deux Mondes*, which vigorously opposed through the previous decade, the 1860's, the rise of the realist and then naturalist movements, both in painting (Courbet and subsequently Manet) and literature (Flaubert and then the Goncourts, and worst of all Emile Zola). This is echoed in Theobald's justification of his method:

> "'An idealist, then,' I said, half jocosely, wishing to provoke him to further utterance, 'is a gentleman who says to Nature in the person of a beautiful girl, 'Go to, you're all wrong! Your fine is coarse, your bright is dim, your grace is *gaucherie*. This is the way you should have done it!' Isn't the chance against him?'"
>
> ("The Madonna of the Future" 152).

Theobald goes on to say, pointing at Raphael's *Madonna della Seggiola*, "cease your irreverent mockery! Idealism is *that*!" (152) — to which the narrator 'H-' replies:

> "There are many people, I know, who deny that his spotless Madonnas are anything more than pretty blondes of the period, enhanced by the Raphaelesque touch, which they declare is a profane touch. Be that as it may, people's religious and aesthetic needs went hand in hand, and there was, as I may say, a demand for the Blessed Virgin, visible and adorable, which must have given firmness to the artist's hand. I'm afraid there is no demand now" (152-53).

Idealism is essentially allusive, the mere real being transformed so that what is depicted alludes either to some ideal form which has not actually been perceived with the eye or to something remembered from the past. There is no need to allude to something which is actually there in front of our eyes.

James may even, conceivably, be alluding, beyond Raphael's madonnas, for which he is perhaps most famous, to the artist's status as a figure in the renaissance humanist movement, when the narrator describes Theobald looking at his model "bending towards her in a sort of Platonic ecstasy" (161) — Raphael, after all, besides portraying madonnas, also portrayed Plato in his mural *The School of Athens* in the papal apartments in the Sistine Chapel in Rome.

Elsewhere in the same tale we find a wealth of strict allusion. There is the use of a surprising number of Latin phrases such as *"aere perennius"* (174) from Horace's *Third Book of Odes* (108), when Theobald is justifying the lasting value of his "ideal" though as yet unproduced Madonna. Theobald's constant activity never gets anywhere, which is in fact an unending deferral of the creative act, of putting theory into practice, and this is ironically pointed up by another Latin quotation, this time from Pliny the Elder, *"Nulla dies sine linea"* (156). Again we need to take into account the general context in which an allusion is made, and this use of Latin may have an influence on what is probably the most famous line from this otherwise rather under-read tale by James: "Cats and monkeys, — monkeys and cats, — all human life is there!" (180). The earlier quotation from Pliny has prepared us for the Classical context. There is Theobald's response to 'H-' ["thrice happy youth" (149; Ovid, 166)] and now 'H-' goes on to refer to the sculptor of caricature busts as "This jaunty Juvenal" (173), as a nod to the possible classical source of the allusion in Juvenal's tenth satire.

According to Brian Southam in *A Student's Guide To The Selected Poems of T. S. Eliot* (Southam 48-52), Eliot, in "Burbank With A Baedeker: Bleistein With A Cigar," appears to be alluding first to "The Aspern Papers" and then "The Madonna of the Future," yet may in fact have been influenced not by the original James texts (though doubtless he had also read these) but by a conflated "pastiche quotation" put together by Ford Madox Ford in his Henry James monograph of 1913, where Ford twice repeats the "cats and monkeys" line. Southam surmises that Eliot may be alluding simultaneously to "The Madonna of the Future" and to the line "goats and monkeys" used by Othello in Act IV Scene III of Shakespeare's play, which, like James's *The Aspern Papers*, is also initially set in Venice.

In *Daisy Miller* of 1878, it is another literary reference sown by another ill-willed hostess in polite society, this time Mrs. Costello, which, as in "The Madonna of the Future," points forward to the central character's demise. Here the American, and more precisely Bostonian, expatriate Mrs. Costello makes a reference to a novel in French which was to become obscure even within the last years of the nineteenth century.

Writing from Rome to her nephew Winterbourne, the anti-hero of the tale, Daisy's fair-weather, stand-offish admirer, Mrs. Costello remarks:

> 'Those people you were so devoted to last summer at Vevey have turned up here, courier and all,' she wrote. 'They seem to have made several acquaintances, but the courier continues to be the most *intime*. The young lady, however, is also very intimate with some third-rate Italians, with whom she rackets about in a way that makes much talk. Bring me that pretty novel of Cherbuliez's—*Paule Méré*—and don't come any later than the 23rd' (332).

This reference goes, as it were, a stage further than that to Balzac in "The Madonna of the Future." There it was left to a secondary character, by whose veracity and perspicacity the reader does not set any great store. Here it is not only a secondary character, but one who is outright ill-disposed towards the heroine of the novel. The mention of *Paule Méré* is every bit as poker-faced or inscrutable as James had been when borrowing the title of Shakespeare's sequence as title for "A Passionate Pilgrim." No more clues than the title are given, except that Mrs. Costello regards the novel as "pretty." Of course there is a quantum difference between Shakespeare and Victor Cherbuliez, but James, in 1879, here expects the reader to pick up on the Cherbuliez *Paule Méré* reference with no more help than we were given to make the connexions with Shakespeare in "A Passionate Pilgrim."

14. Allusions in the Early Stories   165

Yet the implications of Mrs. Costello, arguably the *bête noire* who initiates the ostracisation of Daisy Miller, making this reference, rather than James doing it directly as narrator of the tale, are significant. And a detailed knowledge of Cherbuliez's novel *is* required.[6] Although it is written in French, it differs in a vital respect from almost all the other French authors James was reading. For Cherbuliez was not French by birth but a Swiss from Geneva and moreover a Protestant, indeed a Calvinist. He was simultaneously, as a French speaker, a member of the European cultural order to which James in so many ways aspired throughout his career, and yet also someone who had come from a Protestant background broadly comparable to the culture James had left behind in New England. *Paule Méré*, one of Cherbuliez's early novels, tells the story of a young free-spirited woman, who is ostracised by the repressive Calvinist Swiss community in which she has been brought up, and ends her days fleeing to Italy and dying prematurely, of a broken heart. (Another Protestant admirer, albeit Swiss rather than American, proves himself fickle in his loyalty).

Given these parallels it is surely incongruous in the extreme for Mrs. Costello, who is to remain inimical and unforgiving to Daisy to the end, to, as it were, incriminate herself by making this literary reference to Cherbuliez's novel.

A parallel for what Mrs. Costello is here doing may be found in Shakespeare. In Act I Scene II of *Hamlet*, Claudius, attempting to dissuade Hamlet from excessive grieving for his recently deceased father, says:

> Tis sweet and commendable in your nature, Hamlet,
> To give these mourning duties to your father,
> But you must know your father lost a father,
> That father lost, lost his—and the survivor bound
> In filial obligation for some term
> To do obsequious sorrow. But to persevere
> In obstinate condolement is a course
> Of impious stubbornness,... Fie, 'tis a fault to heaven,
> A fault against the dead, a fault to nature,
> To reason most absurd, whose common theme
> Is death of fathers, and who still hath cried
> From the first corse till he that died today,
> 'This must be so' (185).

---

6 See Pierre Walker 1995, 5-17; Edward Stone 1964, 88-93; and Viola Dunbar 1948, 184-86.

Claudius, having murdered his brother, attempting by rational argument to coax Hamlet out of excessive mourning, ends by alluding to the story of the first murder, and not just a murder but a fratricide, the murder by Cain of Abel, "the first corse." The last thing which he should have mentioned he ends ups divulging. Of course that makes nonsense of what may be called realism in literature. It has to be assumed that Claudius, the plausible human being, is sacrificed here by Shakespeare for the sake of incriminating him in the eyes of the audience. In the seventeenth century (or the nineteenth, for that matter) the readership or audience could be relied on to pick up the biblical reference from Genesis. Or, alternatively, it might be argued that Shakespeare is here giving us not the realism of the conscious world but rather the psychological realism of Freud, according to whom we reveal our most essential truths despite our conscious selves, by saying the very last thing which should come into our heads.

The difference between the Hamlet "Cain" passage and the *Daisy Miller* extract is that the former is an allusion according to the strict definition— an indirect reference—whereas the mention of Cherbuliez is an explicit reference, if only to the title. The first is to the most common work of literature of all—the Bible—whereas the second is to a far from canonical text. But in each case the character is made by the author to incriminate himself or herself.

Today the position is complicated still further. Mrs. Costello makes a reference which is entirely lost on all of us except those who have gone to the lengths of tracking down Cherbuliez's novel in a research library. But even back in the 1870's it was never a reference which in her capacity as a plausible character, in a realistic rather than fantastical or allegorical novel, she should surely have been making in the first place. What she is doing is the equivalent of Brecht's characters remaining on stage even when they are no longer involved in the action—a sort of *Verfremdungseffekt*; or of the character Mrs. Drudge in Stoppard's parodic *The Real Inspector Hound*, who answers the telephone at the beginning of Act I and then proceeds to give, quite uncalled for by the situation, a whole range of background information which is of no use to the person supposedly on the other end of the line (in the supposedly real situation) but of every help to the audience in the auditorium, at this point still in the dark;[7] or to give an

---

[7] "(*The phone rings. Mrs. Drudge seems to have been waiting for it to do so and for the last few seconds has been dusting it with an intense concentration. She snatches it up.*)
MRS DRUDGE (into phone): Hello, the drawing-room of Lady Muldoon's country residence one morning, in early spring?... Hello! – the draw – who? Who did

equivalent from James's own time, Ibsen's maids conveniently filling us in on Rosmersholm's past before he makes his entry (Act I Scene I). Ironically, it is precisely because the other work referred to has now become wholly obscure, both in this case, and in the Dumas *fils* reference in "The Siege of London," that what was an explicit reference has arguably become more indirect and veiled than a formal allusion. I quote here (declining to allude) Christopher Ricks in *Allusion and the Poets*, who in turn cites Eliot on the practice of "difficult" allusions in a letter of 1931 to I.A. Richards:

> That, as you know, is a theory of mine, that very often it is possible to increase the effect for the reader by letting him know a reference or a meaning but if the reader knew more the poetic effect would actually be diminished; that if the reader knows too much about the crude material in the author's mind, his own reaction may tend to become, at best, merely a kind of feeble image of the author's feelings, whereas a good poet should have a potentiality of evoking feelings and associations in the reader of which the author is wholly ignorant
>
> (Eliot, quoted by Ricks 5).

---

you wish to speak to? I'm afraid there is no one of that name here, this is all very mysterious and I'm sure it's leading up to something, I hope nothing is amiss for we, that is Lady Muldoon and her houseguests are here cut off from the world, including Magnus, her ladyship's husband Lord Albert Muldoon who ten years ago went out for a walk on the cliffs and was never seen again—and all alone, for they had no children"(Act I Scene I, 15).

15. *C'est strictement confidentiel*: Buried Allusions in *Confidence* (1879)

Rebekah Scott

Falling between 'Daisy Miller' (1878) and *The Europeans* (1878), on one side, and *Washington Square* (1880) and *The Portrait of a Lady* (1880-81), on the other, *Confidence* (1879) belongs to the early, Austenian phase of James; coruscating, ironic, compact—it goes about its business transparently and unswervingly. Or does it? Already in James, even in 1879, there are the stirrings of his inveterate tendency towards "merciful indirection" (*The Art of the Novel* 306), the kind of indirection that manifests itself in style more than in syntax: in innuendo, euphemism, allusiveness, and the irony that reveals even as it pretends to conceal.

I would like to do two things in this paper. Firstly, to speculate on the role of allusion in the Jamesian imagination and to ask how it contributes to forming "the very atmosphere of the mind" that belongs to the writer of genius. Secondly, I'd like to examine some of the glancing allusions in *Confidence*, including its French allusions, to see if any conclusions can be drawn about the nature and scope of this practice. How far along the scale of winks and nods does the secret, or secretive, allusion have to be before it is merely an unconscious twitch? Can one ever determine the extent to which the buried or glancing allusion is intentional or unintentional, substantial or superficial? And is this effort of determination somehow beside the point?

We are told by the narrator of *Confidence* that its hero, Bernard Longueville, is a man of imagination—witty, suggestive, and, on at least four occasions, "allusive" (30, 40, 80, 100). His best friend, Gordon Wright, is a man of science—stuffy, insensible, plain-speaking; his "every phrase" "march[ed] in stout-soled walking boots" (19). As the narrator says, not without considerable partiality, Gordon's "deficiency" of imagination "was a matter of common jocular allusion between the two young men":

> Bernard had often spoken of his comrade's want of imagination as a bottomless pit, into which Gordon was perpetually inviting him to lower himself. 'My dear fellow,' Bernard [would say], 'you must really excuse me; I cannot take these subterranean excursions. I should lose my breath down there; I should never come up alive. You know I have dropped things down—little jokes and metaphors, little fantasies and paradoxes—and I have never heard them touch bottom!' This was an epigram on the part of a young man who had a lively play of fancy; but it was none the less true that Gordon Wright had a firmly treading, rather than a winged, intellect (19).

Considering that Bernard's quip recalls the narrator's allusion to that other bottomless pit of *The Inferno* and "the Dantean injunction to renounce all hope" (9), made as our hero is weaving his way through the "dark, pestiferous archway[s]" of Siena, it is no wonder that Bernard's little jokes and epigrams fall on deaf ears. They sound so much like insults. Despite the rather one-sided raillery that characterises their relationship, the two men are firm friends when the novel opens. The story takes off when Gordon issues a plea to Bernard to act as his "assistant" in an amorous "experiment" (Gordon's words), designed to sound the depths of a mysterious girl he's been pursuing, Angela Vivian. Somewhat bemused, Bernard agrees to this odd commission. On the train from Venice to Baden-Baden, he muses that "nothing could better express [Gordon's] attachment to the process of reasoning things out than this proposal that his friend should come and make a chemical analysis (a geometrical survey) of the lady of his love" (19). In exasperation, Bernard concludes:

> Gordon's mind [...] has no atmosphere; his intellectual process goes on in the void. There are no currents and eddies to affect it, no high winds nor hot suns, no changes of season and temperature. His premises are neatly arranged, and his conclusions are perfectly calculable (20).

The fundamental problem with Gordon Wright's imagination is, clearly, that it is *scientific*.

If we project forward five years to James's 1884 essay on "The Art of Fiction," we get a sense of what this "atmosphere of the mind" might amount to for a *literary* imagination. In this essay, James argues that the aspiring novelist must make his "impressions" count as "experience"; *this* type of experience, he writes, and only this type, "is the very atmosphere of the mind; and when the mind is imaginative—much more when it happens to be that of a man of genius—it takes to itself the faintest hints of life, it converts the very pulses of the air into revelations" (*Selected Literary Criticism* 85-86). It was certainly not unusual for James to recycle his most felicitous phrases, but it is equally true that this phrase ("atmosphere of the mind") was circulating in the intellectual air of mid-to-late nineteenth-century England. One finds it, for instance, in the plush rhetoric of aestheticism: Walter Pater, in his 1866 essay on Coleridge first published in *The Westminster Review*, describes Wordsworth's "flawless temperament, his fine mountain atmosphere of mind" (*Appreciations* 87). Or in Matthew Arnold's critical introduction to Thomas Gray, first published in 1880 in *The English Poets: Selections with Critical Introductions*, which mentions Samuel Butler's bracing "atmosphere of mind" (*Essays in Criticism: Second Series* 94).

As Leon Edel has gone to great pains to point out, Bernard Longueville is like James in a lot of ways—both temperamental and professional (see *The Conquest of London*). But there is more to it than this. Like James, the narrator tells us that Bernard "had not made much of the law; but he had made something of his talents" (*Confidence* 21); like James, Bernard "was almost always spoken of as 'accomplished' [yet] people asked why he didn't do something" (21); like James, he is a chronicler of his "impressions"; like James, he is a sensualist and a wit (22); like James, Bernard returns to America "as a distinguished stranger in his own land," even a "restless" "wanderer" (115; 119); like James in *A Small Boy and Others* (99-100), he is fond of remembering the way he used to kick the autumn leaves of the Indian Summer along the pavements of New York's Fifth Avenue in his "riotous infancy" (106). One might extend this comparison to ask whether the two are also in agreement about what constitutes "the atmosphere of the mind." Does it hinge for Bernard, too, on "the power to guess the unseen from the seen, to trace the implication of things" (86)—where "implication" is taken to mean both "conclusion" or "consequence" and "implicature," or that which is *implied*? Does it all come down to a susceptibility to "impressions"? Bernard, we know, is always ready with "impressions, opinions, speculations, anecdotes" (35), is always "roaming afield and plucking personal impressions in great fragrant handfuls" (80); has "laid up a great store of impressions and even a considerable sum of knowledge" from his travels (99); and despite his demurral that his "impressions are never fresh" (67), we are made to feel how very far from stale they are, even when they are second-hand—that is to say, the impressions of others.

Due to the secret nature of his undertaking to put the incipient flirt Angela Vivian to the test, Bernard adopts the cloak-and-dagger custom of allusiveness. As soon as he realises that he has already met Angela in Siena, he is confined to "alluding" to their meeting (The narrator actually describes these moments as "allusions": 30, 40). When this fails to get a response, Bernard tries a different kind of allusiveness, one that forms the very fabric of his dissimulation: "He flattered himself that the civil indifference of his manner, the abstract character of the topics he selected, the irrelevancy of his allusions and the laxity of his attention, all contributed to this result [of distracting her from his relentless scrutiny of her]" (80). This time his "allusions" are not to a fleetingly shared past, but to artists, poets, and philosophers, and his recourse to them is only partially motivated by the desire to throw her off the scent of his investigation. Primarily, he alludes in order to *conspire*—not with Gordon this time but with Angela. Their allusion-making resembles other people's love-making: it is a secret language, an emotional heavy weather, very much a part of the upper atmosphere of the mind. Now the comparison between Bernard's methods and James's methods, between the allusiveness of creature and creator, starts to become meaningful.

Of the two available American editions of *Confidence* (Herbert Ruhm's edition of 1962 and William T. Stafford's 1983 Library of America edition), neither is concerned with sourcing allusions. Had they been so inclined, these editors might have begun with the title. In 1857, the American writer Herman Melville published a book called *The Confidence-Man: His Masquerade*. James didn't write about or own this novel, but he would have known of it, and known too that the term "confidence-man" had an American origin: it was coined by the American press in 1859 to describe a notorious confidence-trickster. Melville's novel is one very-extended pun on "confidence," a word that appears upwards of 200 times. (Apart from the word "confidence," which appears, alongside its cognates, in James's novel some sixteen times, other words and phrases associated with confidence-trickery, such as "frank" and "enterprising stranger," reverberate between the two works). James, like Melville, seizes on this word to represent a range of social and economic manoeuvres, both salutary and destructive. Yet James scrutinises the one type of confidence-brokering that Melville neglects in his sceptical novel about loan sharks, shysters, quacks, and evangelists: that is to say, the *love*-con. In transferring *his* con to Europe, James calls up another set of literary antecedents, most of whom are French writers of romance or comedy.

15. Allusions in Confidence 173

Actually, James's edgy romance has an even older, less anxious association with that great anxious romance, Shakespeare's *Love's Labour's Lost*. The two share a motivating conceit, a protagonist's name, a forest setting, a very peculiar joke about "remuneration," and the claim to being, arguably, the least-read work in the author's oeuvre.[1] There are even one or two direct verbal echoes of the play in James's novel. But the relation must not be overstated. It does not suggest itself as a clear source-relation, such as that between *Love's Labour's Lost* and Tennyson's *The Princess*, but as a sub-generic sharing of patterns and preoccupations, signaled by a common set of key words including "study" and "wit." The lovers' sallies of wit do more than invite the old comparison between love and war. For Shakespeare's Biron and Rosaline, Dumaine and Catherine, and Longueville and Maria, and for James's Bernard Longueville and Angela Vivian, Gordon Wright and Blanche Evers, wit is an ambiguous mode of courtship; it is both a stimulant and a scourge. Very often wit is not so much an invitation as a displacement activity for sex, its cerebral equivalent. This lends *Confidence* an admiring collusiveness with *Love's Labour's Lost* that is manifested both in its buried allusions and in its competitive exertion of wit. But before I move on to draw out one or two of these allusions, it is perhaps time to say a word about the name Longueville, since James was such a conscious christener.[2] The name contains the French term for length, *"la longueur,"* a nice conceit given that Bernard takes his time over Angela. Then there is *"la longue-vue,"* which designates a spy glass; Bernard's commission, of course, is to spy on Angela. Apart from Shakespeare's Longueville, Bernard Longueville may claim another French line of ancestry: Victor Cousin. Cousin is the idealist philosopher whom Mrs. Vivian reads amidst the dissipation of Baden-Baden, and who wrote a book entitled *Madame de*

---

1 As noted by Walter Cohen, editor of the Norton edition of *Love's Labour's Lost* (1594-95): "Alone among the First Folio plays, *Love's Labour's Lost* went unperformed between 1642 and 1839, and it remained unpopular until the mid-twentieth century" (738). Famously, Dryden dismissed it as "incoherent." Comparably, Leon Edel dismissed *Confidence* as James's "worst novel" (*The Conquest of London* 385).

2 The Quarto of 1598 has the spelling *Longauill*, or *Longaville* as it appears in most modern editions, a transliteration of the French *Longueville*. Both editions of the play that James owned, the single-volume *Works of William Shakespeare* (1864), edited by William George Clark and William Aldis Wright, and the 10-volume *Works of Shakespeare* (1899), edited by C.H. Herford, have the spelling *Longaville*. However, the Herford edition notes that "The three lords, Biron, Longaville, Dumain [...] derive their names from three conspicuous figures in the war, Henry [IV]'s captains, Marshall Biron and the Duke du Longueville, and the General of the Catholic League, the Duke du Maine" (6).

Longueville (Paris, 1863), a philosophical 'study' of an eighteenth-century Parisian society woman, which James kept in his library—along with Washington Irving's *Journals*, in which there is mention of a Baroness de Longueville who marries a Bernard de Pichon in 1641. (See Edel and Tintner, *The Library of Henry James*). Curiously, James changed the names of his protagonists in the intervening years between his *Notebook* sketch of the novel, where he writes that "their names are perhaps provisional" (6) and indeed where he confuses them, and its first publication in *Scribner's Monthly* from August 1879 to January 1880.

As mentioned earlier, James spent much of the 1870's as a theatre critic, on both sides of the Atlantic. While he could not have been in attendance at Augustin Daly's 1874 production of *Love's Labour's Lost* at the Fifth Avenue Theatre in New York (he was in Florence), it is very likely that a reading of the play was fresh in his mind at the time of writing *Confidence*, since he alludes to one of its incidental jokes—on "remuneration"—in a newsy letter to his father dated 30 March 1880. After discussing his recent fictional projects, James writes:

> I also wrote an article which you will find some day in *Scribner's*, without my name, and which I beg you to keep a religious silence about. The said Scribners [sic] had asked me two years ago, to write a disquisition on the London theatres, to be richly illustrated; but though they were very pressing, I declined, owing to the dreariness of the subject. Since Gilder [Richard, editor of Scribner's] has been abroad, however, he has ardently returned to the charge, offering me so rich a "guerdon or remuneration," as Shakespeare says, that I at last wrote the article, on condition that it should be profoundly anonymous
>
> (*Henry James: Letters 1875-83* 277-78).

The recurring joke in *Love's Labour's Lost* centres on fixing the monetary value of "remuneration": Costard the clown, according to the "remuneration" he is given by Armado for the delivery of a love letter to his sweetheart, assumes the term to be a bombastic Latinism for three farthings, which works out less than the "guerdon" (or reward) of one shilling given to him by Biron for delivering *his* love letter (Act III Scene I, 156-58). (To refer to Scribner's payment in this way is typical of James's tact in financial matters.) This joke on "remuneration" is carried over into *Confidence*: after Bernard has sketched Angela without her permission, rather than apologise for the liberty he has taken, he complains that, since she is by no means a professional model, he is unable to "remunerate" her and she must treat him as "beggar" (14).

Bernard's mock formality in this case clearly expresses itself as flirtation. Indeed, courtship is everywhere presented as a highly literary (if not Latinate) phenomenon proceeding by *coups de grâce* and written "confidences."

In "Henry James and the Poetry of Association," Philip Horne catalogues some of the recurrent if truncated Shakespearean allusions in James, particularly of the kind that have passed into the Jamesian idiom. One of these is the phrase "declined upon a wretch" from *Hamlet*, Act I Scene V, uttered by the Ghost of old Hamlet in reproach of Gertrude for settling on his brother and usurper:

> O Hamlet, what a falling off was there!
> From me, whose love was of that dignity
> That it went hand in hand even with the vow
> I made to her in marriage, and to decline
> Upon a wretch whose natural gifts were poor
> To those of mine.
> But virtue, as it never will be moved,
> Though lewdness court it in a shape of heaven,
> So lust, though to a radiant angel linked,
> Will sate itself in a celestial bed,
> And prey on garbage (47-57).

As Horne notes, James's use of the expression "declined upon a wretch" usually goes unacknowledged, slipping seamlessly into his text without reference or quotation marks, noticeable only through its archaism. We find it re-appearing in *Confidence*, only this time James flags it with *both* a titular reference and scare quotes:

> Gordon knew it must seem strange to so irreverent a critic [as Bernard] that a man who had once aspired to the hand of so intelligent a girl—putting other things aside—as Angela Vivian should, as the Ghost in "Hamlet" says, have 'declined upon' a young lady who, in force of understanding, was so very much Miss Vivian's inferior; and this knowledge kept him ill at his ease and gave him a certain pitiable awkwardness (111).

"Though to a radiant angel [or Angela] linked," Gordon ends up marrying "garbage." This allusion lends Gordon's final choice of the frivolous Blanche for his bride a certain mock-ominousness, which the original melodramatic sketch of the novel in the *Notebooks* vividly fulfils by having Gordon kill his wife. It is enough, at least, to make Bernard "ill at his ease," though *this* phrase ("ill at ease") properly belongs to Cassio (*Othello* Act III Scene III, 30) and not Hamlet.

Dipping back into Philip Horne's repository of stock Jamesian allusions, we find a line from Milton's "L'Allegro" (I 28):

> Jest and youthful Jollity,
> Quips and cranks, and wanton wiles,
> Nods, and becks, and wreathèd smiles,
> Such as hang on Hebe's cheek
> And love to live in dimple sleek.

Horne notices the line "nods, and becks, and wreathèd smiles" surfacing (in a mutant form) in James's 1887 letter to James Russell Lowell ("Henry James and the Poetry of Association" 17-18). Although, in this letter, the reference is clearly to Milton, it is worth pointing out that it may have been a double allusion on James's part, since Lowell himself uses the phrase "wreathed in smiles" in his "Dramatic Sketch," a dialogue between editors about the editorial nightmare of rampant and indeed mutant quotation. The phrase "wreathèd smiles," or "wreathed in smiles" as it appears in *Confidence*, is applied to the newlywed, Blanche Wright:

> On going down to Gordon's house in the country, [Bernard] was conscious of a good deal of eagerness to know what had become of that latent irritation of which Blanche had given him a specimen. Apparently, it had quite subsided; Blanche was wreathed in smiles; she was living in a bower of roses (120).

"Wreathed in smiles" nicely captures the decorativeness of Blanche's "jollity"; it seems a conscious and apt allusion. (Blanche's "bower of roses" may also recall line 22 of the poem: "And fresh-blown roses washt in dew.") But at the same time it is worth noting that the phrase is ubiquitous in the literature of Aestheticism (for example, in *The Picture of Dorian Gray*) and variations on "nods and becks and wreathed smiles" can be found in Sir Walter Scott's *Redgauntlet* (1824), Thomas Carlyle's essay on 'Boswell's Life of Johnson' (1832), and Charles Reade's *The Cloister and the Hearth* (1861), which says as much about the Victorian practice of glancing allusion as it does about James's habits. Similarly, staying with Milton, one wonders just how much can be made of the "forbidden fruit" (136) of Bernard's erotic awakening, or of the peculiarly Miltonic phrase "his sapient faculty," except to signal Bernard's stirrings of guilt over his (potential) sexual betrayal of his friend. If the glancing allusion sets in motion "a train of associations" for James, so that it is useful as a kind of intellectual and affective shorthand, it would appear to have the same function for James's hero. When he is not observing Angela Vivian, Bernard is preoccupied with observing her mother:

'She has the Boston temperament,' he said, using a phrase with which he had become familiar and which evoked a train of associations. But then he immediately added that if Mrs. Vivian was a daughter of the Puritans, the Puritan strain in her disposition had been mingled with another element. 'It is the Boston temperament sophisticated,' he said; 'perverted a little— perhaps even corrupted. It is the local east wind with an infusion from climates less tonic' (56).

This "phrase" with which Bernard "had become familiar" belongs to Thomas Gold Appleton (1812-84), the American epigrammist, who quipped that "A Boston man is the east wind made flesh" (*Oxford Dictionary of Quotations*, attributed). Thomas Gold Appleton, it may be remarked, is best remembered for a one-liner reported by Oliver Wendell Holmes in *The Autocrat of the Breakfast Table* (1858): "Good Americans, when they die, go to Paris" (Ch. 6). This was a witticism that Oscar Wilde made his own in the first act of *A Woman of No Importance* (1893):

> MRS. ALLONBY: They say, Lady Hunstanton, that when good Americans die they go to Paris.
> LADY HUNSTANTON: Indeed? And when bad Americans die, where do they go to?
> MRS. ALLONBY: Oh, they go to America (37).

Perhaps bad Americans in James go to Baden-Baden, along with the bad Russians in Turgenev (*Smoke, or Life at Baden*) and Dostoevsky (*The Gambler*), and the bad Englishwomen in George Eliot (*Daniel Deronda*). James certainly isn't immune to the novelistic (ill-?) treatment of Baden-Baden that promotes a certain continuity between the pathologies of over-confidence at the gaming table and cocksureness in the 'game' of love.

The question of where to draw the line between a glancing allusion and an unconscious appropriation is a difficult and perhaps futile one. In *Allusion to the Poets* Christopher Ricks writes that "there is (as Wittgenstein proposed) nothing self-contradictory or sly about positing the existence of unconscious or subconscious intentions" (Ricks 4), and that, on the matter of *degrees* of intentionality, "[r]eaders always have to decide—if they accept that such-and-such is indeed a *source* for certain lines—whether it is also more than a source, being part not only of the making of the poem but of its meaning" (3-4). I can't help but view these "sources" as a niggling part of the novel's *meaning*, sharing with it, if not a source-relation, then something like a kin-relation—something that establishes an esoteric set of "confidences" between characters as well as between author and reader, and between author and *fellow* author (both living and dead), since the habit of allusion was a vital part of the Arnoldian cultivation of an "atmosphere of mind" (5, 272). Then again, maybe James's buried allusions are meant to *stay* buried, as little private jokes designed to leaven the re-readings that formed the basis of his revisions, in the manner that Bernard's "brilliancy" lay in his "entertaining himself": "Clever as he often was in talking with his friends, I am not sure that his best things, as the phrase is, were not for his own ears" (*Confidence* 10).

16. James and the Habit of Allusion

by Oliver Herford

In this paper I shall trace a single literary allusion through the last dozen years of James's life, and on this basis make some suggestions about the habitual dimension of his allusive practice. Allusion becomes one of James's stylistic habits, I shall be suggesting, not least because it offers him a way of analysing the role of habit in his own life and in others'—a major concern of his late biographical and autobiographical writings. The allusion I shall attend to has a Shakespearean source: Hamlet's line to Gertrude about the Ghost, "My father, in his habit as he lived!" (Act III Scene IV, 130). The pun is not mine—nor indeed exclusively James's, as we shall see. Nor is James alone in alluding to this line. Throughout the nineteenth century it figures as a commonplace of life-writing: again and again, the biographer's stated aim (or achievement, or despair) is to present the dead man "in his habit as he lived"—occasionally, too, the dead woman in hers, though much less frequently. But just that general currency helps to make the allusion a characteristically Jamesian one. James habitually alludes to a small number of the most familiar lines and phrases in English literature, and his relation to those household words gains a particular freshness of invention in contexts of personal retrospect from his accumulated self-consciousness about the interplay of memory and imagination that literary allusion both underwrites and depends upon.

A couple of early instances of the allusion to *Hamlet* will serve to show the conceptual range it covers in a biographical connection. Hazlitt's 1826 essay "Of Persons One Would Wish To Have Seen" recalls a question put in company to Charles Lamb: "'Who is it, then, you would like to see "in his habit as he lived," if you had your choice of the whole range of English literature?'" (33). Lamb chose Sir Thomas Browne and Fulke

Greville "as the two worthies whom he should feel the greatest pleasure to encounter on the floor of his apartment in their night-gown and slippers, and to exchange friendly greeting with them" (33); and in specifying the dress—the habit—of these visitors, or rather their comparative *undress* ("night-gown and slippers"), Hazlitt seems to be making play with the disagreement among editors, performers, and critics of *Hamlet* about what the Ghost should wear in the Closet scene. He appeared in full armour in the first Act, on the battlements of Elsinore; a stage direction in the First Quarto, '*Enter the Ghost in his night-gown*' (after Act III Scene IV, 95), suggests that he may have taken another habit in the meantime.[1] Writing more or less contemporaneously with Hazlitt, Goethe approved of the night-gown as a contrast with—a change out of—the Ghost's earlier "complete steel" (Act I Scene IV, 31): "How much more homely, domestic, and terrible he now appears, in the same form in which he was wont to appear in this chamber, in his night dress, and unarmed!" ("Shakespeare's Critics" 65).[2] The emotional tenor of that ghostly apparition is quite unlike the exchange of greetings envisaged by Lamb in Hazlitt's essay, but both writers emphasise the value of the "homely": indeed it is arguably the Ghost's night-gown that makes this Shakespearean moment available as a focus for the common ambition of biographers to enter into a familiar, "domestic" relation to their subjects. And yet in both fiction and non-fiction James will weigh the biographical fascination of the private life against his awareness of the pervasive publicity of selfhood. When in Chapter 16 of *The Ambassadors* (1903) Mme de Vionnet, splendidly dressed for Gloriani's garden-party, is described as representing to Strether "the idea of the *femme du monde* in her habit as she lived," another Shakespearean reference (not quite an allusion) promptly points up the extent to which her identity is constituted as a social performance on occasions like this one: "Above all, she suggested to him the reflection that the *femme du* monde—in these finest developments of the type—was, like Cleopatra in the play, indeed various and multifold" (200). The "*femme du monde*" is a social "type" or role, and her proper habit is a kind of stage costume.

---

1 The First Quarto (1603) does not present a reliable text of the play, but as a retrospective reconstruction from early performances it has a certain authority with regard to stage directions. The sparer direction of the Folio (1623), just 'Enter Ghost', gave rise to the stage tradition of the Ghost's appearing in full armour in this scene.
2 I quote these remarks as they appear in English translation in an unsigned 1849 survey of Shakespeare criticism; they come from Goethe's essay on an 1825 reprint of the First Quarto, posthumously published in 1833 as "Erste Ausgabe des Hamlet" (see *Goethe's Werke* XIV 61).

16. The Habit of Allusion   181

Goethe's remarks on the Ghost's night-gown assume a criterion of dramatic appropriateness that suits the character's apparel to the immediate setting and context, but we may say too that the clothes in which Old Hamlet "was wont to appear in this chamber" represent a habit in the sense (also current at the time of the play) of "a settled disposition or tendency to act in a certain way […]; a settled practice, custom, usage" (*Oxford English Dictionary*): it was, and is, habitual to him to wear such a thing in such a place. Broadly speaking, nineteenth-century allusions to this line in biographical contexts are drawn to the pun on "habit" because, in pointing to a dimension of behaviour that is regular, customary, and to some extent involuntary (even if, as for the *femme du monde*, the habit is a habit of performance), it helps the biographer's endeavour to represent the whole of a life on the basis of only a few observations or recollections. An anonymous article of 1824 on the "Personal Character of Lord Byron" builds its claim to "peculiar interest" on the writer's having enjoyed "unusual opportunities of observing the extraordinary habits, feelings, and opinions of the inspired and noble Poet": this biographer, who signs himself "R. N.," is "quite sure that, after a perusal of the following paper, the reader will be able to see Lord Byron, mind and all, 'in his habit as he lived':—Much that has hitherto been accounted inexplicable in his Lordship's life and writings is now interpreted, and the poet and the man are here depicted in their true colours" (337). The movement—in successive sentences— from Byron's "extraordinary habits" to "'in his habit as he lived'" treats habitual behaviours as constitutive of a character, and accords them an explanatory value for the representation of that character. In what follows I want to attend a little to James's ways with this pun in connection with the overlapping categories of biography, autobiography and social history that so occupy him in his last works. I shall also try to draw out some reflections on the principles of continuity and recurrence that are embodied for James in any act of alluding, but above all in writing that looks to the past—insofar as an allusion is a return to an earlier form of words that both counts on and renews a tradition of value.³

---

3 Philip Horne has argued that James's several allusions to this line in works published after 1903 share "a double recognition—both of the insubstantiality, deadness and real absence of the thing or person evoked in memories and in works of the imagination; and of the vivid illusion of substance, life and immediate presence to which such evocations give rise" (Horne "The Poetry of Association" 49). This seems to me true of all the instances Horne discusses; indeed it suits one of them, in James's 1907 Introduction to *The Tempest* (see *Literary Criticism: Essays in Literature* 1213), so much better than anything I have found to say about it that I

So far as I am aware, James makes this Shakespearean allusion for the first time (an isolated early instance) in his story "The Author of 'Beltraffio'," which was published in June-July 1884 in the *English Illustrated Magazine* and reprinted the following year in *Stories Revived*. If that was indeed his first ever allusion to "My father, in his habit as he lived!" the timing might be felt to have significance, as his own father had died only eighteen months before in December 1882. I do not intend to consider now whether or not the line had a particular filial resonance for James (incidentally, the words "My father" are *never* part of his allusions to it); but we may observe at least that an association with Henry Sr.'s death would make this a retrospective allusion from the outset, which it certainly is later on. Again, I am not really concerned here to gauge how much of the dramatic context of *Hamlet* should be read into any instance of this allusion. The familial situation in "The Author of 'Beltraffio'" bears some resemblance to the situation adumbrated in the play (a sensitive only son is divided between rival parental claims on his loyalty and affection, and the conflict proves fatal to him); but for my present purpose, where the principal context is rather all the *other* appearances of this line in James's published writing, it will be more productive to begin by considering the manner in which the young American narrator of the story alludes to it.

He has been left alone over tea with Mark Ambient's wife shortly after his arrival at their cottage in Surrey, and takes the opportunity—which he half sees is unwelcome—to praise her husband's writing to her: "'He's magnificent, Mrs. Ambient! There are pages in each of his books that have a perfection that classes them with the greatest things. Therefore, for me to see him in this familiar way—in his habit as he lives—and to find, apparently, the man as delightful as the artist, I can't tell you how much too good to be true it seems, and how great a privilege I think it'" (*Stories Revived* I 14). "'I knew that I was gushing,' he immediately notes, "but I couldn't help it, and what I said was a good deal less than what I felt.'" We might think of the allusion he makes, then, both as a self-conscious flourish of his enthusiasm and as an indirection—a displacement of emotion comparable to his thus declaring something *about* Ambient to a third party when he is "by no means sure that [he] should dare to say even so much as this" directly *to* the novelist. His seeing Ambient in person and "'in this familiar way'" (of course it is *un*familiar to *him*) is taxing as well as exciting, more difficult than reading him.

---

have gratefully left that one out here.

16. The Habit of Allusion

Once out of his youth, James seems to have been beyond awe at meeting anyone; but the narrator of "The Author of 'Beltraffio'" anxiously discriminates, in his first, delighted view of Mark Ambient at home, between the author in person and his differently personal literary achievement. In James's very late commemorative essay "Mr. and Mrs. James T. Fields" (1915), the same allusion combines two distinct causes for wonder at an eminent authorial presence: at its appearance in a place where it might not have been expected (Boston, Massachusetts—"literally"); and again, half a century later, at its *re*appearance in memory, attended by whatever reflections on the value formerly attributed to it. Recalling the transatlantic literary salon maintained by the editor James T. Fields and his wife Annie Adams Fields, a social resource for James in the 1860's, he writes: "I see now what an overcharged glory could attach to the fact that Anthony Trollope, in his habit as he lived, was at a given moment literally dining in Charles Street." James's word "overcharged" drily allows ("now") for the possibility that Trollope was accorded more "glory" in Boston than his literary achievement could justify, or bear; and yet in recalling these "projected assurances and encountered figures and snatched impressions, such as naturally make at present but a faded show," James unabashedly states that "not one of [them] has lost its distinctness for my own infatuated piety" (*Literary Criticism: Essays on Literature* 172). Part of the meaning of "in his habit as he lived" in such contexts, it seems, is that it expresses an infatuation. I would suggest that for James, looking back to his personal past in the works of the fourth phase, that infatuation is not an incidental emotional colouring of retrospect but rather a condition of the kept "distinctness" of his memories; nor is his "piety" incompatible with the critical acuity he displays in handling them. I shall come back to this.

The allusion to *Hamlet* has a special witty aptness at this point in "Mr. and Mrs. James T. Fields," as James has just commemorated the Fieldses' patronage of the French actor-manager Charles Fechter and noted the "delightful roused state under which we"—that is, his own generation of Boston theatre-goers—"grasped at the æsthetic freshness of Fechter's Hamlet in particular" (171). James represents Fechter's audience as delightedly and perhaps unwontedly roused by his performance to make a critical comparison:

> Didn't we react with the finest collective and perceptive intensity against the manner of our great and up to that time unquestioned exponent of the part, Edwin Booth?—who, however he might come into his own again after the

Fechter flurry, never recovered real credit, it was interesting to note, for the tradition of his 'head,' his facial and physiognomic make-up, of a sudden quite luridly revealed as provincial (171-72).

The sense of an aesthetic reaction against a representative American head is present too in the extraordinary passage in Chapter 12 of *Notes of a Son and Brother* (1914) on Andrew Johnson, who became President of the United States in 1865 on the assassination of Abraham Lincoln.[4] James assumes again the "collective" plural voice of the time in pronouncing Johnson "almost too ugly to be borne":

> [F]or nothing more sharply comes back to me than the tune to which the 'esthetic sense,' if one glanced but from *that* high window (which was after all one of many too), recoiled in dismay from the sight of Mr. Andrew Johnson perched on the stricken scene. We had given ourselves a figure-head, and the figure-head sat there in its habit as it lived, and we were to have it in our eyes for three or four years and to ask ourselves in horror what monstrous thing we had done
>
> (*Autobiography* [1956] 491).

James ruefully recalls that "it was open to us to waver at shop-windows exposing the new photograph, exposing, that is, *the* photograph, and ask ourselves what we had been guilty of as a people, when all was said, to deserve the infliction of that form." Johnson's inauguration photograph was taken by Matthew Brady. James's next sentences contrastingly refer to "Lincoln's mould-smashing mask," the "admirable unrelated head" that "had itself revealed a type," thus implicitly arranging a comparison between "*the* photograph" of Johnson and any one of the many photographic images of the former President. That comparison is all to Johnson's disadvantage, but also (obscurely) to his discredit; which of course is terribly unfair. But the trope of the contrasted portraits, and perhaps also the unfairness, return us to *Hamlet* again, and to just the scene in which the ghost appears "in his habit as he lived." A little before this in the Closet scene, Hamlet confronts Gertrude with the likenesses of his dead father and his uncle: "Look here upon this picture, and on this, / The counterfeit presentment of two brothers" (Act III Scene IV, 54-55). The dramatic logic of this gestural allusion casts Andrew Johnson, more unfairly still, as Claudius, not just Old Hamlet's successor but his murderer. And a very little later in *Notes of a Son and Brother* James executes a turn on the word "habit" that recalls

---

4 By a coincidence that James does not remark, the John Wilkes Booth who shot President Lincoln was Edwin Booth's younger brother, and like him an actor and a Hamlet.

his earlier, verbal allusion, as he outrageously suggests that Johnson's personal appearance was "the grand inward logic or mystic law" of his eventual impeachment in 1868, a sequel he rejoices in for its intimations of an improvement in national taste: "What [...] was to be more refreshing than to find that there were excesses of native habit which truly we couldn't bear?" (*Autobiography* [1956] 491).

That is magnificently fanciful—or grotesquely so, looked at from another, lower window. James M. Cox is particularly hard on this passage, complaining that James's elaborate dismay at Johnson's ugliness only dresses up "the easiest, the most utterly complacent and conventional judgments on national politics" (Cox 22). But I would argue that this digression in *Notes* is not meant, as Cox assumes, as a retrospective comment on the politics of the American Civil War and the Reconstruction era, but rather as a demonstration that the record of taste—the record of what can and cannot be borne, aesthetically speaking—may also be counted as a part of the historical record; necessarily a neglected part, James implies, in a society that prejudicially neglects "the 'esthetic sense'." In detailing the failure of his generation to habituate itself to something objectively trivial (the way Andrew Johnson looked American, his lurid "excesses of native habit"), James pays a deliberated tribute of attention to what he calls the "aspects" of the historical moment. "I speak but of aspects, those aspects which, under a certain turn of them, may be all but everything" (*Autobiography* [1956] 491): the sentence itself characteristically turns depreciation to a measured assertion of all but absolute value. James gives ground a little on the complex satisfaction he took in Johnson's impeachment, allowing that "That was at any rate the style of reflection to which the humiliating case reduced me"; and yet the "style of reflection" exemplified by this passage as a whole seems the apt embodiment of his retrospective sense of a "generally quickened activity of spirit" at the time—a quickening he attributes to the shock of Lincoln's death—and of "our having by the turn of events more ideas to apply and even to play with" (491-92). That opportunity, discovered in 1865, is taken up again fifty years later by the play of James's late style, which yet matches its allusive turns at every point to the recollected "turn of events."

His retrospective writing notably rings its changes on "in his habit as he lived" in putting just this question of the value, for an improved acquaintance with the past, of "aspects"—observed and recollected appearances. But it is equally interested in sounds and voices, and frequently sets these registers of remembered sensation alongside one another. In *William Wetmore Story and His Friends* (1903), reproducing an unpublished note by Story's wife on their friendship with the Parisian *salonnière* Mme Mohl, James parenthetically comments:

> What a fortune indeed [...] would have assuredly awaited any chronicler able to produce her image, by the light of knowledge, quite intact and as a free gratuity to his readers; produce it in its habit as it lived, in its tone as it talked, with its rich cluster of associations, and above all with the mystery of the reasons of its eminence (I 365).

The allusion here adds another association to that "rich cluster." James's amplification of the Shakespearean line—"in its habit as it lived, in its tone as it talked"—picks up the verbal detail of Emelyn Story's reminiscence, which characterises Mme Mohl in terms of corresponding idiosyncrasies of dress and speech, and which James immediately quotes: "'Her talk was all her own; nobody was like her for a jumble of ideas and facts, which made her mind much like her clothes, topsy-turvily worn'" (Story I 366). We may take that conversational "jumble" as emblematic of James's retrospective volumes altogether—in his own public characterisations of them, at least, which do not acknowledge the minute detail of these volumes' patterning and cross-referencing, but invoke "the ragbag of memory" and speak of the author's "doubtless now appearing to empty it into these pages"—those of his 1913 memoir *A Small Boy and Others* (*Autobiography* [1956] 41). Or again, at the end of the long passage on Andrew Johnson: "Everything I recover, I again risk repeating, fits into the vast miscellany—the detail of which I may well seem, however, too poorly to have handled" (492). James's handling of detail may sometimes be questioned in these volumes, but surely not on grounds of poverty. It might be noted that Emelyn Story's words as printed in *William Wetmore Story* are not all *her* own: as elsewhere, James rephrases the documentary source so as to smooth down textual oddities. In the manuscript he worked from, Emelyn Story's note on Mme Mohl reads: "Her talk was all her own, nobody like her for a jumble of ideas and facts, like dress like mind, the one and the other infinitely original and clever & topsy [turvy]." [5] That is rather more topsy-turvily expressed than James's version, but arguably truer to both its writer and her subject. It is only in the late non-fiction that such questions of fidelity can arise at all, however,

---

5 Emelyn Story, unpublished manuscript notes. The phrase "& topsy [turvy]" is a cramped insertion above the line, a second thought; indeed my reading of the phrase is conjectural, as only the first three letters of the last word can be plainly made out.

since it is here that James becomes interested for the first time in the *detail* of the past, its habit and tone, as these are preserved by documentary or anecdotal testimony and by personal memory. That development was occasioned by the commission to write the Life of William Story, which James informally received in 1895, not at first recognising it as an opportunity. He took eight years to complete the book, a longer and more frankly resentful procrastination than Hamlet's—and indeed the sense of a duty repeatedly deferred may have contributed something to the prevalence of this ghostly allusion in his subsequent writing. The 1908 Preface to *The Aspern Papers* is in this context an intermediate work, displaying still the caginess of a writer (mostly) of fiction contemplating a change of mode that will entail an obligation to historical fact. Here James recalls learning that Claire Clairmont had "been living on in Florence, where she had long lived, up to our own day, and that in fact, had I happened to hear of her but a little sooner, I might have seen her in the flesh" (*Literary Criticism: French Writers* 1175). He rationalises his sense that he should probably *not* have chosen to see Clairmont even had the opportunity presented itself, as a preservation—for fictional use—of the "romance-value" attaching "to her long survival": his concern was with "the mere strong fact of her having testified for the reality and the closeness of our relation to the past," and he would freely re-invent her situation and her character in writing *The Aspern Papers*.

These considerations perhaps explain the slight oddness of the allusion to *Hamlet* that occurs in this Preface. Unlike the Ghost of Hamlet's father, Clairmont is an unimportunate and unsuspected presence, and unlike him she is a phantom in her own lifetime—partly, as Philip Horne notes, from James's imaginative appropriation of her, "turning her as writers do into a ghost even while she is still in life" ("Poetry of Association" 48), but partly also as the representative of "a dislodged, a vanished society" (*William Wetmore Story* I 14) and a survivor of the Byron-Shelley circle with whom she notoriously associated. James writes:

> The thrill of learning that she had 'overlapped,' and by so much, and the wonder of my having doubtless at several earlier seasons passed again and again, all unknowing, the door of her house, where she sat above, within call and in her habit as she lived, these things gave me all I wanted; I seem to remember in fact [...] my more or less immediately recognising that I positively oughtn't —'for anything to come of it'— to have wanted more
>
> (*Literary Criticism: French Writers* 1175).

These departures from the underlying Shakespearean scenario point up, we might say, the pathos of Clairmont's having been able to make James want so little.

As a novelist, that is. As a biographer and autobiographer, by a marked contrast, he welcomes every recollected detail that comes back to him. These late volumes repeatedly dramatise his sense of being able to remember more than he can really tell; an unexpected fulfilment of the desire he attributes to "[t]he historian" in the Preface to *The Aspern Papers*, a desire for "more documents than he can really use" (1175). A passage in *Notes of a Son and Brother* analogously recalls the welcome repeatedly given throughout the 1860's by the James family in America to George Sand's new novels, imported presumably, and issued in a uniform binding: "oh the repeated arrival, during those years, of the salmon-coloured volumes in their habit as they lived, a habit reserved, to my extreme appreciation, for this particular series" (*Autobiography* [1956] 404). That bibliographical detail now starts an associated memory for James, as the pink covers of Sand's novels are retrospectively revealed as a match for something she once momentously wore:

> The sense of the salmon-coloured distinctive of Madame Sand was even to come back to me long years after on my hearing Edmond de Goncourt speak reminiscentially and, I permit myself to note, not at all reverently, of the *robe de satin fleur-de-pêcher* that the illustrious and infatuated lady [...] *s'était fait faire* in order to fix as much as possible the attention of Gustave Flaubert at the Dîner Magny (404-05).

In the continuum of retrospect, the "vision of a complicated past" afforded James by Goncourt's anecdote (and "recovered even as I write") encounters his grateful recollection of the "social education" that Sand's novels gave him and his family; so that, as he says, "I see that general period as quite flushed and toned by the salmon-coloured covers" (405). Habit in this complex of association signifies a visual appearance or fashion that makes a mark for memory (the salmon-coloured covers, the peach-blossom satin dress), and also personal behaviour in two senses: an isolated act or *coup* that is completely characteristic of the agent (the set that Sand makes at Flaubert), and a regular, habitual course of conduct. It is in this latter sense that the Jameses are remembered reading and discussing Sand *en famille*, their "early complacencies" of American literary response being gradually modified, more or less, by exposure to her writing (405). These are *second* readings, moreover, "renewals of acquaintance" that affirm the family habit of George Sand (404); for they had read her novels once already in serial format in the *Revue des Deux Mondes*. In his essay on the Fieldses, written the next year, James would describe his own relation to the past with the same word he gives to Sand in this passage, "infatuated": he too, in this late, summative writing, is "illustrious and infatuated," and the remembered habit of things receives some of his happiest announcements of infatuation.

In the last chapter of *A Small Boy and Others*, writing of the family's two residences at Boulogne in the mid-1850's, James invokes "a special association, too ghostly now quite to catch again—the sense of certain Sundays" on which he made visits, alone, to a "quite ideally old-world little [...] *musée de province*,"

> ...where I repeatedly, and without another presence to hinder, looked about me at goodness knows what weird ancientries of stale academic art. Not one of those treasures, in its habit as it lived, do I recall; yet the sense and the 'note' of them was at the time, none the less, not so elusive that I didn't somehow draw straight from them intimations of the interesting, that is revelations of the æsthetic, the historic, the critical mystery and charm of things (of such things taken altogether), that added to my small loose handful of the seed of culture
>
> (*Autobiography* [1956] 226).

The exact association in this case is now "too ghostly" for identification, and the artworks the young James looked at steal away, not standing to be remembered in their habits as they lived. Yet the "sense" of his having gone to look at them—and gone "repeatedly," which is to say, for the time, habitually—does live in his memory; and James grants to that sense alone, even without reference to its forgotten objects, a seminal value in the development of the faculties of interest that flower so lavishly in these late volumes. So simply, he shows us, and from so little, can a style and its habits be formed.

V:
PERFORMANCE

17 The Absent Writer in *The Tragic Muse*

Nelly Valtat-Comet

The reading I would like to propose here will focus on one particular element of *The Tragic Muse* that is not foregrounded but implied, and yet informs much of the novel's development—an aspect that belongs more to the fantastic than the realistic vein in James's inspiration, by which I mean the overriding absence of a genius of letters and of an ideal text.

A large proportion of Book I in *The Tragic Muse* is devoted to long and rather sophisticated Oxbridge conversations between, mostly, Nick Dormer, Peter Sherringham, and Gabriel Nash, in various combinations. These conversations offer readers a panorama of views on the arts and on artistic creation, on the current pressure imposed on art by massive and 'vulgar' London audiences, on some of the controversies between classicism, aestheticism, and romanticism in vogue among the English elite of the time. They also fictionalise several theoretical questions perennially dear to James, such as the comparative 'values' of the arts of representation and their inter-relations, the status of "representation" both in its theatrical meaning of "performance" and in the sense of artistic rendering of life, and the personal impact of producing art in the construction of one's identity.

Readers first encounter Miriam as a stroller in the Salon, in company of her mother and Gabriel Nash, through the "agitated perceptions" (29) and the naivety of Biddy Dormer, who becomes scared at her own failure to gauge the strangers, to pin them down to a type and assign them a place in her own world. To her repeated question "who are they?," Nick answers obliquely with a moral *'blanc-seing'*[1] for Gabriel Nash: "he's a gentleman" (31). Nick remembers Nash from Oxford, where he was known for having written "A very clever book [...] A sort of novel [...] with a lot of good

---

1 French for "signature to a blank document."

writing," a novel which obviously involves topics unmentionable to a proper English young lady. Even such evasiveness somewhat reassures Biddy who can adorn Nash with the label "literary character" (32). Nash's double quality as gentleman and novelist is thus offered by Nick as sole answer to Biddy's wonderings on the identities and social placement of Miriam and her mother, so that these two "persons theatrical" (48) find themselves primarily introduced in the text as "female appendages" to a mysterious male novelist figure.

About Gabriel's "book" readers will learn nothing else, but will hear him expatiate on his decision to forget about it and write no more: "Literature, you see, is for the convenience of others. It requires the most abject concessions. It plays such mischief with one's style that really I've had to give it up" (35). It is as if the only novel present in the text as a creation by one of the protagonists were only put forward to be discarded immediately, relegated into an uncertain past previous to the beginning of the story, and an ephemeral *succès d'estime*, nipped in the bud by its own refusal of a readership, condemned by its complicated form, by philistine criticism of its subject, and above all by its author's claim that he wants no more *état civil* or *métier* than just living and feeling the shades of life. The aspiring Miriam will later echo his profession of faith and his haughtiness by declaring "I'm not so fond of reading. I go in for the book of life" (109). There is of course in Gabriel Nash, as in most of James's novelist personae, a lot of Henry James, and a lot of what he criticises or even ridicules. Nash receives a treatment not unlike that given to Mark Ambient, in "The Author of Beltraffio" (1884), who is seen by his easily deluded young American disciple as a genius member of "the guild of artists and men of letters" (867), but equally readable as a very conventional figure of British snobbery. And if Nash's novel can be suspected of much the same 'aestheticism' as "Beltraffio," it is no more than "Beltraffio" offered to the appreciation of James's readers. Nash is thus early dismissed as an author, but continues to exist in *The Tragic Muse* as a critic and an inspired talker, taking upon himself much of the discourse on art, including on literature, inserted in the narrative. A characteristic example occurs when Nash is strolling with Nick Dormer through Paris by night (117). In this page Nash develops the running metaphor (a constant of Jamesian thought) of life as art, and more precisely life as text. But this metaphor also becomes both a pretext and a medium for voicing James's own grievances about the tedious reception and modest commercial profit of his own style and manner.

Nash is also the one who convinces Nick Dormer to renounce politics and espouse portrait painting instead of Julia Dallow. Nash's responsibility in the 'making' of Nick as an artist parallels the way he propels Miriam Rooth onto the European stage and into James's fiction. It makes him a demiurge figure, and I use the term on purpose in its Gnostic sense to underline Nash's status as "a substitute, subordinate or delegate," the one who acts in place of but from a standpoint inferior to the superior instance, that is to say, in a novel, the Author. Here of course we need to recognise a pattern fully explored by Julie Rivkin in her 1996 essay "False Positions, the Representational Logics of Henry James's Fiction," though Rivkin chose to leave out *The Tragic Muse* from the corpus she studied.

Miriam makes her second appearance (her first as aspiring actress) in the drawing room of Honorine Carré, the retired glory of the Théâtre Français whose advice and teachings Peter Sherringham eventually secures for the girl. The description of Madame Carré's *intérieur* is carried out through the perceptions of no less than three focalisers: Gabriel Nash, Nick Dormer, and Peter Sherringham, who in a large part of the novel function as sensitive and intelligent observers (another sort of delegation on the part of James). They are technical '*ficelles*' as well as fully crafted characters, cast much in the same manner as Isabel Archer's 'satellites' in *The Portrait of a Lady* and designed to favour the progressive withdrawal of authorial presence that reached its climax in the novels of James's so-called 'late phase.' While they wait for Madame Carré, Nash's gaze and attention are caught by "the presents, the portraits, the wreaths, the diadems, the letters, framed and glazed, the trophies and tributes and relics collected by Madame Carré during half a century of renown" (83). Henry James is here, as always, faithful to a 19th-century trope that loads with meaning the description of an artist's room. He also entirely exonerates his character-observers from any inclination to voyeurism and to tracking the private life of the woman in the observation of the objects she surrounds herself with. The three of them combined are capable of understanding the meaning of objects, what they point to and, more interestingly, what they fail to represent, or rather represent in absentia. Mostly, Nash ponders for the first of several times in the novel, on the essentially ephemeral, unretainable nature of the theatrical performance, which, in Philip Horne's terms, "transforms behaviour into a work of art" (*The Tragic Muse* xxv):

> The profusion of this testimony was hardly more striking than the confession of something missed, something hushed, which seemed to rise from

it all and make it melancholy, like a reference to clappings which, in the nature of things, could now only be present as a silence: so that if the place was full of history it was the form without the fact, or at the most a redundancy of the one to a pinch of the other—the history of a mask, of a squeak, of a series of vain gestures.

Some of the objects exhibited by the distinguished artist, her early portraits, in lithograph or miniature, represented the costume and embodied the manner of a period so remote that Nick Dormer, as he glanced at them, felt a quickened curiosity to look at the woman who reconciled being alive to-day with having been alive so long ago. Peter Sherringham already knew how she managed this *miracle*, but every visit he paid her added to his amused, charmed sense that it was a miracle and that his extraordinary old friend had seen things he should never, never see. Those were just the things he wanted to see most, and her duration, her survival, cheated him agreeably and helped him a little to guess them. His appreciation of the actor's art was so systematic that it had an antiquarian side, and at the risk of representing him as attached to an absurd futility it must be said that he had as yet hardly known a keener regret for anything than for the loss of that antecedent world, and in particular for his having belatedly missed the great comédienne, the light of the French stage in the early years of the century, of whose example and instruction Madame Carré had had the inestimable benefit. She had often described to him her rare predecessor, straight from whose hands she had received her most celebrated parts and of whom her own manner was often a religious imitation; but her descriptions troubled him more than they consoled, only confirming his theory, to which so much of his observation had already ministered, that the actor's art in general was going down and down, *descending a slope with abysses of vulgarity* at its foot, after having reached its perfection, more than fifty years ago, in the talent of the lady in question. He would have liked to dwell for an hour beneath the meridian (83, emphasis mine).

The passage is strewn with paradoxes: "profusion" / "something missed," "clappings [...] present as silence," "redundancy" of form / "a pinch" of "the fact," and Nash's observations end on a double notion of void and illusion: "the history of a mask, of a squeak, of a series of vain gestures." Nick Dormer and Peter Sherringham are more inclined to seek behind the things the artist as a person, as an actual participant in a period now gone. They express their fascination in much the same terms as the narrator-lodger writes of Juliana Bordereau in *The Aspern Papers* (1888): "The strange thing had been for me to discover [...] that she was still alive: it was as if I had been told Mrs. Siddons was, or Queen Caroline, or the famous Lady Hamilton, for it seemed to me that she belonged to a generation as extinct" (*Complete Stories III* 230). The name of Mrs. Siddons is quoted of course in reference to the fact that she was Sir Joshua Reynolds's Tragic Muse. Then "as she sat there before me my heart beat as fast as if the *miracle* of resurrection had taken place for my benefit" (241). And Juliana Bordereau always hides her face behind a mask. The topos of the mask runs through the two stories. In *The Tragic Muse*, the great absentee, the artist with whom the old actress is a living connection, is not a defunct poet like Jeffrey Aspern, but a "great *comédienne*" whose influence is described in phantasmal terms, whose name is never given, and who later on is given a face and some materiality of existence through pictorial representation in the portrait of Rachel by Gérôme that Miriam admires in the foyer of the Comédie Française. Peter Sherringham's regrets can thus be ascribed to nostalgia, an allegiance to the French classical tradition and a deprecative look on the dramatic art of his time, on both sides of the Channel, an art now given over to melodrama and bourgeois comedy. Hubert Teyssandier asks himself who (is it actors or authors?) can be held responsible for the "descending slope" and the "abysses of vulgarity" in question, and concludes that Peter Sherringham probably means both (171).

At this early point the fictive world of *The Tragic Muse* has already been deprived of its only semblance of a writer-character, and the referent contemporaneous world of European drama is sadly devoid of an author. That vacancy, in the same chapter, when Miriam who has not yet begun her first session of reciting, is described, through Peter as focaliser, with an insistent series of words and grammatical markers indicating a void: "no sentiment in her face—only a vacancy of awe and anguish [...] no spring of reaction" (85), "her persistent vacancy" (90); readers can be tempted to interpret this vacancy as multiple. It is not just the explicit metaphor of the beginner, or a fictionalisation of the controversy, topical since Diderot, on whether acting should mean feeling the emotions of the character one is supposed to perform, but also the indication of a blankness more in keeping with an obsessive theme in Jamesian fiction, that of the missing text by the missing author. After Miriam's disappointing performance in the same episode, this intuition finds itself confirmed, when Peter mentally balances her failure ("no element of interest") with a more favourable impression:

> While Sherringham judged privately that the manner in which Miss Rooth had acquitted herself offered no element of interest, he yet remained aware that *something* surmounted and survived her failure, *something* that would perhaps be worth his curiosity. It was the element of outline and attitude, the way she stood, the way she turned her eyes, her head, and moved her limbs. *These things* held the attention; they had a natural *authority* and, in spite of

their suggesting too much the school-girl in the tableau-vivant, a "plastic" grandeur. Her face, moreover, grew as he watched it; *something* delicate dawned in it, a dim promise of variety and a touching plea for patience, as if it were conscious of being able to show in time more shades than the simple and striking gloom which had as yet mainly graced it (93, emphasis mine).

Peter cannot find the right words. In very Jamesian fashion he resorts to vagueness when describing what is essential. And in the midst of such lexical impotence the choice of the word "authority" cannot be considered trivial. In addition to its connotation of deserved recognition and respect, it also suggests, at this very liminal phase of Miriam's career, a Miriam who is "author of herself,"[2] who can make good use of both the blankness and the "plasticity" Peter recognises in her. At the same time, Peter confesses to himself his own desire to take part in the making of Miriam as actress, to become a sort of Pygmalion (another author figure): "the direction of a young person's studies for the stage may be an interest of as high an order as any other artistic appeal" (96), as if he were ready to compensate for his own lack of artistic inspiration by confusing patronage with actual creation.

De facto, the complex relationship between actor (actress here) and text is explored but obliquely in *The Tragic Muse*. The question of the "authority" of an actor crops up again later (136), and this is what Miriam declares to Peter that she is "going in for." In the same conversation, when Peter says to her "you're an embroidery without a canvas," he has advanced one step: Miriam is no longer total vacuity, but the "canvas" she lacks in Peter's opinion can be read as metaphor for "text." James maintains here the confusion between life as text (obviously Miriam has adopted the trope) and literary text, in the form of a good play, as the necessary medium for drama to exist.

It is only when Miriam already enjoys a certain amount of popularity on the London stage, has gained some confidence in her future and begins rehearsing "an old play, a romantic drama of thirty years before, very frequently revived and threadbare with honorable service" (309), that she herself comes to voice the lack she has been suffering from. She wants to do "the comedy of London life" and deplores the absence, in the English drama, of playwrights capable of putting it into text.

> She saw all round her things she wanted to "do"—London bristled with them if you had eyes to see. She was fierce to know why people didn't take them up, put them into plays and parts, give one a chance with them; she

2 Shakespeare, *The Tragedy of Coriolanus*, Act III Scene III.

expressed her sharp impatience of the general literary bêtise. She had never been chary of this particular displeasure, and there were moments—it was an old story and a subject of frank raillery to Sherringham—when to hear her you might have thought there was no cleverness anywhere but in her own splendid impatience. She wanted tremendous things done that she might use them, but she didn't pretend to say exactly what they were to be, nor even approximately how they were to be handled: her ground was rather that *if she only had a pen*—it was exasperating to have to explain! She mainly contented herself with the view that nothing had really been touched: she felt that more and more as she saw more of people's goings-on (314-15, emphasis mine).

Of course this can be read as one more element of realistic contextualisation, since the London drama of the period was indeed in desperate need for renewal. Here James has Miriam fancy herself author of her own plays and at the same time recognise as not within her range of talent the specificity of the art of play-writing. The resulting feelings are impatience and frustration. She comes to see her own life as subject matter for possible plays. She imagines that the very nagging of her mother might inspire "some play-writing rascal" (385), and later, when she pauses for Nick's second portrait of her, she turns into a convincing storyteller: "Miriam's account of her mother's views was a scene of comedy, and there was instinctive art in the way she added touch to touch and made point upon point" (421). Yet she fails to grasp how much her own life has become romance for all those who take an interest in her. Book 5 ends on Peter Sherrigham's mental engagement in an effort of interpreting the whole situation, his own, that of Miriam, and the interrelations between the various persons of his entourage. And he does so in terms that clearly point to him as a reader figure, enjoying the "fine suspense" of Nick Dormer's "predicament," toying with "the possible" and the "wish to follow out the chain of events" (322). Well into Book 6 an amusing passage stages Gabriel Nash in Nick's studio, caught in the act of trying to pull some strings and grafting fiction of his own on his friends' lives. When Gabriel explains that Peter Sherringham should court somebody else in order to make Miriam jealous, and that it is Nick that Miriam is after, Nick replies in reprobation: "[Y]ou talk like an American novel" (350). For her friends Miriam might be metaphorised as romance or as an interesting show, on and off stage: Peter and Gabriel feel like "a pair of hot spectators in the pit" (351), yet she is a mystery at the same time. For Peter "She was constructed to revolve like the terraqueous globe; some part or other of her was always out of sight or in shadow" (351), and Gabriel develops this planetary vision in a memorable tirade.

Book 8 logically functions as the *dénouement* of precisely that story which seems to have grown so out of hand, both for James (he even inserted a word to this effect in the text), and for Miriam's satellites. It pictures Miriam, not really at the top of the glory imagined for her by her friends and by James, but as a very popular rising star. A star she is indeed, already "lionized" (the word is used as early as 309), and an arch manipulator of her own image. In several short stories ("The Lesson of the Master," "The Death of the Lion" among others), James has developed the theme of the lionisation of artists and their subsequent loss of inspiration. Miriam, on the contrary, seems to capitalise on her own fame, and if she produces an ugly distortion of her artistic variety and ungraspable nature by exploiting the most inartistic aspects of modernity, it is at the expense of no visible encroachment on her talent as actress. The novel of Miriam's life, at that point, has become at once what Henry James abhorred and denounced, a story of fame based on lies and prying into private lives, aimed at ignorant masses, and at the same time the story of a yet-to-be-confirmed great actress.

> She made almost an income out of the photographers—their appreciation of her as a subject knew no bounds—and she supplied the newspapers with columns of characteristic copy. To the gentlemen who sought speech of her on behalf of these organs she poured forth, vindictively, *floods of unscrupulous romance*; she told them all *different tales*, and, as her mother told them others more marvellous yet, publicity was cleverly caught by rival versions, which surpassed each other in authenticity. The whole case was remarkable, was unique; for if the girl was advertised by the bewilderment of *her readers* she seemed to every sceptic, on his going to see her, as fine as if he had discovered her for himself (460, emphasis mine).

For at the end of *The Tragic Muse*, Miriam is still lacking something, and it is implied that her destiny is yet to be delineated. The great modern script she is longing for shows no sign of taking shape, since no reliable author-figure has emerged from the scattering of authorship into fragments of creative impulses in various characters, including Miriam herself. It is through her acting Shakespeare that Miriam's greatness is first established, at Madame Carré's when she recites the part of Constance in *King John* (213). Her great literary reference, as Hubert Teyssandier underlines (177), is Shakespeare's Cleopatra, who embodies the infinite variety of creation and renewal. It is in the role of Juliet that Miriam carries away London audiences as the novel closes, but Miriam still yearns to contribute to the making of a modernity as worthy of esteem, in artistic value, as the great Shakespearian tradition. James will soon take up this theme of the ideal dramatist and the ideal play in the tale entitled "The Private Life" (1891), where Blanche Adney, an avatar of Miriam already celebrated when the story opens, begs lionised novelist Clare Vawdrey to write a play likely to match her best talent as performer, but the ending reveals that Vawdrey is but a social puppet, and his true creative power is exerted by a sort of fantastic double of himself, a ghostly figure who never leaves his study and produces a script that is probably wonderful but that is never brought forth into the world. James certainly had a way of portraying himself in fiction as a sort of Shakespeare figure (the theme is most active in the 1903 story entitled "The Birthplace"). That he was, at the time he wrote *The Tragic Muse*, on the brink of launching himself into a career as a playwright might certainly not be entirely coincidental, but the autobiographical element is not what concerns us here. Desperate attempts to reach, uncover, conjure up the impossible ideal Author constitute one of the main underlying themes running through the whole of James's literary and critical production, and *The Tragic Muse*, despite its relative plethora of artist-characters, is no exception. It is perhaps no coincidence if, though he wrote many tales of the life of letters, James never produced a full-fledged novel with a writer as main protagonist.

18. James and the "Paradox of the Comedian"

Richard Anker

> If she was theatrical, she was naturally theatrical.
> *The Bostonians*, 48
>
> 'What's rare in you is that you have [...] no nature of your own. [...] It's a kind of thing that's a labyrinth'
> *The Tragic Muse*, 138-39.

In order to set the stage, so to speak, for the comedian who will be the principle object of this paper, I would like to quote a sentence from *The Tragic Muse*, in which several important distinctions are made between Miriam Rooth, the comedian in question, and her mother. The sentence is the following:

> The figurative impulse in the mother had become conscious, and therefore higher, through finding an aim, which was beauty, in the daughter
> (*The Tragic Muse* 144).

It is by the mediation of Peter Sherringham's consciousness that James's narrator offers this series of distinctions between Mrs. Rooth and her daughter, the future comedian: the "figurative impulse," native to mother and daughter alike but elevated to consciousness in the daughter alone, converted by her histrionic vocation into art, its aim, or *"telos,"* is what the same reflector, further on in the novel, will qualify as the "strictly mimetic gift" (320) of the young comedian. Miriam Rooth, of course, belongs to a line of Jamesian heroines going back to Christina Light, in *Roderick Hudson*, whose "artful artlessness" ([1983] 269) is the source of Roderick's bewilderment in the novel, ultimately destroying his life in the process of undermining his artistic vocation as a sculptor. As the apocalyptic denouement of this early novel attests, the "figurative impulse" or "mimetic gift" that determines the mystifying character of such heroines as Christina Light—who makes a second appearance in *The Princess Casamassima* where she plays a crucial role in the undoing of Hyacinth Robinson—poses a considerable threat to the stability of the typically male character succumbing to its attraction. Beyond the obvious psychological implications of such seduction, what is at play here is a more essential tension, typical in James, between the rhetorical, or tropological, nature of the text and the phenomenological basis of consciousness.[1] The mystifying character of Christina Light's "artfully artless" behaviour thematically dramatises a pressing formal threat in the writer's perspective, the threat posed by the "deviations" and "differences" constituted by the rhetorical nature of language.[2] The fictional playing out of this tension between the rhetorical and the phenomenological is by no means static in James's work, but is itself inscribed within a teleological movement whereby consciousness gains an increasingly dominant, if illusive, hold over the deviating character of the tropes on which it depends. A certain sublimation of the danger posed by the "figurative impulse" is formally operative from one novel to the next, sublimation which only attains full thematic expression in *The Tragic Muse*, as is attested by the sentence quoted above, in which the difference between mother and daughter is defined not as that between one person endowed with mimetic facilities and another deprived of them, but rather as a redemptive elevation of these facilities, posited as native, in the consciousness-provoking act of furnishing them with artistic intent. This redemptive elevation or sublimation of what is taken to be a native mimetic faculty is perfectly manifest in *The Bostonians*, where Verena Tarrant's "artlessly artful facilities [...] not part of her essence" (366) are successively elevated, even while being subordinated, in a chain of substitutions corresponding to the narrative appropriation of rhetorical drift or deviation. The young heroine's extraordinary oratorical faculty serves as "medium" of the "father's eloquence" (69) in the early pages of the novel, is then raised to the status of feminist port-parole under the tutelage of Olive Chancellor, before finally being channelled into the domestic and

---

[1] See Sheila Teahan's *The Rhetorical Logic of Henry James* for an excellent analysis of the opposition between the rhetorical and the phenomenological in James. This paper disagrees however with her assumption of the absence of a teleological structure in James's work.

[2] The rhetorical foundation of consciousness is perhaps alluded to by James in his preface to *The Golden Bowl*, where he points out that in his rereading of his works in preparation for the New York Edition, "[w]hat was predominantly interesting to note [...] was the high spontaneity of these deviations and differences, which became thus things not of choice, but of immediate and perfect necessity [...]. The deviations and differences might of course not have broken out at all, but from the moment they began so naturally to multiply, they became, as I say, my very terms of cognition" (*Henry James: Literary Criticism II* 1330).

18. The 'Paradox of the Comedian'   205

pseudo-democratic service of her future spouse, Basil Ransom. The dual nature of the sublimation in question, elevating and negating, raising and subordinating at the same time, is nowhere more evident than in Basil Ransom's hypocritical plea demanding that the young heroine sacrifice her vocation as feminist port-parole for the sake of conjugal union with himself; in response to Verena's concern that her oratorical talent risks being squandered in this exchange of the public platform for a private one, Ransom (whose name suggests the appropriation by force or excessive pressure of a value that is by no means his due) replies:

> 'My dear young woman [...] the dining room itself shall be our platform, and you shall mount on top of that. [...] What will become of your charm? [...] It will become about five thousand times greater than it is now; that's what will become of it. We shall find plenty of room for your facility; it will lubricate our whole existence. [...] You won't sing in the Music Hall, but you will sing to me; you will sing to everyone who knows you and approaches you. Your gift is indestructible; don't talk as if I either wanted to wipe it out or make it a particle less divine. I want to give it another direction, certainly; but I don't want to stop your activity. Your gift is the gift of expression, and there is nothing I can do for you that will make you less expressive. It won't gush out at a fixed hour and on a fixed day, but it will irrigate, it will fertilize, it will brilliantly adorn your conversation. Think how delightful it will be when your influence becomes really social. Your faculty, as you call it, will simply make you, in conversation, the most charming woman in America' (375-76).

The change of "direction" that Verena's "artlessly artful facilities" will indeed undergo thanks to Ransom's persuasiveness corresponds with the narrative logic in which the rhetorical or figurative dimension of the text is progressively elevated by, and subordinated to, what James calls the "inner harmony" (*Literary Criticism II* 1105) and "deep-breathing organic form" of the novel (1108). The process in question is obviously, as Derrida would have put it, phallogocentric. In the chain of substitutions leading from serving as a mesmerist's medium, to feminist port-parole, before naturalising themselves in the form of a "really social" vehicle of "conversation," the "artlessly artful facilities" of the young heroine, native and yet "not part of her essence," are progressively essentialised, domesticated, interiorised and given determinate form. A "gift of expression" which "lubricates," "irrigates," and "fertilizes" various forms of social discourse as well as the textual production itself is universalised and personalised at the same time, according to Ransom, by placing itself in the service of an aim loftier and more congenial to the heroine herself than the one it had "adorned" previously. Verena of course bends to the will of her suitor ("It was simply that the truth had changed sides; that radiant image began to look at her from Basil Ransom's expressive eyes" [370]), but the spilled tears evoked in the last sentence of the novel represent in unequivocal terms the price she has had to pay, and will continue to pay, for her sacrifice.

The formal logic that determines James's writing from *Roderick Hudson* to *The Tragic Muse*, but which will undergo significant revision in the later works, at least in the most ambitious of them, is a *sacrificial* logic.[3] More explicitly however than in the previous works, in *The Tragic Muse* this logic ceases to be merely operative and becomes thematised as such, the very meaning of the word "tragic" deriving from the progressively sacrificial nature of the feminine character, in this case Miriam Rooth, constituting the 'structural' or 'organic' centre of the novel. As the tragic muse of the novel, Miriam fully consummates the sacrifice of the "figurative impulse" or "strictly mimetic gift" that determines her own bewildering social identity as well as that of her predecessors, Christina Light and Verena Tarrant. Her artistic sacrifice is precisely what distinguishes her from her mother, not to mention that other socially troublesome and enigmatic figure, Gabriel Nash. While in *The Bostonians*, Verena's mimetic facilities are elevated from the magico-religious service imposed upon them at the beginning to a domestic and pseudo-democratic one at the end, Miriam resists subordination of her faculty to everything but what she calls her "idea": "It isn't to my possible glories that I cling, it's simply to my idea [...]. I like it better than anything else." (436). As mediating figure for the artistic "idea" alone, the "artlessly artful" or "artfully artless" impulse at last becomes fully, or truly, artful, surpassing its previous alienation in the service of religious, political, or conjugal law. The mimetic faculty ceases to mystify from the moment it fulfils its artistic vocation, as is demonstrated by the scene of Miriam's triumph in the role of Juliet at the end of the novel, where Peter Sherringham, brought nearly to the point of madness until then by the blurring of the limits between art and the world, representation and reality, is cured in a moment of cathartic release ("recalled to the real by the very felicity of this experience, the supreme exhibition itself." [490]). The teleological thrust of James's writing at this point, corresponding with the

---

3 One of the more ambitious works in this sense is *The Sacred Fount*, where May Server's sacrifice might be qualified as exceeding the *economy* of sacrifice which is crucial to the closure of Jamesian narrative structure. Similarly, in "The Beast in the Jungle," May Bartram's sacrifice is presented as the possibility of the novella's narrative movement, on the one hand, and irreducible to it, on the other.

18. The 'Paradox of the Comedian'   207

sublimation of the figurative impulse at the origin of his own art, becomes evident if one compares Sherringham's unsuccessful attempt to persuade Miriam to abandon the theatre to marry him with Ransom's successful one to lure Verena Tarrant from the political stage; when Miriam, who refuses to be put in the "box" that her suitor offers her by his marriage proposal, protests that he must let her live, Sherringham responds with the same abusive rhetoric of persuasion that Ransom employed in the previously cited passage:

> 'Let her live? As if I could prevent her living!' Peter cried with unmistakeable conviction. 'Even if I did wish how could I prevent a spirit like yours from expressing itself? Don't talk about my putting you in a box, for, dearest child, I'm taking you out of one. [...] I mean I'll give you a larger life than the largest you can get in any other way. The stage is great, no doubt, but the world's greater. It's a bigger theatre than any of those places in the Strand. We'll go in for realities instead of fables, and you'll do them far better than you do the fables. [...] What I ask you to give up is the dusty boards of the play-house and the flaring footlights, but not the very essence of your being. Your "gift," your genius, is yourself, and it's because it's yourself that I yearn for you. [...] You were made to charm and console, to represent beauty and harmony and variety to miserable human beings, and the daily life of man is the theatre for that—not a vulgar shop with a turnstile that's open only once in the twenty-four hours. [...] You were never finer than at this minute, in the deepest domesticity of private life' (432-34).

That Miriam Rooth, unlike Verena Tarrant, observes without difficulty that the logic employed by her suitor is manipulative, pragmatically serving the ideological and phallocentric interests that men like Ransom and Sherringham represent, attests to the relative supremacy of Miriam Rooth with respect to Verena Tarrant in the mimetological hierarchy established by the formal structure of the two novels. It's the same logic, the same phallogocentrism that informs each of them, but since the chain of substitutions leading from mesmerism to feminist discourse to domestic conversation with Basil Ransom, in *The Bostonians*, is itself surmounted, in *The Tragic Muse*, by the heroine's stubborn devotion to the artistic "idea," Sherringham finds himself confronted with the head of a "medusa" (430) precisely where Ransom's attempt to seduce met with success. Responding to Sherringham's insult that in acting she's immodestly "exhibiting" her "person," Miriam says:

> *'Je vous attendais* with the famous "person"; of course that's the great stick they beat us with. Yes, we show it for money, those of us who have anything decent to show, and some no doubt who haven't, which is the real scandal.

What will you have? It's only the envelope of the idea, it's only our machinery, which ought to be conceded to us; and in proportion as the idea takes hold of us do we become unconscious of the clumsy body. Poor old "person"–if you knew what *we* think of it! If you don't forget it that's your own affair: it shows you're dense before the idea' (439).

"Envelope," "machinery," "clumsy body," "poor old 'person'"—such are the terms designating the material and figural dimension of art as opposed to its "idea." That before the "idea" the spectator should "forget" the "clumsy body" that envelopes it, indeed become "unconscious" of it, shows precisely the extent to which the rhetorical logic of James's writing at this point subordinates the exterior to the interior, the figural to the proper, the material to the ideal. And it is precisely this logic that informs Miriam Rooth's "strictly mimetic gift," or rather the conversion of it, as she succeeds in the course of the novel in distinguishing herself from her mother and becoming a tragic comedian. It is only in the face of the young comedian's stubborn devotion to the idea that Sherringham's plea for the "theatre" of the world versus the stage properly speaking, or for "realities" and the "everyday life of man" instead of "fables," reveals itself as a powerless and hollow mask of words, the self-serving rhetoric that it is, whereas in *The Bostonians* the same discourse was powerful enough to divert an outstanding figurative talent into its ken. Miriam's marriage to her theatre director, Basil Valentine, far from undermining the authority of the artistic bond in relation to the conjugal one, only confirms it: Basil Valentine is as subjugated to the idea that his wife, as a comedian, incarnates, as Basil Ransom coercively gains supremacy over the figurative impulse of his.

The sentence from *The Tragic Muse* that I quoted at the beginning of this paper acquires its full meaning only in the context of the sacrificial logic that determines James's writing at this point. The *tragic* consciousness of the daughter is a consciousness that has knowingly sacrificed its figurative impulse for the sake of the artistic idea. What is sacrificed or, if one prefers, sublimated, is what Diderot famously called the "the paradox of the comedian," the comedian's native lack of identity, or rather, as is the case with the structural centres of James's early novels, their "strictly mimetic" identity, elevated in the narrative process from its origin and subordinated to a greater cause, a higher principle, a more idealised law. The teleological nature of the elevation from impulse to consciousness, from mimesis to art, is rendered explicitly by the use of the word "aim": "The figurative impulse in the mother had become conscious, and therefore higher, through finding an aim, which was beauty, in the daughter." More distinctly perhaps in this sentence than in the grotesque representation of Mrs. Rooth's presumably Jewish identity, James flirts with an anti-Jewishness (not to say anti-Semitism) which consists of stigmatising the Jew *as such*: the Jew with the proverbial 'stiff neck' who refuses to be converted. Perhaps this is why James remains curiously elliptic with respect to the Jewish identity of Miriam's mother; while that of the father is brought up almost with the introduction of Miriam, at the beginning of the novel, we have to wait until near the end of it to read (by the mediation of Dormer's consciousness): "The late Rudolf Roth had at least been, and his daughter was visibly her father's child; so that flanked by such a pair, good Semitic presumptions sufficiently crowned the mother" (414). Despite these "presumptions," nothing permits us to affirm with certainty that Miriam's mother is Jewish, and hence that the "figurative impulse" which does not sublimate itself, refusing to convert itself and to *sacrifice* itself as such, is Jewish. No reader can claim with certainty that Mrs. Rooth, ignorant of the "idea" of beauty and therefore deprived of artistic consciousness, of interiority, dispersing her mimetic "instincts" (414) indifferently in the appreciation of all sorts of spectacles,[4] is Jewish. Dormer's perception of her however is acute, as is appropriate in a portraitist, and his vision of her as a figure of the "immemorial Jewess" (414) testifies to the Judeo-Christian logic of the novel. Read in light of its mimetological structure, and the sacrifice it implies, it is no surprise that the analogy James uses in his preface to describe the "pictorial fusion" of *The Tragic Muse* is a "measureless *Crucifixion*" by Tintoretto (4), meaning that the structural centre of the novel, the figure of the comedian, Miriam Rooth, is Christ-like, analogous to the image of Christ in the painting. Nor is it surprising that James insists, several times in the same preface, and throughout the body of the novel, on the "sacrifice" of the artist.[5]

---

[4] "She found no play too tedious, no *entr'acte* too long, no *baignoire* too hot, no tissue of incidents too complicated, no situation too unnatural and no sentiments too sublime. [...] She delighted in novels, poems, perversions, misrepresentations and evasions [...]" (142-43).

[5] The catharsis Sherringham must undergo at the end of the novel in order to "return to the real" and marry Little Biddy is the result of his inability to accept artistic sacrifice. Speaking with her fellow-artist, Nick Dormer, Miriam Rooth says of Sherringham: "'He wants to enjoy every comfort and to save every appearance, all without making a scrap of a sacrifice'" (418). This criticism is repeated by James himself in the preface: "the promptness with which he [Sherringham] sheds his pretended faith as soon as it feels in the air the breath of reality, as soon as it asks of him a proof or a sacrifice."

Nor that it is before a religious monument, the Cathedral of Notre Dame, that Nick Dormer, early on in the narrative, professes his enthusiasm for art to Gabriel Nash (118). The aesthetic religiosity of *The Tragic Muse* is patent, irrefutable to the extent that one considers seriously the "paradox" comprising its structural centre: "'What's rare in you,' Sherringham says to Miriam, 'is that you have no nature of your own. [...] It's a kind of thing that's a labyrinth'" (138). If in the course of the novel it is precisely this paradox of an identity lacking an identity properly speaking, a character without character, with no nature of its own, the paradox in other words of a purely mimetic nature, that is sacrificed *as such*, that is to say sublimated in the artistic becoming of the comedian, it is not surprising that James's later work will prove to be haunted both by the implications of this sacrifice and by an incessant return of the paradox. Some of the more ambitious of James's later works, including "The Turn of the Screw" and *The Sacred Fount*, will go a long way towards the deconstruction of the aesthetic religiosity (based on a Christian logic of sacrifice) that determines the formal structure of *The Tragic Muse*. The "tragic" acceptance of the sublimation of the "paradox of the comedian" leaves a distinct remainder in this novel in the form of the *difference* between Mrs. Rooth and her daughter, between Jewish exteriority and artistic (not to say Christian) interiority.

Consciousness, in its tragic apprehension of itself, and its apprehension of itself as tragic (Miriam achieving artistic triumph at the end of the novel in the role of Shakespeare's Juliet), can be said to depend upon *the difference of a turn*, upon the twisting of the figurative or mimetic impulse upon itself, on its "elevation," through finding an "aim," which is "beauty," revealed in the final analysis to be nothing other than a representation of the mimetic impulse to itself, that is to say a self-representation. The reason that Jamesian consciousness becomes increasingly self-reflexive, even infinitely so, is that it can never gain complete control over its figurative nature. The sacrificial twisting or turning of the figurative impulse upon itself which ultimately posits, in *The Tragic Muse*, the artistic "idea" as its transcendental correlative, leads to the hyperbolic production of mere phantoms in "The Turn of the Screw," where reflective consciousness is destabilised with every new attempt to gain control over itself. Artistic desire, in *The Tragic Muse*, is mimetic desire now conscious of itself (Miriam on stage imitating the "young passion and young despair" [486] of Juliet, instead of falling in love with her suitor), and it is precisely the renunciation of non-reflexive desire, or instinct, which is tragic. Consciousness-making—that is to say the reflexive turning of the mimetic impulse upon itself, its self-representation—is inherently sacrificial. That this process is also a dizzying one, as later texts such as "The Turn of the Screw" will make clear, is already suggested by Miriam in her attempt to justify to Sherringham her wilful allegiance to the artistic "idea," which she also calls "the *other* side, the grand one [...], the element that makes up for everything"

> 'I'm a contorsionist, and of course there's a hateful side, but don't you see how that very fact puts a price on every compensation, on the help of those who are ready to insist on the *other* side, the grand one [...], the element that makes up for everything?' (440)

The "*other*" side, the meta-physical side of the mimetic twist or turn ("I'm a contortionist"), is the objective or transcendental correlative of consciousness and interiority. If Mrs. Rooth, the comedian's mother, remains deprived of tragic consciousness, forever alienated from the "other" side ("there being no reverse at all to her blazonry" [143]), it is because she remains stubbornly resistant to the sacrificial turning of the mimetic impulse upon itself.[6] But if Dormer's perception of the comedian's mother as a figure of the "immemorial Jewess" is acute, as previously mentioned, it is not only that it refers to the Judeo-Christian logic of sacrifice on which his own aesthetic vision as a portraitist depends. That the Jewish identity of the mother is described as "immemorial" implies that it is irreducible to the representational logic of the novel and older than the consciousness that claims artistic supremacy over it. Refusing to elevate itself towards the beautiful, resisting the sublimating turn that Miriam performs in becoming a comedian, the mimetic impulse of the mother is the 'maternal' resource of the novel's entire system of representation (dramatic, pictorial and narrative); it is older, more primordial, than the theatre which furnishes the cathartic basis, the site of mimetic purification at the core of James's

---

[6] It is precisely such twisting and turning which makes the comedian so appealing as "pictorial object" for the portraitist: "she remained to him primarily a pictorial object, with the nature of whose vicissitudes he was concerned [...] only so far as they had something to say in her face. How could he know in advance what turn of her experience, what twist of her life would say most?" (462). Needless to say, perhaps, Dormer's own success as a portraitist depends upon Miriam's theatrical success as a comedian: "As soon as she [Miriam] stepped on the boards a great and special alteration usually took place in her—she was in focus and in her frame [...]." (382) Pictorial representation and, more generally, the reflector of James's novels, depend upon the "dramatic" sacrifice of the figurative or mimetic impulse.

aesthetic religiosity at this point. One doesn't have to read *The Tragic Muse* from the retrospective point of view of "The Turn of the Screw" to observe that the reflexive (or mimetic) turn of the impulse the daughter inherits from the mother serves as much to occult, or, if one prefers, to repress, the impulse as to 'elevate' it, which is precisely why the 'return' of mimesis as such is inevitable. From a careful reading of *The Tragic Muse* alone one should not be surprised to find Mrs. Rooth making a final, vaguely spectral, appearance as "an undefined shape" (441) lurking just beyond Sherringham's perception, beyond a window-pane, in Miriam Rooth's garden (a scene which prefigures the second appearance of Peter Quint at Bly). Irreducible to perception, and yet constituting the very condition of it, beyond the reflexive or specular basis of consciousness (attested by the presence of the window-pane), the figurative impulse manifesting itself here as a "vulgar ghostly reference" (428) is the first spectre to emerge in James's work in the rigorous sense marking the mimetic deconstruction of the aesthetic. The reference is 'vulgar' to the precise extent that it reveals the imperfect or unachieved sublimation of the figurative impulse by the "idea." Grotesque, because irreducible to the beautiful, the semi-ghostly figure of Mrs. Rooth stands as a sublime reminder of the "paradox" (440) of human identity, resisting the sublimating work of aesthetic form.

It is because the figurative impulse exceeds the self-reflexive capacity of consciousness that the scene at the end of *The Tragic Muse* will repeat itself in James's work. If the condition of being all an artist ("a creature who's absolutely *all* artist" [139], says Sherringham of Miriam Rooth) is precisely to have no nature of one's own, no identity properly speaking, as Diderot had put it in his famous *"Paradoxe sur le comédien,"*[7] and as James understood it in *The Tragic Muse*, the artist will be constrained—contortionist that he or she necessarily is—to repeat the turning of the difference dramatised here as that between Miriam Rooth and her mother. The artistic "idea" will from now on incessantly reveal itself to be the "vulgar ghostly reference" that it discreetly turns out to be in *The Tragic Muse*.

It might well be that James's extraordinary epistemological rigour reaches its pinnacle in "The Turn of the Screw," where the principle of

---

7 For example: " '*A vous entendre le grand comédien est tout et n'est rien.*' '*Et peut-être est-ce parce qu'il n'est rien qu'il est tout par excellence, sa forme particulière ne contrariant jamais les formes étrangères qu'il doit prendre*'" ["You make it sound like a great actor is both everything and nothing at once." / "And perhaps it is because he is nothing that he is the quintessence of everything, as his own form does not prevent him from taking on the foreign ones his roles call for"] (341).

correspondence between the figurative impulse and its "idea," between mimetic performance and the "other side," the metaphysical one, the principle which determines his work up until *The Tragic Muse*, deconstitutes itself with every *turn* in the attempt of the governess, a pastor's daughter, to redeem the figurative impulse in reducing (or raising) it to conscious intent. She lives of course at the mercy of two children touchingly deprived, as she observes, of identities of their own; the orphans of Bly—a mimetic subject being orphaned by definition—Miles (My-less) and Flora—whose name alludes to the rhetorical flowers called tropes—possess, by their very lack of "property," that is to say of identity, a "facility for everything," a "general faculty" compensating for this lack ("They had shown me from the first a facility for everything, a general faculty which, taking a fresh start, achieved remarkable flights" ["The Turn of the Screw" [1999] 63]). This compensating faculty is precisely that of mimesis. Their innocence resides in the fact that they know no distinction between the beautiful and the vulgar, the ideal and the spectral. Only the governess, in accordance with the sacrificial logic of James's own previous work, must distinguish. One is not surprised however that the ghost of Peter Quint turns out to have the aspect of a comedian, reflecting, like the sordid/sublime figure of Mrs. Rooth to Peter Sherringham, her own irreducibly vicarious identity: "He gives me a sort of sense of looking like an actor" (23).

19. Benjamin Britten's Appropriation of James in *Owen Wingrave*

Hubert Teyssandier

Henry James wrote *Owen Wingrave* in 1892, and published it the same year. He later revised it for the New York Edition, where it is included in volume XVII. Benjamin Britten appropriated, and transformed, Henry James's tale in his fifteenth opera, *Owen Wingrave*, which was commissioned by the BBC, and shown in May 1971 as a "television opera," now available on DVD. The first stage performance of *Owen Wingrave* was given at Covent Garden in May 1973. Myfanwy Piper had written the libretto, as she had for Britten's earlier Jamesian opera, *The Turn of the Screw* (1954). Britten's *Owen Wingrave* is, in ideological terms, another statement of the composer's commitment to pacifism, which had also been central to some of his major works, among others *The Rape of Lucretia*, a much earlier opera (1946), and *War Requiem* (1962).

Both tale and opera follow the same story line, and they are both set in the English context of the late nineteenth century. The action begins in London, at the house of Mr. Spencer Coyle, a military instructor, who runs a private teaching establishment for military aspirants cramming for Sandhurst. Mr. Coyle has two sharply contrasted students: one is Lechmere, an uncritical military enthusiast; the other student, Owen Wingrave, is an intellectual, who reads Goethe's poems in James's tale, and Shelley's *Queen Mab* in Britten and Piper's opera. Tale and opera function around this basic contrast, which often lends itself to comic treatment, as Lechmere is a figure of comedy. Owen Wingrave, the scion of a military family, decides to break with the family tradition, and refuses to become an Army officer. He is summoned back to the ancestral seat of the Wingraves, some kind of a 'gothic' place called Paramore, in order to be "straightened out," as his aunt, Miss Wingrave, a "strenuous lady," is made to put it (*Ghostly Tales* 327).

At Paramore, Owen resists all family pressures—both that of his grandfather and of his aunt—and shows no sign of being swayed by 'the voice of the house' nor the presence of the dead. He also resists the pressure of two ladies who live at Paramore: Mrs. Julian, an officer's widow, and Kate Julian, her daughter, who had long been expected to marry Owen. After Owen has been a week in Paramore, showing no signs of submission, the London characters are called for their support, however problematic it might be, on the side of ancestral tradition: these are Lechmere the militarist; Mrs. Coyle, who has sympathy for Lechmere; and Mr. Coyle, who is manifesting an increasing interest in Owen's case against violence and war. They are all invited to Paramore for what is going to prove a very memorable weekend.

In the evening, Kate Julian dares Owen to spend the night in the haunted room, where something ghastly happened long ago. Owen accepts the challenge, to prove that he is no coward, and at his request, Kate locks him in. At dawn the next day, Kate goes to the haunted room, and unlocks the door: Owen's dead body is then discovered, and in both tale and opera, the cause of his death belongs to the unexplained, or the unspeakable.

I.

I shall first discuss the ghostly and its representation, bearing in mind James's well-known artistic aversion to conventional spectral apparitions. His own dramatisation of *Owen Wingrave*, a play entitled *The Saloon* (1908), contains no word nor stage direction that might suggest the introduction of a visible ghost, and when it was performed in 1911, with "a pale, dimly seen figure" appearing on the stage, Henry James expressed his "liveliest disapproval" (*The Complete Plays*, editor's preface). The word "ghost," which is avoided in *The Turn of the Screw*,[1] does occur in *Owen Wingrave*, and the protagonist is made to introduce it: "I've started up all the old ghosts" (336). In this instance, however, the word is not used in its literal sense— that is, not in the sense of what Mrs. Coyle calls "a proved *ghost*" (339). In

---

1 In *The Turn of the Screw*, the word "ghost" occurs only once, in the prologue and in relation to another story ("Griffin's ghost"), but is never used in the course of the main story: Quint and Miss Jessel are never called "ghosts," but "intruders," "visitors," or "visitants."

Owen's remark, the text refers to the souls of the dead, the shadows of the past and Paramore's former glory, not to visible apparitions.

However, at a late stage in the tale, we are made aware that Owen, before the night he meets his death in the haunted room, has spent the previous night there, for unstated reasons of his own—an important detail which is not maintained in Britten's opera: "'I spent all last night in the confounded place'" (350). The information is part of a private exchange between Kate and Owen, but Lechmere, the happy militarist, who has cast himself in the role of Owen's rival for Kate's hand, has been eavesdropping for his own benefit and for the reader's guidance. Though not very shrewd, Lechmere, who is Owen's comic antagonist, has been led to the certainty that, the night before, Owen has had some unaccountable experience in the "confounded" room, as comes out in the ensuing dialogue between Lechmere and Coyle, while Owen is spending his second and ultimate night in the "White Room" (as it is called in James's tale) and may even be already lying dead:

> 'But I'm sure he *did* see something or hear something,' the youth added.
> 'In that ridiculous place? What makes you so sure?'
> 'Well, because he looks as if he had. I've an idea you can tell—in such a case. He behaves as if he had.'
> 'Why then shouldn't he name it?'
> Young Lechmere wondered and found. 'Perhaps it's too bad to mention' (350-51).

As we know from the beginning of the tale, Lechmere, contrary to Owen, is "as a general thing uninspired" (259). So what he thinks he has read in Owen's face can hardly be taken for a reliable judgment. On the other hand, Owen has been making jokes about the "White Room," calling it "'an awful sell,'" but at the same time he has shown signs of embarrassment when told by Lechmere that he did not believe that (347). Mr. Coyle, who is showing more and more sympathy for Owen's pacifist opinions and has far greater insight than Lechmere, is here anxiously trying to make sense of what Lechmere thinks he has found out. Following a familiar Jamesian strategy, the text is here hovering over something that cannot be named.

Ironically, Lechmere, in his lame remark ("'too bad to mention'"), comes quite close to saying all we can assert about the haunted room. The ghostly, whatever it is, is associated with one of the worst forms of evil: the ugliness of violence and war, which the Wingrave family has been perpetuating throughout the ages, and which will eventually cause the death of the one who tries to oppose it. Owen Wingrave is another doomed fighter, like all his ancestors, though a fighter in the cause of peace. In the sentence that concludes the New York version, Owen appears as a dead soldier, lying on the ground he has helped to conquer: "He was all the young soldier on the gained field" (352).[2]

Within the tale that leads to Owen's death, the legend of Paramore, which is brought to the reader's knowledge as Mr. Coyle is relating it to his wife, functions as an inset tale within the main tale. The legend is about two of Owen's ancestors, Colonel Wingrave and his son, who both lived and died in the eighteenth century, in George II's time (339). The boy was stricken to death by his father in the haunted room at Paramore, because he had refused to take up the challenge of another boy and to fight against him, and in the very same room, the father's dead body was discovered the morning after. Owen's death duplicates, in a double way, the legend of Paramore: like his young ancestor, he has refused to conform to the family tradition, and he dies the same inexplicable death as the boy's father.

In their rendering of the ghostly, Britten and Piper preserve the silence and mystery in which Henry James has enshrouded it—a noticeable difference of treatment compared with their operatic transposition of *The Turn of the Screw*, where the "visitants" hold major singing roles. The dead Wingrave ancestors, as they appear to Owen and to the audience, are silent spectral presences becoming visible in the darkness of Paramore. I shall for the moment restrict myself to the libretto and the score, in particular as regards the stage directions, which clearly indicate that the ghostly must, in some way or other, be made visible. It is clear from the libretto and the score that there are ghostly apparitions in the opera, although they do not utter a word in reply when Owen addresses them. They intervene only in Act II, and the stage directions only mention them at the point when Owen, who has been formally disinherited by his grandfather, is left alone on the stage, all the other characters having gone to bed in some kind of funereal procession, each holding a light, up the staircase that leads to the upper level of the stage, from which they disappear into the corridors. The scene (Act II Scene I) uses the two levels of the stage, the upper level being also called "the gallery," as on the Elizabethan stage. "Gallery" is simultaneously used in the sense of picture gallery (where the ancestral portraits cover the wall); the lower level is the drawing room.

---

2 The earlier version read: "He looked like a young soldier on a battle-field."

After all the family and guests have gone up the stairs, "Owen goes up to the portraits" (*Score* 243), and starts apostrophising his painted ancestors:

> Now you may save your scornful looks
> and turn your faces to the wall [...]
> Now I am nothing, I bid you all farewell
>
> (*Libretto* 33).

Then Owen turns away from the portraits, to sing his peace aria or soliloquy ("'In peace I have found my image [...]'"), and as he concludes with the words: "'I am finished with you all,'" the stage directions read: "Apparitions of the old man and the boy appear to Owen," and he addresses them in *Sprechstimme*: "'Ah! I'd forgotten you! Come on then, come on I'll tell you'" (33). The spectral presences are those of earlier Wingraves, a father and his son, around whom the legend of Paramore has been woven: the boy beaten to death, and the father found inexplicably dead the morning after the son's murder. "The boy turns and looks at Owen" (*Score* 258), then "the apparitions disappear into the [haunted] room" (*Score* 260). After they are gone, "Owen sinks into a chair in the shadows." Not only are the two spectral figures explicitly called "apparitions," they are also given faces, since they are listed in the cast of the original television opera, as "Colonel Wingrave, an apparition" (played by Peter Pears) and "Young Wingrave, his son, an apparition." Of course there may be different ways of staging the apparitions, but it seems difficult, in the case of the opera, to represent them as Henry James would have wished for his play *The Saloon*: greater darkness in the midst of darkness.

In the original television version, the ghosts actually appear twice, the first apparitions occurring right at the beginning of Act II, which opens with a ballad, sung by a tenor voice, and accompanied by a "distant chorus of boys' voices." The tenor voice is that of a character called "The narrator" (for which there is no basis in James's tale), and the legend of Paramore, which in the tale is related by Mr. Coyle, is here conveyed in ballad form, an old narrative poetic form, revived in the days of Romanticism, which Myfanwy Piper has used as an inset narrative, which goes through all the circumstances of the boy's cruel murder and the father's mysterious death:

> There was a boy, a Wingrave boy,
> A Wingrave born to kill his foe,
> Far away on sea and land
> The Wingraves were a fighting band (25-26).

While the legend of Paramore is being sung, the narrator and the distant chorus are invisible, and we are shown, inset in the main color film, "slow-motion mime in sepia, the use of monochrome strikingly evoking an earlier historical period" (John Evans 237). In the inset monochrome film, there are three spectral figures, the father, his son (the earlier Owen), and another boy, the playmate against whom he refuses to fight, and all the episodes in the legend are mimed: the challenge, the Wingrave boy crossing his arms as a sign that he will not fight, the father taking his son by the hand, marching him up the stairs and beating him to death, until the sepia film finishes with a close-up on the head of the dead father lying on the floor.

In the television film, the reappearance of two of the spectral figures (the father and son) continues the sepia film that has illustrated the ballad, with the difference that this time the silent slow-motion miming is watched by Owen, who, just before the ghosts disappear, addresses the boy with compassion, and as his father takes him into the "White Room," views himself, not without hubris, as having won against the family tradition.

II.

The prominent role played by painted portraits in Britten's opera amounts to an extensive development of Henry James's pictorialism, as we can observe it at work in *Owen Wingrave*. The tale hints at an indefinite number of portraits, summing up the family history on the walls of Paramore: they are part of "the family circle," as Miss Wingrave calls it (336). The portraits intervene at a fairly late stage in the tale (in penultimate section 3), when the weekend guests have joined the family at Paramore, and they mark the beginning of the crucial and terminal episode. Owen refers to the portraits as stern judges manifesting their disapproval of his resolution: "The very portraits glower at me on the walls" (336). In James's tale only one portrait can be visualised with some distinctness, as Mr. Coyle shows it to his wife: "On the staircase as they went her husband showed her the portrait of Colonel Wingrave—a representation, with some force and style, for the place and period, of a gentleman with a hard handsome face, in a red coat and a peruke" (340).

We are told that Sir Philip looks like him—an ominous sign, especially as we know that this is the Wingrave ancestor that struck his son to death. From what Mr. Coyle has told his wife earlier on (339), we can date the portrait:

it is an eighteenth-century painting, from the days of George II's reign. The text does not say nor imply that his son is represented with him on the same canvas, but ghostly apparitions, which the text of the tale never mentions, begin to take shape in Mr. Coyle's own personal imagination: "[…] if one should have the courage to walk the old corridors of Paramore at night one might meet a figure that resembled him roaming, with the restlessness of a ghost, hand in hand with the figure of a tall boy" (340). Mr. Coyle may well imagine it, but Henry James is not going to represent it. The portrait however is central to the tale, and in some way contains it all, as it refers to a point in time that contains the whole of time, past, present, and future.

In Britten's opera, the pictorial idea it borrows from Henry James is developed on a very large scale from the very beginning after only a few bars of music. Instead of a traditional overture, the opera starts with a prelude combining music and pictures, described as follows in Myfanwy Piper's libretto: "Prelude: The family portraits at Paramore. Ten are seen, of which the fifth is a double portrait" (5).

In the original television film, the first shot is a close-up on the Wingrave coat of arms: a massive shield, with swords and other weapons arranged symmetrically across it, on top of it a medieval helmet, the metallic folds of military banners on both sides—all of a dull grey. Then the ten portraits mentioned in the libretto are shown one after the other in their thick wooden frames, each bearing the date when it was painted, the first being that of Owain Wyngrave, Knight of Paramore, c. 1536, all rough paintings with the colours all gone, except for a trace of faded red here and there. The fifth portrait—a double portrait—represents a man and a boy, and the camera slowly zooms in on the face of the boy, called Owen. The date of the painting is 1652—during the reign of Charles II. In Britten and Piper's operatic version of the tale, the legend of Paramore has been pushed back to the early years of the Restoration period, shortly after the Civil War. The last portrait shown is that of the protagonist's father, Colonel Oliver Wingrave, dated 1875.

At this point there is a cross-fade from the image of the father to Owen's face, and he is thus introduced as one more portrait continuing the series, which is another way of making the same point as Henry James in the last sentence of the New York version: "He was all the young soldier on the gained field." Then the camera zooms away from Owen's face, and he appears sitting in a room (with more military paintings in it), half-listening to Mr. Coyle, who is explaining the battle of Austerlitz with tin soldiers, on a map spread on his desk. At this point the dramatic action begins, and Mr. Coyle's voice is the first to be heard, as in the tale.

The Wingrave coat of arms, and some of the portraits, in particular the double portrait and the portrait of Owen's father, are made to reappear recurrently. As to the double portrait, during Owen's soliloquy, the two spectral figures are distinctly seen detaching themselves from their painted images, which they duplicate, and walking away hand in hand, as Mr. Coyle imagines them in the tale; they disappear into the haunted room, where Owen is eventually going to rejoin them.

The visual display, which the opera allows, combined with the impact of the music, prevents the ironic distancing which Henry James continually maintains, with its subtle balance between comedy and tragedy, and Britten's opera is a more somber work than James's tale. But both opera and tale function around the same ambiguity: the protagonist refuses to follow the line of his ancestors, but he does follow it all the same, and he dies a violent death, although what kills him is beyond words and defies representation.

III.

Britten combines several kinds of music writing, which refer to different periods in the history of music: Schönberg and the twelve-tone system, based on specific arrangements of all the twelve degrees of the chromatic scale; the tonal music of the great operatic tradition from Mozart to Richard Strauss; and the far older, late medieval tradition of church music with its eight modes.

Britten introduces, as early as the opera's prelude, a first schönbergian twelve-tone row, and this takes us back to the portraits, and the question of their exact number. They are said to be ten, but as one of them is a double portrait, this brings the total up to eleven. Further, since Owen is made to appear looking like one more portrait, the correct total is twelve. So the portraits work in conjunction with the twelve-tone music, which is heard in the very first bars, even before the first portrait has appeared. A first twelve-tone series opens the opera, over three bars, and the notes, played on the piano, with percussion accompaniment (including two drums) are arranged in harshly dissonant chords, which make up a refrain that is going to be heard throughout the opera. The chords, which make up a two-beat military march, indicated as "Martial," are arranged according to a "nightmare rhythm" which leads to the appearance of the portraits, and will be heard again repeatedly, for example at the beginning of Owen's soliloquy.[3] So the dissonant military march, bristling with false relations, is the music of the Wingraves. Then another twelve-tone row appears as the portraits are shown, each with its own cadenza, and each portrait introduces a new pitch in the series, so that the notes pile up until we reach the total of eleven, and when Owen is seen, the one chromatic pitch that has so far been missing (D) is introduced by one of the horns.

However, the music of Owen Wingrave is not all twelve-tone series, and as we watch Owen for the first time, we enter the tonal system, with a horn motif in D, wavering between D major (two sharps) and D minor (one flat). As John Evans has pointed it out, Owen's tonality is "the central pivot" around which the other tonalities are arranged (235). The conflicts around him are reflected in the tonalities ascribed to those who show sympathy for him or hostility against him: Mr. Coyle's tonality is A major and Mrs. Coyle's is E major (tonalities with sharps); on the other hand, Lechmere is often made to sing in B flat, and Sir Philip in E flat. So the conflict around Owen is musically rendered through a sharp/flat contrast.

Fig. 1 Kate Own.
But on — ly found the blood — soaked brack-en and trampl-ed   grass.
Ex.1 fig. 265 @ 1973 by Faber Music ltd. Reproduced by kind permission of the publishers

Leaving out most details concerning tonalities, I shall mention at this stage that the ambiguous relationship between Owen and Kate is rendered through tonal contrast (Kate's G flat against Owen's D). However their voices, both in the medium range (mezzo-soprano and baritone), sing in proximate registers, and at one point, in the course of what appears first as an uncertain love duet, before it turns into a quarrel, they both sing in the same (somewhat funereal) key of C minor, and for a brief while their two musical lines are made of the same notes, exactly one octave apart (*Score* 265 fig. 1). However,

---

3 The phrase "nightmare rhythm" occurs in the manuscript sketches of Benjamin Britten for *Owen Wingrave*, and Arnold Whittall, in his article on "Britten's Lament: The World *of Owen Wingrave*," points out how the "nightmare rhythm" reappears in the score as Owen speaks to the portraits (Whittall 148-52).

the words they sing speak of "blood-soaked bracken and trampled grass" — the marks left by two rival stags "fighting for their chosen hind." It does seem that a grim kind of desire is part of Kate's violence, as she is still trying to bring back Owen to the tradition and religion of Paramore. The tragedy of it is that the duet seals Owen's doom, and the comedy of it is that the rival stag is Lechmere.

Fig. 2 The Ballad.
Fig. 196 @ 1973 by Faber Music ltd. Reproduced by kind permission of the publishers

With Act II, in which this scene is contained, Britten has introduced from the beginning still another kind of music writing, which is modal, and refers back to distant times. The words of the ballad which relates the legend of Paramore ("There was a boy, a Wingrave boy [...]") are sung to music written in one of the church modes — a mode in G (as for ghostly), and as soon as it begins to be heard, the ballad's modal melody is perceived as completely different from all the music that has been heard so far in the opera.[4] It is obviously not twelve-tone music, and it uses a system of intervals (starting with a second followed by a fifth) that makes it sound unlike any tonal arrangement (fig. 2). It is a doleful, eerie melody, accompanying a tale of ancient days, a ghostly music heard as if coming from far away. The ballad starts on a D (the reciting note), which of course relates the mode to Owen's key: it is indeed both the story of the seventeenth century Owen and of his late nineteenth century namesake. So the modal system is here related to the tonal. The chorus of boys' voices starts with a succession of semitones, also heard on the accompanying trumpet, and sings the refrain that concludes each stanza: "Trumpet blow, Paramore shall welcome woe." Then the chorus becomes a second narrative voice, while the trumpet sounds a final military flourish. The overall effect is chromatic, owing to the frequency of ascending and descending semitones, so that transitions are easy with the twelve-tone music system.[5]

---

4 Technically, the mode used here is the mixolydian: the note on which it ends is G, its ambitus is gg, and its tenor is D (Don Michael Randel, *The Harvard Dictionary of Music* 533).
5 This is effected in particular through what Arnold Whittall has analysed as a "wedge-shaped idea," which also appears in Britten's Owen Wingrave sketchbooks:

The resort to the ballad form had been foreshadowed at the beginning of Act I, as Lechmere joyfully sings the first line of a traditional ballad: "The Minstrel boy to the war is gone / In the ranks of death you'll find him" (*Score* 15). That was however a different tune, not at all doleful. Later in Act II, Owen is heard singing the Paramore ballad tune derisively, to deride Lechmere who has been flirting outrageously as well as comically with Kate Julian: "And with his friend, young Lechmere played" (*Score* 236). The ballad tune is going to be heard one last time, after Owen's death and Kate's shriek of horror. This time, only the first stanza is heard, with the tenor voice, the chorus of boys' voices, and the trumpet. As the music fades away into silence, the last words heard are "Paramore shall welcome woe."

The opera has begun with the coat of arms of the Wingraves, in its medieval splendor — an image that sums up the glory of Paramore, but we have not been given any more clues than in Henry James's tale as to the possible significance of this odd place name, apparently derived from the French (*"par amour"*). The emphatically doleful way in which the name is sounded and repeated at both ends of Act II, echoing as it were the funereal cry of Poe's *Raven*, combines contradictory associations of tragic sorrow and subversive irony. The ancestral coat of arms has no motto, but Lechmere's triumphant outcry in Act I (*"La Gloire c'est Tout"*) would be more suitable than *"Par Amour."* The absent motto is in itself a significant blank.

IV.

In *Owen Wingrave*, Benjamin Britten's second and last Jamesian opera, there seem to be strong affinities with the art of Henry James, and not only with the tale that is here transposed. While maintaining his opera within the same late nineteenth century context as James's tale, Britten also evinces a Jamesian sense of the past as regards both distant historic times, and the history of his art. While dealing with the contemporary scene, James's tale reverberates dim sounds of earlier periods — the Napoleonic wars, the "crowded Indian past" (323), the Indian mutiny, Hannibal and Julius Caesar,

---

it is made of two lines that diverge from a single pitch or converge on one. To quote Whittall: "This idea is notable for its tonal elusiveness [...] The last of [Britten's] sketches closes on a chord that verticalizes four prominent notes from the Ballad's modal melodic line [G—D—E—B], and this found its way directly into the score of the opera [...] (Fig. 236)" (149-50).

226   Henry James's Europe

Marlborough and Frederick (328). In *Owen Wingrave*, Britten uses and alters musical forms that are part of the great operatic tradition: both the military march that introduces us to Paramore, and the chorus of boys' voices that seals its doom rewrite Mozartian structures, although their former associations have been altered. Britten also goes further back, beyond the seventeenth century, to the times of pre-tonal music—modal music having its origins in very distant times.

In dramatic terms, the opera and the tale are fairly close to each other, and James's 'scenic' method, which often resorts to dialogues and confrontational exchanges, and uses conscious theatrical effects from the first scene to the last, easily lends itself to stage transposition, although James was unfortunate when he himself turned *Owen Wingrave* into a play. Britten's opera is often remarkably close to the tale, from Coyle's initial words ("Upon my words you must be off your head!") to the final catastrophe. However, in the opera, Coyle's apostrophe to Owen (*Score* 24) is delayed by the "prologue," and the beginning of scene one; at the end the music continues beyond the discovery of Owen's dead body. Operas are expected to have some kind of "overture," or, as was the case in the earliest operas (Monteverdi), a "prologue" for one or more singers. *Owen Wingrave* begins with an extended prologue that serves as overture, introducing a whole set of musical motifs, and a sequence of images that concentrates centuries of historic time from the days when the family coat of arms was designed to the late nineteenth century. Operas are also expected to have a finale, and while the tale comes to an abrupt end on the image of Owen's dead body, in the opera the music goes on, after the catastrophe has happened. The ballad is resumed, serving as low-keyed finale, and the boys' voices, fading away, 'ghostlily,' lead to the barely audible, ultimate G that concludes the mode used in the ballad (fig. 3), after the tenor voice has stopped, and the trumpet has ceased its muted fanfare.

Fig. 3 Fig. 295. Fading away, calando...
@ 1973 by Faber Music ltd. Reproduced by kind permission of the publishers

VI:
AUTHORSHIP AND SELF-REPRESENTATION

20. Narrative Heterogeneity as an Adjustable Fictional Lens in *The American Scene*

Eleftheria Arapoglou

Henry James returned from England to the United States in late August 1904, after nearly a quarter of a century's absence from his native land. As Leon Edel records in the last volume of James's biography *The Master: 1901-1916*, James's reasons for returning to the U.S. and for writing about his homeland were not uniform. His motives included personal nostalgia and artistic interest, as well as practical and financial considerations. In the period between 1902 and 1904, while James still resided in England, he contacted several people—among them his brother William, as well as his friends Grace Norton and William Dean Howells—to inform them of his return plans. He revealed to them his powerful urge to revisit America and the necessity of expediting his business interests in view of the forthcoming collected edition of his works.

When James first left the United States in 1875, he was turning away from a country he judged too unsophisticated to sustain a novelist of manners. His criticism of Nathaniel Hawthorne's work as undernourished in *Hawthorne* (1879) justifies James's turn to the "denser, richer, warmer, European spectacle" on the grounds of his disdain for the "cold, and light and thin something belonging to the imagination alone" which America evoked in authors at the time (*Hawthorne* [New York, 1967] 55). James then felt that Europe's structures of life and literature, validated by the long process of history, could grant his material the solidity of specification. Contrary to his claims in *Hawthorne* in which he minimises America's artistic effect, James's *Notebooks* for November 1881 stress that, even though at the time the American writer had to "deal, more or less, even if only by implication, with Europe," otherwise he would be considered "incomplete," "a hundred years hence—fifty years hence perhaps he [would] doubtless be accounted [incomplete] for neglecting America" (Matthiessen 214). In other words, even at a time when Europe monopolised James's creative interest, America did not cease to constitute a pole of attraction, which would soon reclaim the author

Not fifty, but merely twenty-five years later, James felt the urge to shift his focus from the European to the American scene. In a 1902 letter to Grace Norton, James qualified "the idea of seeing America again and tasting the American air" as "a vision, a possibility, an impossibility positively romantic" (Edel *Henry James V*, quoted by Fargnoli 312). Three years later, and following his tour of America, James's *Notebooks* dated 29 March 1905 from Coronado Beach, California, testify to his "inward accumulation of material" and express a wish:

> I shall be able to [plunge] my hand, my arm, in, deep and far, and up to the shoulder—into the heavy bag of remembrance—of suggestion—of imagination—of art—and fish out every little figure and felicity, every little fact and fancy that can be to my purpose
>
> (Matthiessen 237).

James's "arm" fished into "the bag of remembrance" during his journey across America, which began in September and ended in December 1904. However, his ultimate "purpose," a book recording his experience of revisiting America, was realised at Lamb House in Sussex, where James returned in July 1905.

The author composed *The American Scene* out of the sixteen travel impressions that appeared in various magazines up to 1906. "New England" was the only section that was composed while James was still in the United States. The pieces that had appeared as magazine instalments formed the basis of the book along with four previously unserialised chapters. *The American Scene* follows James's visit to New England and New York—chronologically spanning from September to December 1904—as well as his journey to Florida, and concludes with the author heading north of Florida on the Pullman train. James's tour of the Midwest—including Mississippi, St. Louis, Chicago, and Indianapolis—and of California and the Pacific Coast—Coronado Beach, Monterey, San Francisco, and the journey up to Oregon and Seattle—do not form part of the narrative. These impressions were initially scheduled to appear separately as a second volume, but were never published.

Throughout *The American Scene*, references to America as the center of James's creative orientation abound. The chapter on Richmond opens with a comment on the autobiographical narrator's renewed fascination with his homeland: "Europe had been romantic years before, because she was different from America; wherefore America would now be romantic because she was different from Europe" (*American Scene* [1993] 655). "The restless analyst" of the Richmond chapter admits to the freshness and romance of Europe in the past as conducive to the making of impressions more varied and "of a higher intensity" than those gathered on the American scene (654). However, at present, a long absence from America and stay in Europe have dulled James's fascination with the Old World and rekindled his attraction to his homeland as a new locus of interest.

In my view, the two central themes around which the narrative of *The American Scene* centers—repatriation and the challenge to identity posed by a belated view of American culture—highlight the significance of the cultural geographical context of the Jamesian text. More specifically, in this paper I am going to focus on the ways in which James's re-territorialisation of the physical and socio-cultural American landscape determines his identity (re)configuration within a modern frame. Usually, the spatial grounding of a narrative has a specific referent. Nevertheless, in the case of *The American Scene*, this spatial referent is not a static place but an itinerary. If we take into consideration the fact that James the author collects his impressions as he is crossing the country, we can see why James the narrator subsequently presents his readers with kinetic, constantly shifting, travel impressions. Furthermore, James's own positioning within the narrative, which lacks fixity because of the multiple narrative personas he adopts, grants the text a dynamic, kaleidoscopic outlook. Consequently, narrative structure and stance defy the aspect of stasis and fixity in James's construction of geographical as well as social space.

As I will argue in this paper, James's social, political, economic, cultural, and aesthetic sense of modernity testifies to the spatial and temporal divides in his approach to America. James as both the author and narrator of *The American Scene* speaks from a liminal space. This space is delineated and necessitated by his topographical and temporal in-betweenness. On the one hand, his aesthetic and literary attachment to the Victorian European scene clashes with his emotional and social proximity as a native of the pre-industrial American scene. On the other hand, his long absence from his homeland stirs in him a nostalgic inclination to the rural, agrarian past of his memory, which conflicts with the urban, industrial reality confronting him. As a result of this ambivalent positioning, James's record of his travel impressions revels in ambiguity. More specifically, at the same time that his native consciousness urges him to ground himself in the physical landscape of his homeland, his extended absence and subsequent detachment from America de-familiarise the country's socio-cultural landscape. As a result of this oscillation between instinctive familiarity and affected estrangement, the narrative of *The American Scene* does not simply record traveling as a leisure activity. Rather, it establishes traveling as a modern social gesture of cultural significance and a moral statement on modern American reality.

The most obvious illustration of James's ambivalent narrative stance in the face of modern America is the text's narrative heterogeneity, identified in the constantly shifting perspectives. The narrator's vacillating positioning has stirred much discussion. The fact that, soon after the first few pages of the book, the straightforward first-person narrator of the opening sentence suddenly turns to third-person (with the narrator assuming multiple guises such as "the returning visitor," "the cold-blooded critic," "the spectator," "the incurable eccentric," "the victim," "the starved story-seeker," "the perverted person," "the palpitating pilgrim," "the ancient contemplative person," "the restless analyst"— the last one outnumbering the rest) along with the fact that narration is placed in the past, establish a clear distinction between author and narrator: James writing in Lamb House versus James traveling and collecting impressions in the United States. Stuart Hutchinson sees these "titles" as veils that, in James as in Hawthorne, shield the "inmost Me" in "an unknowable world" where identification becomes impossible (Hutchinson 134). Nevertheless, I see the poise and 'shielding' of the detached analyst continuously threatened by the autobiographical context of the narrative, which is constantly reinforced. James's narrative grounding on locations that hold a personal interest to him—because they are associated with his youth—and his focus on intimate moments of his journey—as, for example, the detailed, profoundly emotional, accounts of his visits to past family residences—deeply implicate him, too, as part of the American scene and as object of literary representation. In fact, I believe that James exults in the ambiguity and ambivalence of his positioning within the narrative as a means of constantly adjusting his fictional lens to the contradictions, modalities, and oscillations of his personal and socio-cultural geography.

My view on the book's narrative structure is reinforced by a prefatory claim James himself makes that anticipates and justifies the narrative shifts to follow. In the *Preface* to *The American Scene*, James admits to the textual dialogue between his remembered or re-imagined past as a native of America and the experienced present of his encounter with the country as a visitor. He actually presents this dialogue as a narrative merit when he confesses: "I felt no doubt [...] of my great advantage on that score" (*The American Scene* [1993] 353). For this reason, on the one hand, he admits to the long years of "continuous absence" that allowed him the "time" to become "almost as fresh as an inquiring stranger," "the most earnest of visitors," while on the other, he tones down the impression of distance and estrangement by identifying himself as a "native" (353). Subsequently, he defines his advantage as the co-existence of "the freshness of eye, outward and inward" that his years of absence have affected with the acuteness of vision that he possesses as an "initiated native" (353). By asserting a double positioning, as simultaneously the "initiated native" and "the inquiring stranger," James implicitly claims an enlarged perspective. To justify this perspective, he mentions "the longest list of questions, the sharpest appetite for explanations and the largest exposure to mistakes" that he announces will help him "take his stand" (353). This amalgamation of detachment and intimacy that James endeavors to achieve subsequently affects narrative tone, fusing documentation with imagination, history with autobiography, report with fiction.

Stuart Johnson views James's narrative fusion positively, as the "key to the interest and pathos" of James's characterisation in general. Indeed, the discourse of outsider and insider that Johnson applies to the discussion of such Jamesian characters as Lambert Strether and Chad Newsome can also be applied to James's position as the author and narrator of *The American Scene*. James is geographically both an outsider and an insider to the American scene. He is an outsider by the fact of his extended absence in Europe and his penetration into the heart of European life that resulted in some of his most brilliant novels set in the European scene. Nevertheless, he is also an insider because of his "initiated native" status, which allows him an intuitive proximity to his subject. Edna Kenton, in her 1943 essay "Henry James in the World," coins the term "dispatriation" to refer to James's oxymoronic combination of nearness and remoteness, as she feels that the term "expatriate" cannot express the particularities of James's absence from his homeland and does not accurately describe the author's status with respect to his home country. Kenton draws on the definition James himself gives in "The Story-teller at Large: Mr. Henry Harland" of the dispatriate as the citizen of the world whose detachment in viewpoint of, rather than severance or lack of interest in, his birth land grants his artistic creation what Kenton judges the right point of view.

Among the contemporary critics who have discussed James's identification in *The American Scene*, Posnock's argument on James's self-representation—embedded as it is in cultural criticism, historical context, and social thought—also probes into James's positioning "between cultures" (*The Trial of Curiosity* 8). Similarly to Kenton, Posnock highlights the fact that James, as an expatriate, is "neither wholly European nor wholly American" (7). More specifically, the critic reveals that James refused to identify himself as a New Englander, and considered himself a New Yorker, removed from Boston's "cultural idealism" and from "class loyalties" of any kind (9). Furthermore, in his essay "The Politics of Nonidentity: A Genealogy," Posnock contends that "[t]hroughout *The American Scene*, James's effort is to exemplify, in his own marginal, oscillating status as returning native and stranger, an alternative mode of being" (40). There, the critic places James's idiosyncratic identitarian thinking in the context of his discussion of the political responsibility of intellectuals, and claims that Henry James shares with Randolph Bourne, John Dewey, Theodor Adorno, and Michèl Foucault "a paradoxical effort that engages in public life and upholds intellectual responsibility while resisting conventional modes of engagement and responsibility" ("The Politics of Nonidentity" 42). Whereas I agree with Posnock that James's self-representation in *The American Scene* challenges static notions of fixed identity, I view James's oxymoronic identification as a correlative of his spatial awareness. James's floating selfhood, lacking "impermeability and fixity," signifies his liminal positioning within a modern world where dividing lines are blurred, distinctions have collapsed, and forms are lacking ("Breaking the Aura" 36).

The multiplicity and fluidity of the personas James adopts in the narrative course is a correlative of the American scene's overall transience. Paradoxically, the ever-changing, and thus ephemeral, nature of the landscape is the only constant value in modern America. Thus, James engages in spatio-temporal *flânerie*, seeking to approach the country and establish spatial as well as temporal divides. However, the modern character of his experience of American landscape and society destabilises these divides. As Marshall Berman has argued, "[m]odern environments and experiences cut across all *boundaries of geography*" (Berman 15, emphasis mine) and modernity pours humans into "*a maelstrom* [...] of perpetual disintegration and renewal, trouble and anguish, ambiguity and contradiction" (345, emphasis mine). In the light of Berman's claim, the spatial transformation and impermanence to which James becomes a witness during his tour of his homeland testify to America's modernisation—social, economic, political, cultural. Everywhere he goes the "restless analyst" is confronted with the predicament of the modern, mobile man who is unable to establish geographical roots in an evanescent cosmos. As Anthony Giddens has written, the effect of the great dynamic forces of modernity is that places are no longer the clear supports of identity (92). In *The American Scene*, modernisation progressively erodes spatio-temporal frontiers and borders: home becomes an impossibility in a world of dissolving boundaries and expanding horizons, the present is disengaged from the past, and the distinction between private and public spaces breaks down. Consequently, fixed and unitary identity concepts are undermined as the native James returns to America as an alien. James's dispatriate status urges him to strengthen his sense of self by revisiting what he thinks will be an accessible past. His urge is not unjustifiable if we interpret it as an essentially modern need to establish an expressive relationship to the past by identifying territorial locations that function as nodes of association and continuity. Indeed, James's experience of the social aspect of modernity cuts through his drifting from present to past and projection into the future—temporal as well as spatial.

As Homi Bhabha has argued, modern humans experience ambiguity of identification because they are faced with "the moment of transit where space and time cross to produce complex figures of difference and identity, past and present, inside and outside, inclusion and exclusion" (Bhabha 158). Thus, this crossing of the spatial and the temporal in the American scene's modern context produces the liminal space that James is called to inhabit. The in-betweenness and ambivalence of James's positionality display, but also displace, designations of identity founded on what Bhabha terms "the binary logic through which identities of difference are often constructed," because they defy the dualism of fixity versus flexibility (Bhabha 159). Ultimately, James's experience of the American scene, as well as his role in the narrative process, reveals his simultaneous status as the observer and the self-observed. James's double status as subject and object of observation and critique, along with his defiance of fixed and unitary concepts of identification, foregrounds the intentional, invented, multiple, relational and often oxymoronic qualities of James's identity as both the text's narrator and author. This is why I conclude that *The American Scene* can best be read as a musical composition, with the multiplicity of voices playing together at the same time, as a polyphonic symphony charged with intentional contrapuntal variations. In this fictional "*capriccio,*" the many individual voices shaping the narrative are neither dissonant nor cacophonous. Rather, they form and inform each other as they take radically different shapes and still maintain harmonies.

21. James's Faces: Appearance, Absorption and the Aesthetic Significance of the Face

Jakob Stougaard-Nielsen

On 27 June 1906, James wrote to his literary agent, James B. Pinker, that he had found the right image for illustrating the first volume of his New York Edition: the "very good & right (beautifully done) photographic portrait" by Coburn (Horne *A Life in Letters* 435). Coburn shot three profile portraits from which James selected the smallest as the one best suited for his purpose.[1] James also offered directions to Coburn on how to crop the chosen photograph for the desired effect, suggesting that it should be "reduced down *to above* the resting hand — that is to about the middle of the trunk" (Saltz 258).[2]

In James's letters we witness an author far from uninterested in (though often troubled by) the visual appearance of his literary texts and his own literary (if not physical) image. From Kaplan's biography, we learn that throughout his life, James had an uneasy relationship both with photography as an art form and with his own appearance captured in such reproductions. In a letter, for instance, James wrote: "I am terribly

---

[1] One of the profiles was printed in A.L. Coburn's *Men of Mark*, an *en-face* photograph is reprinted in Peter Buitenhuis's *The Grasping Imagination*. William Veeder has reprinted seven other photographs taken by Coburn on this occasion in *Henry James – Lessons of the Master*. See also Charles Higgins (664) for a discussion of the photographs resulting from this session.

[2] See Bogardus (10) and McWhirter (275) for references to this letter. The original letter is kept in the Henry James Collection at the University of Virginia Library, Charlottesville.

unphotographable & have fewer accumulations of that sort of property than most people" (Kaplan 299). Kaplan maintains that James would only confront the camera occasionally and selectively, due to his highly developed vanity (Kaplan, as a narrative motif, has James posing in front of mirrors examining his appearance), and "whether painted or photographed, he did not like how he looked" (299).

It is no surprise then, that I have only been able to find three other occurrences of James's face prefacing his texts in early editions: a drawing by Sargent in the second volume of *The Yellow Book*, a photographic portrait accompanying the serialised version of *The Ambassadors*, and, curiously, the apparition of Coburn's profile in Lubbock's 1917 edition of James's unfinished novel *The Sense of the Past*, a novel in which a ghostly portrait from the past plays a significant role. It is surprising, however, that James chose so blatantly to 'face' his authorised literary testament in the visual paratext of the New York Edition.

In the frontispiece, the author is looking to the right toward the title page, which is visible only through the transparent paper veil of the tissue-overlay. At least so the profiled face appears in its reproduction in the New York Edition. In the photograph James is merely posing as if he is looking out of the frame at something invisible to the camera. In the frontispiece reproduction the gaze is provided with an object: the black letters on the veiled whiteness of the title page. While the reader scans the author's face for expressive signs, the reproduced eye of the author may be contemplating "the veiled face of his Muse" that James, in the preface to Volume I, *Roderick Hudson*, claims is the reward of a growing artistic experience made visible through his own experience of re-reading and re-seeing his novels and tales ([1980] xxxix). The reader may also imagine that the author's gaze is directed not only to the title page, but toward all the texts and images that follow in the twenty-four volumes of the entire Edition.

The author is absorbed in his gaze. If not entirely indifferent, his gaze at least expresses a certain impatience with the reader. It directs the reader to proceed without hesitation, and to 'listen' to the words that follow with a seriousness and attentiveness suggested by the author's steadfast-gazing eye, which is kept in dark shadow beneath his arching forehead and protruding eyebrow.

Naturally, the conventional iconic value of the frontispiece author portrait as symbol or imprimatur precludes 'reading' the face of the author, but this portrait seems, on the contrary, to invite reading, even as

James blatantly avoids the gaze of the beholder. The face wants to be read through its photo-*graphic* textuality of black and white tonal qualities, the central ear as a readable cipher (a physiognomic sign of identity), the right forehead as the cranial site of the imagination. The expression of the eye, where all facial readings must begin and end, is the expression of an absorbed reader.

If pictures want anything from their spectators, as W. J. T. Mitchell has recently suggested, they want to arrest the motion of the reader's eyes (36). James's face urges the reader to halt in front of it, and to conform to the gaze and the profile of the author. The absorbed gaze of the author is what attracts the beholder. As Michael Fried points out in *Absorption and Theatricality: Painting and Beholder in the Age of Diderot* (1980), it is the very significance of absorption in painting that it brings the reader to halt in front of it, keeps him or her spellbound and unable to move (Fried 92). According to Mitchell and Fried's exploration of Diderot's doctrine of "absorption" (defined as the realisation of an unawareness of the beholder in a painterly or theatrical tableau), pictures want "a kind of mastery over the beholder," to bind the observer to the picture with a spell comparable to the arresting stare of Medusa: "The painting's desire is to change places with the beholder" (Mitchell 36). The picture, in other words, wants to turn the beholder into a picture and the picture itself into a beholder. All visual objects and portraits in particular want to come alive in our imagination, and not only the ones similar to Pygmalion's: Poe's "Oval Portrait;" Wilde's *Picture of Dorian Gray*; or, indeed, James's ghostly portrait in *The Sense of the Past*. Paintings and sculptures are always partly materialisations of human ways of seeing, and in this sense they "stare back at us."

James's face in the frontispiece portrait both wants something from the reader/beholder and fulfills a reader's desire to see the face of the author in the book. It establishes identity between the authority and the text it 'faces,' but it is also indifferent to being seen. In fact, it does not want to be seen; it renounces any direct sign of desire through its absorbed indifference to the beholder, the stone-like face's anti-theatrical "absorption" in its own internal drama—maybe it does not even want to be seen? (Mitchell 45)

As in the modern aesthetics Fried is excavating, the paradox of the figure of absorption is comparable to the "double-consciousness" explored by James in *The Ambassadors*.[3] The term defines Strether's burdensome

---

3 *The Ambassadors* was originally published in 1903 and later revised and reprinted in the NYE as Volumes XXI and XXII, 1909. Rosenbaum has based his edition on the text of the NYE.

errand in Europe, and may be found as an adequate term to apply to the absorbed face in the frontispiece: "He was burdened [...] with the oddity of a double-consciousness. There was detachment in his zeal and curiosity in his indifference" (18).

James's represented face is doubly conscious of being the object of the reader's gaze, of placing itself in the field of such a gaze, and of desiring to detach itself with an indifferent expression worn with much zeal. Strether's sense of representation as "ambassador" in Europe conforms to the representational logic of absorption also readable in the face of the author: its curious indifference, its half-willingness to be seen and, in turn, to represent.

In Julie Rivkin's 'revision' of the theme of renunciation in "the logic of delegation" as textual dynamic in *The Ambassadors*, we find a confluence of the thematic and the formal, compositional, function of ambassadorship. Rivkin states that "James invites us to see Strether's role as substitute or delegate for another absent authority, James himself" (Rivkin 57). I will add that this logic of delegation extends to include the author of the New York Edition preface as well, and may also be extended to include the first frontispiece, the author's half-willingness to represent himself and his text, and his avoidance of coming face to face with the reader, by delegating the authority of the writing author to an author-as-reader, to exist through intermediaries.

Although the paratextual devices of the frontispiece author portrait and the facsimile signature in the first volume of the Edition on their "face-value" make claims for authorial identity, authenticity, originality, and intimacy, the texture of this profiled face and the absorbed gaze of the author affect the reader differently. The affect recalls the logic of authorial delegation that James conceived with his "central-consciousness" narrative technique; the author is speaking through masks of both others and himself or from under a veil.

In the preface to *The Golden Bowl*, James refers to his narrative voice as radically impersonalised, as a voice or impression of somebody else. In this final preface of the New York Edition, where James elaborates on his experience of revising his novels and tales and where he presents the reasons for including Coburn's photographs as frontispieces, James defines such a narrator as "the impersonal author's concrete deputy or delegate, a convenient substitute or apologist for the creative power otherwise so veiled and disembodied" (*The Golden Bowl* [1987] 19).

In *The Ambassadors* this delegation of narrative authority is negotiated in the novel itself in its dramatisation of the supplementary constitution of the self and the possibility for self-perception. In the Edition the delegation of authority, textual authority as well as authorial self-perception, is visually figured in the profiled, disembodied face in the frontispiece. We find that the profiled face and its absorbed gaze direct the reader's attention toward the delegation of narrative voice crucial to James's late novelistic discourse.

Meyer Schapiro, in a meticulous study of faces in medieval art, suggests a grammar of facial representations that throws light on the correspondence between James's profiled face and his practice of narrating through deputies. The profile is, according to Schapiro, "like the grammatical form of the third person, the impersonal 'he' or 'she'" (38). The profiled face is not like the *en face* portrait appropriate as a symbol or as a carrier of a message beyond its own appearance. Instead, the profile is absorbed in its own represented space where its legibility rests in its actions in the shared space of the image; it does not want to be seen, as Mitchell suggests. The face in the frontispiece *represents* the author in the same way that the central-consciousness narrator functions as the author's representative—the profiled face is the author's delegate, his final apology.

Face-reading, or the face as a master-trope of reading, has received prominence partly for its visualisation of the very process of interpretation: fragments are connected to make a whole and surfaces are analysed for the interiors they give access to and mask.

Throughout his career, James invested much in the typology of characters as most prominently recognisable in their facial features. In the novels, we find persistent references to physiognomy. *The American* opens with an elaborate physiognomic scrutiny of Christopher Newman's face as he sits absorbed in the Louvre:

> The gentleman on the divan was the superlative American [...] His complexion was brown and the arch of his nose bold and well-marked. His eye was of a clear, cold gray [...] He had the flat jaw and the firm, dry neck which are frequent in the American type [...] It was the eye, in this case, that chiefly told the story; an eye in which the unacquainted and the expert were singularly blended. It was full of contradictory suggestions; and though it was by no means the glowing orb of a hero of romance you could find in it almost anything you looked for.
>
> (*The American* [1978] 2-4).

In *The Ambassadors*, Chad's face reveals to Strether's scrutinising gaze a change in his character:

> [T]he inscrutable new face that he had got somewhere and somehow was brought by the movement nearer to his critic's. There was a fascination for that critic in its not being the ripe physiognomy, the face that, under observation at least, he had originally carried away from Woollett [...] It was as if in short he had really, copious perhaps but shapeless, been put into a firm mould and turned successfully out
>
> (*The Ambassadors* [1994] 96-97).

This is a change that recalls Roderick Hudson's central statement, "surely I haven't the same face?" ([1980] 64).

Strether experiences a similar change of "the elements of Appearance" upon his arrival in England before the dressing-glass of his hotel room. Here, confronted with his own face, "[n]othing could have been odder than Strether's sense of himself" (*The Ambassadors* 20). Like his sense of Chad's face, his own had been "disconnected from the sense of his past." Strether's critical scrutiny of Chad's face and 'story' in Paris is, of course, as much an attempt to restore the knowledge of his own self. The instrument readily available to this critic of inner knowledge is physiognomic interpretation, or face-reading, which is revealed to be a mode of aesthetic reading that perceives of faces as molded, designed sculptural representations. Physiognomic reading allows both for a description and knowledge of others' characters and of one's own.

Face-reading as portrayed in *The Ambassadors* further attests to the centrality of interpretation as both a visual and cultured activity wherein as much is revealed about the physiognomic reader as the face of the other. Subjecting the other to the scrutinising gaze of the physiognomist reveals one's own face as open to such reading, to become the observed and not the observer, as the social-detective narrator realises in *The Sacred Fount* (1901), a novel centrally concerned with the interpretation and misreading of appearances: "Hadn't everyone my eyes could at present take in a fixed expressiveness? Was I not very possibly myself, on this ground of physiognomic congruity, more physiognomic than anyone else?" (157).

The meaning bestowed upon the face, in James's turn of the century conception, is produced by the observer, by a way of looking, and not by any essence leaving its trace on the face: "you could find in it almost anything you looked for." It is especially the eye that produces this mirror effect revealing more about the gaze than the face.

21. The Aesthetic Significance of the Face

The frontispiece portrays not only an absorbed face, but also the type of observer that engages it; it is deeply immersed in a modern aesthetics of the face, but also in a mode of face-reading that since Aristotle has been given the same name as the object it studies: physiognomy.

The face as a primary subject in the history of art, and the figurative significance of the face as being poised vulnerably somewhere between surface and substance, is also what we find in Georg Simmel's understanding of "the aesthetic significance of the face" in his 1901 essay bearing that title. To Simmel the importance of the face in both the arts and in our cultures, is closely tied to its ability to signify the 'soul,' and that access to the soul goes by way of an aesthetic reading of the ways in which a face obtains symmetry and unity between its disparate elements and expressions. The face gives the beholder an impression of something 'behind' the face that provides this unity of form to the face. However, if we follow Simmel's "rhetorical basis or his technology of the face," the 'behind' is actually revealed to be an 'in front' or, more precisely, a self-generative *face-giving* that could be compared to Levinas's conception of "the face of the other" and Deleuze and Guattari's machines of *faciality* (Siegel 105). This is what Simmel writes about the structuring and aesthetic form-giving of the face as a pertinent symmetric and unified expression of the soul, as the soul's mirror, as a symbol for, and an interpreter of personality as *Appearance*:

> [T]he eye epitomizes the achievement of the face in mirroring the soul. At the same time, it accomplishes its finest, purely formal end as the interpreter of mere appearance, which knows no going back to any pure intellectuality *behind* the appearance
>
> (Simmel 281).

The eyes in the visually represented face are the devices that structure the very pictorial space in which the mirroring of the soul takes place. The represented eye sees appearances before they are subject to interpretation. It is because the represented eye structures the visual space (in the same way Schapiro determines the profile instead of referring to something 'behind') that appearance, according to Simmel, may lead to "the veiling and the unveiling of the soul" (281).

As a master trope in the many "sciences of identity" in the past centuries, as in James's works, the face presents a surface or a canvas that no longer discloses interiority. Such a face of pure appearance, "which knows no going back to any pure intellectuality *behind* the appearance," Jonathan Crary suggests, is already conceivable and visually representable as early as in the

1860's in the works of Manet: "In much of Manet's work the face, in its casual amorphousness, becomes a surface that no longer discloses interiority or self-reflection, an unsettling site of pictorial effects traceable through the next two decades into the late portraits of Cézanne" (Crary 92).[4]

James was particularly preoccupied with facial 'systems' of representation at the time of his work on recollecting, annotating and revising his collected works. While designing his own literary testament, and while he was engaged in re-writing and re-packaging his literary works, he was also remediating his own image, and contemplating the very process of remediating the aesthetic significance of his face. In the first decade of the twentieth century we find, in James's critical and epistolary work, a prominence of sculpted faces and busts, testifying to his aesthetic concern with what he termed, the "whole face-question" and "a system of face."

In 1906, James was explicitly thinking in terms of the aesthetic remediation of the face in sculpture through photographic reproduction as evidenced in his epistolary correspondence with the young American-Norwegian sculptor Hendrik Andersen.

A stream of letters was exchanged between them (Kaplan 448).[5] The letters, as requested by James, often included photographs of the sculptures, or "Kodaks," that Andersen had just completed of family and friends who visited his Rome studio. The letters and photographs were not only the media through which James would have to peruse and communicate his thoughts on Andersen's works; they also served as substitutes for the intimacy that James longed for with the young sculptor.[6] It was not only Andersen who sent photographs. On 7 September 1900, James enclosed a photograph of his new facial appearance: "P.S. I enclose a poor little Kodak-thing of *my* brother and me. He is thin & changed & I am fat & *shaved*!" (Gunter 33). This example further testifies to the relentless reinvention and examination of his own visual appearance, his own bearded or beardless face, in words and in photographs that he for some reason did not find "terrible" enough to refrain from sending to his young friend in exchange for photographs of statues. James's changed facial appearance at the turn of the century and his relentless examination of his

---

4 See also Michael Fried, *Manet's Modernism*, for a discussion of Manet's work that "rebuffs or at least strongly resists all attempts at hermeneutic *penetration*" (Fried 401).
5 According to Kaplan, their relationship was mostly an epistolary friendship.
6 See the letter from James to Andersen from May 1906: "I look at your kodaks (as I suppose them) over again, while I write and they make me groan, in spirit, that I'm not standing there before the whole company with you" (Nadel 93).

own physical image in photographic reproductions points to the importance of the visual representation of the face to James as aesthetic object, and as a currency in social and private communications. In fact, according to Kaplan, James always initiated a friendship by exchanging photographs (503).

On 31 May, half-way between James's two sittings for Coburn in 1906, James responded to a previous letter that Andersen had included, apart from "three 'kodak-views' of [Andersen's] self, [his] mother and the friend," "[n]umerous little photographs of [Andersen's] work" (Edel 402). James is reluctant about going into details about the sculptures but would do so if they were not so far apart. He further writes: "I should go down on my knees to you for instance, to individualize and detail the *faces*, the types ever so much more—to study, ardently, the question of doing that—the whole face-question" (402). A few months later, James again complained about Andersen's way of doing his sculptured faces, the types, the "whole face-question," in a letter dated 20 July. James responded to a new set of photographs, "2 Kodak-figures," that Andersen had included in his latest letter: "They are very beautiful to me, as to everything but their faces—I am quite impertinently unhappy (as I told you, offensively, the last time) about your system of face" (412). From these two letters we find the suggestion that around the time when James was contemplating the question of illustrations—that is, when he was collaborating with Coburn on the first frontispiece—he was corresponding, through letters and photographic reproductions of sculptures, with another young visual artist engaged in the aesthetic significance and execution of the face in sculpture, the "whole face-question" or a "system of face."[7]

Though Andersen was unsuccessful, James still suggested that he should turn his attention to the face; more precisely, James suggests that Andersen "do [his] *bust!*"

> You ought absolutely to get at Busts, at any cost of ingenuity—for it is fatal for you to go on indefinitely neglecting the *Face*, never doing one, only adding Belly to Belly—however beautiful - & Bottom to Bottom, however sublime. It is only by the Face that the artist—the sculptor—can hope *predominantly* & steadily to live—& it is so supremely & exquisitely interesting to do!
>
> (Gunter 61).

---

[7] Eve Kosofsky Sedgwick has also pointed to the similarity between some of the formulations in the prefaces to the New York Edition and his letters addressed to the "younger men"—among them Hendrik Andersen, Jocelyn Persse, and Hugh Walpole: "This sanctioned intergenerational flirtation represents a sustained chord in the New York Edition" (Kosofsky Sedgwick 218).

There seems then to be strong evidence for the fact that James was thinking about the representation of his face in sculptural terms in 1906, and it is as such that the reader meets the thrice removed remediation of the author's bust in the frontispiece. James's recasting of his face, as a rebirth of his literary career in a renewed 'friction with the market,' his encounter with his past work and his aesthetics, seem intricately interwoven with the personal and artistic (predominantly epistolary) relationships of patronage he maintained with the two much younger visual artists. It is as if these two youths, Coburn and Andersen, function as discursive mirrors in which James negotiates his own physical and artistic appearance in written letters and photographs of and to himself as a younger other.

The photographed, sculpted face of the author that we encounter on the threshold to his literary testament is, then, deeply invested in aesthetic and hermeneutic issues, which James explored in works immediately preceding the New York Edition and in the famous prefaces: the investigation of social surfaces and the interpretive constructivism central to so many of his main characters. It is also a playful presentation of the author figure. It both offers the author's face to the reader as a traditional sign of textual authority and authenticity, and simultaneously refuses to reveal anything behind its mere appearance, testifying to James's narrative strategy of authorial impersonality. James was, throughout his career, unwilling to include frontispieces and especially photographs of himself in his published work, but in the author portrait for the first volume of the Edition, he found a way to weave his own face into the fabric of his work—beardless and 'busted'— at one and the same a figure that does not give anything away and a very personal document reflecting his relationship with two younger visual artists and his own art of the novel.

22. From Copying to Revision: *The American* to *The Ambassadors*
Paula Marantz Cohen

More than thirty years ago, Leo Bersani challenged the conventional psychological approach to Henry James's work. He argued that in James's writing "human relations implied what we call human feelings into existence" but that these feelings were "the elaborations of surfaces—they have no depth" (Bersani *A Future...* 148). In my own 1991 book, *The Daughter's Dilemma: Family Process and the Nineteenth-Century Domestic Novel*, I supported this view by applying a family systems-theory approach to *The Awkward Age*: tracing patterns of interaction *among* characters rather than digging for psychic depths *in* characters. Since then, critics like Christopher Lane and Eric Savoy have explored Jamesian surfaces from the angle of queer theory. This essay is yet another attempt to trace surface patterns in James's writing by looking at how the processes of copying and revision contributed to the evolution of his work.

My point of departure is James's relationship to his older brother William. I wish to use that relationship, not as Leon Edel did as the way into some sort of primal scene, but, rather, as the basis for a set of surface coordinates. For I see the position of Henry to William as a temporal gap that would become a spatial one: a difference in age that would become a separation in space, and that would have repercussions for James's late fiction.

These coordinates—of younger brother and of expatriate American—are, I contend, connected to the processes of copying and revision. "Copying" involves the representation of an antecedent exterior element, seen as more authentic, more "real" than the copy. "Revision," by contrast, operates with the idea of reworking what is already within the arsenal of representation. The move from copying to revision in James's work describes the development of complexity in his artistic design, which is to say, the development from his earlier to his late style.

Copying is the starting point for Henry James's art insofar as it arose out of his initial position as William's younger brother. There is no mystery, no secret in this relationship as I am considering it here. William, by the simple virtue of being older, was situated as a logical vehicle for emulation. In an often cited passage from *A Small Boy and Others*, James described how he perceived his early position with respect to his brother: "I never for all the time of childhood and youth in the least caught up with or overtook him. He was always round the corner and out of sight" (9). The phrasing here suggests a competitive pursuit, as so many critics, including Edel and Howard M. Feinstein, have argued. But I want to read the line in a somewhat different way—to see the pursuit as a desire initially to *copy* the older brother. In this context, the gap in age becomes the gap between the original and the copy; the older brother "around the corner and out of sight" becomes the space where projection can happen, where the imaginative life can develop.

The second part of my idea is derived from another anecdote that James describes toward the end of *A Small Boy and Others*: that "most appalling yet most admirable nightmare of my life" of being chased by "a dimly-descried figure" in the Galerie d'Apollon of the Louvre, then finding that the chase has been reversed and he is pursuing the figure that had initially pursued him (349). If, in the original statement about his brother, Henry can be understood to be pursuing William in order to copy him, in the dream, he describes a shift in the order of creativity: from a drive to copy a real sibling, to a back and forth process with the self and a ghost—or, as I see it, with a past self and a present self.

The first anecdote, significantly, is a recollection; the other is a dream (or an alleged dream). One is about a relationship to a real sibling; the other is about a recursive process, only possible when time and distance had separated James not only from his brother but also from a body of his own work that he could return to.

Just as the conceit of the copy was grounded in the relationship to the older brother, so one can say that the distance between them, initially simply one of a gap in age, became translated concretely into the real distance between America and Europe. This distance, of course, grew out of copying: James copied his brother first, in choosing an artistic career; then, in moving to Europe after his brother had left and come back to America.

22. The American to The Ambassadors

Still, only when James settled in Europe did he acquire sufficient material to make possible the next stage in this pattern—that of his returning on his own work for the purpose of revision, and by so doing, creating the density of the major phase.

I want to illustrate this idea by looking at two novels, *The American* and *The Ambassadors*, written more than 25 years apart, which, with a certain neatness (admittedly, for my purposes, an over-neatness), define the process I have in mind.

The American, James's second published, self-standing novel, was written just before his move from Paris to London. Hence, it stands as a transitional work between a looking back and a looking forward—a looking to the older brother and a looking to his own work for inspiration.

Christopher Newman, the protagonist of *The American*, is the sort of character that a younger brother might create in an effort to produce a copy of a revered older brother. Here is part of the opening description of Newman: "Decision, salubrity, jocosity, prosperity, seem to hover within his call; he is evidently a practical man, but the idea, in his case, has undefined and mysterious boundaries, which invite the imagination to bestir itself on his behalf" (*The American* [1971] 4). Add to this, the following descriptive passage, which evokes William even more distinctly:

> He had turned his hand, with his brain in it, to many things; he had been enterprising, in an eminent sense of the term; he had been adventurous and even reckless, and he had known bitter failure as well as brilliant success; but he was a born experimentalist [...]. His most vivid conception of a supernatural element in the world's affairs had come to him once when [...] misfortune was at its climax; there seemed to him something stronger in life than his own will. But the mysterious something could only be the devil, and he was accordingly seized with an intense personal enmity to this impertinent force (19-20).

This is a wonderfully simplified rendering of William's famous existential crisis, a "copy" of that early struggle as a hero-worshipping younger brother would tend to see it.

If *The American* thus sets forth a simplified copy of William James in Christopher Newman, the novel as a whole lays out the coordinates of the international theme as simply as one is likely to see it in James. The opening scene in the Louvre gives these to us in the terms I have been using:

> 'I have bought a picture,' announced Christopher Newman to his friend Mr. Tristram.
> 'Bought a picture?' said Mr. Tristram, looking vaguely round at the walls.

> 'Why, do they sell them?'
> 'I mean a copy.'
> 'Oh, I see. These,' said Mr. Tristram, nodding at the Titians and Vandykes, 'these, I suppose, are originals?'
> 'I hope so,' cried Newman. 'I don't want a copy of a copy' (14).

The idea of the copy is thus introduced and placed wittily before the reader. The question of what is copy and what is original is raised in this scene, but it is a mild, transparent paradox when compared to how complex the issue will become in late James where the emphasis will indeed shift to the *copy of a copy*—and beyond, in a prolonged series of iterations. For the paradoxes at work in *The American* are still traceable to a simple binary opposition with a clear emphasis on one side. The novel begins by appearing to elevate Europe at Newman's expense: the site of great art in the face of which Newman looks gullible and naïve—"an undeveloped connoisseur," as he is referred to:

> He had looked [...] not only at all the pictures, but at all the copies that were going forward around them, in the hands of those innumerable young women in irreproachable toilets [...] and if the truth must be told, he had often admired the copy much more than the original (1-2).

James is making fun of Christopher Newman here—younger brothers can do that so long as the basic hierarchy remains intact—and, of course, it does. As Richard Poirier observed: "In no other novel is James's comedy so insistently at the service of his hero, even when, as in the early scenes, it affectionately makes fun of him" (Poirier xi). Newman's inability to value the original over the copy in the paintings around him is not only connected to his appreciation of the young women doing the copying, but also—and extending from this—a more fundamental authenticity. As we are told: he "was a powerful specimen of an American. But he was not only a fine American; he was, in the first place, physically, a fine man" (2).

The loyalties of the novel are here made explicit. For the paintings in the Louvre, even though they are masterpieces by Titian and Van Dyke, are indeed copies of originals, the originals being the actual flesh-and-blood people they portray. And in this context, it is Newman who is the original: indisputably, "a fine American and a fine man"— much finer than the furtive, artificial types that will come to surround him from among the French nobility.

James thus spells out the emphasis he has in mind here, which reflects the position of himself to his brother: the American, the original man, is superior to the European copy, which is, in this context, the copy of life. The older brother at home in America remains the original to the younger brother living abroad and using him and America as an artistic resource.

The American is James's most accessible novel, beautifully uncluttered in its humor—one of the few novels, one could say, capable of being read and appreciated by his older brother. It is, in short, a novel written at a point before the older brother had been rendered obsolete—or, rather, had been assimilated so fully into representation as to become so. Yet reading the novel, we can see how this is poised to happen. Newman's heroism, though never compromised, leads to disappointment for him and tragedy for the woman he loves. It is a scenario that we see could be revised with a different emphasis—as it will be in later novels. In other words, the potential for recursiveness in the design is already present. With the completion of *The American*, James would move from Paris to London, and this, in my admittedly simplistic genealogy, would begin a revisionary process—that copying of copies, to use Newman's terminology—that would reach its apotheosis in *The Ambassadors*.

In James's Preface to *The Ambassadors* he invokes but immediately *revises* the advice that Strether gives to Little Bilham inside the novel: He cites the lines which begin "Live all you can; it's a mistake not to," as constituting the "grain of suggestion" that got him writing the novel. James cites the lines, ending as they do with: "Do what you like so long as you don't make [my mistake]. For it was a mistake. Live! Live!" (*The Ambassadors* [1909] v). He notes Strether's reference to his own "mistake," only to proceed with a revision of this viewpoint when he says that Strether was "perhaps after all constitutionally qualified for a *better part* […] so that the business of my tale and the march of my action […] is just my demonstration of this process of vision" (vi, emphasis mine). James here makes explicit the shift that has occurred since the writing of *The American* and, indeed, a shift of the position stated by his character inside *The Ambassadors*. He sidelines the idea of Strether's "mistake" in not "having his life" and moves to assign him a "better part," which is to say, Strether's "reparation" for his "mistake" through a "process of vision." The "original" has been definitively superseded by the "copy." Life may seem the paramount value to Strether, but to his creator, the belated "process of vision," Strether's—and his own— *re*-vision makes reparation, indeed, more than rectifies any past mistake by providing a "better part."

By the time we arrive here, significantly, revision is occurring on multiple, interconnected levels: There is the revision of Strether's idea with respect to his mission: the desire to bring home the young American, Chad Newsome, becomes a determination to make him stay in France. And there is the revision of *that* idea as articulated in the Preface—the call to "live" superseded by a "better part," which is not related to Chad but to Strether in his acquisition of a "process of vision."

These various forms of revision pertain to my larger idea, namely that *The Ambassadors* is a revision of *The American*. This can be understood in the following respects: Chad Newsome is a revision of Christopher Newman as spelled out in his name alone: Not Christopher for the great original explorer but a vogue-ish Chad; not a new man, but "new-some"—the product of existing materials revised to produce something "somewhat new"—the recycling of what exists in a new context. In the dream that James tells in his autobiography, the apparition chasing him is suddenly being chased by him. But the point seems to me not a simple reversal but a metaphor for recursiveness: how the past self becomes incorporated into the new self in an endless, revisionary cycle. In *The Ambassadors*, Strether comes to Europe to retrieve the wayward Chad Newsome to American values only to find himself converted to European ones (and hence, in a sense, turned on and pursued *by* Chad). Then, once converted, Strether is transformed into a pursuer again, determined to keep Chad in Europe. Yet he returns to America likely to continue in this back and forth motion as his imagination works in the service of a new "process of vision." Chad is the younger Jamesian self re-imagined not as the pursuer of the idolised older brother but as an apparition that serves the imaginative elaboration of the older self, the mature artist. The very slightness of Chad in the novel underlines his role as a shadow self—a ghost serving the Jamesian surrogate in his initiation into a "better part"—making the novel not only a revision of *The American* but an allegory of artistic development as well. Again, to cite James in the Preface: "There is the story of one's hero, and then, thanks to the intimate connexion of things, the story of one's story itself" (*The American* [1971] x).

I realise of course that I am simplifying egregiously, failing to tackle all that seems so different about the two narratives. My point is a partly metaphorical one. *The American* partakes of a period ending in the 1880's, when James had done sufficient "copying" to have an arsenal established for revision. But there is also a sense in which I believe the two novels can be viewed together, as the echo of Christopher Newman in Chad Newsome suggests. One can do the same with a pairing like *Portrait of a Lady* and *The Golden Bowl*, *The Bostonians* and *The Awkward Age*, and *Washington Square* and *The Wings of the Dove*—of course, these probably could be shuffled into other combinations. The point is that while one may draw a one-to-one correspondence between certain Jamesian works, one can also assume a continual revisionary process, in which James used all that he had done as his stock material once he had reached a certain point in his development.

What remains to be asked is whether there was any 'new' material introduced once James had hunkered down at Lamb House and entered his major phase? Everything, of course, depends on what one calls "new"— and I suppose I would argue that it is only "new-some." James often referred to the "germ" or, as he calls it in the Preface to *The Ambassadors*, "the grain of suggestion" ([1909] v) that served as the basis for his fiction. I would call this germ or grain the site upon which his revision of existing themes could be carried out. It must, as he explained, be quickly removed from reality so as to leave room to be imaginatively worked over. It is no longer the copying, then, but the space between that has become central to the creative process. This is borne out by the difficulty James experienced editing William's letters after his death. Instead of writing a biography to include with the letters, he felt compelled to write his own autobiography instead and to revise his brother's letters to suit his own vision. As has been noted, the work "is empty at the center" (Olney 46), where William should have been—or, as James wrote in another context, explaining the development of character in his fiction: "I had in a word to draw him forth from *within* rather than meet him in the world before me, [...] and [in order] to make him objective, in short, had to turn nothing less than myself inside out" (*Autobiography* [1983] 455). This turning of the self inside-out seems another configuration for the self-chasing and being chased by an apparition of the self.

I will conclude by invoking a detail unearthed by Adeline Tintner in an essay some years ago: William James, it seems, had a portrait done in 1863 in the pose of Titian's *Portrait of the Man with a Glove*. Henry, no doubt, knew of the portrait and may have had it in mind when he wrote the scene in *The American* in which Christopher Newman is introduced as a "fine man," implicitly more authentic than even the priceless Titians and Van Dykes in the gallery. Significantly, that particular portrait by Titian, whose pose William copied for his own in 1863, appears again in *The Ambassadors*. Here, it is the one painting that Strether looks at closely during a trip to the Louvre early in the novel, just before he is about to meet Chad Newsome for the first time and register the "conspicuous improvement" that the young man has undergone. When he does meet Chad, we are told that he is affected "as he might have been affected by some light, pleasant, perfect work of art." In Chad Newsome, the *copy of the copy* is being set before Strether, and it causes him to revise his vision. To spell this out mechanically: We have the original older brother, the copy of the older brother in Christopher Newman, the copy of the copy, or more correctly, the revision of the copy in Chad, and the re-vision of Chad by Strether. Finally, in yet another recursion, we have Strether as re-seen by James in his Preface, not as the failure he professes to be when speaking of his "mistake," but as a revised sensibility recouped to a "better part." If we go back to the Preface of *The American* we find James enumerating the problems he sees with the novel, and concluding in the final paragraph that whatever success it achieves must be ascribed to its hero, Christopher Newman. James writes: "clinging to my hero as to a tall, protective, good-natured elder brother in a rough place, I leave the record to stand or fall by his more or less convincing image" (xxiii). James needed his older brother as a template when he wrote *The American*, but by *The Ambassadors* he had worked a revision on that real person that fit the world of romance he had created over the course of his literary career. While he was unhappy with his revision of *The American* for The New York Edition, he would call *The Ambassadors* "quite the best, all around, of my productions" (vii). The later novel was the truly comprehensive revision of the former. In a way, for James, it rendered the former obsolete, much as had been the case for the older brother long before.

23. Friction with the Publishers, or How James Manipulated his Editors in the Early 1870's

Pierre A. Walker

This volume appears to take its theme from the prominence today in American literary studies of what is variously called trans-Atlantic or transnational studies. As Paul Giles wrote in the 2003 *PMLA*: "American literature should be seen as no longer bound to the inner workings of any particular country or imagined organic community but instead as interwoven systematically with traversals between national territory and intercontinental space" (63).

As a James scholar, and in fact as one who carries two passports, I completely endorse what Lawrence Buell has called this "recent Americanist push to think 'beyond' or 'outside' the confines of nationness" (Buell 90). But at the same time—and again as a James scholar—I'm inclined to shrug my shoulders and ask: "So what?" It has always seemed obvious to me that James "travers[ed] [...] national territory and intercontinental space," to use Giles's words again, and did so through his fiction, his non-fiction, and his personal and professional relationships, so many of which were trans-Atlantic and maintained through correspondence that literally traversed "intercontinental space" (63).

What I want to focus on here is James's very practical intercontinental 'traversals' as he worked in the mid-1870's to place the serial versions of *Roderick Hudson* and *The American* in American periodicals at the most favorable terms possible. In placing these two serials, he worked first *Scribner's* and then the *Galaxy* against the *Atlantic Monthly* and established a pattern of manipulating his editors and publishers.

While James was living in Florence in March 1874, he received a letter from Josiah Holland, editor of *Scribner's*, in which Holland invited James to submit a novel for serialisation in his magazine. Rather than replying directly, James immediately began to use Holland's invitation as leverage to get his novel serialised in the *Atlantic Monthly*. He explained to his parents (in a letter dated 9 March 1874) that, all else being equal (in other words, the money), he felt "under a tacit pledge" to offer a novel first to the *Atlantic*; doing otherwise would be "unfriendly" to William Dean Howells, the *Atlantic's* editor and James's friend and mentor (*Complete Letters* 133).

Therefore what James did was to write two separate answers to Holland, one declining and the other accepting Holland's invitation. He sent these answers home to his father with instructions to forward the appropriate one to Holland pending the outcome of negotiations with Howells. Then he wrote to Howells and put the question to him as a "grim" matter of business: would the *Atlantic* match Holland's offer and serialise a twelve-monthly installment novel, beginning in November 1874, for twelve hundred dollars? (*Complete Letters* 137).

Six weeks later, when he received a letter from his father "enclosing Howells's acceptance of my story for the Atlantic," James learned that the answer was "yes" (*Complete Letters* 150). *Roderick Hudson* began its serial run in the January 1875 issue of the *Atlantic*, which appeared in late December 1874 (not November). Serialisation concluded with the November 1875 issue, at which point James Osgood published the book edition. Thanks to leveraging the invitation from *Scribner's*, James achieved what he wanted: $1,200 for the serial rights to his novel, publication commencing in the late fall of 1874 (which was important, since payment only started with publication), and exposure in the more prestigious *Atlantic*.

For his next novel, *The American*, James played not *Scribner's* but the *Galaxy* off against the *Atlantic*. On 1 December 1875, having just settled in Paris, James wrote to the editors of the *Galaxy*, the brothers Francis Pharcellus Church and William Conant Church, proposing they serialise the novel he was working on:

> I propose to take for granted, as soon as I can, that you will be ready to publish, on receipt of them, the opening chapters of a novel. I have got at work upon one sooner than I expected, & particularly desire it to come out without delay
>
> (*Life in Letters* 61).

The language with which James makes his proposal is striking: "I propose to take for granted" that you will "publish, on receipt" and "without delay" "the opening chapters" of my new novel. In simple terms: publish my novel right away!

We don't know how the Churches replied, but James wrote his mother on 11 January 1876 that "I expect to begin a novel in the April *Galaxy*: to run thro' nine numbers—to December" (*Life in Letters* 65). He then sent the Churches the first two installments of *The American*, and on 8 February 1876, James wrote his brother William that he was still "working at the novel I have begun for the *Galaxy*" (*Correspondence of William James* 254).

But even as he sent the *Galaxy* the first two installments of *The American*, James was beginning to play this magazine off against the *Atlantic*. Howells had written James on 16 January 1876, inviting James to submit a new serial novel to the *Atlantic* (*Letters, Fictions, Lives* 115). James received this letter just after he mailed the first installment of *The American* to the *Galaxy* and just before mailing the second one. On 3 February 1876, the day before he mailed the second installment, he wrote to Howells. He explained that for financial reasons he needed to have a serial begin as soon as possible, that he had assumed that the *Atlantic* would not be able to begin a serial of a new James novel until June or July, that he assumed the new novel would begin to appear in the March or April *Galaxy*, and therefore that since "it was the money question that had to determine me" he had not considered writing Howells about serialising *The American* in the *Atlantic*. However, James added, had Howells written "some weeks before," his "extreme preference to have the thing appear in the Atlantic might have induced me to wait till the time you mention." But, James suggested, all was not lost. For one, James proposed serialising his next novel after *The American* starting in the January 1877 *Atlantic*. But more importantly, James hinted that the serialisation of *The American* in the *Galaxy* was not entirely settled. James complained of the Churches' "insufferable *nonchalance*, […] neglect and ill-manners" for having "left me very much in the dark as to whether my conditions are acceptable to them" (James was asking $150 per installment). He had, therefore, "written to them [i.e. the Churches] that if they are not satisfied they are immediately to forward my parcel [of manuscript] to you" (*Letters, Fictions, Lives* 115).

Only a fragment of this letter to the Churches has survived. But we know from James's next extant letter to the Church brothers (of 3 March 1876) that he had written them to insist on publication beginning as soon as possible and on $150 per installment.

In spite of having, at the beginning of February 1876, written to the Churches to spell out his terms, and in spite of his having indicated in his letter of 3 February to Howells that the Churches had not as yet accepted his conditions, on 4 February he mailed the second installment to the *Galaxy*. It is only in March 1876 that it becomes apparent that the Churches were not meeting James's expectation of almost immediate publication. In his letter of 3 March 1876, James replied to a now lost letter from the Churches of 18 February. In his reply, James made it as clear as he could that $150 per installment was his price, and that while he had "hoped" that the first installment would appear in the "April" number (though he first wrote "March"), he now expected it to appear in the "May" issue (though he had first written "April"). If the *Galaxy* could not meet these conditions, he wrote, "I must forego the pleasure of having the story appear in the Magazine." In that case, he added, "I shall be obliged to you […] for despatching [the manuscript…] without even a day's delay […] to my father" in Cambridge (*Henry James Letters* 31).

Eleven days later, James still did not know the outcome. He wrote to William on 14 March that "there is a hitch" in the *Galaxy's* serialisation of *The American* "thro' their threatening delay of publication." Henry explained that he had instructed the Churches, in case of a delay, to send the manuscript to Henry James Sr., who "would make it straight over to Howells." "I don't know how it will turn out," he added, "& meanwhile it annoys me" (*Correspondence of William James* 257).

The uncertainty lasted only two or three weeks more. Howells, in the meanwhile, had negotiated directly with the Churches. He had written the Church brothers on 29 February 1876, suggesting that if "you can't use Mr. James's new serial, conveniently, wont you turn it over to me? I should be very glad to get it, and you may for editorial reasons, be glad to get rid of it, and so I make bold to ask for it." The Churches did not reply immediately, and Howells wrote them again on 5 March 1876: "I should be glad to know within a week what your decision in regard to Mr. James's story is." Howells and the Churches reached an agreement shortly thereafter. Someone at the *Galaxy* wrote on Howells's second letter: "Mss sent per Exh Mch 11/76," apparently referring to an exchange of materials between the *Galaxy* and the *Atlantic*. The installments James had already sent the *Galaxy* were transferred to Howells, and *The American* began its serial run in the *Atlantic* in the June 1876 issue, concluding with the issue of May 1877.

23. Friction with the Publishers

James learned during the first days of April 1876 of the arrangement between Howells and the Churches. He wrote to Howells on 4 April that he was "very glad now that you have got hold of my story" and "very well pleased that you should have made your proposal to Church" (*Letters, Fictions, Lives* 117). Given the minimum ten days it took letters to travel between Paris and Boston, Howells must have heard back from the Churches around the middle of March, about the time that they had received James's 3 March letter to them, where James had repeated as clearly as possible his terms of $150 per installment and almost immediate publication.

That's the story of James's placing the serial version of *The American*. Eight months later, on New Year's Day 1877, James wrote to James Osgood to offer him the book version of *The American*. Nothing exceptional here, as Osgood had published all three of James's books to date. "I have delayed writing to you longer than I intended," wrote James, "to ask you whether you are disposed to publish as a volume my novel of *The American*." Nothing exceptional here, as I say, except for the tone James then takes: "I suppose I may safely assume that you will do so, and that you will offer the same terms as for *Roderick Hudson*" (Rosenbaum 533-34). Notice how James takes for granted, much as he did when he first wrote the Churches to offer them the serial of *The American*, that his correspondent will allow James to dictate his terms. Perhaps this was James's way of dealing with editors and publishers by appearing to query them from a position of strength rather than as a supplicant, young author.

What must have motivated Howells and James in the *Roderick Hudson* and *American* incidents is clear: James, with his pressing need to keep up with reimbursements to his father, who was advancing the costs of James's European travels, needed to generate a steady income through constant publication. In addition, James stood to gain through serialising his novels in the *Atlantic*, possibly the most prestigious American literary magazine at the time. Howells, apparently, wanted to solidify James's situation as an "*Atlantic* author," which explains the steps he took to arrange with the Churches the transfer of *The American* from the *Galaxy* to the *Atlantic*.

What is not as clear is what motivated the Churches. The *Galaxy* already had a long serial novel running at the time James wanted them to begin *The American*: William Black's *Madcap Violet*, which began serialisation in the *Galaxy*'s January 1876 issue and concluded in the January 1877 issue. So making room just then for the serial of James's *The American* was no doubt a genuine editorial problem for the *Galaxy*. But there was probably an additional problem, one we catch a glimpse of if we note some of James's derogatory remarks to others about the Churches. For instance, in his 4 April [1876] letter to Howells, James stated that the "conduct" of the Churches "remains to me a mystery" (*Letters, Fictions, Lives* 117). James's work had been appearing in the *Galaxy* practically since its inception ("A Day of Days" appeared in the magazine's fourth issue, of 15 June 1866). Perplexity at and dissatisfaction with the editors of the *Galaxy* were persistent themes for James, and we can tell why from a remark in his 26 October 1873 letter to Henry Sr.: "I am sorry to hear such accounts from you of the dishonesty of Sheldon & Church" (*Complete Letters* 63). Sheldon, here, is the publisher Isaac Sheldon, whose New York publishing company had owned the *Galaxy* since 1868. James's correspondence with the Churches suggests that Sheldon exercised a considerable degree of control over the Churches' editorial decisions, especially over the purse strings. This becomes clear if we consider James's last dealings with the Churches, before the *Galaxy* ceased to publish in 1878.

Not content with having worked *Scribner's* in 1874 and the *Galaxy* in 1876 against the *Atlantic*, James did it again in 1877 with *The Europeans*. On 26 May 1877, having now established himself in London, James wrote to William Church to propose that the *Galaxy* serialise his next novel. "Shall you be disposed," James wrote, "to begin a serial novel [...] on the month of January next?" He added, though, and in a slightly less compliant tone: "Will you let me know as to this without delay?" James broke off negotiations about this proposed serialisation in August, because Sheldon would not unambiguously endorse the terms of publication. Adopting an angry tone, James wrote in an unpublished letter of 27 August 1877:

> You say that you are not to be in the least responsible for payment & that I am to look for it to Messrs. Sheldon, to whom you have sent my letter for acceptance. [...] You say that t̶h̶e̶i̶r̶ the printing of my story will be equivalent to acceptance, on their part, of my terms; but I cannot proceed with it in this uncertainty, and as I cannot afford to wait for further interchange of letters, I must consider our negotiations as interrupted—or rather, as at an end. [...] What if Messrs. Sheldon should signify their non-acceptance by not printing my opening chapters & I should be left with them on my hands?

Apparently it was Sheldon the publisher, and not the Church brothers, who decided the *Galaxy's* terms with its authors. James's queries to the Churches about serialising therefore had to be approved by Sheldon. We know this from notes written by *Galaxy* editorial staff on the back of James's 26 May 1877 letter to William Church, where James offered *The*

Europeans. One note says: "See letter of Sheldon & Co of July 3," and the other: "Respectfully respond to Mssrs Sheldon & Co. As Mr. James has just published a novel [*The American*, in fact] which has attracted more attention than any for a long time published I should second this if possible."

One can easily picture the Churches' difficulty when they found themselves in competition with Howells for James's work. The Churches could not agree directly to terms with James; they needed first to have Sheldon's approval. This explains why they appeared to leave James "in the dark" about his terms for serialising *The American*. Howells, on the other hand, could negotiate directly with his author on behalf of the *Atlantic*. James, needing to pay his way in Paris in 1876 and London in 1877, could not afford to wait for Sheldon to make up his mind. No wonder *The American* and *The Europeans* were serialised in the *Atlantic* and not the *Galaxy*.

If he knew that the Churches could not act without Sheldon's approval, James may have made proposals to the Churches expecting to wait some time for their definite reply. In the meanwhile, James could have exploited their delay with overtures to Howells. Or perhaps James was simply lucky, lucky that the Churches couldn't give immediate answers, lucky that Howells could, and lucky that Howells was anxious to publish as much of James's work as he could. Whatever the truth may be, James succeeded in placing *Roderick Hudson*, *The American*, and *The Europeans* in the prestigious *Atlantic* and at terms he deemed favorable. We have to conclude that in spite of the distance across the Atlantic Ocean, James worked to obtain the most favorable conditions from his magazine editors, and that he relished doing so. Just as "Daisy Miller" completed its two-installment run in the *Cornhill* and just as *The Europeans* was beginning to appear in the *Atlantic*, James wrote his mother in an unpublished letter of 4 July 1878:

> Leslie Stephen came to see me the other day to ask me for a serial novel for the Cornhill; & I had the superior vantage of replying to him that I was engaged to furnish my next to Mcmillan. So you see I am in a superior position, being able to work the 2 leading [British] magazines against each other. But don't breathe a word of this; I do nothing save discreetly.

Thanks to the work of Michael Anesko and others, we know that James was diligent at the practical aspects of publishing and making a living as a writer. While Anesko (41) and Leon Edel (*Henry James V* 160-61 and 245-47) have already outlined for us James's dealings in relation to the serialisation of *Roderick Hudson* and *The American*, I don't believe anyone has described in quite as much detail as James's complete letters provide the manipulations James undertook in order to place these serial novels. Furthermore, I think my more detailed account shows that James wrote his early novels when he knew where they would appear. In March 1876, when it was not clear who would serialise *The American* and when, James suspended work on it (*Letters, Fictions, Lives* 117); as soon as Howells had sealed the deal, he went right back to work; "I am now actively at work upon it," as he wrote his father on 11 April 1876, after he heard from Howells that the *Galaxy* turned *The American* over to the *Atlantic* (*Henry James Letters* 39). Let me conclude, therefore, by suggesting to critics planning to work on these novels that they bear in mind that James wrote them (at least wrote the first drafts) knowing precisely who his audience would be.

24. Losing Oneself: Autobiography, Memory, Vision

John Holland

Henry James begins *A Small Boy and Others* by explaining why he found it difficult to respond to a request. Having been asked, shortly after William's death, to write a memoir of his brother, he is forced to explain that he cannot do so in a direct and simple way, for he is not the master of his own thoughts. The very attempt to recall his experiences with his older brother has immersed him in a flood of associations. Since "it was to memory in the first place that my main appeal for particulars had to be made," the request leads him "to live over the spent experience itself" and thereby to see the associations from the past "beg[i]n to multiply and […] swarm" in his mind (3). Fascinated by these memories, he finds that he cannot dissociate those of William from the thousands of others that are enveloping him, "so inseparably and beautifully they seemed to hang together and the comprehensive case to decline mutilation" (3). Instead, then, of writing a memoir of his brother, he delivers himself to these associations, luxuriating in his memories of the sights that had fascinated him in his childhood and now do so again.

This essay seeks to examine certain qualities of Jamesian thought and the effects that they have on the author's attempt to represent his younger self in *A Small Boy and Others* and *Notes of a Son and Brother*; their fundamental result is to render the author foreign to himself. The fiction to which James had devoted much of his life is marked by a state in which, in the words of Sigmund Freud, "the thought-process itself [has] becom[e] sexualized"; the very act of thinking can, in certain circumstances, become a source of jouissance" ("Notes" 124). In the novels and stories, one of the results of this libidinalisation of thinking is a recurring concern with ambiguity; works such as "The Turn of the Screw" and *The Sacred Fount* stand as what the narrator of the latter book might well have called "perfect palaces of thought": texts whose extreme epistemological ambiguity makes them the perfect vehicles for the jouissance of thinking (Holland 140). Since each detail of these works can be read either as confirming or as working against the theories constructed by their first-person narrators, they can afford one the joy of an almost infinite contemplation and analysis of their details, in the fortunately fruitless attempt to reach a definitive conclusion (Rimmon xi-xii). Peter Brooks, in extending this problematic to James's own life, has recently remarked that he is "not so convinced as some critics that James was 'unhappy' (whatever that means) with his life, including his version of sexuality" precisely because of his "epistemophilia"—because of the *jouissance* that the author invested in thinking and knowing (Brooks *Henry James Goes to Paris* 124). This essay seeks to analyse what results from this *jouissance* when James, near the end of his life, tries to transform his own experience into a text. The form that James adopts in order to recount his life both exemplifies this enjoyment and seeks to counter it in a fashion that arouses a fundamental anxiety.

In the autobiographies, the libidinal qualities of his thought are manifest from the opening pages, and that they are derived, in this case, from his memories of the act of looking. In the opening pages of the autobiographies, the memories that most entrance the author are those concerned with vision. For example, James treats the reader to a lovingly detailed description of the marble facade of his grandmother's house in Albany and the pinkish-red front of the dame-school that was to be found across the street from it; indeed, he even pauses to consider the ways in which his memory has played tricks on him, before noting to himself, "I lose myself in ravishment before the marble and the pink" (9). Shortly afterward, remembering the "New York *flâneries*" that he had once undertaken, the author now recreates in his mind—and on paper—what his younger self had seen, and thus can re-experience these sights as "pictures." As he exclaims, "Wonderful altogether, in fact, I find as I write, the quantity, the intensity of picture recoverable from even the blankest and tenderest state of the little canvas." While recalling the way in which the child had "dawdle[d]" in the street and "gaped" at the sights, the author finds that "I positively dawdle and gape here—I catch myself in the act" (17).

In lingering over these memories, the author shows the extent to which seeing, like thinking, has become eroticised; he describes the young boy as someone for "whom contemplation takes so much the place of action" and shows that the act of looking had, from the earliest moments, been the object of a libidinal investment (17). The older narrator is now able to recuperate, through the process of thinking and remembering, something of the jouissance that he had once derived from his childhood acts of seeing. Having plunged into the torrent of associations and then catching himself in the act of gaping at them, the author is continuously startled by the enjoyment that he derives from them.

This experience of enjoyment in re-seeing childhood experiences may have been a necessary condition for beginning to compose the autobiography, but it is hardly a sufficient condition for the production of the books that we now have. The jouissance of thinking may have freed the author from the alienating request that he write a memoir in which he would have figured only as a subsidiary character. To immerse himself completely in his own memories, however, would be a way of cutting himself off from others: of writing a book entirely for himself, while failing to take into account any consideration of possible readers. Now, the autobiographies are, on the contrary, texts that manifest a careful consideration for the reader; at each moment when the author risks losing himself entirely in his memories, he finds himself pulling back from this position in order to address the reader: to place the various pictures that he has succeeded in recapturing within enough of a context that the movement of his thought remains fairly comprehensible for the reader. What makes the book intelligible for us, then, is the intervention of another force: a principle for the production of the text that goes in the opposite direction from the solitary jouissance that the author has been describing, a principle that opens the text to others.

James describes this principle much later, in *Notes of a Son and Brother*, where he attempts to state one of the methods that he has used to compose these texts. He reveals that he had long been "haunted" by the wish to relate "The personal history [...] of an imagination" and would gladly have done so, if he "could first [have] 'ca[ught]'" this imagination (455 and 454). Finally, after years of waiting for this figure to arrive, "It happened [...] that he was to turn up [...] in a shape almost too familiar at first for recognition" for, he discovers, he was *himself* the figure that he had been seeking (455). According to this description, James, in finding what he wants, recognises only tardily that he is really seeing himself:

[This character] had been with me all the while and only too obscurely and intimately—I had not found him in the market as an exhibited or *offered* value. I had in a word to draw him forth from within rather than meet him in the world before me, the more convenient sphere of the objective (455).

The task of the autobiographer is to take this obscure and intimate figure and to make him "objective."

James's description of this discovery raises a number of questions. First of all, his use of the term, "objective," may seem surprising. Was it not, indeed, the concern with recapturing his *subjective* experience that underlay his early discussion of the method of following the intricate paths of associations wherever they took him? What, if any relation exists between the determination not to cut the threads of association and this new emphasis on an objective presentation? Paul John Eakin has suggested that the views expressed in the two passages are mutually incompatible and indeed, "cancel each other out" (Eakin 61).

In opposition to Eakin's contention, this essay seeks to argue that much of the disturbing power of the autobiographies derives from the tension and interaction between the methods discussed in the two passages. The second passage suggests that for James, an autobiographer should not simply be content with following out the path of his associations; the results of the method that this passage unveils, however, disturb our intuitive spatial sense of the world, reverse the visual relations established by the first method and entail an identification that the narrator can never fully occupy. In our everyday lives, we tend to make a relatively simple distinction between inside and outside: our subjective 'selves' are located on the inside and the world of others on the outside. According to the second method, however, the autobiographer must present his younger self not as if it were a part of himself—a source of his memories—but as a character in a book, and thus, in a sense, as someone else. He must therefore narrate the work from a position that tries to be fundamentally *external* to that self; this is the sense of the injunction to make this portrayal objective, as if he were seeing that self "in the world before me."

This "objective" method of presentation also reverses the polarities of vision established by the associational method. If the first of these procedures presented the boy as the one who looks and the author as a man whose memories consist, in large part, of what the latter has seen, the second places the young Henry under the gaze. The younger self, according to James's schemes, would serve as the center of interest that lights up the stage on which he has been placed. "[W]ouldn't the *light* in which [this character] might so cause the whole *scene* to unroll inevitably become as fine a thing as possible to represent?" (455, emphasis mine). What these passages suggest is that in writing these books, James is imagining that his younger self is being looked at. *A Small Boy and Others* and *Notes of a Son and Brother* are written from the position of an author who has revisited his experiences and remembers the early joy that he has taken in looking, and who is now seeking to reverse the polarities of vision: he is trying to turn the young boy who looked into someone who, rather than seeing, is seen.

This impulse to transform the seer into the seen is a project that is obviously fraught with problems, not least because, for the narrator, it involves an identification that is fundamentally impossible. If the narrator is to present the young boy "objectively," as a figure who is external to himself, he is obliged to identify with someone else, someone for whom the child is indeed a separate figure: the reader. At bottom, it is only the reader, and not the autobiographer, who is fully distinct from the young Henry and who is thus able to see him from a more purely external position. The objective method, then, involves a continual attempt on the part of the author to see his younger self as a reader would be likely to see him. James acknowledges the difficulties of this situation when he notes that "objectivity, the prize to be won," could "just be frightened away by the odd terms of the affair" and that "It is of course for my reader to say whether or not what I have done *has* meant defeat" (455). Such an attempt is, of course, fundamentally impossible, for how can he ever know how his younger self is seen from the reader's perspective? The subjective experience of losing oneself, which had begun merely as an inability to master the progression of his thoughts, now takes the form of a far more radical self-estrangement.

The formal conditions by which this text was produced seem sufficiently unusual that they invite certain speculations. It can be asked whether the position in which the author places himself must not necessarily lead, for him, to a sense of unease. First of all, what can we imagine to be the effects of the technique of bringing the gaze to bear upon the small boy? If the author had at first been overwhelmed by his memories of this boy, the objective method introduces a sense of distance between himself and his earlier self, making the latter figure seem less immediate, its memories less overwhelming and its concerns less pressing. Now, the greater the distance that the author puts between himself and us, on the one hand, and the boy on the other, the smaller the latter will seem to us; indeed, if we are placed at an enormous distance from him, we will see him as little more than a point. This is all the more the case since what we see is the young boy in the act of looking; we catch him, in the words of Jacques Lacan, in the position of a subject "sustaining himself in a function of desire" (Lacan 85). The autobiographies trap the child in this position, thus sometimes producing the effect of making him seem like a small, trivial and even slightly pathetic figure. This reduction, indeed, may not be without discomfort for the author, who, for all his claims to distance and objectivity, cannot, of course, definitively cut his ties with the young boy.

The second source of unease manifests itself in two passages in his description of the objective method, passages that hint at a feeling of the uncanny, which Freud defined as the sense that something that is familiar and intimate is also utterly foreign. The first of these is the experience of not recognising himself as the figure that he had been seeking—the figure who embodies the principle of active imagination—followed by the sudden shock of self-recognition. The second proceeds in the opposite direction; instead of involving the sudden understanding that what had seemed foreign was actually intimate, it renders strange what had once been familiar. In order to make his presentation of himself objective, James asserts that "I [...] had to turn nothing less than myself inside out" (455). This statement, when taken literally, creates a disturbing image of a thoroughgoing defamiliarisation of the body, and in doing so, radicalises the already existing disturbance of our sense of space. It allows us to imagine the transformation of the body into a sort of topological figure that can be made unrecognisable by a series of manipulations: a reversal that places the outside of the body on the inside and the inside on the outside. The "objective" method had begun by requiring that the narrator see his younger self as an external figure, and the result of this attempt is that inside and outside have become entirely reversed for him. This image highlights the radical way in which what was most familiar to James is made alien to him by the form that he has imposed upon himself in writing this autobiography; the effect of this way of writing is to make James foreign to himself. With this latest evocation of an encounter with the alterity that exists within what is most familiar to us, we are not far from the territory of anxiety, if anxiety is taken to be the encounter with something that bears an intimate relation to oneself, while at the same time seeming radically other.

The threshold into anxiety pure and simple is crossed only once in the autobiography: in the famous nightmare set in the Galerie d'Apollon. In the autobiography, the dream becomes related to the process by which the text was written; one may presume that the origin of the dream itself, which occurred years after James's first sight of the Louvre, is connected with his earliest responses to Europe. Not the least of the ways by which Europe distinguished itself for the young Henry was that it was the place in which he found himself under the gaze in a particularly marked way. This is not simply because his obviously foreign appearance frequently attracted what the narrator calls "the from-head-to-foot stare" and a "curiosity void of sympathy" from the boys in the cities in which he wanders (*Autobiography* [1983] 174). It is also because Henry's febrile agitation, occasioned by his encounter with a Europe about which he had dreamed for years, endowed his inanimate surroundings with a living agency that enabled them, in a sense, to look at and even to speak to him. Overwhelmed by the sense of style conveyed to him by Paris, he felt as if "every low-browed vitrine" was expressing a "dark message" in a "sinister way": "Art, art, art, don't you see? Learn, little gaping pilgrims, what *that* is!" (191). Henry feels that he is caught and seen in the very act of looking and one can easily suppose that his "small scared consciousness" reacted in an even more intense way to the Galerie d'Apollon (198).

In the context of the autobiography, however, the nightmare becomes related to the unease that the author feels in directing the gaze upon his younger self and to the anxiety that renders his own body foreign to himself. In this text, the dream takes on the status of a founding myth, for it dramatises an element of alterity that is continuously evoked by this act of narration, an element that must be avoided if the story is to be told, but which also threatens constantly to return. It shows us an anxiety that marks the encounter with what is unrepresentable and ties the latter inextricably with the difficulties of representing oneself.

In this nightmare, James depicts for us, in the same sentence, two logically distinct moments:

> The lucidity, not to say the sublimity, of the crisis had consisted in the great thought that I, in my appalled state, was probably still more appalling than the awful agent, creature or presence, whatever he was, whom I had guessed [...] to be making for my place of rest.

The terms in which he describes his shadowy persecutor—an "awful agent, creature or presence"—are words of a calculated vagueness; they do not endow this 'visitant' with any particular characteristics and they suggest that the dreamer cannot know what sort of entity is pursuing him (197). Indeed, they are precisely not terms that would be used to describe an alter ego, and they open up the possibility that this thing is not even human. What pursues the dreamer is something that, in a sense, stands just on the threshold of representation: the author cannot name what it is and cannot give it a specific description.

It is only in a separate, logically distinct moment—although it is to be found in the same sentence—that the dreamer confers upon this persecutor the status of a mirror image; imagining that this entity has all the same feelings that he does and that their roles are interchangeable, he can cease to be the pursued and can become the pursuer. The dream acts, then, to reduce the anxiety provoked by the sense of alterity; it does so precisely by reducing this sense of otherness and transforming it into something that resembles the dreamer.

In this scene, the elements of the uncanny that had been latent in James's earlier formulations come to full fruition. What happens in the nightmare responds to the anxiety-provoking idea of rendering his own body unrecognisable by turning it inside-out and destroying its normal human aspect. The dream attempts to allay the anxiety brought by this idea; the threatening alterity is dispelled in this conversion of otherness into similitude. The dream constitutes a myth that gives the author a sense of "life-saving energy" and guarantees to him, even when the act of writing threatens him most strongly with a sense of self-estrangement, that the "danger" posed by this encounter with otherness can be overcome (196). Yet in achieving this victory over anxiety, the dream also creates a curious ambivalence. The only way that James can defeat the figure is to identify with it and for this reason, its defeat is also his own; indeed, the state to which he reduces it is related to the procedure to which he subjects his younger self. To place the boy under the gaze and thus to catch him in his own little acts of looking and enjoying constantly runs the risk of making him seem small, trivial and diminished. It is precisely this reduction that the entity is forced to undergo in the dream. Paul John Eakin has claimed that the dream "culminates in an act of self-display" in which the dreamer demonstrates his power to his antagonist, but it should be noted that there is never a confrontation in which these two figures look at each other face to face (Eakin 81). Instead, the author describes the "retreat" of a "dimly-descried figure," who, after James opens the door, runs away and is seen at such a distance that he has been reduced to nothing more than a "diminished spot" (196-97). What the dreamer sees is not an alter ego that would resemble something like a mirror image, a figure whose body would correspond closely to his own. Instead, the entity, having been reduced to little more than a small point, falls victim to the state of diminishment and reduction to which the system of vision that dominates the autobiography has always threatened to subject the small boy. The vanishing of this figure is one final consequence of a form that imposes on the subject the imperative of losing himself.

Bibliography of Works Cited

A. Works by Henry James

"A Day of Days." In *Galaxy* 1 (15 June 1866), 298-312.
"A French Watering Place." In *Parisian Sketches*. Edel, Leon and Dusoir Lind, Ilse (eds.). London: Rupert Hart-Davis, 1958.
A Small Boy and Others. New York: Charles Scribner's Sons, 1913.
Autobiography. Dupee, Frederick W. (ed.) Princeton: Princeton University Press, 1983.
— Dupee, F. W. (ed.). New York: W. H. Allen, 1956.
"Benvolio." In *Henry James. Complete Stories 1874-1884*. New York: The Library of America, 1999, 82-125.
Ce que savait Maisie, Yourcenar, Marguerite (trans.). Paris: Laffont, 1947.
Collected Stories. Vol. I. London: Everyman's Library, 1999, 2 Vols.
Complete Stories 1864-1874. Strouse, Jean (ed.). New York: The Library of America, 1999, 5 Vols.
Complete Stories 1892-1898. Osgood Edition. 1893. New York: The Library of America, 1996.
Confidence. 1879. Ruhm, Herbert (ed.). New York: Grosset and Dunlap, 1962.
— Stafford, William T. (ed.). New York: The Library of America, 1983.
"Correspondance de Gustave Flaubert." 1893. Rpt in *Henry James: Literary Criticism, Volume II*: 295-314.
"Correspondance de H. de Balzac." 1877. Rpt in *Henry James: Literary Criticism, Volume II*: 68-90.
"Daisy Miller." In *Cornhill Magazine* 37 (June 1878), 678-98; 37 (July 1878), 44-67.
English Hours. Whitefish, Minnesota: Kessinger Publishing, 2005.
"George Sand: The New Life." 1902. Rpt. in *Henry James: Literary Criticism, Volume II*: 755-75.
Hawthorne. 1879. London: Macmillan, 1967.
— Tanner, Tony (ed.). New York: St. Martin's, 1967.
Henry James: A Life in Letters. Horne, Philip (ed.). London: Allen Lane, 1999.
Henry James: Literary Criticism, French Writers. Other European Writers. The Prefaces to the New York Edition. Edel, Leon Edel (ed.) with the assistance of Mark Wilson. New York: The Library of America, 1984, 2 Vols.
Henry James: Novels 1871-1880: Watch and Ward, Roderick Hudson, The American, The Europeans, Confidence. William Stafford (ed.). New York: The Library of America, 1983.
"Her and She: Recent Documents." 1897. Rpt in *Henry James: Literary Criticism, Volume II*: 736-55.

"Honoré de Balzac." 1875. Rpt in *Henry James: Literary Criticism, Volume II*: 31-68.
Italian Hours. Auchard, John (ed.). University Park, Pennsylvania: Pennsylvania State University Press, 1992.
— Auchard, John (ed. and intr.). New York-London-Victoria-Toronto-Auckland: Penguin Books, 1995.
Letter to Francis Pharcellus Church or William Conant Church, 27 August [1877]. MS. *Galaxy* Correspondence. William Conant Church Papers. Manuscripts and Archives Division, New York Public Library, New York.
Letter to Mary Walsh James, 4 July [1878]. MS. James Family Papers. bMS Am 1094 (1869). By permission of the Houghton Library, Harvard University, Cambridge Massachussetts.
Letter to William Conant Church, 26 May [1877]. MS. *Galaxy* Correspondence. William Conant Church Papers. Manuscripts and Archives Division, New York Public Library, New York.
Letters, Fictions, Lives: Henry James and William Dean Howells. Anesko, Michael (ed.). New York: Oxford University Press, 1997.
Letters of Henry James. Lubbock, Percy (ed). London: Macmillan, 1920, 2 Vols.
Letters of Henry James. Edel, Leon (ed.). Cambridge, Massachussetts: Harvard University Press, 1974-84, 4 Vols.
"Owen Wingrave" (New York edition). In *The Ghostly Tales of Henry James*. Edel, Leon (ed.). New Brunswick: Rutgers University Press, 1948, 311-52.
Parisian Sketches. Edel, Leon and Dusoir Lind, Ilse (eds.). London: Rupert Hart Davis, 1958.
Preface to *The Awkward Age*, Vol. IX. 1908. Rpt. in *Henry James: Literary Criticism, Volume II*: 1120-37.
Preface to *The Ambassadors*. In *The Novels and Tales of Henry James: New York Edition*. Vol. XXI.
Preface to *The American*. In *The Novels and Tales of Henry James: New York Edition*, Vol. II.
Preface to "The Siege of London," "An International Episode," "The Pension Beaurepas," "A Bundle of Letters," and "The Point of View." *The Novels and Tales of Henry James*. Vol. XIV, 1909.
Preface to *What Maisie Knew*, "The Pupil," and "In the Cage." *The Novels and Tales of Henry James*. Vol. XI, 1908.
Preface to *What Maisie Knew*, Vol. XII. 1908. Rpt. in *Henry James: Literary Criticism, Volume II*: 1156-172.
"Roderick Hudson." In *Atlantic Monthly* 35 (January-June 1875): 1-15, 145-60, 297-313, 422-36, 515-31, 644-58; 36 (July-December 1875): 58-70, 129-40, 269-81, 385-406, 553-70, 641-65.
— Boston: Osgood, 1876.
— Oxford: Oxford University Press, 1980.
— (1876). *Novels 1871-1880*. New York: The Library of America, 1983.
Stories Revived. London: Macmillan, 1885, 3 vols.
"The Acting in Mr. Irving's *Faust*." In *The Scenic Art*. Wade, Allan (ed.). London: Rupert Hart-Davis, 1949.
The Ambassadors. London: Methuen, 1903.
— The Novels and Tales of Henry James: New York Edition, Vol. XXI.
— 1903. New York: Penguin, 1986.
— London: Penguin Books, 1987.

—   Rosenbaum, S. P. (ed.). New York: Norton, 1994.
—   Oxford: Oxford World's Classics. 2009
"The American." In *Atlantic Monthly* 37 (June 1876): 651-73; 38 (July-December 1876): 15-31, 155-70, 310-29, 461-74, 535-50, 641-57; 39 (January-May 1877): 1-18, 161-75, 295-311, 412-25, 530-44.
—   Boston: Osgood, 1877.
—   1879. New York: Bantam Books, 1971.
—   Tuttleton, James W. (ed.). New York and London: W.W. Norton & Company, 1978.
The American. Novels 1871-1880. New York: The Library of America, 1983, 513-872.
The American Scene. 1907. London: Granville, 1987.
—   Howard, Richard (ed.). New York: The Library of America, 1993.
—   New York: Penguin Books, 1994.
The Art of the Novel. New York: Scribners, 1947.
'The Art of Fiction.' In *Henry James: Selected Literary Criticism.* Shapira, Morris Shapira (ed.). Harmondsworth, England: Penguin, 1968, 78-97.
The Aspern Papers (New York edition) (with *The Turn of the Screw*). Introduction by Kenneth B. Murdoch, London: Everyman's Library, 1963.
"The Author of *Beltraffio*." In *Complete Stories,* Vol. II (1874-1884).
The Awkward Age. New York: Scribner, 1907.
"The Beast in the Jungle." In *The Complete Tales of Henry James* Vol. 11. Edel, Leon (ed.). Philadephia: Lippincott, 1964, 12 Vols. 351-402.
"The Birthplace." In *Complete Stories,* Vol V (1898-1810).
The Bostonians. 1886. 2nd eds. New York: Oxford University Press, 1998.
The Complete Letters of Henry James 1872-1876, Vol. II. Walker, Pierre A. and Zacharias, Greg W. (eds.). Lincoln: University of Nebraska Press, 2009, 3 Vols.
The Complete Notebooks of Henry James. Edel, Leon and Powers, Lyall (eds.). New York and Oxford: Oxford University Press, 1987.
The Correspondence of William James: William and Henry 1861-1884, Vol. I. Skripskelis, Ignas K. and Berkeley, Elizabeth M. (eds.). Charlottesville: University Press Virginia, 1992-2004, 12 Vols.
"The Europeans." In *Atlantic Monthly* 42 (July-October 1878), 52-72, 155-77, 262-83, 404-28.
The Ivory Tower. In *The Novels and Tales of Henry James,* Vol. XXV. New York: Charles Scribner's Sons, 1937.
The Golden Bowl (2 Vols.). In *The Novels and Tales of Henry James.* Vols. XXIII and XXIV. 1909.
—   Harmondsworth: Penguin, 1987.
"The Long Wards." In *The Book of the Homeless.* Edith Wharton (ed.). New York: Scribner's, 1916. 115-25.
The Notebooks of Henry James Mattheissen, Francis O. and Murdock, Kenneth B. (eds.) New York and Oxford: Oxford University Press, 1947.
The Portrait of a Lady. More, Geoffrey (ed.). Harmondsworth: Penguin, 1986. (Savoy)
—   London: Everyman, 1995.
"The Private Life." In *Complete Stories,* Vol. IV (1892-1898).
The Question of Our Speech. Boston: Houghton-Mifflin, 1905.
The Sacred Fount. New York: Charles Scribner's Sons, 1923.
"The Saloon." In *The Complete Plays.* Edel, Leon (ed.). London: Rupert Hart-Davis, 1949, 641-74.

The Sense of the Past. Percy Lubbock (ed.). *The Novels and Tales of Henry James.* Vol. XXVI.

"The Story-teller at Large: Mr. Henry Harland." In *The American Essays of Henry James.* Edel, Leon (ed.). Princeton, New Jersey: Princeton University Press, 1990.

The Tales of Henry James, Vol. II (1870-1874). Aziz, Maqbool (ed.). Oxford: Clarendon Press, 1978, 348-82.

The Tragic Muse. 1890. New York Edition (1908). Horne, Phillip (ed.). Place: Penguin Books, 1995.

"The Turn of the Screw." *The Novels and Tales of Henry James.* Vol. XII. New York: Charles Scribner's Sons, 1908.

— *and Other Stories.* Oxford, New York: Oxford University Press World's Classics, 1992.

— New York Edition. 1908. In *The Norton Critical Edition.* 2nd eds. Esch, Deborah and Warren, Jonathan (eds). New York and London: W.W. Norton and Company, 1999.

The Wings of the Dove (2 Vols). *The Novels and Tales of Henry James.* Vol. XIX and XX.
— Harmondsworth: Penguin, 1965.

"Travelling Companions," *Complete Stories, 1864-1874. What Maisie Knew.* Adrian Poole (ed.). New York: Oxford University Press, 1998.

William Wetmore Story and His Friends. London: Thames and Hudson, 1903, 2 Vols.

B. Works by other authors

Adams, Henry. *The Education of Henry Adams*. Boston and New York: Houghton Mifflin Company, 1918.

Albers, Christina. *A Reader's Guide to the Short Stories of Henry James*. New York: Hall, 1997.

Anderson, Quentin. "Why R. P. Blackmur Found James's *Golden Bowl* Inhumane." In *ELH (English Literature History)* 68: 3 (2001), 725-43.

Anesko, Michael. *"Friction with the Market": Henry James and the Profession of Authorship*. New York: Oxford University Press, 1986.

Appiah, Kwame Anthony. *Cosmopolitanism: Ethics in a World of Strangers*. New York: Norton, 2007.

— *The Ethics of Identity*. Princeton: Princeton University Press, 2007.

Arnold, Matthew. "Civilization in the United States." *The Complete Prose Works of Matthew Arnold*, Vol. X. Super, R. H. (ed.). Ann Arbor: University of Michigan Press, 1977.

— *Essays in Criticism: Second Series*. London: Macmillan, 1865.

Ascham, Roger. *The Schoolmaster* in *English Works*. Wright, William A. (ed.). Cambridge: Cambridge University Press, 1904.

Auchard, John. "Introduction" to Henry James's *Italian Hours*. Auchard, John (ed.). New York-London-Victoria-Toronto-Auckland: Penguin Books, 1995, ix-xxxii.

Augé, Marc. *Le temps en ruines*. Paris: Galilée, 2003.

Balzac, Honoré de. *Cousin Pons* in *La Comédie Humaine*, Dufief, Pierre and Dufief, Anne-Simone (eds.). Paris: Omnibus, 1999.

— *Louis Lambert* in *La Comédie Humaine*, Vol. XI, 589-692. Gallimard: Paris, 1980, 20 Vols.

Banta, Martha. "Introduction." In *New Essays on the American*. Banta, Martha (ed.). Cambridge: Cambridge University Press, 1987, 1-42.

— "Men, Women, and the American Way." In *The Cambridge Companion to Henry James*. New York: Cambridge University Press, 1998, 21-39.

— (ed.). *New Essays on* The American. New York: Cambridge University Press, 1987.

— "The Quality of Experience in *What Maisie Knew*." In *New England Quarterly* 42 (1969), 483-510.

Battilana, Marilla. *Venezia sfondo e simbolo nella narrativa di Henry James*. Milano: Laboratorio delle Arti, 1971.

Bell, Millicent. *Meaning in Henry James*. Cambridge, Massachussetts and London: Harvard University Press, 1993.

Berman, Jessica. "Feminizing the Nation: Woman as Cultural Icon in Late James." In *Henry James Review* 17: 1 (1996), 58-76.

Berman, Marshall. *All That Is Solid Melts into Air: The Experience of Modernity*. New York: Penguin, 1988.

Bersani, Leo. *A Future for Astyanax: Character and Desire in Literature*. Boston: Little, Brown, 1976.

— "The Jamesian Lie." In *Partisan Review* 36: 1 (Winter 1969), 53-79.

Bhabha, Homi. "Border Lives: The Art of the Present." In *Defining Travel: Diverse Visions*. Roberson, Susan (ed.). Jackson, MI: University Press of Mississippi, 2001, 157-66.

Black, William. "Madcap Violet." *Galaxy* 21 (January-June 1876), 102-10, 149-64, 293-317, 461-85, 602-23, 738-61; 22 (July-Dec. 1876): 21-42, 169-87, 303-08, 457-77, 581-603, 725-47; 23 (Jan. 1877): 30-42.

Blackmur, Richard P. *The Art of the Novel: Critical Prefaces By Henry James*. New York: Charles Scribner's Sons, 1934.

Blanche, Jacques-Émile. *Portraits of a Lifetime*. Clement, Walter (trans. and ed.). London: Dent, 1937.

Bogardus, Ralph F. *Pictures and Texts: Henry James, A.L. Coburn, and New Ways of Seeing in Literary Culture*. Ann Arbor, Michigan: UMI Research Press, 1984.

Bourdieu, Pierre. *Distinction. A Social Critique of the Judgment of Taste* (1979). Nice, Richard (trans.). Harvard: Harvard University Press, 1987.

— *The Rules of Art: Genesis and Structure of the Literary Field*. Emanuel, Susan (trans.). Stanford: Stanford University Press, 1996.

Bowen, Ray P. "Balzac's Interior Descriptions as an Element in Characterization." In *PMLA* 40: 2 (June 1925), 289-301.

Brissenden, Robert F. *Virtue in Distress: Studies in the Novel of Sentiment from Richardson to Sade*. London and Basingstoke: The Macmillan Press, 1974.

Britten, Benjamin, cond. English Chamber Orchestra. *Owen Wingrave; A Television Opera* (1971). Dir. Brian Large and Colin Grahame. A BBC Recording. The Britten-Pears Collection. London: Decca, 2009.

— Libretto. *Owen Wingrave. An Opera in Two Acts*. Op. 85. Music by Myfanwy Piper based on the short story by Henry James. Study Score (1970). London: Faber Music, 1995.

Britzolakis, Christina. "Technologies of Vision in Henry James's *What Maisie Knew*." In *NOVEL: A Forum on Fiction* 34 (Summer 2001), Providence: Novel Corporation, Brown University, 369-90.

Brontë, Charlotte. *Jane Eyre* (1847). London: J.M. Dent and Sons, 1922.

Brooks, Peter. *Henry James Goes to Paris*. Princeton, New Jersey: Princeton University Press, 2007.

— *The Melodramatic Imagination*. New Haven: Yale University Press, 1976.

— *Reading for the Plot: Design and Intention in Narrative*. Cambridge, Massachussetts: Harvard University Press, 1984.

Buffet, Warren. "To the Shareholders of Berkshire Hathaway." March 2, 1990. <http://www.berkshirehathaway.com/letters/1989.html>.

Buell, Lawrence. "Fictive Nation-Building on the Grand Scale: Contested Templates for the 'Great American Novel.'" In *English Now: Selected Papers from the 20th IAUPE Conference in Lund 2007*. Thormälen, Marianne (ed.). Lund, Sweden: Centre for Languages and Literature, Lund University, 2008, 90-101.

Buitenhuis, Peter. *The Grasping Imagination: The American Writings of Henry James*. Toronto: University of Toronto Press, 1970.

Burrows, Stuart. "The Golden Fruit: Innocence and Imperialism in *The Golden Bowl*." In *The Henry James Review* 21: 2 (2000), 95-114.

Buzard, James. "A Continent of Pictures: Reflections on the "Europe" of Nineteenth-Century Tourists." In *PMLA* 108: 1 (January 1993), 30-44.

Byron, Lord. *A Self-Portrait. Letters and Diaries 1798 to 1824*. Quennell Peter (ed.). London: Murray, 1950.

Cargill, Oscar. "The First International Novel." In *PMLA* 73 (September 1958); 418-25.

— *The Novels of Henry James*. New York: Hafner, 1971.

Castle, Terry. *The Female Thermometer: Eighteenth Century Culture and the Invention of the Uncanny*. Oxford, New York: Oxford University Press, 1995.
Chambers Twenty-First Century Dictionary. Robinson, Mairi (ed.). Edinburgh: Harrap, 1999.
Chinitz, Lisa G. "Fairy Tale Turned Ghost Story: James's *The Turn of the Screw*." *The Henry James Review*. Vol. 15: 3 (Fall 1994): 264-85.
Clegg. Jeanne. *Ruskin and Venice*. London: Junction Books, 1981.
— "Superficial pastimes, fine emotions and metaphysical intentions: James and Ruskin in Venice." in *Henry James e Venezia*. Perosa, Sergio (ed.). Firenze: Olschki, 1987, 159-70.
Coburn, Alvin Langdon. *Men of Mark*. New York: Mitchell Kennedy, 1913.
Cohen, Paula Marantz. *The Daughter's Dilemma: Family Process and the Nineteenth Century Domestic Novel*. Ann Arbor, Michigan: University of Michigan Press, 1992.
Coryat, Thomas. *Coryat's Crudities*. Glasgow: James MacLehose & Sons, 1905, 2 Vols.
Cox, James M. "The Memoirs of Henry James: Self-Interest as Autobiography." In *Studies in Autobiography*. Olney, James (ed.). New York: Oxford University Press, 1988.
Crary, Jonathan. *Suspensions of Perception: Attention, Spectacle, and Modern Culture*. Cambridge, Massachussetts: The MIT Press, 2001.
De Man, Paul. *The Resistance to Theory*. Minneapolis: University of Minnesota Press, 1986.
Diderot, Denis. "Paradoxe sur le comédien" (1830). In *Œuvres esthétiques*. Vernière, P. V (ed.). Paris: Classiques Garnier, 1988.
Dunbar, Viola. "A Note on the Genesis of *Daisy Miller*." In *Philological Quarterly* 27 (1948), 184-86.
Eagleton, Terry. *Criticism and Ideology*. London: Verso, 1978.
Eakin, Paul John. *Fictions in Autobiography: Studies in the Art of Self-Invention*. Princeton: Princeton University Press, 1985.
Edel, Leon. *Henry James. A Life*. New York: Harper and Row, 1977.
— *Henry James, Vol. II. The Conquest of London: 1870-1883*. London: Rupert Hart-Davis, 1962, 5 Vols.
— *Henry James, Vol. V. The Master: 1901-1916*. New York: J.B. Lippincott, 1972, 5 Vols.
— Introduction. *Stories of the Supernatural* (formerly *Ghost-Stories*). New York: Taplinger Publishing Company, 1970.
Edel, Leon, and Tintner, Adeline R. *The Library of Henry James*. Ann Arbor: UMI Research Press, 1987.
Eliot, T.S. "Portrait of a Lady." *Prufrock and Other Observations*. London: The Egoist, Ltd., 1917, 17-23.
Evans, John. "A Case for Pacifism." In *The Britten Companion*. Palmer, Christopher (ed.). Cambridge: Cambridge University Press, 1984, 227-37.
Fargnoli, Joseph. "Henry James's *The American Scene*: A Vade Mecum for Writing American Culture." In *American Transcendental Quarterly (ATQ)* 2 (1988): 312-26.
Feinstein, Howard M. *Becoming William James*. Ithaca: Cornell University Press, 1984.
Fielding, Henry. *Amelia*. 1759. Rpt. Whitefish, Montana: Kessinger Publishing, 2004.
Follini, Tamara L. "James, Ruskin, and *The Stones of Venice*." In *Tracing Henry James*. Ross, Melanie H. and Zacharias, Greg W. (eds.). Cambridge: Cambridge Scholars Publishing, 2008, 124-36.
Franklin, Benjamin. *Autobiography*. New York: P. F. Collier, 1909.

Freedman, Jonathan. "Introduction: The Moment of Henry James." In *The Cambridge Companion to Henry James*. Freedman, Jonathan (ed.). Cambridge: Cambridge University Press, 1998. 1-20.

— *Professions of Taste: Henry James British Aestheticism, and Commodity Culture*. Stanford: Stanford University Press, 1990.

Freud, Sigmund. "Notes Upon a Case of Obsessional Neurosis." In *Case Histories II: The 'Rat Man,' Schreber, 'Wolf Man,' a Case of Female Homosexuality*. Richards, Angela (ed.). Strachey, Alix and Strachey, James (trans.). London: Penguin Books, 1979, 31-128.

— "The Uncanny." In *Art and Literature: Jensen's Gradiva, Leonardo Da Vinci and Other Works*. Dickson, Albert (ed.). Strachey, Alix (trans.). Harmondsworth, Middlesex: Penguin, 1985, 335-76.

Fried, Michael. *Absorption and Theatricality: Painting and Beholder in the Age of Diderot*. Berkeley: University of California Press, 1980.

— *Manet's Modernism, or, the Face of Painting in the 1860's*. Chicago: University of Chicago Press, 1996.

Fussell, Edwin. *The Ambassadors: Gloire Complete, The French Side of Henry James*. New York: Columbia University Press, 1990.

— *The French Side of Henry James*. Cambridge: Cambridge University Press, 1993.

Genette, Gérard. *Figures of Literary Discourse*. Sheridan, Alan (trans.). Oxford: Blackwell, 1982.

Giddens, Anthony. *The Consequences of Modernity*. Cambridge: Polity, 1990.

Giles, Paul. "Transnationalism and Classic Amerian Literature." In *PMLA* 118 (January 2003), 62-77.

Goethe, Johann Wolfgang von. *Goethe's Werke. Vollständige Ausgabe letzter Hand*. Stuttgart: Cotta, 1827-42, 60 vols.

Goldstein, Laurence. *Ruins and Empire. The Evolution of a Theme in Augustan and Romantic Literature*. Pittsburgh: University of Pittsburgh Press, 1977.

Greene, John Patrick. "Balzac's Most Helpless Heroine: The Art Collection in *Le Cousin Pons*." In *The French Review* 69: 1 (October 1995), 13-23.

Greenslade, William. "The Power of Advertising: Chad Newsome and the Meaning of Paris in *The Ambassadors*." In *ELH (English Literary History)* 49 (Spring 1982), 99-122.

Gunter, Susan E. and Jobe, Steven H. (eds.). *Dearly Beloved Friends: Henry James's Letters to Younger Men*. Ann Arbor, Michigan: University of Michigan Press, 2001.

Haviland, Beverly. *Henry James' Last Romance. Making Sense of the Past and the American Scene*. Cambridge: Cambridge University Press, 1997.

[Hazlitt, William.] "Of Persons One Would Wish To Have Seen." In *New Monthly Magazine* 16 (January 1826), 32-41.

Higgins, Charles. "Photographic Aperture: Coburn's Frontispieces to James's New York Edition." In *American Literature* 53 (1982), 661-75.

Hillis Miller, James. *Versions of Pygmalion*. Cambridge and London: Harvard University Press, 1990, 23-81.

Hoeveler, Diane Long. *Gothic Feminism: The Professionalization of Gender from Charlotte Smith to the Brontës*. University Park, Pennsylvania: Pensylvania University Press, 1997.

— "Romancing Venice: the courtship of Percy Shelley in James's *The Aspern Papers*." In *Tracing Henry James*. Ross, Melanie H. and Zacharias, Greg W. (eds.). Cambridge: Cambridge Scholars Publishing, 2008, 155-67.

Holland, John. "The Palace of Thought." In *Critical Essays on Jacques Lacan*. Ragland-Sullivan, Ellie (ed.). New York: G.K. Hall, 1999, 119-41.
Horace. *The Complete Odes and Epodes* West, David West (trans.). Oxford: Oxford University Press, 1997.
Horne, Philip. *Henry James: A Life in Letters*. Harmondsworth: Penguin, 1999.
— *Henry James and Revision*. Oxford: Clarendon Press, 1990.
— 'Henry James and the Poetry of Association.' Unpublished doctoral thesis, University of Cambridge, 1982.
— 'James Among the Poets.' In *Henry James Review* 26: 1 (2005), 68-81.
— (ed.) Introduction. Henry James. *The Tragic Muse* (1890). New York Edition (1908). London: Penguin Books, 1995, vii-xxix.
Horne, Alistair. *Seven Ages of Paris*. New York: Vintage, 2004.
Howells, William Dean. Letter to Francis Pharcellus Church or William Conant Church, 29 February 1876. MS. *Galaxy* Correspondence. William Conant Church Papers. Manuscripts and Archives Division, New York Public Library, New York.
— Letter to Francis Pharcellus Church or William Conant Church, 5 March 1876. MS. *Galaxy* Correspondence. William Conant Church Papers. Manuscripts and Archives Division, New York Public Library, New York.
Hutchinson, Stuart. *The American Scene: Essays on 19th-century American Literature*. New York: St. Martin's, 1991.
Hutchison, Hazel. "The Other Lambert Strether: Henry James's *The Ambassadors*, Balzac's *Louis Lambert*, and J. H. Lambert." In *Nineteenth-century Literature*, 58: 2 (September 2003), 230-58.
Ibsen, Henrik. *The Master Builder, Rosmersholm, Little Eyolf, John Gabriel Borkman*. Ellis-Fermor, Una (trans.). Harmondsworth: Penguin, 1969.
Irwin, William. 'The Aesthetics of Allusion'. *The Journal of Value Inquiry* 36: 4 (2002).
Izzo, Donatella. *Henry James*. Firenze: La Nuova Italia, 1981.
— *Portraying the Lady: Technologies of Gender in the Short Stories of Henry James*. Lincoln: University of Nebraska Press, 2001.
Jackson, J. B. *The Necessity for Ruins and Other Topics*. Amherst, Massachusetts: University of Massachusetts Press, 1980.
Johnson, Stuart. "American Marginalia: James's *The American Scene*." In *Texas Studies in Literature and Language* 24: 1 (1982), 83-101.
Kaplan, Fred. *Henry James: The Imagination of Genius*. London: Sceptre, 1993.
Karénine, Wladimir. *George Sand: Sa vie et ses oeuvres*. Paris: Plon, Vols. I and II, 1899; Vol. III, 1912, 4 Vols.
Kenton, Edna. "Henry James in the World." In *The Question of Henry James*. Dupee, F.W. (ed.). New York: Holt, 1945. 131-37.
King, Kristin. "Ethereal Milly Theale in *The Wings of the Dove*: The Transparent Heart of James's Opaque Style." In *The Henry James Review* 21: 1 (2000), 1-13.
Kipling, Rudyard. "France." *Rudyard Kipling's Verse: Inclusive Edition, 1885-1918*. Garden City, New York: Doubleday, Page & Co., 1919. 336.
Kristeva, Julia. *Word, Dialogue and Novel* and *Revolution in Poetic Language* in Moi, Toril (ed.). *The Kristeva Reader*. New York: Columbia University Press, 1986.
Lacan, Jacques. *The Four Fundamental Concepts of Psycho-analysis*. Miller, Jacques-Alain (ed.). Sheridan, Alan (trans.). New York: Norton, 1978.
Lamartine, Alphonse de. *Confidential Disclosures*. Plunkett, Eugène (trans.). New York: D. Appleton & Co., 1849.

Lanchester, John. "Cityphobia." In *London Review of Books* 30: 20 (23 October 2008), 3-5.
— "Melting Into Air, or, Before the Financial System Went Bust, It Went Postmodern." In *The New Yorker*, 10 November 2008, 80-84.
Lane, Christopher. "Jamesian Inscrutability." In *The Henry James Review*. 20:3 (1999), 244-54.
Lapham, Lewis. "Achievetrons." In *Harper's Magazine* 318: 1906 (March 2009), 9-11.
Lawrence, D.H. "The 'Jeune Fille' Wants to Know" (1928). In *Phoenix II*. London: Heinemann, 1968, .
Levinas, Emmanuel. *Totality and Infinity. Essay on Exteriority*. Lingis, Alphonso (trans.). Pittsburgh: Duquesne University Press, 1969.
Lucking, David. "Romance as Irony in *The American* by Henry James." In *Quadreni* 2 (1980). Ist. Di Lingue e Lett. Straniere, Univ. degli Studi di Lecce, 93-115.
Lustig, Tim. "James, Arnold, 'Culture' and 'Modernity'; or A Tale of Two Dachsunds." In *The Cambridge Quarterly* 7:1 (2008), 164-93.
— Introduction. *"The Turn of the Screw" and Other Stories*, Oxford, New York: Oxford University Press World's Classics , 1992.
McWhirter, David (ed.). *Henry James's New York Edition: The Construction of Authorship*. Stanford: Stanford University Press, 1995.
Mamoli Zorzi, Rosella. "The Text is the City; the Representation of Venice in Two Tales by Irving and Poe and a novel by Cooper." in *RSA Rivista di Studi Anglo-americani* 6:8 (1990), 285-300.
— "Intertextual Venice: Blood and Crime and Death Renewed in Two Contemporary Novels." In *Venetian Views, Venetian Blind*. Pfister, Manfred and Schaff, Barbara (eds.). Amsterdam: Rodopi, 1999, 225-36.
— "'A Knock-down Insolence of Talent': Sargent, James, and Venice." In *Sargent's Venice*. Adelson, Warren; Gerdts, William H.; Kilmurray,Elaine; Mamoli Zorzi, Rosella; Ormond, Richard; and Oustinoff, Elizabeth. (eds.). New Haven: Yale University Press, 2006, 140-59.
— *In Venice and in the Veneto with Henry James*. Venezia: Supernova, 2005.
Marivaux, Pierre. *False Admissions, Successful Strategies, La Dispute*. Wertenbaker, Timberlake (trans.). London: Oberon, 1997.
— *Les Fausses Confidences*. Mason, H. T. (ed.). Oxford: Oxford University Press, 1964.
Marotta, Kenny. "*What Maisie Knew*: The Question of Our Speech." In *ELH (English Literary History)* 46 (1979), Baltimore: The Johns Hopkins University Press, 495-508.
Melchiori, Giorgio G. "Locksley Hall Revisited." *Review of English Literature* 6 (October 1965), 9-25.
Melville, Herman. *The Confidence-Man: His Masquerade*. 1857. Parker, Hershel (ed.). New York: Norton, 1971.
Méral, Jean. *Paris in American Literature*. Long, Laurette (trans.). Chapel Hill: University of North Carolina Press, 1989.
Milbank, Alison. "Gothic Femininities." In *The Routledge Companion to Gothic*. Catherine Spooner and Emma McEvoy (eds.). London and New York: Routledge, 2007. 155-63.
Mitchell, William J. Thomas. *What Do Picvtures Want? The Lives and Loves of Images*. Chicago: University of Chicago Press, 2005.
Moretti, Franco. *Modern Epic: The World System from Goethe to Garcia Marquez*. London: Verso, 1996.

— "Conjectures on World Literature." In Prendergast, Christopher (ed.). *Debating World Literature*. London: Verso, 2004.
Mulhallen, Jaccqueline, *The Theatre of Shelley*. Cambridge: Open Book Publishers, 2010.
Muratov, Pavel. *Obrazy Włoch [Images of Italy]*. Hertz, Pawel (Polish trans.) Warszawa: Panstwowy Instytut Wydawniczy, 1972.
Nadel, Ira B. "Visual Culture: The Photo Frontispieces of the New York Edition." in *Henry James's New York Edition: The Construction of Authorship*. McWhirter, David (ed.), Stanford: Stanford Uuniversity Press, 1995, 90-108.
Nashe, Thomas. *The Unfortunate Traveller and Other Works*. Stearns, John Barry (ed.). Harmondsworth: Penguin, 1971.
Nedelmann, Birgitta. "Oggetti d'arte – oggetti artigianali: Il problema dello stile di vita" in Borsari, Andrea (ed.). *L'esperienza delle cose*. Genova: Marietti, 1992, 193-207.
O'Gorman, Francis. "'Fabulous and Illusive': Giorgione and Henry James's *The Aspern Papers*." In *The Henry James Review*, 27 (2006), 175-87.
O'Hara, Daniel T. *Empire Burlesque: The Fate of Critical Culture in Global America*. Durham: Duke University Press, 2003.
Olney, James. "Psychology, Memory, and Autobiography: William and Henry James." In *The Henry James Review* 6:1 (1984), 46-51.
Oltean, Roxana. *Eternal America. Henry James and the Globalizing Imagination*. Bucharest: The University of Bucharest Press, 2007.
— "'I Longed for a New World': Colonial Hysteria, *The American*, and Henry James's Paris." In *Henry James Review* 24 (2003), 269-80.
— *Spaces of Utopia in the Writings of Henry James*. Bucharest: The University of Bucharest Press, 2005.
Orlando, Francesco. *Obsolete Objects in the Literary Imagination: Ruins, Relics, Rarities, Rubbish, Uninhabited Places, and Hidden Treasures*. Yale: Yale University Press, 2006.
Oxford English Dictionary. 2nd Edition. Volume II. Oxford: Clarendon Press, 1989, 20 Vols.
Ovid. *Ars Amatoria (The Art of Love)*. Book II. Yalden, Thomas (trans.). London: Wordsworth Classics, 2000, 3 Books.
Parkinson, Edward J. "'The Turn of the Screw' and its Critical Interpretations, 1897-1979. 1991 Doctoral Thesis, Saint Louis University. <www.turnofthe screw.com>.
Pater, Walter. *Appreciations, with an Essay on Style*. London: Macmillan, 1889.
Paumgarden, Nick. "Arithmetic Department: In for It." In *The New Yorker*, 17 November 2008, 43-4.
Pearson, John H. "Repetition and Subversion in Henry James's *The Turn of the Screw*." *The Henry James Review*. 13/3 (Fall 1992): 275-91.
Pemble, John. *Venice Rediscovered*. Oxford: Clarendon Press, 1995.
Perrot, Jean. *Henry James: une écriture énigmatique*. Paris: Aubier Montaigne, 1982.
Petry, Alice Hall. "Jamesian Parody: *Jane Eyre* and *The Turn of the Screw*." *Modern Language Studies*. Vol. 13/4, Henry James Issue (Autumn 1983): 61-78.
Pety, Dominique. *Les Goncourt et la collection: de l'objet d'art à l'art d'écrire*. Genève: Droz, 2003.
Pfister, Manfred (ed.). *The Fatal Gift of Beauty. The Italies of British Travellers. An Annotated Anthology*. Amsterdam: Rodopi, 1996.
Piper, Myfanwy. *Owen Wingrave. An Opera in Two Acts*. Set to Music by B. Britten Op.

85. London: Faber Music, 1971.

Poirier, Richard. Introduction. *The American* by Henry James. New York: Bantam Books, 1971.

Posnock, Ross. "Breaking the Aura of Henry James." In *Henry James's New York Edition: The Construction of Authorship*. McWhirter, David (ed.). Stanford: Stanford University Press, 1995, 23-38.

—. "The Politics of Nonidentity: A Genealogy." In *Boundary 2* 19:1 (1992), 34-68.

—. *The Trial of Curiosity: Henry James, William James, and the Challenge of Modernity*. New York: Oxford University Press, 1991.

Powers, Lyall (ed). *Henry James and Edith Wharton, Letters 1900-1915*. New York: Scribners, 1999.

Praz, Mario. *La carne, la morte e il diavolo nella letteratura romantica* (1930). Firenze: Sansoni, 2003.

"R. N." "Personal Character of Lord Byron." In *London Magazine* 10 (October 1824), 337-47.

Randal, Michael. *The Harvard Dictionary of Music*. 4th eds. Cambridge, Massachussetts: The Belknap Press, 2003.

Ricks, Christopher. *Allusion and the Poets*. Oxford: Oxford University Press, 2002.

Rimmon, Shlomith. *The Concept of Ambiguity: The Example of James*. Chicago: University of Chicago Press, 1977.

Rivkin, Julie. *False Positions: The Representational Logics of Henry James's Fiction*. Stanford, California: Stanford University Press, 1996.

Robb, Graham. *Balzac*. New York: W. W. Norton, 1994.

Rodas, Julie M. "On the Spectrum : Rereading Contact and Affect in *Jane Eyre*." *19th Century Gender Studies*, 4.2 (Summer 2008). <http://ncgsjournal.com/issue42/rodas.htm>

Rosenbaum, S. P. "Two Henry James Letters on *The American* and *Watch and Ward*." In *American Literature* 30 (1958-1959), 533-37.

Rowe, John Carlos. *Literary Culture and U.S. Imperialism: from the Revolution to World War II*. New York: Oxford University Press, 2000.

Saltz, Laura. "Henry James's Overexposures." In *Henry James Review* 25 (2004), 254-66.

Savoy, Eric. "Subjunctive Biography." In *The Henry James Review*. 27:3 (2006), 248-56.

Sawyer-Lauçanno, Christopher. *E. E. Cummings: A Biography*. Naperville, Illinois: Sourcebooks, 2004.

Schapiro, Meyer. *Words and Pictures: On the Literal and the Symbolic in the Illustration of a Text*. 1973. Berlin: Walter de Gruyter Publishers, 1983.

Schiller, Friedrich. *Der Geisterseher*. Stuttgart: Philipp Reclam, 1996; French edition, *Le Visionnaire*. Preface par Pierre Péju, Paris: José Corti, 1996.

Schneider, Daniel J. 'The Figure in the Carpet of Henry James's *Confidence*.' In *The Henry James Review* 4: 2 (1983), 120-27.

Schwarz, Daniel R. "A Humanistic Ethics of Reading." In *Mapping the Ethical Turn: A Reader in Ethics, Culture, and Literary Theory*. Davis, Todd F. and Womack, Kenneth. Charlottesville: University of Virginia Press, 2001, 3-15.

Sedgwick, Eve Kosofsky. "Shame and Performativity: Henry James's New York Edition Prefaces." in *Henry James's New York Edition: The Construction of Authorship*. McWhirter, David (ed.). Stanford: Stanford University Press, 1995, 206-39.

Shakespeare, William. *Hamlet*. Jenkins, Harold (ed.). London: Methuen, 1982.

— *Love's Labour's Lost*. Cohen, Walter (ed.). *The Norton Shakespeare*. New York:

W.W. Norton & Co., 1997, 733-802.
— *The Oxford Shakespeare: Hamlet.* Hibbard, G. R. (ed.). Oxford: Oxford University Press, 1987.
— *The Works of William Shakespeare.* Clark, William George Clark and Wright, William Aldis (eds.). The Globe Edition. Cambridge and London: Macmillan & Co., 1864.
— *The Works of Shakespeare*, Vol. I. Herford, C.H. Herford (ed.). London: Macmillan & Co., 1899, 10 vols.
"Shakespeare's Critics: English and Foreign." In *Edinburgh Review* 90 (July 1849), 39-77.
Shelley, Percy Bisshe. *The Poetical Works.* London: Ward, Lock & Co., n.d.
Sherman, Daniel and Irit Rogoff (eds). *Museum Culture: Histories, Discourses, Spectacles.* London: Routledge, 1994.
Siegel, James T. "Georg Simmel Reappears: 'The Aesthetic Significance of the Face.'" *Diacritics* 29 (1999), 100-13.
Simmel, Georg. "The Aesthetic Significance of the Face." In *Georg Simmel, 1858-1918.* Wolff, Kurt H. (ed.). Columbus: Ohio State University Press, 1959, 276-81.
Southam, Brian. *A Student's Guide to the Selected Poems of T S Eliot.* London: Faber & Faber, 1994.
Stephens, Winifred (ed.). *The Book of France.* London: Macmillan, 1915.
Stone, Edward. *The Battle and the Books.* Athens: Ohio University Press, 1964.
Stoppard, Tom. *The Real Inspector Hound.* London: Faber & Faber, 1970.
Story, Emelyn. Unpublished manuscript notes. Harry Ransom Humanities Research Center, The University of Texas at Austin, MS (Story, EE), Works [Anecdotes and reminiscences].
Tambling, Jeremy. *Henry James.* New York: St. Martin's Press, 2000.
Tanner, Tony. *Venice Desired.* Cambridge: Harvard University Press, 1992.
Teahan, Sheila. *The Rhetorical Logic of Henry James.* Baton Rouge: Louisiana State University, 1995.
Teyssandier, Hubert. "Modèles et représentations dans *The Tragic Muse.*" In *Henry James ou le fluide sacré de la fiction*, Geoffroy-Menoux, Sophie (ed.). Paris: L'Harmattan, 1998.
Thoreau, Henry David. *Walden.* Boston: Beacon Press, 2004.
Tinayre, Marcelle. *Avant l'Amour*, Paris: Calmann-Lévy, 1897.
Tintner, Adeline R. "Henry and William James and Titian's Torn Glove." In *Iris: Notes in the History of Art* 1 (February 1982), 22-24.
— "Henry James and the First World War: The Release from Repression." *Literature and War: Reflections and Refractions.* Trahan, Elizabeth W. (ed.). Monterey: Monterey Institute of International Studies, 1985.
— *The Book World of Henry James. Appropriating the Classics.* With a foreword by Leon Edel. Ann Arbor, Michigan: UMI Research Press, 1987.
— *The Cosmopolitan World of Henry James: An Intertextual Study.* Baton Rouge, Louisiana and London: Louisiana State University Press, 1991.
— *The Museum World of Henry James.* Ann Arbor, Michigan: UMI Research Press, 1986.
— "'The Old Things': Balzac's *Le Curé de Tours* and James's *The Spoils of Poynton.*" In *Nineteenth-century Fiction* 26:4 (Mar 1972), 436–55.
— "The Spoils of Henry James." In *PMLA* 61:1 (March 1946), 239-51.
Veblen, Thorstein. *Theory of the Leisure Class* (1899). New York: Penguin, 1994.

Veeder, William. *Henry James – The Lessons of the Master: Popular Fiction and Personal Style in the Nineteenth Century*. Chicago: University of Chicago Press, 1975.
Venezia nell'Ottocento. Pavanello, Giuseppe and Romanelli, Giandomenico (eds.). Milano: Electa, 1983.
Venn, Couze. *Occidentalism. Modernity and Subjectivity*. London: Sage Publications, 2000.
Wade, Allan. *Henry James: The Scenic Art: Notes on Acting and the Drama, 1872-1901*. London: Rupert Hart-Davies, 1949.
Walker, Pierre A. "'Adina': Henry James's Roman Allegory of Power and the Representation of the Foreign." In *The Henry James Review*. 21: 1 (Winter 2000), 14-26.
— *Reading Henry James in French Cultural Contexts*. De Kalb, Illinois: Northern Illinois University Press, 1995.
Ward, Susan P. "Painting and Europe in *The American*." In *American Literature* 46:4 (January 1975), 566-73.
Watson, Janell. *Literature and Material Culture form Balzac to Proust: The Collection and Consumption of Curiosities*. Cambridge UK: Cambridge University Press, 1999.
Weissman, Steven R. "Bernanke Nods at Possibility of Recession." *The New York Times*. April 2, 2008.
Wharton, Edith. *A Son at the Front* (1923). DeKalb: Northern Illinois University Press, 1995.
Whittall, Arnold. "Britten's Lament: The World of *Owen Wingrave*." In *Music Analysis*, 19:2 (2000), 145-66.
Wilde, Oscar. *A Woman of No Importance: A Play*. 1893. Leipzig: B. Touchnitz, 1909.
Williams, Raymond. *Marxism and Literature*. Oxford: Oxford University Press, 1977.
— "The Metropolis and Modernism." In *Universal City: Urban Experience in Modern European Literature and Art*. Edward Timms and David Kelly (eds.). Manchester: Manchester University Press, 1985. 13-24.
Woodward, Christopher. *In Ruins*. London: Chatto and Windus, 2001.
Woolf, Virginia. *The Common Reader, First Series, Annotated Edition*. 1925. Andrew McNeillie (ed.). Fort Washington, PA: Harvest Books, 1984.
Wullschlager, Jackie. *Chagall, Love and Exile*. St. Petersburg: Léon Bakst, 1909-1911; London: Allen Lane, 2008.

Index

adaptation 157, 158, 226
Adorno, Theodor 234
Albee, Edward 158
Allart, Hortense 7
allegory 19, 20, 21, 25, 33, 37, 38, 166, 252
allusion 9, 10, 43, 79, 83, 167, 178, 189
Americanisation 83
Americanism 114
American language 81, 91
American values 120, 125, 252
Andersen, Hendrik 246
Anesko, Michael 131, 261
antiques 77, 139, 144. *See also*: collecting / collector
Arnold, Matthew 4, 66, 67, 171, 178
art (work of art, *objet d'art*) 3, 44, 73, 88, 140, 145. *See also*: collecting / collector
Ascham, Roger 108, 109, 110
Atlantic Monthly, The 256
Austen, Jane 169
autobiography 61, 65, 91, 115, 136, 149, 171, 179, 181, 189, 201, 231, 233, 253, 271. *See also*: James, Henry: *Notes of a Son and Brother*

Babylon 45, 76, 80
Bakst, Léon 16
Balzac, Honoré de 4, 6, 7, 40, 51, 107, 136, 137, 144, 161, 162, 164
 Cousin Pons 143, 145
 Louis Lambert 134
Banta, Martha 23, 72, 86
Barrès, Maurice 62
Battilana, Marilla 105
Bellini, Giovanni 93
Bell, Millicent 147, 152
Benjamin, Walter 114

Bennett, Alan 158
Bergson, Henri 97
Berman, Jessica 72
Bernanke, Ben 54
Bhabha, Homi 235, 236
bildungsroman 127, 128. *See also*: *künstlerroman*
Blanche, Jacques-Emile 8
Boston, Massachusetts 29, 73, 103, 125, 134, 135, 164, 177, 183, 234, 259
Boulogne, France (city) 81, 86, 87, 189
Bourdieu, Pierre 43, 48, 50
bourgeois society 44, 141, 197
Bourget, Paul 8
Bourne, Randolph 234
Brissenden, Robert 149
Britten, Benjamin
 Owen Wingrave 226
 Rape of Lucretia, The 215
 Turn of the Screw, The 215
 War Requiem, 215
Britzolakis, Christina 83
Brockden Brown, Charles 106
Brontë, Charlotte
 Jane Eyre, 154
Brooke, Rupert 63
Brooks, Peter 40, 74, 75, 264
Broughton, Rhoda (letter to) 61
Browning, Robert 97, 104, 105, 107
Buell, Lawrence 255
Buffet, Warren 53, 55
Butler, Samuel 171
Byron, Lord 108, 106, 132, 181, 187

Cameron, Elizabeth 8
capitalism 40, 41, 45, 72, 73, 77, 83
Capri, Italy (city) 101
Carlyle, Thomas 176
carnivalesque, the 149, 150

catachresis 57
Cézanne, Paul 244
Cherbuliez, Victor 166
Church, Francis Pharcellus and William Conant 261
Churchill, Winston 62
citizenship (U.S. vs. European) 17
civilisation 38, 62, 69, 113, 117, 120
Civil War, The 185, 221
class 50, 234
　educated, the 160
　leisure, the 42
　middle, the 39, 40, 42, 140
　upper, the 47, 82
　working, the 41
cliché 15, 75
Coburn, Alvin Langdon 237, 238, 240, 245, 246
Coleridge, Samuel Taylor 171.
　collecting / collector 30, 33, 37, 43, 47, 76, 141, 142, 145, 195, 232
consumption/consumerism 10, 43, 50, 77, 142, 144
Cooper, James Fenimore 106
Coryat, Thomas 108, 110
cosmopolitanism 17, 19, 37, 75, 83
Cotes, Mrs. Everard 3
Cox, James M. 185
Crevecoeur, Michel Guillaume Jean de 134
Cummings, E.E. 64
cynicism 4, 34, 140, 141, 142, 143

Dante Alighieri 170
deconstruction 52, 55, 75, 210, 212
defamiliarisation 148, 268
déjà vu, feeling of 148, 154
DeKoven, Marianne 71
Delacroix, Eugene 108
Deleuze, Gilles 97, 243
Derrida, Jacques 18, 55, 205
desire 39, 42, 43, 45, 47, 50, 66, 74, 79, 85, 86, 94, 126, 128, 140, 188, 198, 211, 224, 239, 268
De Staël, Germaine 128, 129, 131
destiny 16, 87, 142, 150, 200
Dewey, John 234
Diaghilev, Sergei Pavlovich 16
Dickens, Charles 107
Diderot, Denis 197, 208, 212, 213, 239
　'absorption', 239

'Paradoxe sur le comédien.' *See*: drama / acting
Dorval, Marie 7
Dostoevsky, Fyodor 177
Doumic, René 4
drama / acting 108, 111, 138, 160, 176, 197, 199, 201, 213
dream 24, 56, 119, 130, 139, 153, 248, 252, 271
Dreyfus Affair, the 8
Dumas fils, Alexandre 160, 167
Durand, Marguerite 15

Eagleton, Terry 49
Eakin, Paul John 266, 270
economy
　economics 9, 30, 39, 44, 50, 57, 72, 73, 76, 83, 133, 134, 172, 231, 235
　'narrative economy' 53, 55
Edel, Leon 99, 100, 105, 131, 147, 171, 174, 229, 230, 245, 247, 248, 261
editors, negotiations with 172, 174, 255-262
Eliot, George 177
Eliot, T.S. 14, 15, 158, 164, 167
Emerson, Ralph Waldo 130, 134
epiphany 36, 57, 88
eroticism 79, 176, 265
ethics 38, 41, 51, 125, 145
　'Cosmopolitan Ethics' 37
Etty, William 107
Euclide 25

facial expression 245
failure, sense of 9, 16, 124, 132, 134, 138, 185, 193, 197, 249, 254
fairy tale / children's story 154
fantastic, the 91, 102, 125, 126, 166, 193, 201
Feinstein, Howard M. 248
Fetcher, Charles 183
Fielding, Henry 148, 153.
Flaubert, Gustave 15, 162, 188
Florence, Italy (city) 8, 97, 99, 101, 104, 107, 161, 174, 187, 256
Ford, Ford Madox 164
Foucault, Michel 18, 234
France, Anatole 62
France (James's impressions of) 69, 80
　language 91
　theatre 172, 183, 197

Franklin, Benjamin 136
Freud, Sigmund 57, 115, 150, 166, 263, 268
Fried, Michael 240
Fussell, Edwin 80, 160
futures / futurity 53, 57

Galaxy, The 137, 255, 262
Galbraith, John K. 53
gender relations 16, 80, 83, 151. *See also*: women, portrayal of
Geneva, Switzerland (city) 116, 165
Germany (James's impressions of) 63
Giddens, Anthony 235
Gide, André 62
Giles, Paul 255
globalisation 18, 19, 24, 28, 33, 37, 53, 76, 83
Goethe, Johan Wolfgang von 128, 129, 132, 180, 181, 215.
Goncourt, Edmond de 75, 142, 162, 188
Gothic fiction 106, 119, 147, 150, 216
Greenslade, William 74
grotesque, the 34, 115, 141, 185, 209, 212
Guattari, Félix 97, 243
Gyp 9, 15

Harper's Magazine 128, 131
Haussmann, Baron Georges Eugene 75, 79
Haviland, Beverly 37
Hawthorne, Nathaniel 66, 229, 232
Hayez, Francesco 108
Hazlitt, William 180
heterogeneity, narrative 236
Hetzel, Jules 4-6
Hillis Miller, James 19, 89
Hoeveler, Diane L. 105, 149, 150
Holbein the Younger, Hans 28
Holland, Josiah 256
Holmes, Oliver Wendell 177
Horace 163
Horne, Alistaire 75
Horne, Philip 16, 108, 110, 160, 175, 176, 181, 187, 195, 237
Howells, William Dean 130, 131, 229, 262
humanism 19, 163
Husserl, Edmund 97
Huxley, Aldous 158

identity
  national 66, 72, 77, 83, 91, 95, 113, 115, 116, 236
  personal 17, 45, 48, 65, 73, 74, 124, 126, 130, 180, 193, 206, 213, 246, 267, 271
impressionism 39, 44, 45, 48, 50, 68, 98
International Theme (American Innocence Abroad, U.S. vs. Europe) 24, 38, 75, 115, 234, 249
Irving, Henry 3
Irving, Washington 106, 174
Irvin, William 159
Irwin, William 157
Italy (James's impressions of) 102, 93-112, 143
Izzo, Donatella 114, 145

James, Alice 99, 125, 130, 131
James, Garth Wilkinson 124, 125, 130
James, Henry (works and correspondence)
  Ambassadors, The 17, 25, 28, 29, 37, 40, 50, 66, 71, 80, 125, 132, 133, 136, 180, 238, 242, 249, 254
  American Scene, The 67, 91, 236
  American, The 20, 24, 26, 29, 71, 79, 120, 241, 254, 255, 262
  A Small Boy and Others 65, 134, 171, 186, 189, 248, 264, 267
  Aspern Papers, The 111, 164, 187, 188, 197
  Awkward Age, The 15, 24, 247, 253
  Birthplace, The 201
  Bostonians, The 203, 206, 208, 253
  Church, Francis Pharcellus (letter to) 257
  Confidence 178
  copying phase 254
  Cotes, Mrs. Everard (letter to) 3
  Daisy Miller 20, 166, 169, 261
  Europeans, The 169, 262
  Fullerton, Morton (letter to) 131
  Golden Bowl, The 28, 37, 40, 137, 204, 240, 253
  Hawthorne 67, 116, 230
  Italian Hours 102, 104, 107, 113
  Ivory Tower, The 37
  Lowell, James Russell (letter to) 176
  New York Edition 9, 17, 19, 110, 152, 157, 159, 204, 215, 218, 221, 237, 238, 240, 246, 254

290   Henry James's Europe

Notes of a Son and Brother 134, 185, 189, 263, 267
Parisian Sketches 6, 67
Portrait of a Lady, The 17, 20, 22, 137, 169, 195, 253
portraits / frontispieces 246
Princess Casamassima, The 203
Question of Our Speech, The 91
revision phase 254
Roderick Hudson 204, 206, 238, 242, 256, 259, 262
Sacred Fount, The 206, 210, 242, 264
Saloon, The 216, 219
Sense of the Past, The 38, 61, 238, 239
Spoils of Poynton, The 42, 137
Sturgis, Howard (letter to) 61
Tragic Muse, The 71, 201, 213
Washington Square 169, 253
What Maisie Knew 5, 8, 9, 10, 24, 42, 91
William Wetmore Story and His Friends 107, 187
Wings of the Dove, The 18, 22, 32, 35, 40, 111, 135, 253
Yellow Book, The (periodical) 5, 238
James, Robertson 125, 130
James Sr., Henry 124, 174, 182, 256, 258, 259, 260, 262
James, William 75, 100, 131, 229, 244, 254, 257, 258, 263
Jewish faith 82, 130, 210, 211
Johnson, Andrew 186
Johnson, Stuart 233
Jonson, Ben 9, 110. Kaplan, Fred 238, 245

Karénine, Wladimir 4, 6, 14
Keats, John 100, 114.
Kenton, Edna 233
Kierkegaard, Soren 151
Kipling, Rudyard 62, 63
Kristeva, Julia 124, 125, 127, 130, 133, 136
künstlerroman 129, 136

Lacan, Jacques 52, 53, 57, 268
Lamb House, Rye 230, 232, 253
Lambinet, Emile 73
Lanchester, John 53, 55
Lane, Christopher 247
Lauth, Frédéric 15
Lawrence, D.H. 11
Leroux, Pierre 4

Levinas, Emmanuel 19, 24, 28, 33, 37, 243
London, England (city) 9, 10, 13, 15, 30, 35, 63, 66, 77, 80, 81, 82, 86, 99, 107, 109, 159, 174, 215, 216, 249, 251, 260, 261
  the London stage 86, 174, 193, 198-200
Loti, Pierre 62
Lubbock, Percy 61, 62, 63, 68, 238
Lustig, Tim 66, 68, 147
Lyons, France (city) 116

Malory, Thomas 158
Manet, Edouard 162, 243
Marx, Karl 40, 97
masculinity 74, 83, 128, 148, 150, 151
Mawr, Bryn 90
melancholy 8, 20, 21, 22, 23, 28, 29, 36, 37, 38, 99, 106, 118, 138, 142, 145, 196
memory 45, 94, 97, 101, 104, 114, 116, 126, 128, 150, 179, 183, 187, 189, 232, 271
Méral, Jean 27, 66
Milton, John 10, 178
Mitchell, W.J.T. 239, 241
modernisation / modernity 53, 55, 71, 75, 76, 83, 100, 200, 201, 235
modernism 9, 15, 39, 40, 71, 73, 83, 100, 231
monuments 98, 117, 210. *See also*: ruins
morality / immorality 3, 9, 11, 14, 18, 29, 48, 52, 74, 88, 120, 125, 232
Mozart, Wolfgang Amadeus 114, 222, 226.
Muratov, Pavel 94
Murillo, Bartolomé 114
Musset, Alfred de 4

Nabokov, Vladimir 24, 95
Naples, Italy (city) 102
Napoleon Bonaparte 47, 65, 225
Nashe, Thomas 108, 110
Nedelman, Birgitta 144
New York City 32, 37, 64, 67, 171, 174, 230, 234, 260, 264
New York Tribune, The 5, 67
Nietzsche, Friedrich 18, 96
Nijinsky, Vaslav 16
Norton, Grace 229

Old World values 80, 114, 115, 116
Olney, James 253
opera 67, 139, 226
Orlando, Francesco 113, 120

Osgood, James 256, 259
otherness 19, 24, 26, 28, 29, 30, 35, 37, 73, 74, 76, 79, 150, 211, 242, 243, 268, 270

Paër, Ferdinando. *See*: *Griselda*
painting 15, 21, 23, 26, 31, 71, 73, 83, 94, 95, 98, 105, 108, 111, 128, 137, 142, 163, 195, 209, 219, 222, 238, 239, 250, 254
Paris, France (city) 8, 15, 16, 24, 27, 41, 45, 47, 63, 67, 80, 88, 107, 123, 125, 126, 127, 129, 131, 132, 138, 140, 159, 174, 177, 194, 242, 249, 251, 256, 259, 261, 269
  Faubourg Saint Germain 44, 79
  Le Louvre 65, 241, 248, 249, 250, 254, 269
Parkinson, Edward 148
parody 134, 135, 147, 148, 153, 166
Pater, Walter 171
Pearson, John 151
Pemble, John 105
perception / misperception 6, 37, 39, 45, 47, 49, 72, 80, 85, 87, 101, 104, 108, 120, 183, 193, 195, 209, 241
Perugia, Italy (city) 96
Petry, Alice Hall 147
photography 185, 200, 238, 240, 246
Piper, Myfanwy 216, 220, 221. *See also*: Britten, Benjamin
Pius IX, Pope 99
Pocock, Isaac. *See*: *Don Juan*; *Libertine, The*
Poe, Edgar Allan 239
Poirier, Richard 250
Pope, Alexander 10
Posnock, Ross 234
possession,
  material 37, 50, 73, 77, 137, 139, 140, 143, 144, 145
  supernatural 149, 153
postmodernism 55
prosopopeia 56
Proust, Marcel 8, 15

Radcliffe, Ann 105, 147, 150
Raphael 163
Reade, Charles 176
realism 37, 40, 51, 115, 120, 126, 128, 129, 147, 151, 162, 166, 193, 199
revision 9, 37, 79, 108, 178, 206, 240, 248, 249, 254
Revue des Deux Mondes, La 162

Richards, I.A. 167
Richardson, Samuel 149
Ricks, Christopher 167, 177
Rieman, Bernhard 25, 28
Rivkin, Julie 195, 240
Robb, Graham 126
romantic drama 198
romanticism 44, 45, 87, 88, 90, 95, 106, 108, 128, 142, 193, 230, 231
romantic novel / archetype 128, 129, 149, 152, 154, 219
Rome, Italy (city) 66, 97, 101, 116, 138, 139, 142, 163, 164, 244
Roosevelt, Theodore 72, 73
Rossini, Gioachino Antonio 139
Rousseau, Jean-Jacques 4
ruins 120
Ruskin, John 105, 107

Sand, George 4, 6, 7, 14, 15, 16, 110, 188, 189
Sargent, Henry 31, 105, 238
satire 8, 10, 15, 163
Savoy, Eric 247
Schapiro, Meyer 241, 243
Schiller, Friedrich 107.
Scott, Walter 176
Scribner, Charles 9, 68, 174, 255, 256, 260
sculpture 163, 203, 239, 242, 246
self / selfhood 18, 24, 26, 30, 31, 37, 53, 65, 101, 114, 145, 151, 152, 180, 210, 234, 235, 241, 242, 248, 252, 253, 271
Serao, Mathilde 102
sexuality 16, 44, 48, 57, 72, 73, 74, 78, 81, 82, 84, 85, 88, 101, 104, 109, 110, 111, 147, 149, 150, 151, 173, 176, 263, 264
Shakespeare, William 5, 105, 106, 107, 108, 151, 157, 158, 159, 164, 165, 166, 173, 174, 180, 198, 200, 201, 210
  Hamlet 114, 159, 166, 175, 187
  Love's Labour Lost 175
  MacBeth 108, 159
  Measure for Measure 159
  Merchant of Venice, The 108, 159
  Othello 108, 114, 164, 175
  Tempest, The 158, 181
Shelley, Percy 100, 103, 104, 105, 107, 187, 215
Simmel, Georg 243

sophistication 16, 40, 53, 55, 67, 76, 118, 152, 177, 193, 229
Southam, Brian 158, 164
Stephens, Winifred 63
Strauss, Richard 222

Tanner, Tony 105
taste 41, 42, 47, 48, 50, 67, 90, 138, 143, 159, 185
Tennyson, Alfred Lord 173
Teyssandier, Hubert 197
theatre *See*: drama
Thoreau, Henry David 134, 136
Tinayre, Marcelle 15, 16
Tintner, Adeline 20, 63, 105, 124, 253
Tintoretto 98, 209
Titian 107, 250, 254
Tolstoy, Leo 10
Trollope, Anthony 183
Turgenev, Ivan 177

United States (James's impression of) 236. *See also*: Americanism

Van Dyke, Anthony 250
Veblen, Thornstein 42, 48
Venice, Italy (city) 30, 94, 99, 101, 111, 164, 170
Veronese, Paolo 107, 111, 114
Virgil 148
vulgarity / vulgarisation 6, 9, 41, 44, 76, 83, 86, 97, 100, 131, 140, 193, 196, 197, 207, 213

Wagner, Richard 97
Walker, Pierre 66, 160, 165
Walpole, Hugh 68, 245
Watteau, Jean-Antoine 24
Wells, H.G. 62, 63
Wharton, Edith 7, 16, 61, 62, 63, 64, 65, 66, 68
Wilde, Oscar 8, 176, 177, 239
Williams, Raymond 19, 76, 97
women, portrayal of 71-80
Woodward, Christopher 115
Woolson, Constance Fenimore 97
Wordsworth, William 171.
World War I 37, 62, 64, 69, 72
World War II 75, 215

A new approach to academic publishing

OPEN BOOK PUBLISHERS is dedicated to making high quality research less expensive and more accessible to readers around the world. Set up and run by academics, we produce peer-reviewed monographs, collected volumes and lecture series in the humanities and social sciences.

Open Book speeds up the whole publishing process from author to reader. We offer all the advantages of digital texts (speed, searchability, updating, archival material, databases, discussion forums, and links to institutions' websites) without sacrificing the quality of the traditional university presses.

All Open Book publications are available online to be read free of charge by anyone with access to the internet. During our first year of operation, our free digital editions have been accessed by people in over 120 countries, and are being read by as many people per month as many traditionally printed titles will reach in their entire published life.

We are reliant on donations by individuals and institutions to help offset the production costs of our publications. As a Community Interest Company (CIC), we do not operate for commercial profit and all donations, as with all other revenue we generate, will be used to finance new Open Access publications.

For further information on what we do, how to donate to OBP, additional digital material related to our titles or to order our books, please contact the Managing Director, Dr. Alessandra Tosi (a.tosi@openbookpublishers.com) or visit our website:

www.openbookpublishers.com